The CARRY ON story

The CARRY ON story

ROBERT ROSS

REYNOLDS & HEARN LTD
LONDON

For my best friend: this is the first one you've missed, Dad.
And, at last, to the special lady that made that 'old man' very happy,
my beautiful soul mate, Melanie. I've kept the best for you!

FRONTISPIECE: Producer Peter Rogers and director Gerald Thomas
announce the production of *Carry On Teacher* in 1959.

CONTENTS PAGE: The Chayste Place girls from *Carry On Camping* (1969),
headed by Elizabeth Knight, Georgina Moon, Jackie Poole,
Barbara Windsor, Sandra Caron, Valerie Shute and Jennifer Pyle.

First published in 2005 by
Reynolds & Hearn Ltd
61a Priory Road
Kew Gardens
Richmond
Surrey TW9 3DH

© Robert Ross 2005, 2006, 2008
Reprinted 2009

The Carry On films were produced by Peter Rogers.
© 2008 licensed by Granada Ventures Ltd.

The Carry On films are protected under copyright.
1958 to 1966 films are distributed by Canal Plus Image UK Ltd.
1966 to 1978 films are distributed by Granada Ventures Ltd.

A CIP catalogue record for this book is available from the British Library.

ISBN 978 1 905287 61 1

Designed by Peri Godbold.

Printed and bound in India by Replika Press.

CONTENTS

ACKNOWLEDGEMENTS

'They're here again!' exclaimed the poster for *Carry On Cabby*. And here is another book about the Carry On films. It has been over a decade since my first book on the subject; *The Carry On Companion* was my love letter to the series, packed with cast and crew lists, and affectionate critical opinions. *The Carry On Story* is very different. This book contains the facts about the making of the films, largely derived from the Gerald Thomas Collection held in the archives of the British Film Institute. This is also the story of the Carry Ons as told to me by the people that made those films so great.

Over the last ten years a lot of these heroes have become valued friends. For interviews, both past and present, I most warmly thank a great many people. Norman Hudis tickled my hospitalised dad pink with a huge basket containing a sample of every fruit known to mankind. Jack Douglas stepped into Jim Dale's shoes at the eleventh hour for my first book launch and has never let me down since, however many times I have asked him for 'one more favour'. The late Norman Rossington shared endless showbiz memories back 'on location' in Guildford forty years on from *Carry On Sergeant*. After a National Film Theatre screening, Bob Monkhouse bumped into me in the foyer and accepted my blurted 'I've written a Carry On book!' with a rummage in his plastic carrier bag – 'What this one?' The ever-cheerful, carefree and cavalier Alec Bregonzi... a trip to the NFT isn't the same now you are gone. Terence Longdon wrote a letter to this eleven-year-old fan pondering that perhaps we would meet one day – it was great when we did. Then, there's Leslie Phillips, a scholar and a gentleman to the tips of his fingers; the ever-gracious and graceful Shirley Eaton, the image of the 1950s

stunner I worshipped during Sunday afternoon repeats; and the delirious and delectable Sally Geeson, my beloved 'ND' and Sid's surrogate daughter; the incomparable Liz Fraser; the eternally humble Lance Percival; the timelessly bewitching Fenella Fielding; and Bernard Cribbins, forever disarmingly supportive. The jack of all trades, master of all them, Jim Dale has been a dear friend and an inspiration. And I must thank that self-effacing pro Peter Gilmore, and the late Ed Devereaux, for an amusing correspondence, and the unflappable and cuddlesome Julie Stevens. The late Norman Mitchell was quite simply the nicest man in showbusiness. The late Joan Sims had an endless supply of cherry cake and cola – Joan was always as sweet as her refreshments. Not forgetting the spirited Barbara Windsor, the ageless Anita Harris and the equally ageless Hugh Futcher! Dilys Laye gave her unflagging enthusiasm for the subject and the late Patsy Rowlands had a warm word for everybody and was a relentless lover of life. The late Frankie Howerd – thanks for being 'the greatest'... and for never going too far. The late Dave Freeman who greeted praise and blame and treated both those impostors the same. Larry Dann is a fund of energy, stories and kindness and Jack Gardner one of the most vital of backroom boys. I'm grateful to the philosophical Richard O'Callaghan for saying 'yes' to the commentaries; and to the tops Jacki Piper, for being a very special friend with a very special place in my heart. There are many more, from Kenneth Williams to Julian Clary, who have always smiled in the right places and treated this Carry On historian with kindness.

Special thanks for this book must also go to Janet Moat and Vicky Hedley of the British Film Institute's Special Collections department. Ever helpful and ever agreeable to another trawl through the archives, this book would not have been possible – or as lavish – without them. The Carry On copyright-holders have been just as helpful: grateful thanks to Caroline Raudnitz at Granada Ventures, and to John Herron and Dennis Hall at Canal Plus. Thanks also to Vic and Gary at the London Postcard Company for the scans of so many Carry On posters from the Rank years. And Michelle Skinner for so much.

A warm embrace to Alan Coles and Henry Holland, who always keep me sane with the perfect combination of great company and the unity of hops. I'm similarly grateful to Rosalind Tapping and Edgar Locke for finding Harry, and Sandra Turner and Jon Webster, for helping me know my farce from my elbow. Thanks also to copy editor Steve Tribe, indexer Ian Crane and scanning supremo Andrew Godfrey for their sterling work behind the scenes.

And another special thank you to my 'boss', Marcus Hearn. A schedule that never let up and a thousand and one things to iron out were made a pleasurable breeze with you as a comrade-in-arms, old friend. I think we did it! And to our right-hand woman, Peri Godbold, who has designed this book with care, affection and the spirit of Carry On in every page. I think the three of us know how skilled they all were making the Carry Ons in such a short space of time.

Finally, to Gerald Thomas, whom I only met twice, and Peter Rogers, whom I have met so many times I've lost count. I hope I've done you proud this time. Without those two gentlemen, what follows would not have been possible.

FOREWORD

Joan Sims looks set to tuck in to the cake as Terence Longdon, Susan Beaumont, Gerald Thomas, Joan Hickson and Peter Rogers celebrate Ann Firbank's birthday.

I've said it before and I'll no doubt say it again, as long as they continue to publish books about the Carry Ons and either interview me or ask for forewords such as this. And what I'll say is that when the life story of jazz musician Mezz Mezzrow (*Really The Blues*) was published, transcribed from his own tape-recorded memories, he commented: 'I thought I was just playing the music I loved but now it turns out I was being significant.'

Before we leave the jazz mode, let's tie it all off with a quote from Benny Goodman: when asked what happened to swing, he said, 'We played it too long and too loud.'

Well, evidently, with the publication of this handsome volume, the chroniclers of the Carry Ons haven't yet reached saturation limit. The fascination with these movies, in college courses, websites, fan-mags and the like, continues at a truly amazing rate. And, to pick up on Mr Mezzrow's modest assessment of his place in musical history, all I can say is that I just thought I was writing as funny as I knew how, for colleagues Peter Rogers and Gerald Thomas, and I know their ambitions were set no higher than that also: but it turns out we, in our own blithe way, were being 'significant' too.

We didn't sit down and decide, after exhaustive intellectual analysis, that live-theatre vaudeville was dead or dying but that didn't mean that the British public's appetite for hearty, undemanding laughter had died with it, so let's turn our joint efforts toward a form of it in the cinema. Someone must have idly taken the commercial hint from *The Army Game*'s popularity on television and surmised that a modest movie on the same time-worn comedic possibilities inherent in army life, might earn a bob or two on the big screen.

The rest has been told so often that it's not even worth a few recalling lines here. But I won't forget in a hurry that first year when Britain's box-office top three winners were *Dunkirk*, *The Bridge on the River Kwai* and *Carry On Sergeant*.

The three pictures could not have summed up Britain better if they had set out deliberately to do so: in fact, if anyone had concocted such a trilogy, it could have been so self-consciously self-loving as to be nauseating. But there you had them – a British army rescued from total disaster by an improvised fleet of little boats; a group of British POWs undergoing inhuman treatment and whistling bollocks as they entered hell; and a bunch of unwilling, grumpy British conscripts laughing at themselves and the army and yet becoming citizen-soldiers of high quality, without self-congratulation and almost in spite of themselves.

So it went – these stolid and unbelievable British contradictions – with *Nurse*. Married to a nurse, I always fretted greatly over the ridiculous and again typically British anomaly of their lives: in the few minutes before a doctor could be summoned to an emergency in a ward, they were trusted, and indeed expected, to take life-or-death decisions, and yet were mistrusted by an insultingly dated system which compelled them to be in bed by 10.00 pm. Stalwart and skilled women on duty, treated as potentially naughty girls in their own scant time.

In Britain, are such blatantly differing attitudes cause for protest unto mutiny? Not often. More typically, they're ultimately laughed at by us and this is what baffles so much of the rest of the world. Yet, in country after country, via our films, they found the way we, er, carried on, amusing too.

Bottom line: in those early Carry Ons all we did was reflect our country and its ways from one of its most individual points of view: humour. The trick is that, like Mr Mezzrow, we didn't know we were being significant and making a sociological point. Thank God.

On a personal level, I was lucky. I was in on it when we had all the easy, familiar, down-to-earth targets to poke fun at: Army, Hospital, School, Police Force. A Helping Hands Agency

(*Regardless*) stretched a little beyond the familiar (though I'm still very fond of the *39 Steps* sequence in that one), and *Cruising* served its purpose but didn't have, I thought, the general application to most peoples' lives that army service and the cops did.

The subsequent Carry Ons, mostly under the untiring pen of Talbot Rothwell, developed a new and hilarious level to which I could not aspire. Someone recently dug up a draft of *Carry On Spying*, which was the last attempt I made at the genre under my original six-year contract. I wish I hadn't read it! It was an appalling script, tired and uninspired, written by one who was running on empty and flying on automatic pilot (and all other clichés of that kind). It was time for me to move on: it was clear to all concerned that, for me, if a theme wasn't real, I couldn't feel.

But I will never forget those first six scripts, not only because they transformed my career, took me to Hollywood etc, but also for what they were: sheer joys to write and then to wonder at the sympathy and fidelity of the makers and the actors.

I must hope that this book provokes similar memories in its readers. Certainly, its author, Robert Ross, who began enjoying the films at the age of two (blimey, was that, after all, the mental age we were aiming at?!), bids fair, with this effort, to become the definitive Carry On historian.

Norman Hudis
California,
December 2004

The triumvirate that created Carry On – director Gerald Thomas, writer Norman Hudis and producer Peter Rogers in a joyous reunion at Pinewood studios.

INTRODUCTION

I n 1962, after half a dozen Carry On comedies produced over half a decade, an enthusiastic publicist by the name of Tony Hill planted his tongue very firmly in his cheek. He predicted:

'In the year 2008 when Mr Ripley's successor is still declaiming Believe it Or Not, the story of the very first Carry On may be told to coincide with its fiftieth anniversary year. Under the heading of "Do You Know?" one can envisage Ripley's column symbolising the then current title. Imaginatively, let's call it "Carry On Levitating" because, by that time, this may possibly be the only recognised method of reaching the moon, mercury or, by the same means, solving the rush-hour problem of getting from Marble Arch to Mansion House without undue delay. With a little nostalgia, the historian will delve into the archives and without actually shouting "eureka", is almost certain to come up with the information that the very

first Carry On, *Sergeant* that is, in its pristine state, was titled "The Bull Boys". A line in the script, what else but *Carry On Sergeant* was adopted as a much more intriguing title and, such was its success, thus was the Carry On series born. In this space probe age, six Carry On subjects have been made currently culminating in *Carry On Cruising*, the first in colour. Who knows (except Ripley II) when other contemporary subjects might come under the microscope through a legacy handed down by producer Peter Rogers and director Gerald Thomas, abetted by screenplay writer Norman Hudis. Chronologically this might read "Carry On Cowboy", "Carry On Commonwealth", "Carry On Chaos", "Carry On Carnage", "Carry On Phoenix", "What A Carry On" and so on (but not "ad nauseum"). By this time Anglo Amalgamated Film Distributors might have changed their name to Inter Planetary Films Incorporated. Meanwhile, just for the record, to date these are the six Carry Ons which serve as a foundation for the future.'

The first six Carry Ons were, indeed, joined by a comic western, as well as adventures with Cleo and Columbus, and ribald antics while *Camping*, *Loving* and even going *Up the Khyber*. Now, in the year 2008, Tony Hill's comic observations take on the air of a misunderstood prophet. The Carry Ons are still very much with us. A resurrection of the series is always just around the corner. The merchandising of the franchise is at fever pitch. In their homelands, Hattie Jacques and Charles Hawtrey are as vital and vibrant dead pop culture icons as Marilyn Monroe and James Dean. The Carry Ons are a part of the British way of life and part of what makes us the nation we are in the eyes of the world. We are an island where bosoms make an amusing 'bong!' noise when knocked and lecherous men hitting retirement age can lustfully look up a teenage girl's skirt without getting arrested. The Carry Ons, an archive of saucy seaside postcards come to life, remain the backbone for corny, nudge, nudge, groan-worthy comedy.

This is their story. Through original correspondence, bright and cheerful promotional material, behind-the-scenes photographs and exclusive, first-hand memories, the treasure trove that follows is what makes the Carry Ons carry on.

Filming patient Frankie Howerd and nurse Valerie Van Ost in December 1967.

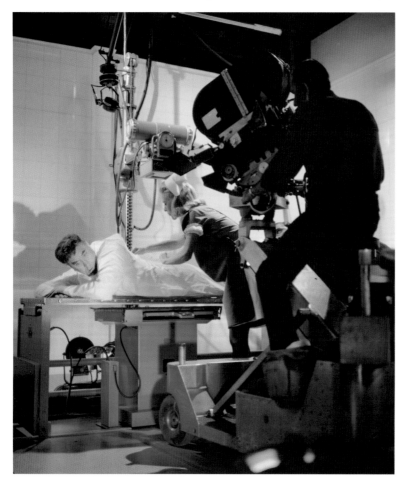

Like those other multi-talented and very British heroes, Noel Coward and Winston Churchill, Peter Rogers is proudest to be known simply as a writer. During the war, his work was performed on the London stage and adapted for BBC radio, but it was in 1942 that he entered the film business. Writing five-minute dramas for J Arthur Rank's Religious Films Unit, he was 'gagging up Jesus Christ!'

Gerald Thomas had studied to be a doctor, before war service with the Royal Sussex Regiment put paid to his medical career for good. Upon demobilisation in 1946, he secured a job in the cutting rooms of Two Cities Films at Denham Studios.

Rogers had landed a job as the film editor of World Press News. A press reception at the Savoy in 1947 introduced him to Sydney Box, who had just been appointed to take over Gainsborough Studios. 'When I asked him for an interview, he said, "You write it and I'll sign it!"' recalls Rogers. 'He then said he was planning a film called *Holiday Camp* and asked if I had any ideas. I hadn't, but promised to send him some.' On the basis of his ideas, Box offered Rogers a full-time contract as a scriptwriter for Gainsborough Pictures. The young writer accepted.

The following year, Rogers contributed to a spin-off film, *Here Come the Huggetts*, and

Producer Peter Rogers and director Gerald Thomas prove it isn't only ladies that lunch, during the making of *Carry On Cabby* (1963).

A trade advertisement for *Here Come the Huggetts*, the first spin-off from the 1947 comedy drama *Holiday Camp*. Peter Rogers wrote material for both.

Costume designer Julie Harris and producer Peter Rogers on the Pinewood set of *You Know What Sailors Are!* (1953). Carry On star Shirley Eaton is second in line.

Peter Rogers (seated), producer of *To Dorothy a Son*, is joined by (kneeling) production supervisor Al Marcus and (sitting behind) director Muriel Box and American star Shelley Winters. Stood at the back are first assistant director Ernie Morris, third assistant director John Draper, director of photography Ernest Steward (with a helpful book, *Comedy Films*), star John Gregson and camera operator Bob Thompson.

married Sydney Box's producer sister, Betty. Thomas had graduated to assistant editor, working on Laurence Olivier's *Hamlet* and the John Mills thriller *The October Man*. In 1949, he received his first credit as editor, on the Margaret Lockwood melodrama *Madness of the Heart*. Rogers, meanwhile, was associate producer on three films with Betty: the Basil

Radford and Naunton Wayne spy comedy *It's Not Cricket*; a bleak domestic drama, *Don't Ever Leave Me*, starring Jimmy Hanley as the ruthless abductor of Petula Clark; and the marriage bureau portmanteau *Marry Me!*, starring David Tomlinson and Susan Shaw.

A steady stream of films gainfully employed both men before a professional breakthrough in 1952. Rogers produced his first film, the Venice Film Festival prize-winning Children's Film Foundation release *The Dog and the Diamonds*, and Thomas was appointed editor, by his older brother Ralph, for the Richard Todd thriller *Venetian Bird*. The film was produced by Betty Box, Ralph's collaborator since *The Clouded Yellow*, in 1950. The associate producer was Peter Rogers. Rogers continued to produce popular comedy subjects such as the Donald Sinden naval romp *You Know What Sailors Are!* and the daring *To Dorothy a Son*, with John Gregson and Shelley Winters. Thomas was still happily employed editing his brother's films, notably the hugely successful Dirk Bogarde comedy *Doctor in the House* and the tense submarine adventure *Above Us the Waves*, starring John Mills.

But, by the mid 1950s, the Box family had bought up Beaconsfield Studios and Rogers had been put in charge of production. Although the original intention for all the family to make films at Beaconsfield never came to fruition, Peter kept the studios going for two years with only one empty day in the production schedule. Although overseeing such offerings as the Barbara Shelley horror film *Cat Girl*, the train heist drama *The Flying Scot* and the popular Roger Moore television series *Ivanhoe*, he wanted to emulate his wife and have a permanent director at his side. He requested Gerald Thomas.

'It wasn't as easy as I thought it would be. I couldn't persuade the distributor to accept Gerald as a director, so, as he was under contract, I used him on a second feature at Beaconsfield and wrote one or two scripts for the Children's Film Foundation to keep us going.' Their first collaboration was the Children's Film Foundation's *Circus Friends*, starring Carol White and Alan Coleshill in the emotive tale of an abused circus horse rescued from destruction.

Rogers continued to produce feature films. His sister-in-law, Muriel Box, directed the romantic comedy *Passionate Stranger*, starring Ralph Richardson and Margaret Leighton, while Compton Bennett was recruited as director for *After the Ball*, the biopic of music hall star Vesta Tilley with Pat Kirkwood. The second feature thriller that hit the jackpot for Rogers and Thomas was *Time Lock*, an atmospheric adaptation of Arthur Hailey's story of a boy who is accidentally trapped inside a bank vault by his distraught father, played by Robert Beatty. It

was shot in just three weeks on a budget of £30,000, but the team managed to convincingly set the story in Canada. Helped by the brooding performance of his Canadian star, Rogers had a persuasive diatribe with the authorities that saw traffic on the main route to Slough diverted to the opposite side to create the illusion of

Muriel Box (centre) with her husband Sydney and Grace Moore at the Cannes Film Festival in 1946.

Writer Richard Gordon, Ralph Thomas, Gerald Thomas, Betty Box and Muriel Box pictured during the production of *Doctor in the House* (1953).

Hattie Jacques and Tommy Steele – both stars of Peter Rogers films.

of *Vicious Circle*. A skilful adaptation of the Francis Durbridge thriller *The Brass Candlestick*, it starred John Mills as the hounded Dr Latimer.

Two further crime films followed in 1958. John Clarke starred as a corrupt bank clerk in *Chain of Events*, while *The Solitary Child* cast Philip Friend as the suspicious Captain James Random, marrying Harriet (Barbara Shelley) just two years after being acquitted of the murder of his first wife.

It was actually a hastily made 1957 biopic of Tommy Steele that sealed the future for Rogers and Thomas. A Herbert Smith production, with Rogers as executive producer, *The Tommy Steele Story* was a stylised depiction of the rise and rise of Britain's first rock 'n' roller and it made fifty times its own production costs on its initial release. So popular was the star that Steele's lyricist and composer, Lionel Bart, approached Rogers with an idea for another film vehicle, loosely based on *The Prisoner of Zenda* – the cinemagoer would get two Tommys for the price of one in *The Duke Wore Jeans*. Another

driving on the right-hand side of the road! *Time Lock* was a major box-office hit, and the distributors finally recognised Thomas as a director, endorsing the partnership's production

Eric Barker and William Hartnell inspect a shower of national service recruits in *Carry On Sergeant*.

instant hit, it was the first comedy produced by Peter Rogers and directed by Gerald Thomas.

Beanconsfield Studios had produced twelve films under the auspices of Peter Rogers. Incredibly, all were made for a total budget of £180,000. Thus with a tight budget and a hit comedy under his belt, it was little wonder he was considered the saviour of a much-rejected story outline by playwright R F Delderfield. Originally the property of Peter's brother-in-law, the outline ran to over 200 pages, double the length of a normal British feature film. Leslie Caron had been approached to play the passionate ballerina who pines when her dance partner is enlisted in to the army but, even with an international star attached, the project could not find a producer willing to take it on. The script was provisionally saddled with a title lifted from the lyrics of wartime favourite 'Bless 'Em All': either 'The Long and the Short and the Tall' or 'This Side of the Ocean'. The central

character was Mike Ellison who, with his best friend 'the Tank', struggled to survive army life away from his lady and dance. 'The background will be for the most part amusing but the thread quite serious,' it was noted, with 'one-third laughter, one-third documentary, one-third exciting incident building up to the climax.'

By May 1957, the project was simply referred to as the 'National Service Story'. By the following month, it had become 'The Bull Boys'. In pre-production, it was recorded that 'the author has considered transferring the action abroad but has rejected this.' Peter Rogers was superficially conscious that this was not 'just another war story on Malta, or Egypt, or Cyprus', as well as cannily aware that exotic location filming would inflate the budget. In a statement that stands as a remit for the whole series it would inspire, he proudly declared: 'This is a British story and ought to be set in Britain throughout.'

Opposite: William Hartnell and Bob Monkhouse chat in the officers' mess at the Queens Barracks, Guildford. Fellow *Carry On Sergeant* stars Terence Longdon and Gerald Campion mingle with real-life soldiers.

CARRY ON SERGEANT (1958)

Blushing bride Mary Sage (Shirley Eaton) is distraught when her husband Charlie (Bob Monkhouse) receives his call-up papers during the wedding breakfast. En route to Heathercrest National Service Depot, he chats to weedy Horace Strong (Kenneth Connor), a fellow recruit who doesn't bode well for Sergeant Grimshawe (William Hartnell). Grimshawe is retiring from the army and takes on a £50 bet with Sergeant O'Brien (Terry Scott) that his last bunch of squaddies will be his first champion platoon. With beady-eyed inspection from Captain Potts (Eric Barker) and disgruntled support from Corporal Copping (Bill Owen), Grimshawe struggles to take his squad through basic training. What with failure Herbert Brown (Norman Rossington), upper-class cad Miles Heywood (Terence Longdon), rock 'n' roller Andy Galloway (Gerald Campion), delicate flower Peter Golightly (Charles Hawtrey) and supercilious James Bailey (Kenneth Williams), his attempts seem doomed. Moreover, Mary is determined to spend her wedding night with her husband and blags a job in the NAAFI, while Horace spends most of his time complaining to Medical Officer Captain Clark (Hattie Jacques). It is only the love of doe-eyed NAAFI girl Norah (Dora Bryan) that makes him a man, just as the squad are inspired to become real soldiers for their departing Sergeant.

With memories of warfare mellowing and National Service in its death throes, the Britain of the late 1950s was full of fun-pokers poking fun at the military. Terry-Thomas and Ian Carmichael did it satirically for the Boulting brothers in *Private's Progress* and Norman Wisdom added sentimental slapstick for *The Square Peg*. It was, however, the ITV situation comedy *The Army Game* that had captured the imagination of the nation. A contemporary comment on the lazy, ineffectual and corrupt soldiers that reluctantly went through the motions, it was a series that naturally inspired and worried producer Peter Rogers in equal measure.

Having been rejected from the army with the words 'Better get back to the theatre – you're no bloody good here!' William Hartnell had made a professional career out of hard-nosed characters, often in khaki. He had become the definitive screen Army Sergeant in such unforgettable British films as Carol Reed's *The Way Ahead* (1944), the biopic of William Friese-Greene *The Magic Box* (1951) and *Private's Progress* (1956). He had been an obvious choice for the aptly named Sergeant-Major Percy Bullimore in *The Army Game*. Departing the show after the second series, he landed the lead role in *Carry On Sergeant*.

Similarly, Charles Hawtrey had been abandoned from the Granada series and gratefully grabbed the chance of spin-off film work. Hawtrey had starred in the hastily released feature version of *The Army Game* from Hammer Film Productions, *I Only Arsked*. That film also recruited Norman Rossington, reprising his television role of Private 'Cupcake' Cook. 'Out of the blue I received a letter on 29 January 1958 which said that from mid-March they wouldn't be renewing my contract,' revealed Rossington. 'I don't know if Gerald Thomas, Peter Rogers and Norman Hudis created *Carry On Sergeant* with *The Army Game* in mind, but when they heard I was sacked, they asked me to play Herbert Brown.'

Peter Rogers had certainly had *The Army Game* in mind when he had picked up the option on a script called 'The Bull Boys'. With *The Army Game*'s instant success from June 1957, Rogers decided to turn 'The Bull Boys' into an all-out comedy based around the life, loves and losses of a bunch of raw recruits thrown into National Service. He approached

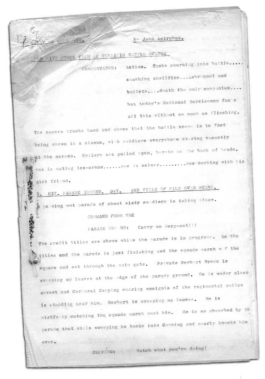

the celebrated agency Associated London Scripts and its roll call of writers headed by Ray Galton, Alan Simpson, Johnny Speight, Eric Sykes, Spike Milligan and John Antrobus. Eric 'had had an unfortunate experience with a film producer and had vowed never to work with another one for as long as he lived!' recalls

Rogers, 'and Spike was completely insane. He was brandishing a loaded revolver above his head and bellowed "I can't see anybody just now. I'm just about to kill myself!"'

John Antrobus, who was then on the Granada payroll writing scripts for *The Army Game*, seemed the most sensible bet in every sense. The draft that he prepared, however, was heavily rewritten, and the eventual writing credit was given to Norman Hudis, with 'additional material by John Antrobus'.

Rogers decided to set up production at Pinewood and thus join his wife, Betty Box, who was resident at the illustrious studios with two profitable sequels to *Doctor in the House* already in the can. The pre-production meeting at Pinewood clearly laid down the Carry On ground rules of 'waste not, want not'.

Left: Although elements of the John Antrobus script were retained, Peter Rogers wrote: 'What he wrote was really a radio script and I want him to read the present script as much for his guidance as anything. If after reading it he still insists on the percentage we suggested as an encouragement I will be very surprised.'

Opposite: A drilling for Terence Longdon, Bob Monkhouse, Norman Rossington, Gerald Campion and Kenneth Williams. Charles Hawtrey seems to be the butt of the military ranting from real-life Sergeant-Major Douglas Fairbanks.

ON LOCATION

The wedding sequence was filmed with doubles and crowd artistes by the second unit one morning at Beaconsfield Church, and then Harefield Church. They were back at Pinewood Studios by 1.15 pm that afternoon. After camera tests at Slough station, the unit travelled to Taplow in order to film the train journey from Slough to West Drayton for back projection during the Bob Monkhouse and Kenneth Connor train sequence. During filming at the Queens Barracks, Whateley Road, Guildford, William Hartnell and Gerald Thomas stayed at the Angel Hotel, High Street, Guildford.

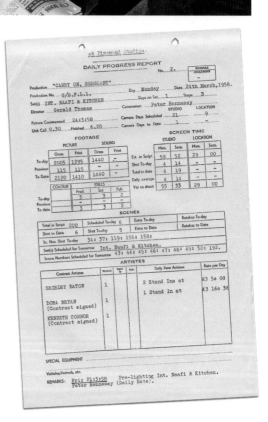

Reluctant squaddie Bob Monkhouse and sickly recruit Kenneth Connor filmed the train carriage scene over 28 and 31 March 1958.

The very first daily progress report from a Carry On film, detailing the filming of 24 March 1958.

Wedded bliss... but it won't last for Shirley Eaton and Bob Monkhouse.

On location, Norman Rossington was amused by 'the actor Patrick Newell [who went on to play "Mother" in *The Avengers*]. He was supposed to be in the film. He was a very posh chap. He turned up on the first morning in his Rolls-Royce and caught sight of the Sergeant who was going to drill us for the film. It was the same Sergeant from when he was in the army. "There's no way I'm going to be drilled by him again," he said, promptly got back in his car and drove off. He was never in the film. Having not been in the army myself, I didn't appreciate that the square of the barracks that soldiers drill on is holy ground. One morning I was walking across it and got a right telling off from the real Sergeant!'

William Hartnell, it would seem, was just as unforgiving. Although Hartnell was given top billing, Bob Monkhouse, playing newlywed recruit Charlie Sage, had 'argued and reasoned and blustered to get my name above the much more experienced and recognisable player but to no good effect. To some bad effect, however. Bill Hartnell had been informed of my demand and didn't like my uppishness one bit. From the first day of filming he made it quite clear that he had it in for me. During the rehearsal scenes together he would pause after I

spoke my lines, shake his head a little in mild disbelief, sigh, and look at Gerald Thomas with a bleak air of expectation. I don't think Gerry knew what Bill was finding wrong with my efforts but he just had to respond somehow to the implicit disapproval from such a seasoned actor.'

A budding cartoonist and gag writer, Monkhouse had made his first broadcast on Ralph Reader's *Gang Show* in 1947, breaking into television in *New To You* the following year.

With his long-time writing partner Denis Goodwin, Bob created and starred in the BBC television sketch series *Fast and Loose* and, by December 1956, ITV was presenting *The Bob Monkhouse Show*. *My Pal Bob*, a BBC sitcom on its second series in January 1958, clearly displayed the comics' clout. He and Goodwin shot the show on film and leased the programme to the BBC for one showing only.

Also new to the cast were man of many faces Kenneth Connor and Alec Bregonzi, a familiar effete and superior stooge for Tony Hancock on television. Bregonzi recalls: 'It was the very first film I ever did so I was full of apprehension. I was one of the kit issuers and had a dialogue scene with one of the principals (who never did another Carry On), Bob Monkhouse. Unfortunately it hit the cutting room floor and I think that must have been quite late in the day because the billing I have certainly wouldn't have been as good just for the sequence that is left (when all of us kit out Kenneth Connor). You can imagine how disappointed I was having been excited by the credits and then to

see me virtually an extra in what was left, although I was in rather good company.'

The actual military uniforms were put together by costume designer Joan Ellacott. William Hartnell was so impressed with his uniform that he officially requested to keep it after shooting was completed so he could do the gardening in it!

At £77,956, *Carry On Sergeant* has always been considered a very small picture indeed but, in comparison to the recent productions from Peter Rogers which were averaging at around £20,000 each, the first Carry On was actually something of an epic for the producer. The military's full cooperation was appreciated and the budget was ploughed into the production rather than the props. Just a fortnight before shooting began at Pinewood Studios, Rogers penned a lengthy thank you and further request to Major Michael Forbes explaining that 'Eastern Command has responded very well to your prompting and we have been allocated the Queens Barracks for our shooting. However one little problem still worries me. I am experiencing great difficulty in obtaining the correct "props" for the film and although the people at the Queens Barracks are willing to supply them, your permission is necessary before this can be effected. For your guidance I am sending you with this letter a list of our essential requirements.'

Major Michael Forbes was clearly amused and amazed at the film's lengthy requirements, suggesting that 'any deficiencies will have to be produced from theatrical agencies unless Headquarters Eastern Command can help in

Straight from *The Army Game* and a film star with twenty five years' experience, William Hartnell was the lead in the first Carry On comedy.

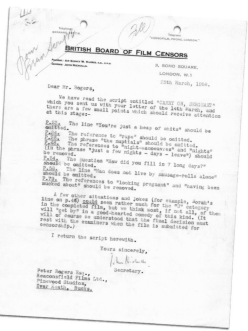

This censors' note reveals that biblical references were not considered to be suitable dialogue for a comedy. It was the first of many battles the Carry On production team had with the BBFC.

Bill Owen MBE (1914-1999)

A manager of a Warners holiday camp and for many years strongly associated with the Unity Theatre, Bill made his first film appearance in *The Way to the Stars* (1945) under his real name of Bill Rowbotham. An impressive performance as a demobbed spiv in *Dancing with Crime* (1947) landed him a contract with Rank and roles in *Easy Money* and *Once a Jolly Swagman* (both 1948). At Ealing Studios, he starred as a discredited jockey in *The Rainbow Jacket* (1954), a corrupt black marketeer in *The Ship That Died of Shame* (1955) and opposite Harry Secombe in *Davy* (1957). He proved a reliable player during the formative years of the series. Although Peter Rogers wanted him as a Carry On regular, Bill declined in order to tackle Ko-Ko in *The Mikado* at Sadler's Wells and the lead role in John Osborne's *Luther* at the Phoenix. In 1966, he wrote the West End musical *The Match Girls* and worked under Lindsay Anderson at the Royal Court. However, he was most popular in BBC television comedy, playing Bob's father-in-law in *Whatever Happened to the Likely Lads?* (1973-1974) and, from 1973, the scruffy rascal Compo in *Last of the Summer Wine*. He was filming that show's millennium special, 'Last Pigeon and Post', at the time of his death.

Carry On credits: *Sergeant, Nurse, Regardless, Cabby*
Autobiography: *Summer Wine and Vintage Years – A Cluttered Life*

Bill Owen as the forthright Helping Hand, Mike Weston, in *Carry On Regardless* (1961).

Cyril Chamberlain, as the Bren Gun Sergeant, shows how to handle your weapon in a lecture for the raucous raw recruits.

which case you should send them a list of the facilities that cannot be produced by the Queens at Guildford.' Well into production, Peter Rogers responded, on 1 April: 'There seems to have been some confusion, misunderstanding, misapprehension, miscalculation or mis-tery

concerning our requirements for this film. Everything seems to have sorted itself out and, as far as the eye can see, everything in the garden is lovely, ship-shape and hunky-dory. In fact we are seriously thinking of pulling up the ladder, Jack.'

Not slow on the uptake, Forbes quickly replied: 'I assume having been written on that date, means that there is a glorified muddle and that you are now going to ask for the entire British Army to come and sort things out because once again the film company has got itself into their usual unforeseen mess.'

Another 1 April 1958 letter from Peter Rogers was to the British Board of Film Censors. Having noted that 'a few situations and jokes could seem rather much for the U category in the completed film, but we think most, if not all, of them will "get by" in a good-hearted comedy of this kind,' there were a few required edits that mystified Rogers. He wrote: 'Can you tell me what it is about the line "Man does not live by sausage-rolls alone" to which you object? ... I feel sure that when you see the finished film you will see that it has all been shot in the sense of good clean fun.'

The BBFC explained that 'We raised objection to the line "Man does not live by sausage-rolls alone" because we usually dislike parodies of well-known Bible phrases. If it can be slightly rephrased it would avoid giving offence to anyone.'

For Norman Rossington the film had been a blessing. Not only had he gratefully picked up a decent wage packet for his role but: 'while I was filming, Granada had loads of mail complaining that I had been taken out of *The Army Game* and I was reinstated. I got £50 an episode from then on, up from £33 a fortnight.' Not only that, but Rossington would return, with *Army Game* cohort Michael Medwin in tow, for a brief cameo in the already planned follow-up to *Carry On Sergeant*.

TITBITS

Spotted amongst the recruits are *Love Thy Neighbour* bigot Jack Smethurst, *Supercar* voice artist Graydon Gould and that qualified bounder James Villiers.

Born to a naval family on Armistice Day, Connor made his first stage appearance at the age of two, as a barrel-organ monkey in one of his father's concert parties. He later formed a comedy double act with his brother. As a student of the Central School of Drama, Connor emulated Laurence Olivier by winning a Gold Medal on his graduation at the age of nineteen, although he would later point out that Olivier only tied for his!

He made his first film appearance, as a post boy, in the village murder mystery *Poison Pen* (1939). Trained in machine-gunnery and signalling, he 'fought against the foe in 1940 in Europe until I was slung into the sea at Dunkirk'. While waiting for the second front, he joined 'Stars in Battledress', appearing with Wilfrid Hyde-White in Terence Rattigan's *Flare Path* and, with the Allied forces in Italy, touring in *Someone at the Door*, with Geoffrey Keen. While in Cairo, Connor received a cable from producer William Devlin asking him to play Scrutt in *Beaux Statagem* at the Bristol Old Vic, and he became part of the company upon his demobilisation in 1947.

From 1951, he was a regular on BBC radio, supporting Ted Ray in *Ray's A Laugh*, with a gallery of grotesques including the ineffectual Sidney Mincing and the vague odd job man, Herbert Toil. He had also made a return to films; memorably playing the bewildered cab driver with Katie Johnson in the Ealing comedy classic *The Ladykillers* (1955). His skill for comic voices made him a natural cohort of the Goons, joining the team on television for *Idiot Weekly Price 2d*, *A Show Called Fred* and *Son of Fred*. He subbed for Peter Sellers and Harry Secombe in *The Goon Show* ('Who is Pink Oboe?' and 'The £50

Cure' respectively, both 1959). He starred in *The Black and White Minstrel Show* for three seasons, with other light entertainment television credits including *Hi Summer*, *Summer Time* and *Don't Say A Word*.

On stage, he took over from Kenneth Williams in the revue *One Over the Eight* and scored a West End triumph as Hysterium in *A Funny Thing Happened on the Way to the Forum*. Starring opposite Frankie Howerd and Jon Pertwee, it ran for over 500 performances at the Strand Theatre from October

1963. Connor directed the touring production, with Charles Hawtrey as Hysterium.

On television, he starred as crooked maintenance man Gus Fogg in the 1966 *Comedy Playhouse*: 'Room at the Bottom', with a full series the following year. He was also applauded as the bigamist in Somerset Maugham's *The Round Dozen*. On film, he joined the ensemble of Eric Sykes' comedy *Rhubarb, Rhubarb* and played Swallow in *Captain Nemo and the Underwater City* (both 1969). On radio, in the 1970s, he starred with Leslie Phillips in *Will the Last Businessman Who Leaves the Country Kindly Turn Out the Lights*, while in the 1980s he guest starred as Whatsisname Smith in *Rent-a-Ghost*. A favourite of David Croft, Connor played Monsieur Alfonse, the funeral director with the 'dicky ticker' in *'Allo, 'Allo* (1985-1992), Sammy the scruffy children's entertainer in *Hi-De-Hi* (1986-1988) and Professor Heinrich Van Manheim in *You Rang, M'Lord?* ('Labour or Love', 1990). He played superstitious actor Mossop alongside Hugh Paddick in *Blackadder the Third* ('Sense and Senility', 1987) and gave a moving turn as a jilted groom obsessed with his wasted wartime romance in *Made in Heaven* (1990). His last role was as Mr Warren, with Jeremy Brett and Betty Marsden, in *The Memoirs of Sherlock Holmes* ('The Red Circle', 1994).

Carry On credits: *Sergeant, Nurse, Teacher, Constable, Regardless, Cruising, Cabby, Cleo, Up the Jungle, Henry, Again Christmas, Matron, Abroad, Christmas '72, Girls, London!, Christmas '73, Dick, Laughing*: 'The Prisoner of Spenda', 'The Baron Outlook', 'Orgy and Bess', 'One in the Eye For Harold', 'The Nine Old Cobblers', *Behind, Laughing*: 'Under the Round Table', 'The Case of the Screaming Winkles', 'And in My Lady's Chamber', 'Short Knight, Long Daze', 'The Case of the Coughing Parrot', 'Who Needs Kitchener?', 'Lamp-Posts of the Empire', *England, Laughing, Emmannuelle*

CARRY ON NURSE (1959)

Local newspaper reporter Ted York (Terence Longdon) is rushed to hospital for an appendix operation and is immediately attracted to glamorous Nurse Dorothy Denton (Shirley Eaton). The hospital is ruled by the formidable Matron (Hattie Jacques) but the men's ward is packed with eccentrics like constant radio listener Humphrey Hinton (Charles Hawtrey) and pompous bookworm Oliver Reckitt (Kenneth Williams). Accident-prone Nurse Stella Dawson (Joan Sims) is forever in trouble with the Sister (Joan Hickson) and at the beck and call of troublesome patient, the Colonel (Wilfrid Hyde-White). Brave, bruised boxer Bernie Bishop (Kenneth Connor) displays an irrational fear of life in the ward and even the arrival of the ever-cheerful Jack Bell (Leslie Phillips) can't lift his spirits. But Bell himself gets moody. He's desperate to get his bunion operation over with as quickly as possible in order to whisk his coy girlfriend, Meg (June Whitfield), off on a romantic weekend. And he's not adverse to Reckitt's attempt at practical surgery. At first! But all's well that ends well. And even Nurse Dawson gets her cheeky own back on the Colonel thanks to a strategically positioned daffodil...

It is fair to say that a series was never fully intended. As Peter Rogers has often commented, 'We were never that arrogant. You can't assume the public is going to like what you do and say, right we will make a series. We made one film. It was popular. So we made another, and another, and another. Then you have a series!'

The project that eventually became *Carry On Nurse*, the film that made *Carry On Sergeant* the first of something very big indeed, was in the pipeline way before the army comedy was shot. As with 'The Bull Boys' before it, Peter Rogers was offered a threadbare piece entitled 'Ring For Catty'. Written by Patrick Cargill and Jack Beale, the property was bought by Sydney Box's production company Anglo American Associates Ltd in June 1956, and shelved for future production. Over a year went by until Eric Glass, Cargill and Beale's agent, revealed on 29 October 1957 that film industry heavy-weights Richard Attenborough and John and Roy Boulting had expressed serious interest in 'Ring For Catty', even before the first stage production at the Lyric in London. Sydney Box paid a further £1000 for the film rights and he assured Glass: 'We have also agreed that the authors of the play should be invited to write or collaborate on the writing of the screenplay on reasonable terms to be mutually agreed upon.' Just days after *Carry On Sergeant* had wrapped, 'Ring For Catty' was officially registered by Peter Rogers. Crucially, Rogers also registered two alternative titles. One was simply 'Nurse', the other *Carry On Nurse*. A sequel, if not a series, had indeed been envisaged long before the 'first' film had been commercially released.

While the screenplay would be singularly credited to Norman Hudis, Cargill and Beale were paid £2000 and promised an on-screen 'based on a play by' credit and a two and a half per cent royalty from the profits. By the time Norman Hudis had delivered his final draft, the film bore little resemblance to the play from which it was adapted. In fact, it was more like an affectionate hymn to the scriptwriter's nearest and dearest.

The majority of the saucy hi-jinks and medical madness was gleaned from true stories related by Hudis' wife, nurse Rita, the model for the delicious Nurse Dorothy Denton in the film. It is no surprise that cheerful reporter Ted York is Hudis' autobiographical appearance in the series. Indeed, like York, Hudis had experienced an emergency appendix operation during a useful, fact-finding stay at the Peace Memorial Hospital, Watford: 'It was rich in natural, earthy humour.' It was fitting, therefore, that Shirley Eaton and Terence Longdon looked set for a romance away from the bedpans as the film came to a close. The surging crescendo as affection blossoms signals that, right up to the wire, this was destined as the touching end to the picture.

Until Peter Rogers decided to usurp it with the celebrated daffodil in lieu of a rectal thermometer gag! This wasn't included in the first draft of the script and it's a low brow visual image that Norman Hudis is happy to credit to another, his mother-in-law Ethel Goode. 'Born in Ireland and a very lively lady indeed, she was greatly experienced in polishing off a jar or two with friends and neighbours and swapping stories both true and otherwise, but always deeply amusing. Ever a snapper-up of well-considered non-trifles, the story was on paper before the air around us had a chance to change back from the bright blue she had created with the yarn.'

It was a raucous shoot. Peter Rogers recalls Hattie Jacques getting a fit of the giggles. 'When one wag on the set made a noise like a

champagne cork popping out of a bottle, as she lifted up the daffodil, she was a complete goner. Gerald tried take after take, but she couldn't keep a straight face. We had to abandon the shoot for the day.' Despite this, it was only during the editing that the producer realised the scene's impact. Already a canny producer, it was this knack for tasteful vulgarity that kept the films on track.

It is for that reason that several important, issue-led exchanges were blue-pencilled from the script. Notably, one with Ted's editor coaxing his impassioned writer: 'What we want is a couple of nice articles with everything the reader expects. Smooth, selfless efficiency – dedicated

Opposite: The shapely legs of Susan Stephen help Kenneth Connor and Cyril Chamberlain find the cure for all ills. Fellow patients Brian Oulton and Ed Devereaux miss the entertainment.

That's a funny way to take a temperature – Hattie Jacques delivers one of the classic Carry On gags.

ON LOCATION

During the pre-production meeting on 27 October 1958, Gerald Thomas explained that the first two days 'would necessitate outside shooting. This work, however, would all be done within the studio grounds.' The frontage of Haven Hospital is the front of Heatherden Hall, Pinewood Studios, while the gardens outside the restaurant doubled for the ward garden. The ambulance drives through Framewood Road and Wexham Street, Fulmer, Buckinghamshire.

Kenneth Connor, Terence Longdon and Cyril Chamberlain relax between scenes at Pinewood Studios.

nurses and doctors – angels of mercy – ladies with lamps – cool hands on fevered brows – you know. A little laughter – a little sadness – a little...' 'A load of bull. There's absolutely no sentimentality involved – that's what makes these kids great. I've reported things as they are – in a completely typical ward. And I've got some stuff – off the record – about nurses' pay – that'd turn the ink in your veins to blood.'

In terms of pay, actor Terence Longdon pocketed a healthy £900 for his work on the film, while 'his' feet were paid five pounds and five shillings! As Terence explains: 'For the scene when Joan Sims gives me a complete body wash, she comments about how foolish she now feels about having earlier called me a baby! To avoid problems with the censors, Gerry Thomas had to include a shot of my huge feet

Both Joan Sims and Wilfrid Hyde-White would also star in the film *Life in Emergency Ward 10* in 1959.

just in case the audience got the right idea and thought Joan was referring to some other big part of my anatomy! Sadly, my feet weren't big enough! During the editing a stunt double was brought in and it's his feet that appear in the film. He was Bernard Bresslaw.' Identified as simply '1 double for Terence Longdon' on the contract, Bresslaw was at Pinewood Studios filming *Too Many Crooks* when he obliged and, on 20 January 1959 on 'B' Stage, made his first, unofficial, appearance in the Carry Ons.

For Shirley Eaton, the film was a blessed event in more ways than one: 'At that particular moment in time I found out I was expecting our first baby. I was twenty-two years old and overjoyed by the fact I was going to become a mother. I told everyone on the set one morning and received many warm congratulations. In my personal opinion, I think *Carry On Nurse* was the best of all the Carry On films, because it showed so well the humorous happenings

DOCTOR, DOCTOR!

On 6 November 1958 director of cinematography Reginald Wyer had a bad cough and was replaced by Harry Waxman. Newcomer Joan Sims was accident prone both on and off the screen: on 2 December 1958, during action, she fell against a trolley sustaining a cut to her right leg. She reported to First Aid and had two stitches in the wound. Sent home, she returned to film the following day.

that could go on in a typical men's surgical ward of that era. I loved every minute of shooting. The whole cast were often beset by bouts of giggling as each day's filming progressed.'

As with the military in the previous film, the nursing fraternity was turned to for assistance. For 'loaning us the numerous items of hospital equipment', the Bermondsey Work Group Hospital Management Committee was awarded twenty-five guineas for their Nurse Comfort

following day. For Connor, it wouldn't prove the only discomfiture. Playing his on-screen son was real-life son Jeremy, tempted into pretending that Susan Shaw was his mother in return for a present Gerald Thomas had dangled from the back of the camera. The joke concerned Connor's boxing prowess, with the little lad giving his father a quick jab, but, recalled Connor, 'He gave me a right cut. We had rehearsed a left. I was down on the floor, blood pouring from my nose! And there was Gerry saying, "Very good Jeremy. Very realistic!"

For most of the time, Connor and the cast of patients had it easy. The typical day

Left: Can someone smell gas? Kenneth Connor starts to feel woozy and Leslie Phillips flakes out.

Below: The first draft of the script shows Norman Hudis injecting some social comment, which was cut from the final draft.

Bottom: Rank starlet Susan Shaw joins Kenneth Connor and his son Jeremy.

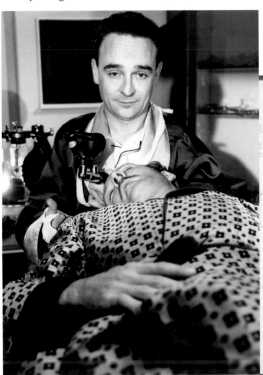

Fund, while the Central Middlesex Group Hospital was given a donation of fifteen guineas. Clearly, the Royal National Orthopaedic Hospital was less crucial to the production. Their nurses had to find comfort in a single guinea.

Even on the first day of production, 3 November 1958, medical assistance was gratefully received. After shooting had wrapped for the day a sister from King Edward VII Hospital, Windsor, arrived at the studio to mould plaster casts around Kenneth Connor's forearm. The process was completed by early evening, in readiness for an early start the

TRAILER

'Cor, What a Carry On! From the squad that gave you *Carry On Sergeant* comes its roaring laughing successor.'

Shirley Eaton (1937-)

Shirley Eaton in a captivating pose for *Doctor At Large* (1957).

Having made her debut in revue at the age of twelve, Shirley tasted adult stardom opposite Dora Bryan in *At the Lyric*, which 'funnily enough was presented at the Lyric Hammersmith!' She proved whistle-worthy decoration in *You Know What Sailors Are!* (1953), *Doctor in the House* (1954) and *Three Men in a Boat* (1956), before landing leading roles. She was blackmailed by Dennis Price in *The Naked Truth*, starred opposite Frankie Howerd in Hammer's *Further Up the Creek* and was recruited into the Carry On squad. She again worked with Bob Monkhouse in *Dentist on the Job* and the comedy play *Come Blow Your Horn* at the Prince of Wales Theatre. On film, she was the blonde eye candy in the Sid James and Kenneth Connor comic horror *What a Carve Up!* Her most iconic role was as the ill-fated Jill Masterson in the James Bond adventure *Goldfinger*, forever to be remembered as the girl suffocated by gold paint. Subsequently she appeared in an all-star production of *Ten Little Indians* (1966) with *Carry On Nurse* guest star Wilfrid Hyde-White, the Bob Hope film *Eight on the Lam* (1967) and several other international romps before concentrating on her family. She has fond memories of her time on the Carry Ons, 'working with my fellow madmen!'

Carry On credits: *Sergeant, Nurse, Constable*
Autobiography: *Golden Girl*

director, the actor protested: 'I'm a professional thespian. I don't do that sort of thing!' Photographic evidence was required and, the next time Williams dozed off, a banana was placed in his hand and a piece of cardboard reading 'Spare a copper Guv for an ex actor available on HP to careful users' laid across his bed sheets. Confronted with this, the outraged actor complained that it was a fake.

He, at least, was only joking. Guest star Wilfrid Hyde-White was very much unamused by reaction he got from the world-famous daffodil scene. Originally written as a millionaire maharajah, his role as the troublesome Colonel netted him the top acting salary of £2000. On stage since 1922 and in films since the early 1930s, he was disgusted that his integrity was being questioned by this lewd sequence. Having featured in such classics as *Quartet* (1948), *The Third Man* (1949) and *The Browning Version* (1953), he considered the scene detrimental to his subsequent career. In fact, the bottom is never on screen. The risqué joke is completely in the mind.

And it stayed in the mind of many contented cinemagoers. Over ten million tickets were sold, making *Carry On Nurse* the most successful film in Britain for 1959. Even more amazingly, this economically made British comedy was taken to the heart of American audiences with thousands of plastic daffodils being snapped up in theater foyers. It was rude health at its most successful.

The first of many memorable drag sequences for Charles Hawtrey, here becoming a sister of mercy with Stephanie Schiller and Ann Firbank.

consisted of rolling out of bed, getting out of pyjamas, getting to Pinewood, putting on some different pyjamas and getting back into a bed on set. For Kenneth Williams all this exertion proved too much. Caught napping by his

TITBITS

On 19 December 1958, the respected racing broadcaster Raymond Glendenning recorded a specially written horserace commentary for the opening scene, as ambulance men Fred Griffiths and Anthony Sagar hurtle to the finish post.

Norman Hudis (1922-)

tepney-born Hudis started his writing career at the age of sixteen, when he was appointed the junior reporter on the *Hampstead and Highgate Express*. In a deleted exchange from his most successful screenplay, *Carry On Nurse*, Terence Longdon's character, Ted York, spoke on his behalf when he explained: 'When you're sixteen, you call yourself a journalist. When you're my age – reporter.'

After two years on the 'Ham and High', Hudis volunteered for the Royal Air Force in 1940. Although he was rejected for flying duties on medical grounds, he served five and a half years in the RAF. For his last two years he was stationed in Cairo as an official correspondent on the reporting staff of the *Air Force News*, covering the entire Middle East area.

Upon his demob, Hudis joined the Rank Publicity Division as a studio publicist. Having been contracted as an apprentice screenwriter at Pinewood Studios, Hudis took six weeks to write his first play, *Here is the News*, for an under-thirties theatre group in Leatherhead. Based on Peron's suppression of the newspaper *La Prensa*, it was also performed at the White Bar Theater, Connecticut, USA. His second play, *The Powder Magazine*, was produced for a repertory company and then performed for BBC television.

At Pinewood, he was faring less well. None of his scripts had been filmed. With invaluable experience but nothing tangible to show for it, Hudis decided to resign and went freelance as a second co-feature writer on such films as *West of Suez*, *Face in the Night*, *Hour of Decision* and *Passport to Treason*, for Monty Berman and Bob Baker. At Beaconsfield Studios, Peter Rogers

signed him up for 'The Mail Bag Robbery'. Later changed to *The Flying Scot*, Hudis' script concerned petty criminal Ronnie Cowan (Lee Patterson) and his attempted robbery of half a million Bank of Scotland pound notes from a London-bound train. A well-made second-feature thriller directed by Compton Bennett, the film made back its meagre budget of £20,380 with ease.

Even more economic was *The Tommy Steele Story*, which came in at just £17,500. Hudis, a rock 'n' roll illiterate, wrote the screenplay and saw the film gross over three and a half million pounds. It even did well in America,

basking in the light of the Bill Haley hit, *Rock Around the Clock* (1956) and spearheading the British invasion as *Rock Around the World*. The film's success catapulted Hudis into the front line of British film writers and made him a natural to polish up the army comedy Peter Rogers had been planning to make.

Carry On Sergeant was, of course, the result, 'which, in the words of distributors and cinema managers, turned out to be one of the funniest and most successful comedies for many, many years.' Of his time on the series, 'two phrases stick in my mind to this day. "It's not what we expected," from Peter, and Gerry saying "I agree with whatever Peter thinks!" It became a joke between us.'

As well as nine more comedy films for Peter Rogers and Gerald Thomas, Hudis created the ITV situation comedy *Our House* (1960-1962) which starred Hattie Jacques, Charles Hawtrey, Joan Sims, Norman Rossington and Bernard Bresslaw. Hudis subsequently worked in Hollywood, writing for hit television series such as *The Man From U.N.C.L.E.* ('The Five Daughters Affair') and *Marcus Welby M.D.* ('Hell is Upstairs', which was nominated for a Best Episode, Drama Award by the Writers' Guild of America (West)).

He has latterly worked in animation, writing the film *A Monkey's Tale*, and working as story editor and writer on the German series *Waldo*. His play, *Dinner With Ribbentrop*, was premiered at the Rude Guerilla Theater in Santa Ana.

Carry On credits: Sergeant, Nurse, Teacher, Constable, Regardless, Cruising

Autobiography: *No Laughing Matter – How I Carried On*

CARRY ON TEACHER (1959)

Maudlin Street School Headmaster William Wakefield (Ted Ray) has his heart set on a position in a brand new school. The behaviour of his current charges, notably cane-worthy joker Robin Stevens (Richard O'Sullivan), makes him yearn for a change even more. Everything rests on a trouble-free visit from inspector Felicity Wheeler (Rosalind Knight) and child psychologist Alistair Grigg (Leslie Phillips). But the kids have other ideas. They blow up a miniature rocket belonging to science master Gregory Adams (Kenneth Connor) and play up the sexual tensions within Romeo and Juliet *during a lesson with English Literature master Edwin Milton (Kenneth Williams). They collapse the piano of Music master Michael Bean (Charles Hawtrey) and even provide Physical Training mistress Sarah Allcock (Joan Sims) with a pair of shorts several sizes too small. Much to Grigg's delight! And they pepper the noticeboard with saucy pictures, which caretaker Alf (Cyril Chamberlain) removes with gusto. After the sabotage of the musical staging of* Romeo and Juliet, *Maths mistress Grace Short (Hattie Jacques) realises that the children are reacting against the departure of the Headmaster they love. An emotional Mr Wakefield decides to stay.*

The first totally original Carry On script, Norman Hudis' treatment was delivered in November 1958. Already, familiar actors from the previous two films were sensing the possibility of long-term employment.

Norman Hudis wrote to Peter Rogers relating that 'Michael Medwin mentioned to me that he's been approached for an option for a role in the next Carry On. In the original storyline – and indeed in this treatment – there isn't really a spot for him. Bill Owen has also mentioned the possibility of an option to me and the same applies to him. I'm sure (if these statements by the actors are correct) that we'd all rather have parts written in for them at the beginning instead of trying to graft them onto a complete film later on.' Bill Owen was considered for the gym master Harold Short ('unless there's a strong desire to feature Terence Longdon in this role)' while Medwin was earmarked for the revolutionary Ellis Hackenschmidt.

By 11 February 1959, Peter Rogers had already mapped out his planned casting for the film, a fortnight before the trade showing of *Carry On Nurse* and less than a year since *Carry On Sergeant* had started production. Rogers wrote to Anglo Amalgamated: 'The subject, the script of which has already been submitted to you, is planned to start production at Pinewood Studios on 9 March 1959. As in the other two Carry On films the cast will be Kenneth Connor, Kenneth Williams, Charles Hawtrey, Joan Sims, Hattie Jacques, Rosalind Knight and Leslie Phillips. The newcomer to the team will be Ted Ray (subject to contract). I propose to make this film at a budget not exceeding £85,000.' Sims and Phillips had, in fact, only appeared in the previous film, as had Rosalind Knight.

The daughter of actor Esmond Knight, she had attended the Old Vic School from the age of fifteen and studied there during its last two years in existence. In 1955, she landed a walk-on part in Laurence Olivier's film of *Richard III*. However, she relished her radio work on *Ray's A Laugh* with Ted Ray and Kenneth Connor, and claimed her ambition was to work with Kenneth Williams.

Left: Kenneth Connor, the undisputed star of vintage Carry On, in a publicity pose as science master Gregory Adams.

DOCTOR, DOCTOR!

Concerned about her recurring weight problem, the production costs included a slimming and relaxation course at a Hertfordshire health farm for Joan Sims, a course she had to fit in with her West End stage commitment to *Breath of Spring*. However, on the first day of filming, 9 March 1959, Joan reported to First Aid complaining of acute pains in her right leg. The studio doctor, Dr Danger, bound the leg to ease the pain. The medical report states that after shooting it was decided that as it 'was very inconvenient for Miss Sims to rest at home the producer decided that she should be admitted to Windsor Hospital in order to obtain the maximum rest and to have treatment if necessary. It is also adjacent to the studio thereby saving travelling time. She was admitted at 10.00 pm Monday evening. The schedule has been rearranged to allow Miss Sims the maximum number of days off before resuming work.' She was back at work three days later.

Opposite: Hello! Joan Sims looks set to give in to the raffish charms of Leslie Phillips.

ON LOCATION

Drayton Secondary School in West Ealing doubled for Maudlin Street School for location filming on 6 and 7 April. On 12 April 1959 production manager Frank Bevis thanked the education committee explaining: 'We erected our own school entrance in the playground but this has now been struck and cleared away and I have since been to see Mr Drydon, who was a great help, and have been around the school with him to see that everything has been left in the same condition as we found it.'

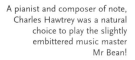

A pianist and composer of note, Charles Hawtrey was a natural choice to play the slightly embittered music master Mr Bean!

Julia Lockwood and Leslie Phillips in *Please Turn Over*.

Guest comedian Ted Ray had been born in Liverpool, the son of stage comic Charlie Alden. A star for over twenty years, he was much admired by Peter Rogers because 'he had made the whole nation laugh during the war.' However, Rogers's handwritten notes on the script reveal that his original casting choice was Eric Barker, commenting about the actor that 'age OK – not a Mr Chips but a vigorous man'. In the end, Ted Ray's performance was more sentimental than authoritarian although, off camera, he was one of the keenest practical jokers the series would ever employ. Leslie Phillips remembers 'Ted saying "You've got my number!" "What number?" I replied. "That number, UMD 412. That's the number I've always wanted." He was talking about my car registration! Every time I saw Ted he would say "You've still got that number." On the last day I got the prop-master

to make up a set of car registration plates bearing the number. They stuck one on the back of Ted's car but couldn't finish the wheeze before Ted returned. That night I got a phone call from the police saying they had stopped a man claiming to be the comedian Ted Ray and he appeared to be driving my car. "However," continued the policeman, "the front of the vehicle appears to be Mr Ray's car!" It was Ted on the phone and he burst out laughing!'

Once again, Rogers turned to the obvious authorities for help, penning a letter to Dr C E Gurr of the Middlesex Education Centre, on 13 February 1959: 'I have been in touch with Mr Wilson and Mr Rose of the Ealing Education Authority with regard to facilities for shooting a film comedy entitled *Carry On Teacher*. Mr Wilson has suggested that I write to you personally to put the case before you. You will notice from the script that the school has been given a fictitious name to shoot on the outside of an existing school, which will not be recognisable in the film. I would plan to shoot the film during the school holidays and would produce my own crowd of children and teaching staff so that none of your actual staff would be required. I would like to point out that this is intended as a completely harmless comedy and I look forward to your permission to use one of your schools for background.'

The BBFC was less cooperative when surveying the shooting script. 'They said that they didn't like the idea of Leslie Phillips saying the name Allcock because it would sound too rude,' recalls the actor ruefully. 'The entire crew

Please Turn Over

Norman Hudis adapted the hit West End comedy *Book of the Month* by Basil Thomas for this Peter Rogers comedy that contrasts the home life of Jo Halliday (Julia Lockwood) and the fantasy version as depicted in her bestselling raunchy novel. The film was released in 1959 and featured Ted Ray, Joan Sims, Leslie Phillips, Dilys Laye and Charles Hawtrey.

were walking round Pinewood proving they could say Allcock without sounding filthy but I couldn't. It was the "k" sounds. The flatter I made it the filthier it became!' It was a battle that Peter Rogers would fight and fight again. 'We both enjoyed it as a matter of fact! The censors knew what sort of film we were making and we would put in jokes deliberately. If that one was cut out, we had another one in the next scene. It was a bargaining system!'

The producer was less indulgent of his scriptwriter's flights of social consciousness. Struck from the final draft was a teacher's thought on: 'Heard of the Miners Dream of Home? This is the Teachers Dream of School.' Even the stage directions for when Wakefield

Cyril Chamberlain (1909-1974)

A prolific stage and screen actor who remains the most underrated of Carry On stars, Chamberlain chalked up appearances in the first seven films, including the supporting role of Alf the caretaker in *Carry On Teacher* and an arresting cameo in *Carry On Regardless*. Having made his stage debut in 1931, he made his first films just before the war, memorably playing a BBC broadcaster in the Will Hay comedy *Ask A Policeman* (1939). After war service, he became an indispensable part of British film's collection of character stars. He was notable as the petty criminal in the Norman Wisdom comedy *Trouble in Store* (1953), the gruff father obsessed with television in *Simon and Laura* (1955) and the bemused chess-playing policeman friend of Alastair Sim in *The Green Man* (1956). A popular comic stooge for Arthur Lucan, he notched up three *Old Mother Riley* titles, ... *In Business*, ... *In Society* and *Old Mother Riley's Jungle Treasure* between 1940 and 1951. He sparred with George Formby in *Spare a Copper* (1940) and joined Frankie Howerd's gang in *The Great St. Trinian's Train Robbery* (1966). Very much part of the pool of talent utilised by Peter Rogers and Betty Box, he appeared in *Marry Me!* (1949), *You Know What Sailors Are!* (1953), *Doctor at Sea* (1955), *The Tommy Steele Story* (1957), *Upstairs and Downstairs* (1959) and *Raising the Wind* (1961), notching up over 150 film appearances before his retirement in 1966. In his later years he ran an antiques business in Watlington and hosted the television series *Treasure Chest*, in which he talked about family heirlooms.

Carry On credits: *Sergeant, Nurse, Teacher, Constable, Regardless, Cruising, Cabby*

his films. Sadly, he was under contract with ABC Pictures. 'They never used him,' complains Peter Rogers, 'but because he was being employed in our pictures it was an embarrassment for Anglo Amalgamated. ABC threatened to scupper the distribution of the Carry Ons and so we had to find somebody else. It was a bitter blow. Ted was a fine artiste and a good friend but we had to find someone else.' That someone else was Sid James.

Cyril Chamberlain as the dependable Thurston in *Carry On, Constable* (1960).

The heavily annotated draft outline from Norman Hudis.

appears before the schoolchildren were not safe from Rogers's editing. 'Except for the lack of cloth caps, it looks rather like one of those shots from an early Russian film in which a group of workers gather round a bright-eyed revolutionary leader, hanging on his every word.'

Despite steering clear of this politically themed imagery, Rogers was clear about one thing. Ted Ray was the perfect leading man for

TITBITS!

Future stars Richard O'Sullivan, Carol White and Larry Dann appear as schoolchildren. All were under the auspices of the Malone Corona Stage School, including twenty-four crowd girls, a group which numbered tail-end Carry On babe Diane Langton among them, and one boy musician, Terry Cook. The children recorded a rendition of 'Ten Green Bottles' in Pinewood's Theatre 1 on 16 March 1959.

CARRY ON, CONSTABLE (1960)

With a flu epidemic depleting the police force, Sergeant Frank Wilkins (Sid James) can't wait for the arrival of three new recruits. Unfortunately, he gets the dashing playboy Tom Potter (Leslie Phillips), the superstitious Constable Charlie Constable (Kenneth Connor) and the haughty Stanley Benson (Kenneth Williams). The arrival of the effete Timothy Grose (Charles Hawtrey) and his budgie Bobby is the final straw. The incompetent Inspector Mills (Eric Barker) blames his sergeant as a catalogue of catastrophes mount, from Benson attempting to arrest a CID man (Victor Maddern) to Potter pushing Inspector Mills into his garden pond! Potter does, however, help Sally Barry (Shirley Eaton) through pre-wedding tensions, and the matchmaker Sergeant Laura Moon (Hattie Jacques) helps Constable Constable find love and fulfilment with WPC Gloria Passworthy (Joan Sims). Eventually, the new boys in blue bag the criminals and Sergeant Wilkins is promoted!

An unashamed rehash of *Carry On Sergeant*, the title *Carry On, Constable* had previously been considered as early as August 1958, just as *Sergeant* was released. On 1 September 1958 John Antrobus received a down payment for a story outline; three months later, on 2 December 1958, Beryl Vertue confirmed a deal with Peter Rogers that included rights for a script as well.

Antrobus would land a supporting role in the film (as one of the citizens hassling Sid James at the film's start) but another writer would take his place. The film would ultimately be 'based on an idea by Brock Williams', although the writer's treatment bears little comparison to the finished article.

Williams' proposal starts with a violent bank robbery told in flashback. The ancient and wheezing Constable Henry Gubbins relates his adventure from twelve years previous to wide-eyed new recruit: Police Constable George Gulp. The grip of gangland violence perpetrated by the dreaded Spineza gang would form the backbone of the plot as Gubbins reveals: 'What a chase that was. I got two bullet holes in me helmet that day. Lucky it was a couple of sizes too big or I'd have been a goner.'

Brock Williams' notes included a tentative casting suggestion, with the character of Ron written for Leslie Phillips, Mate for Kenneth Connor, Sweeney for Charles Hawtrey, Chalky for Cyril Chamberlain, Dusty for Bill Owen, Lofty for Terence Longdon and Sherlock for who else but Kenneth Williams. Brock also suggested casting *Carry On Nurse* starlet Ann Firbank as his female lead, Sylvia Grant.

Even at this stage, it would appear to have been the kiss of death for writers to construct

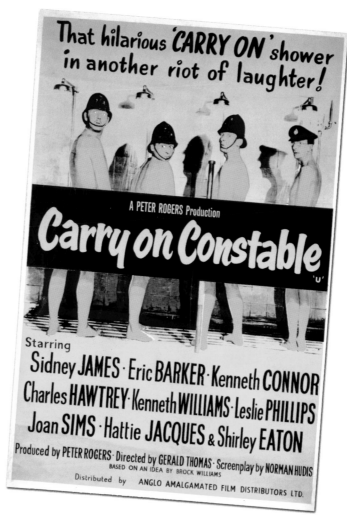

characters for particular members of the gang. 'I want writers to write good characters. I'll cast it!' was Peter Rogers' maxim. On Williams' treatment the producer confined his noted comments to a terse: 'not enough for Connor'. In fact he was so adamant on this point that he wrote it twice.

After all this activity it is perhaps unsurprising that Norman Hudis was asked to return to the fold. Hudis was contracted to write the script on 21 September 1959 and

Bernard Spence was paid £500 for additional work on 2 February 1960.

Hudis had to work fast. On 2 November 1959 the pre-production meeting heard from 'Mr Gerry Thomas and 'Mr [Frank] Bevis' who 'intimated that there would be approximately fourteen days' location in the Ealing area before the production came into the studio. No night

Opposite: Cyril Chamberlain, Esma Cannon, Kenneth Williams and Sid James filming on location in Ealing.

Shirley Eaton is alarmed by Leslie Phillips' undercover investigation.

DOCTOR, DOCTOR!

The progress report for 2 December 1959 records that: 'Leslie Phillips was unwell on arrival at studios, and was sent home by studio doctor. The order of shooting had to be changed and Kenneth Connor did not work.' The following day Leslie was 'still indisposed and unable to work' while on the 4th the unit was 'unable to continue shoot owing to indisposition of Leslie Phillips.' He returned on 7 December. It could have been down to sleepless nights, for Leslie's fourth child, Roger, was born during the production. Leslie was given a gift of a policeman's helmet to use as a rocking cradle!

ON LOCATION

On 9 November 1959, the unit arrived at 'Oakhurst', St Stephens Road, Ealing, at 7.30 am, the location for the neglected house of thieves tracked down by Leslie Phillips, Kenneth Williams, Kenneth Connor and Charles Hawtrey. Work was wrapped up at 6.05 pm and completed the following day. Sid James joined the cast on 11 November, filming outside the Postmen's Office, Manor Road, West Ealing, with Phillips, Williams, Hawtrey and Connor. Later that same day, Williams filmed his one-day scene with Victor Maddern at the same location.

On 17 November Irene Handl, Williams and Hawtrey filmed on Lothair Road, South Ealing, while two days later Esma Cannon filmed her road-crossing sequence. On 11 December 1959, the 'unit commenced work at Hanwell location [Parish Church, for Hawtrey's cat rescue] and travelled back to Pinewood location at 12.30. On completion of street sequence unit moved onto 'D' stage at 3.30pm.'

Gerald Thomas sees to the location catering for star Sid James.

Finally, on 16 December 1959, Charles Hawtrey jumped on to his scooter on Lothair Road and the Eric Barker lily pond sequence was filmed. Kenneth Connor stands outside the public convenience at South Ealing Station and accompanies Joan Sims over the railway station footbridge. The actual police station is the Public Library in Cherrington Road, Hanwell.

shooting was envisaged at this stage but it would be necessary to have several early calls. Phil Hobbs would be catering for the location. On the completion of the location shooting the production would come into the studio on 'D' stage.'

Already using its past successes as shorthand, it was noted that this film would be similar to others in the Carry On series. On 29 October 1959 production manager Frank Bevis had written to the superintendent at Ealing police station: 'Referring to my visit to your station yesterday ... there are several locations needed for this picture and we are shooting these around the Ealing area commencing Monday 9 November. We would very much appreciate it if you would detail a police officer to us during this period to control spectators etc should we attract attention from passers by. In the past when we have had police cooperation the company has always made a substantial donation to the police widows and orphans fund. This procedure we will gladly follow in this instance unless of course you have other suggestions as to how we can show our appreciation for your help.'

Watch Your Stern

Kenneth Connor headlined this Peter Rogers comedy as hapless Seaman Blissworth. Written by Alan Hackney and Vivian Cox, who had been a witness at the wedding of Peter Rogers and Betty Box, the

similarities with radio's *The Navy Lark* were heightened by the 'silly ass' performance of Leslie Phillips. Joan Sims, as Connor's love interest, and Sid James as the bewhiskered Chief Petty Officer Mundy give exemplary support.

In the event, bad weather scuppered the planned schedule. Joan Sims first day on the film was 12 November 1959 and, after just three days of location filming, 'the unit travelled to an Ealing location but owing to thick fog decided to move back to Pinewood at 11.40 am, started shooting on Pinewood Estate at 12.13 and moved into Police Canteen on 'D' Stage at 2.50.' The following day was similarly affected, before a renewed location schedule with firm studio cover backing was put together.

While Gerald Thomas was trying to second-guess the elements, Peter Rogers was back at Pinewood acknowledging expert advice. On 1 December 1959 he wrote to George Eyles of the Institute of Advanced Motorists. 'I feel that it is time that I wrote to you and came to some understanding regarding the technical advice and research which you have given us on our film 'Carry On, Constable'. If you remember we did discuss a figure when you came down to the studio with Brock Williams and I am really wondering how you would like the payments made. But to avoid the harsh world of

No kidding

In this 1960 comedy Leslie Phillips and Geraldine McEwan star as a couple who convert a country mansion into a holiday home for the children of the very wealthy, including sexy teen Vanilla (Julia Lockwood). The film was based on the novel by Valerie Anderson and co-written by Norman Hudis. The home itself would become very familiar to Peter Rogers. A vacant Beaconsfield property, Dirk Bogarde bought it and named it 'Drummer's Yard'. A year later, he sold it to Rogers.

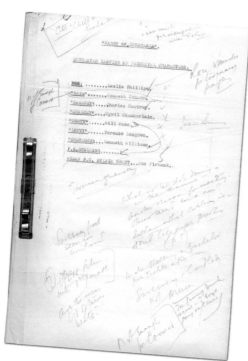

commerce perhaps you would come down to the studios and have lunch with me and Gerald one day, and help us with our parade sequence. If I give you a day or two notice perhaps you can fit it in. I hope so.'

In a letter of 17 December 1959 Eyles thanked the producer, 'for your kind hospitality on my recent visit to Pinewood. I very much

enjoyed seeing the parade sequences which were extremely well carried out, also the "rushes" (is that correct?) and I have no doubt that the end product will be hilarious. However, there is one point about which I am rather disturbed. I am given to understand that there is a possibility that you may change the name of the film to 'Carry On Copper', and I feel that this would be a grave error from the point of view of thousands of police officers and their families, who will undoubtedly enjoy the film as much as I will. The term 'copper' is a term of derision and is invariably used in a most uncomplimentary

Brock Williams' suggested casting for his, largely unused, version of the film.

Sid James gets an unexpected soaking.

Raising the Wind

An unashamed reworking of *Doctor in the House* for music students, even the academy location of University College Hospital in London's Gower Street, was the same in this 1961 Peter Rogers comedy. And James Robertson Justice stars as the irascible but ultimately warm Sir Benjamin. With a script by composer Bruce Montgomery, Paul Massie and Jennifer Jayne do sterling work as the romantic leads, struggling through the frustration, financial problems and musical elation of life as a student.

context, one could almost say it is a method of expressing contempt for the police force, which I am sure is anything but your intention. '*Carry On, Constable*' is a friendly title and will in my opinion convey to the picture going public that this, like the previous Carry On films, is good friendly fun.' Never one to offend the cinema-going public, Peter Rogers conceded the point.

Things didn't go quite so smoothly on the casting front. Young Paul Cole, who as the

cheeky Atkins had stolen many of the classroom scenes in *Carry On Teacher*, had filmed a one-day role as an equally cheeky barrow boy on 11 November 1959. Sadly, the scene was cut from the finished film. Hitting the cutting room floor too was Ronald Adam, best remembered as Alec Guinness's furtive boss in *The Lavender Hill Mob* (1951). He had filmed his bit as a motorist on 17 November.

Jeremy Connor was unable to play Irene Handl's son because he was too fond of Charles Hawtrey to plough his scooter into the actor on camera! Appropriately, the film's criminal element was also to prove unreliable. On 18 November, Herby Nelson was not available to play his part as '3rd crook' so the role was recast. On 8 December 1959 it was noted that 'Michael Balfour although contracted to us on first call accepted work from another studio and therefore must not be paid the balance of his contract, ie one day's rate. Jack Taylor and Eric Boon were called to the studios but unable to work due to Michael Balfour's absence.'

Boon, a friend of 'everybody's friend' Sid James, was one of the greats in the fight game, boxing five nights a week at boys' clubs in London. The figurehead of pugilism, however, was undoubtedly Freddie Mills who lamented that he had to miss the much anticipated Henry

Kenneth Williams and Charles Hawtrey go undercover as Ethel and Agatha.

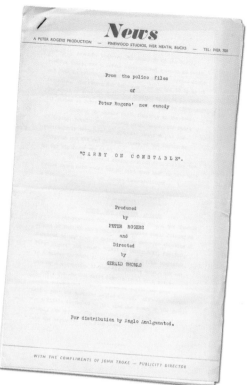

News

A PETER ROGERS PRODUCTION — PINEWOOD STUDIOS, IVER HEATH, BUCKS — TEL: IVER 700

From the police files

of

Peter Rogers' new comedy

"CARRY ON CONSTABLE".

Produced
by
PETER ROGERS
and
Directed
by
GERALD THOMAS

For distribution by Anglo Amalgamated.

WITH THE COMPLIMENTS OF JOHN TROKE — PUBLICITY DIRECTOR

Leslie Philips OBE, CBE (1924-)

A model and child actor from the mid-1930s, Leslie returned to acting after war service and created the role of Tony in the hit West End comedy *For Better, For Worse*. Supporting roles opposite Norman Wisdom in *Just My Luck* and Bill Travers in *The Smallest Show on Earth* (both 1957) led to a stint in Hollywood as the silly ass in *Les Girls* (1958). On his return to England he played more of the same in the BBC radio series *The Navy Lark* (1959-1977) and began a run of starring comedy film vehicles, notably as the hapless romantic in *Doctor in Love* (1960), *Doctor in Clover* (1966) and *Doctor in Trouble* (1970). Throughout the 1970s Leslie directed and starred in stage farce and cavorted with a glamorous parade of totty on film in the likes of *Don't Just Lie There, Say Something* (1973) and *Spanish Fly* (1975). A conscious effort to tackle more serious roles resulted in theatrical productions of Shakespeare (as Falstaff with the Royal Shakespeare Company) and Chekhov (in *August*, under the direction of Anthony Hopkins). His one-man show, *On the Whole It's Been Jolly Good*, won plaudits at both Edinburgh and Hampstead. His best television role was as the scheming Jimmy Blake in *Chancer* (1990-1991). Always busy, he was a lusty Major Godfrey Teal in the *Midsomer Murders* episode 'Painted in Blood', the ill-fated Wilson in *Lara Croft: Tomb Raider* (2001), the caddish safecracker in the BBC sketch show *Revolver*, the voice of the sorting hat in the *Harry Potter* films and an award-winning performance opposite Peter O'Toole in *Venus*.

Carry On credits: *Nurse, Teacher, Constable, Columbus*
Autobiography: *Hello*

Cooper v Joe Erskine fight on 17 November because he had to be up bright and early for filming the next day.

Perhaps Marianne Stone did stay up late because on 18 November she wasn't available to fulfil her £25 contract for the role of 'Agitated Woman'. Hilda Fenemore was cast, although Stone did make a contribution to the film. On 17 December 1959 she redubbed Lucy Griffiths for the role of the manic spinster Miss Horton, who suspects a break-in next door and telephones the police. It was the last day of studio time, culminating with Ted Ray's son Robin completing his two days' work as a distraught store manager.

The film's trade show, on 17 February 1960, marked the start of a new era for Carry On. And the start of a new decade in which the series would flourish. Despite Kenneth Williams' first

TITBITS

For the scene where Kenneth Connor believes a murder is being committed (filmed at 39 The Avenue, West Ealing), an extract of radio material was especially recorded by actors Mary Jones and Frederick Treves. Charles Stanley remained uncredited for his role as the newspaper man, as did Arnold Diamond as the Police Commissioner and Robert Howell as the boy in the street.

impression that 'it was mediocre and tired. I think everyone knew it', the *Monthly Film Bulletin* proved exceedingly prophetic when it noted: 'the Carry On series looks like becoming an anthology of all the slap-and-tickle music hall jokes that have ever been cracked.'

A tickety-boo publicity shot of Leslie Phillips as happy-go-lucky RAF officer Jimmy Cooper in *Very Important Person* (1961).

CARRY ON REGARDLESS (1961)

Frustrated Unemployment Agency worker Sam Twist (Kenneth Connor) has nothing to offer regular jobseeker Montgomery Infield-Hopping (Terence Longdon). Multi-linguist Francis Courtenay (Kenneth Williams) can't get a job either, nor burly Mike Weston (Bill Owen) or delicate Gabriel Dimple (Charles Hawtrey). The ladies, Lily Duveen (Joan Sims) and Delia King (Liz Fraser) are so desperate they even barge into the men only department. But there isn't any work. Monty finds something in the newspaper and quietly creeps away, but all the jobseekers follow him and even Sam Twist leaves his depressing post for more job satisfaction. The advert leads them to Bert Handy (Sid James), Miss Cooling (Esma Cannon) and the Helping Hands Agency. Life is never dull. Courtenay walks a chimp, poses for a beekeeper's helmet advert and mistakes a group of schoolgirls for Chinese tourists. Twist ends up on a train in the middle of a spy adventure right out of The 39 Steps *and in a seductive situation with Penny Panting (Fenella Fielding). Dimple encounters the wrong sort of bird at a strip club while Lily gets drunk at a wine tasting. All the Hands are put to good use at an Ideal Home Exhibition. Later they inadvertently wreck a deserted mansion belonging to their landlord (Stanley Unwin). But, he's pleased with the mess. Helping Hands gets a new ninety-nine-year lease and it's carry on regardless for the cheerful workers!*

I t was almost a year after the release of *Carry On, Constable* before shooting commenced on the next film in the series. By that time, Carry On had become something of a phenomenon.

Eager fans would bombard the Carry On office with suggestions for everything from 'Carry On Pig Farming' to 'Carry On Stamp Collecting'.

A more pressing issue was that other film companies were gainfully employing the familiar Carry On actors in rival knockabout comedies. Indeed, *Dentist on the Job*, with its vintage *Carry On Sergeant* cast of Bob Monkhouse, Shirley Eaton, Kenneth Connor, Eric Barker and Charles Hawtrey, was reissued in America as *Carry On TV*. And George Minter's Renown Pictures had attempted to register the title *Carry On Doctor* with the British Film Producers Association. A 'comedy relating to medical practice based on a book by G Stuttard', it caused Joyce M Briggs to write a letter to the Rank Organisation: 'This sounds a very deliberate attempt to cash in on the success of *Carry On Nurse* and maybe also the Doctor subjects. I don't know whether there is anything one can do to stop them. I would think it doubtful but it certainly seems pretty bad form.'

Meanwhile, in America, Warwick Films had already title-registered both 'Carry On Doctor' and 'Carry On Intern'. Clearly, Peter Rogers had to react quickly in order to protect his growing empire. In a memo to Nat Cohen at Anglo

Amalgamated, Rogers suggested a blanket quote that 'unless it is a Peter Rogers production distributed by Anglo Amalgamated it is not a genuine Carry On.' Still, more legally binding precautions were taken: that November, a selection of titles, including *Carry On Regardless*, were registered. And J Arthur Rank himself had appointed Cyril James of Walt Disney Productions to arbitrate the official ownership of the name Carry On. Crucially, although Val Guest's naval comedy *Carry On Admiral* had hit cinemas a year before the production of *Carry On Sergeant*, 'the committee noted that the film was trade shown by the applicant on the 16th April 1957 but that the title was not registered with the British Film Producers Association scheme.' Peter Rogers was able to register *Carry On Doctor* and rest assured that *Carry On Regardless*, on general release on 26 March, would not be threatened by unofficial Carry On comedies.

On 8 November 1960, the day before filming began, Rogers explained to Stuart Levy at Anglo that 'in submitting the enclosed budget for this production you will notice that the cost has increased somewhat since the last Carry On.' A £5,000 increase in cast budgets was among the many reasons given, although he was at pains to point out that: 'You will notice that the only sacrifice towards any saving in the cost of production have been made by me and Gerald. Our fee on the last two films was £7,500. In this production I have put them at £5,000

because I vaguely remember a slight lunchtime battle with you and Nat [Cohen] over this. I am anxious to know whether or not you feel such a sacrifice is justified bearing in mind the increased responsibilities and difficulties connected with this production.'

The pre-production had certainly been troublesome, particularly in terms of the other acting commitments of the film's stars. A letter from Charles Hawtrey's agent to casting director Betty White on 20 May 1960 gives an idea of the difficulties: 'This will confirm that you have employed Charles Hawtrey, to play one of the leading parts in a production in the Carry On series, his engagement to commence on November 14 1960 and to be for a period of not less than four weeks. You acknowledge that he will be appearing in a TV series entitled *Our House* prior to his engagement and it is possible that should you require his services on the 7 November he might be available but this we

Opposite: The magnificent seven from the Helping Hands Agency cause havoc.

Joan Sims, tricked in to drinking neat gin during the filming of this scene, puts a stop to the wolfish suggestions from Nicholas Parsons.

DOCTOR, DOCTOR!

Kenneth Williams received an unexpected Christmas box on 'A' stage on 21 December 1960. For the Ideal Homes Exhibition scene, Kenneth had to appear to fly from a swing into a bubble bath containing Joan Sims. Perched on a twelve-foot-high rostrum, Kenneth accidentally fell backwards and did his nether regions some damage. Screaming 'Oh my parts!' he was sent off to the medical department. With no sign of his return, Gerald Thomas eventually found him, 'lying on a table with his trousers down, while a nurse slapped handfuls of Savlon on to the injury! As she gently massaged it in Kenneth was moaning softly "Oh lovely, lovely!" "Come on Kenny," I said, "that's enough of that. There's work to do!"

ON LOCATION

As the pre-production meeting of 22 November 1960 noted, 'there would be three days local location at Windsor, West Drayton and Yiewsley.' The shoot must have been delayed since, on 6 December, the 'chimps party at Windsor was held up because of rain'. As a result, the unit was back at the studio by 2.00 pm. Again, on 12 December, 'shooting on location at Windsor was held up because of bad weather and the unit returned to the studio at 1.30 pm to shoot interior Delia's bedsitting room which was completed except for inserts of alarm clock.' Bus driver Tony Sagar, cabbie Fred Griffiths and the chimps were all on stand-by, but were released before the afternoon was out. The Helping Hands Agency is situated on the corner of Park Street, Windsor and the house where the chimp lives is 11 Clarence Crescent. Kenneth Williams 'attacked' the Corona schoolgirls in Windsor Riverside Station on 15 December 1960.

Job-seekers Terence Longdon and Bill Owen see the funny side of Kenneth Connor's frustration.

Pinewood daffy with Donald Houston, Ronald Lewis, Juliet Mills, Donald Sinden, Kenneth Williams, Amanda Reiss, Andrew Ray and Lance Percival.

cannot let you know until a little nearer the date. You agree to co-star his name alphabetically with other co-starred artists, no other artist's name to be in larger type and his name to be not less than in fourth position. This will apply likewise to all paid advertising and publicity. For his service you will pay Mr Hawtrey £2000 for four consecutive weeks any days thereafter £100 a day and a maximum of £50 per week.'

On the same day, 'Welacts Limited for the service of Hattie Jacques' had agreed a fee of

£1,400 for the actress to play a leading role in the film. However, when the film finally went into production, illness prevented Hattie's involvement save for a one-day cameo role as the frosty-faced hospital sister. Hattie pocketed £100 for her loyalty to the brand name although 'it is understood this artiste does not require any screen or publicity credit.' Hattie's indisposition meant it was necessary to rewrite the script, giving some of Hattie's material to Joan Sims's role of Lily Duveen and restructuring

Twice Round the Daffodils

A more sedate and thoughtful adaptation of *Ring For Catty*, the inspiration for *Carry On Nurse*, the film stars Juliet Mills as the devoted nurse, Catty. Here only Kenneth Williams, as TB patient Henry Halfpenny, and Joan Sims as his loving sister Harriet are present from the recognised Carry On team. Anglo was uneasy about the depiction of TB, as Norman Hudis recalls: 'We believed that the subject could include comedy moments because we were under the impression that the disease had been virtually eliminated. It turned out that 5,000 people died of tuberculosis that year. The kindest headline we got was "Carry On Coughing"!'

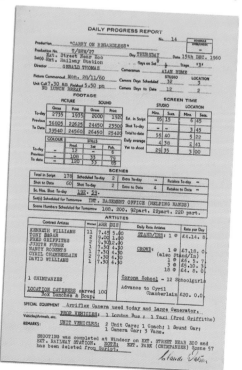

Hattie's character, Delia King, to fit the shapely figure of newcomer Liz Fraser.

Because of the changes, Betty White had to negotiate a new and very reasonable deal for the film's star attraction, Sid James. That November, his representative Phyllis Parnell wrote: 'I have discussed this with Sidney and he is quite agreeable to your suggestion ... he will be available to you for a further week on the above production, making it a guarantee of one day per week for four weeks commencing 28 November, and three complete weeks from on or about 28 December for a guaranteed sum of £2,600 and thereafter at a daily rate of £200. With regard to the one day per week from 28 November he has agreed to make himself available to you on Friday.'

Unusually for a vintage Carry On, there was a lot of material cut for reasons of timing or, in the case of Eleanor Summerfield, of supposed public decency! 'I was always cutting her out of one film or another' recalls Peter Rogers, 'she was a wonderful artiste but she never seemed to get off of the cutting room floor!' In a lengthy sequence with Charles Hawtrey, she played friendly housewife Mrs Riley, who is obsessed with talking in her sleep. While her husband is away, she wants a Helping Hand to write down what she says. Confusion reigns, as this brief extract from Norman Hudis's shooting script illustrates:

Mrs Riley: I'm in the mood.
Gabriel: Are you?
Mrs Riley: I know I am.
Gabriel: Oh, do you.?
Mrs Riley: That's why I'm so keen to get to bed.

Gabriel: Mrs Riley!!!
Mrs Riley: There are nights when I know it's going to happen at its most effective.
Gabriel: You don't say.
Mrs Riley: I've got it!
Gabriel: I should think you have!
Mrs Riley: What does it matter what you are?
Gabriel: It takes all sorts to make a world – yes.
Mrs Riley: Mr Pimple.
Gabriel: Dimple.
Mrs Riley: You'll be able to do your part from the wardrobe.
Gabriel: You flatter me, madam.

Ronald Adam, cut from *Carry On, Constable*, again earned himself £40 for a day's work that

No stranger to the boxing ring himself, Sid James chats to Carry On regular Tom Clegg during a break from filming on Pinewood's 'B' Stage.

Eleanor Summerfield and a shocked Charles Hawtrey in a scene censored from *Carry On Regardless*.

Liz Fraser (1933-)

Cornering the market in blonde bombshells with a heart, Liz was part of Tony Hancock's television repertory company and subsequently played Sid James's girlfriend in the BBC situation comedy *Citizen James* in 1960. On film, she excelled opposite Sid in *Desert Mice* (1959) and *Double Bunk* (1961), played a stripper in *Doctor in Love* (1960) and, in the same year, played Peter Sellers' daughter in *I'm All Right, Jack* and his girlfriend in *Two-Way Stretch*. She bewitched Norman Wisdom in *The Bulldog Breed* and toyed with Lloyd Lamble in *The Pure Hell of St. Trinian's*, but proved she was more than just a pretty face in the bleak thriller *The Painted Smile* (1961) and the domestic drama, *The Family Way* (1966). On television, she guest starred in *The Avengers* ('The Girl From Auntie', 1966), *Randall and Hopkirk (deceased)* ('It's Supposed to be Thicker Than Water', 1969) and *The Goodies* ('Caught in the Act', 1970), before returning to film as Ian Lavender's mother in *Dad's Army* (1971). A glut of sex comedies followed, with Liz seducing Barry Evans in *Under the Doctor* (1976) and Robin Askwith in *Confessions From a Holiday Camp* (1977). She gave impressive performances as a heartbroken mother pickled in gin in *Miss Marple* ('Nemesis', 1987) and a cancer victim in *Eskimos Do It* (1988). In 2000, she was still as seductive as ever as Compo's secret love in *Last of the Summer Wine* ('Surprise at Throstlenest' and 'Just a Small Funeral').

Carry On credits: *Regardless, Cruising, Cabby, Behind, Laughing*

A seductive Liz Fraser during publicity for Carry On Cruising.

would never be seen by the cinema-going public. Ian Whittaker was originally contracted for £15 to play the tobacconist's assistant who eases Kenneth Connor's addiction. Subsequently, the part was recast, with Angus Lennie taking on the assignment for £12. Sadly, in the event, the interior tobacconist's scene was cut anyway, as

was a nudist camp sequence which saw Carl Conway's sterling performance as 'man in nudist club' lost from the final print. Having been the celebrated stooge of Sid Field and Norman Wisdom on film and stage, Jerry Desmonde was clearly nearing the end of his tether. He stepped into the minor role of smooth-talking actor Martin Paul when Benny Hill cohort and *Criss Cross* quiz host Jeremy Hawk couldn't fulfil his £50 contract. Sheila Hancock, rehearsing the Kenneth Williams revue *One Over the Eight*, also had to pull out of the film. She was originally hired to play the fussy owner of the chimpanzee for a fee of £50. With an increase of £10, Ambrosine Phillpotts was cast in her stead.

Further expense was incurred when Stanley Unwin and the gang completed the dilapidated house sequences. As the call sheet details, 'the rushes showed a scratch on the negative which will necessitate re-takes of part of today's shooting.' Kenneth Williams 'got the giggles when we did the sequence with Stanley Unwin. His extraordinary gobbledegook delighted me. He played a property developer who talked of building sumptuous apartments fit for a king. This came out as "Luckshe flabberblock dangly chandelery, Harry the Acres and Kathering of Arabolde." The dialogue always flowed trippingly on cue, and when I said to Gerald, "Marvellous the way he knows his lines," he replied. "Certainly, nobody else does".'

The Iron Maiden

The Maiden in question here wasn't the glamorous tease of Anne Helm as American airline heiress Kathy Fisher, but a massive traction engine. This 1962 Peter Rogers comedy was scripted by Vivian Cox and Leslie Bricusse. Michael Craig stars as Jack Hopkins, an energetic and enthused aircraft designer who obsessively tinkers with engines in his spare time. It was understandably considered a 'poor man's *Genevieve*'. Joan Sims and Jim Dale can be spotted in enjoyable cameos.

Charles Hawtrey (1914-1988)

The son of a Hounslow motor mechanic, Hawtrey's love of performing started early. At the age of six he was writing and directing plays that he would perform in his back garden with his school friends. He charged one penny for admission and this money went on sweets and payment for his actors.

By 1922, he had made his first film, cast by actor and director Donald Crisp in *Tell Your Children*. He made his professional stage debut in December 1925, playing a street boy in *The Windmill Man*, at the Boscombe Theatre, Bournemouth and, as 'Master Charles Hawtrey – the Angel Faced Choir Boy' he recorded on Columbia and Regal Records. Taking his stage name from the late actor-manager Sir Charles Hawtrey, in December 1928 he played William in a production of Hawtrey's fantasy *Where the Rainbow Ends*. He remembered that his 'challenge as an actor was to find the fine line between farce and comedy. It took me years of practice.'

By 1935, he had starred in the musical short *Kiddies On Parade* and played an irritating schoolboy in the Will Hay comedy *Good Morning, Boys!* The following year, he played Slightly in a stage production of *Peter Pan* and tried to impress his girl with his knowledge of turtles in Alfred Hitchcock's *Sabotage*. But it was Will Hay that became his mentor and he appeared with the comic in *Where's That Fire* (1937), *The Ghost of St. Michael's* (1941) and *The Goose Steps Out* (1942).

Further film offers at Ealing included two George Formby vehicles, *Much Too Shy* (1942) and *Bell-Bottom*

George (1943) and a memorable supporting role as the put-upon, piano-pumping pub worker in *Passport to Pimlico* (1948). On radio, he remained a *Children's Hour* favourite in partnership with Patricia Hayes as *Norman and Henry Bones, Boy Detectives*. The serial ran from 1943 until 1960. On film, he directed *What Do We Do Now?* and *Dumb Dora Discovers Tobacco* in 1945 and played a succession of cameo roles, including a victim of con artist Frankie Howerd in *Jumping For Joy* and a hassled radio disc jockey in the Benny Hill comedy *Who Done It?* (both 1955).

Thereafter, Carry On dominated, although his eccentric artist in *What A Whopper!* (1961) and the 1963 situation comedy *The Best of Friends*, with Hylda Baker, were notable exceptions. Gerald Thomas was aware of his star's impact on first appearance. 'Way back in the beginning, Charles' shock entrance was an accident,' he recalled in 1967, 'but realising the potential I set out deliberately to "shock" and now Charles' first appearance is carefully planned.' Hawtrey pondered, 'In a way it's terrible. Often my first line of dialogue, funny though it may be, is completely lost.'

In the 1970s, Hawtrey starred in stage farce and pantomime, notably playing Muddles in Aubrey Phillips's productions of *Snow White and the Seven Dwarfs*. Happily retired in Deal, he made one last television appearance, as Clarence, the Duke of Claridge, in *SuperGran* ('The State Visit', 1987).

Carry On credits: *Sergeant, Nurse, Teacher, Constable, Regardless, Cabby, Jack, Spying, Cleo, Cowboy, Screaming!, Don't Lose Your Head, Follow That Camel, Doctor, Up the Khyber, Camping, Again Doctor, Up the Jungle, Christmas '69, Loving, Henry, Again Christmas, At Your Convenience, Matron, Abroad*

CARRY ON CRUISING (1962)

Captain Wellington Crowther (Sid James) is not impressed when his ship, the SS Happy Wanderer, is full of new faces. The midshipman Leonard Marjoribanks (Kenneth Williams), Dr Arthur Binn (Kenneth Connor) and seasick chef Wilfred Haines (Lance Percival) make him nervous. He hopes to take control of a new luxury liner and this cruise is destined to be his swansong on the Wanderer, but things look black when new barman Sam Turner (Jimmy Thompson) can't mix the Captain's favourite drink, an Aberdeen Angus. Saucy passenger Glad Trimble (Liz Fraser) is having a break from men while looking for a boyfriend for her bosom buddy Flo Castle (Dilys Laye), although one look at the hunky Jenkins (Vincent Ball) changes Glad's mind. Dr Binn falls under the spell of Flo and even serenades her, although he mistakenly declares his undying love to the ship's resident drunk (Ronnie Stevens). As time runs out, Marjoribanks and Glad match-make, Flo gets over her girlish crush on Captain Wellington and Haines concocts an unspeakable cake to celebrate his Captain's tenth year in the job. Captain Crowther is moved by the occasion but, impressed with his new recruits, he has already decided to stay with the ship and turn down the captaincy of a brand new vessel.

Anglo Amalgamated were aware that Carry On was a hot property, but it lacked, in Anglo's opinion, one vital ingredient: colour. Peter Rogers was happy to oblige – 'It was their money' after all. Indeed, the budget for *Carry On Cruising* weighed in at £145,403, a whopping £30,000 more than *Carry On Regardless*. Still, as the Helping Hands agency comedy packed them in across the country, it was uncertain what the next subject was going to be.

Michael Pertwee had scripted a draft for a 'Carry On Flying', simply referred to as 'the Flying Story' in a memo to Peter Rogers on 2 June 1961: 'I think we should be able to get what we want except that if you decide not to go on with the screenplay you will get no rights in the treatment. I think that it is fair because if you did get rights in the treatment and not have a screenplay written Michael will have spent a lot of time on it and not be able to do it for anyone else.' Rogers has since dismissed suggestions of a 'Carry On Flying' (and of a tentatively suggested 'Carry On Smoking', concerning firemen), citing the risk of a tragedy hitting the news while the film was on general release.

Far safer was a vague notion from Carry On star Eric Barker concerning a film based around a coach tour of Europe. This was modified to a Mediterranean cruise ship by Rogers and on 12 July 1960 Barker was commissioned to write a thirty- to forty-page treatment entitled 'Carry On At Sea'. Barker had had three novels published by the time he was twenty-one, written lyrics and sketches for André Charlot's revues and written and produced two plays. In addition, one of his short stories had been included in P G Wodehouse's celebrated anthology *A Century of Humour*. The draft was headed 'Carry On Sailor (or Cruising)', and Barker suggests Miles Malleson for the role of Lord Tolsworth. The story starts with Tolsworth addressing a shareholders' meeting of the Ocean Navigation Company. Business is bad and just one senior captain can be selected as Commodore of the Fleet in charge of the SS *Felicity*. The hapless Rodney Booth, son-in-law of Tolsworth (with no casting suggestion by Eric Barker), sets up an off-screen football match between the crews of the rival captains, but one of the coaches hits a bus and all of Captain Blythe's crew end up in Sidcup Hospital. Although the overall feel is more like *Watch Your Stern*, which Barker had just acted in for Peter Rogers, the *Cruising* treatment does include a new crew being hastily summoned and that's where Barker earned his 'from a story' credit on the finished film and promotional materials. The treatment suggests an intriguing, gentle comedy that casts 'Ken Connor' as communist communications man Lofty Long and Hattie Jacques as the seductive Felicity Tolsworth, trying to save her marriage while besotted by Long. Leslie Phillips was penned in for Chris Fletcher who is assigned the job of chaperoning Felicity on the voyage. The sexy Dr Tempest was planned for Liz Fraser, complete with plenty of attention from the randy crew, and 'Dickie Wattis' was Barker's choice for Tolsworth's subservient lackey Kearns. 'Kenny Williams' as Clement Bagpuize and 'Sid James' as Sid Jackson, 'a tough sea-dog, ticking off horses' were recruited and in this early extract, Rodney continues to gather the vessel's skeleton crew:

CLOSE-UP OF LEONARD TOWSLE ('Charlie Hawtrey') PEERING

AFFECTIONATELY THROUGH HIS STEEL-FRAMED GLASSES AT SOMEONE JUST OFF SCREEN

Leonard: Who loves his beautiful baby girl, then? Papa does. Yes, he does then. And who loves her Papa? Beautiful baby does. Yes, she does, then.

PHONE BELL RINGS. HE PICKS UP RECEIVER

Leonard: Who? Oh. Yes, I'll hold on.

RODNEY BOOTH TAKES PHONE FROM SECRETARY (MISS HAMMERTON)

Rodney: Rodney Booth here.

Leonard: Come on, give papa a kiss then.

RODNEY REACTS

Rodney: Hullo. Is that Seaman L Towsle's house?

Opposite: Ship of Fools: Sid James, Kenneth Connor and Ed Devereaux confront a supposedly drunk Kenneth Williams.

Gerald Thomas chats with two of his stars, Kenneth Connor and Lance Percival

Kenneth Connor goes where the sun don't shine to inject seasick chef, Lance Percival. Kenneth Williams gets the point of the joke.

Dilys Laye grapples with a reluctant Sid James.

Leonard: Oh. Yes, sir. Rather. What can I do for you, m'm?

Rodney: Well, this is the Ocean Navigation Company. Is your husband there, Mrs Towsle?

Leonard: (HURT) This is my husband, that is to say, I'm not married. This is Seaman Towsle speaking.

Rodney: Oh, I'm so sorry. Well, I can offer you your old job on the *Ophelia*, if you can sail immediately?

Leonard: Oh, how too utterly fabulous. Back with my lovely old deck games, and the darling old quoity-woities. I'll be there, on the dot, what!

RODNEY REPLACES RECEIVER, SHAKING HIS HEAD EXPRESSIVELY.

Leonard: Hear that, my

darling baby? Papa's back in work. That means he can buy gorgeous things for his girl out in the exotic East!

CAMERA TRACKS BACK TO SHOW THAT HE IS ADDRESSING MOLLIE. A VERY TATTY ELDERLY PARROT IN A CAGE.

Mollie: Go, man, go.

In Norman Hudis's shooting script, Captain Sid James's new crew is already in operation as the film starts. When Kenneth Connor's character, Dr Arthur Binn, explains that he has come from Consolidated Marmalade he continues, in material cut from the film, that it was a 'Jammy job! Chuff chuff – 'cept when they're overcome by the fumes.' 'Who?' 'The workers. Hours at a stretch over a vat of seventy thousand steaming oranges, gives 'em the pips so to speak!'

'Captain' Gerald Thomas couldn't resist a subtle in-joke during the scene: his clipboard includes the names of the new recruits as well as several members of the film crew listed as 'officers': 'Third Officer J Causey' (Assistant director Jack), 'Fourth Officer D Lovell' (Camera operator Dudley), 'Junior Fourth Officer A Hume' (Director of photography Alan).

Kenneth Williams repeated loud and often that this film was a huge disappointment. He would drop his chin, flare his nostrils and tell any chat show host who cared to listen that he had been promised an all-expenses-paid Mediterranean cruise as part of the production. This seems to fly in the face of Peter Rogers' tight rein on the budget and dislike of foreign location filming but, indeed, one pre-production meeting (of Thursday 4 January 1962) did mention the possibility of ocean liner footage being filmed in Gibraltar, although, by then, a unit consisting of Gerald Thomas, Bill Hill and Alan Hume had already filmed the relevant material on the MV *Braemar Castle*, Tilbury Docks.

Filming proper began at Pinewood on 8 January 1962. Certainly, with the respected production designer Carmen Dillon aboard, all that was needed was a ripe imagination. Having worked at Fox-British Pictures at Wembley Studios from 1935, Dillon had often collaborated with director Anthony Asquith. She also worked on Laurence Olivier's *Henry V* (1944), *Hamlet* (1948) and *Richard III* (1956), but relished the release that the Doctor and Carry On comedies gave her. Her construction of the deck of the SS *Happy Wanderer* on Pinewood's 'A' stage was a masterpiece. A tank was set into the floor of the sound stage, featuring tiled surround backed by a large mural depicting Neptune and the

TITBITS

Keith Peacock, an ex-physical training instructor for the Army Physical Training Corps in Catterick was employed to train Vincent Ball as the butch gym instructor. Jan Williams, soon to massage the clavicles of Robert Shaw in the James Bond film *From Russia With Love*, is an uncredited passenger. At Denham Studios on 8 February 1962 the Italian/English balladeer Robert Cardinali recorded the song that makes Liz Fraser and Dilys Laye go weak at the knees.

denizens of his underwater world. Six and a half feet at its deepest end and twenty-four-feet long, it contained 50,000 gallons of chlorinated water heated to 86°F. This may have looked impressive on-screen, but it left several actors uneasy, particularly the diminutive Esma Cannon, who couldn't swim! Gerald Thomas planted an expert swimmer off camera during her pool sequence, just in case she got into difficulties. Liz Fraser, on the other hand, perfected a twist-action swimming style that was dubbed 'the Liz Fraser Keep Up or Otherwise I Go Down Stroke'.

Sound mixer Bob MacPhee had worked as a ship's wireless officer and even been on a course of instruction under Marconi. The radio on the film set was a fully working model. Continually egged on by the crew to send messages to real ships, he managed to resist the temptation.

But Peter Rogers was never once tempted to indulge one of his regular actors. Charles Hawtrey, originally offered the role of the seasick chef Wilfred Haines, had proved too demanding. Requesting a star on his dressing-room door and better billing than for previous films, Gerald Thomas insisted that: 'It was a difficult situation. But with the best will in the world we just could not bill him above Sid James, for example.' In the end, Hawtrey's role went to Lance Percival, who had forged a close working relationship with Kenneth Williams in the West End revue *One Over the Eight* and had proved himself a resourceful radio and cabaret performer since forming his own calypso orchestra in 1957. Despite being his only foray into the Carry On series, Percival's ability to slot into the established team and knuckle down for the tight schedule won Rogers' respect. He also saved some money on the budget: Percival was paid just £600; Hawtrey's fee would have been nearer the £4,000 that Sid James earned. This figure, despite securing him 'star screen credit', was eclipsed by the £4,500 Kenneth Connor made and the £5,000 Kenneth Williams received.

Dilys Laye skilfully stepped into the vacant shoes of Joan Sims. After a lengthy West End run in the revue *The Lord Chamberlain Regrets!* alongside *Cruising* guest star Ronnie Stevens, Joan was, apparently, exhausted. A close friendship with a Pinewood carpenter had done her no favours with Peter Rogers – the relationship had lasted over the filming of *Carry On Regardless* and *Twice Round the Daffodils*, resulting in Rogers advising her that he disliked his artistes fraternising with the crew.

The box office receipts proved beyond a shadow of a doubt that a Carry On could still

Dilys Laye (1934–)

Having studied at the Aida Foster school, Dilys recreated Elizabeth Bergner's celebrated role of *The Boy in The Burning Bush*. She wowed audiences in Wales during a twelve-week run of one-night stands for the Arts Council under the direction of Kenneth Tynan. After repertory experience at Bromley and work at the Bristol Old Vic, she starred for a year on Broadway in *The Boy Friend*. Returning to the West End, she appeared in the revue *For Amusement Only* and, deciding to settle in London, joined Joan Sims in the revue *Intimacy at 8.30*. *And So To Bed*, *High Spirits* (again with Sims) and *The Tunnel of Love* followed. Having made her film debut as the Young Trottie in *Trottie True* (1949), she played the sexy school girl Bridget in *Blue Murder at St. Trinian's* (1957) and decorated Betty Box and Peter Rogers comedies, *Doctor at Large* (1957), *Upstairs and Downstairs* (1959) and *Please Turn Over* (1959). In 1965, she starred opposite Sheila Hancock in the BBC series *The Bed-Sit Girl* and featured in Charlie Chaplin's cinematic return, *A Countess in Hong Kong* (1967). She wrote and appeared in the 1981 domestic sitcom *Chintz* for Granada, played Maxine Palmer in *EastEnders* from 1994 to 1995 and guested as Isabel Stephens in *Coronation Street* (2000-2001).

Carry On credits: *Cruising, Spying, Doctor, Camping*

make money, even without the complete roster of the regular faces that had enlivened earlier films. And it was nearly 1963, the year when Britain learned how to swing...

Above: Dilys Laye poses as a sexy secretary in a promotional shot from *Doctor At Large* (1957).

Left: Peter Rogers and Gerald Thomas frame Anglo Amalgamated's Nat Cohen with one of the props!

CARRY ON CABBY (1963)

Cheerful taxi firm owner Charlie Hawkins (Sid James) is happy in business but unhappy in love. Despite his best intentions, his wife Peggy (Hattie Jacques), feels neglected. Ineffectual ex-serviceman driver 'Pintpot' (Charles Hawtrey) joins the company and there is a revolt when Flo (Esma Cannon) attempts to cover an emergency fare for her sick husband, Smiley (Bill Owen). Gullible unionist Allbright (Norman Chappell) calls for action so Flo backs down. It becomes a real battle of the sexes when Ted Watson (Kenneth Connor) feuds with his canteen girl, Sally (Liz Fraser). While rushing back to take his wife out for an anniversary dinner, Charlie is stopped by a nervous man (Jim Dale), desperate to get his expectant wife to hospital. Peggy drowns her sorrows with Sally and, with Flo in tow, hatches a plan for a rival, all-female cab company, Glam Cabs. Soon business is booming and Charlie's old black cabs are obsolete. Drivers walk out, Charlie hits the bottle and Ted 'drags up' to infiltrate the enemy camp. A radio airwaves war rages until Sarge (Cyril Chamberlain), picks up a Glam Cab distress signal from Sally and Peggy. The chancer Dancy (Peter Gilmore) and his gang have kidnapped the girls and their takings. It's down to Charlie, his men and their army training techniques to save the day.

In April 1962, *Carry On Cruising* went on general release and writer Norman Hudis still had two years left on his contract with Peter Rogers. But, as with previous films, other writers were welcomed, nay encouraged, to deliver treatments, draft scripts and hopeful suggestions.

Having seen his client, John Jowett, earn from *Carry On Nurse*, Kevin Kavanagh wrote to Rogers on 25 June 1962: 'With the thought that perhaps the props of *HMS Defiant* may still be lying around, Talbot Rothwell has written the enclosed storyline for a screen comedy. It strikes me this could be a completely new look for the Carry On gang, and I hope it will amuse you'. This missive is arguably the most crucial in the continuing cult and clout of Carry On. It introduced both the series' most prolific writer and, with the suggestion of an historical naval comedy, the entire concept of the period costume Carry On.

Peter Rogers was clearly taken with the suggestion, replying: 'Thank you for Talbot Rothwell's idea for a Carry On. I will read this eagerly as I admire Rothwell's work.' So much so, that the producer optioned the offered work and assigned the writer to another pending comedy film, based on a treatment that Sid Green and Dick Hills had fleshed out during their time writing the second series of *The Morecambe and Wise Show* for ATV. On 1 June 1963 the pair received £3000 for the basic idea, although another writer would contribute the all-important chase finale, as Kevin Kavanagh noted. On 30 November 1962 he wrote to Peter Rogers: 'Further to our conversation yesterday this to confirm our agreement that Talbot Rothwell will work on the "Taxi" project – sorry, I don't know the correct title – for a fee of £1,750. This fee to include the rights of the "chase" sequence which is the property of Sid Colin. This fee shall be payable as to £1,000 on signature of contract, and the balance on delivery. Just to remind you, too, that you kindly agreed to pay now the balance of £1,500 due on "Poopdecker, RN" ("Up the Armanda")'

At one stage the film, now entitled 'Call Me A Cab', was to be credited to Richard Michael Hills and Sidney Charlie Green and the shooting script to Talbot Rothwell and Sid Colin. In the end, Colin would receive no credit, only money. His script, 'The Streets of Town', was registered

Speedy work as Kenneth Connor gets to grips with Marian Horton at Pinewood Studios.

by Peter Rogers but never filmed, but the finale was indeed lifted for the 'Taxi' project. Rothwell, a friend and colleague of Colin for many years, was happy to remunerate the writer from his own fee. On Christmas Eve 1962, within weeks of signing the contract, Rothwell delivered his finished script.

By the New Year, the original title had been removed from the screenplay; it was now officially recognised as 'Carry On Cabbie' or 'Carry On Cabby', both spellings being used. It certainly wasn't a quickie as has often been suggested. Despite returning to black and white production, the budget saw an increase of just under £5,000 from *Carry On Cruising*. It was clear from the outset that Rothwell's style was broader and more reliant on innuendo than his illustrious predecessor, as witnessed in this sequence, sadly deleted, between cheeky Kenneth Connor and grumpy Bill Owen:

Ted: Don't laugh so much you'll bust something. You don't want to have to wear one of those belts do you now?

Top: Shameless product placement, as the new Cortina is draped with Glam Cab drivers.

Opposite: You're not in the Army now – Kenneth Connor castigates a gloomy Bill Owen as the accident-prone Charles Hawtrey tries to look innocent.

TITBITS

Penelope Lee and Michael Graham, who played the couple snogging in the back of Milo O'Shea's cab, went uncredited. So did Joan Green, who played Jim Dale's pregnant wife, Frank Lawless as the estate agent and Geoffrey Colville as the printer besieged with work printing cut-price cab fare flyers. The Glam Cab girls included unheralded members Maris Tant, Joanna Ford, Anabella McCartney, Sally Ann Shaw, Olive Milbourne and Alexandra Dore.

Nurse On Wheels

In his last film for Peter Rogers, Norman Hudis adapted the novel *Nurse is a Neighbour* by Joanna Jones. He was told that Joan Sims had been cast as the new county district nurse, Joanna Jones herself, and the role was written accordingly. Unfortunately Sims put on weight before production and Rogers reluctantly had to recast. Because of her rocky love affair with farmer Henry Edwards (Ronald Lewis), the producer felt 'Joan just wasn't suited for that role at that time.' She was replaced by Juliet Mills and offered any other female role in the script for the same top billing salary. Joan chose Deborah, the vicar's daughter.

Smiley: I already do. The old woman gave it me for Christmas.
Ted: That's what I like to see. A marriage based on mutual truss.

Trust was key when it was confirmed that Mr S Trotter of the London General Cab Company would be happy to help with 'the hire of cabs, the museum and whatever "props" he can supply for studio use.' During the making of the film, cabbies were employed as driving extras and advisers. Charles Hawtrey certainly needed all the help he could get. Having never learned to drive, he crammed in one-hour lessons three times every day for three weeks, passing the test on the Friday before shooting

Prince Charles holds court with the King of Carry On, Sid James, on location in Black Park.

began. 'At least I knew that one part of the film would be easy enough,' he reflected, 'the part where I had to ram a taxi with my scooter!' But, despite the crash, bang, wallop of production, for one veteran cabby, Bert Leavy, it was all 'very boring' except for the hands of poker on set. Another returning veteran was Ron Digby, who had been Chief Electrician at Teddington Studios from 1939 until 1948. He was anything but bored, enthusing, 'It's good to be back. And though there's no one to touch Will Hay, these youngsters certainly know a thing or two. I reckon Sid would make a pretty good cabby.'

Sid James, Kenneth Connor and Charles Hawtrey would have been rather mystified to

ON LOCATION

The pre-production meeting of Monday 18 March 1963 revealed that the film would incorporate a lot of exterior filming. The first day, Monday 25 March, saw the unit on Pinewood's Car Park 1, which doubled as Charlie Hawkins' yard. On Friday 29 March, the unit then moved to Windsor. A prefab cabbie shelter was constructed at the studio and taken to Windsor, while an extended day had been scheduled at Windsor South Railway Station. It was outside the station that Michael Ward and Kenneth Connor filmed their mincing vignette. Town Street, Windsor was extensively used, notably for the Sid James' encounter with Ambrosine Phillpotts, filmed on 3 April 1963. On 9 April, a municipal building near the railway station stood in for the mortuary that a confused Charles Hawtrey drives up to. The lavish motor showroom was situated at Maidenhead Authority Limited, Bath Road, Taplow, and they were informed that 'the picture is a first feature

comedy being made at Pinewood Studios, starring Sidney James and Hattie Jacques.' The car chase was filmed on Seven Hills Road, Black Park Road and Fulmer Common Road, Fulmer.

Esma Cannon (1906-1972)

Nobody played bewildered, twittering innocence better than the diminutive Esma Cannon. Her role as the dogmatic Flo was her final film appearance before retirement, but she reflected: 'Until now, I've always played fluttery parts. My height made it difficult to play anything else. But as Flo I really do get a chance to show that little women can be a character to reckon with.' She had made her debut in opera at the age of four in *Madame Butterfly* and continued on stage, memorably in a Francis Laidler pantomime at the Victoria Palace. She started in films in the 1930s, appearing in the George Formby comedy *I See Ice!* (1938) and the village crime thriller *Poison Pen* (1939), and had made her television debut as a village maid in *Love From a Stranger*. She could play perfect variations on her bemused spinster roles, memorably as the lovesick victim of Dennis Price in *Holiday Camp* and the mute serving maid, Lindy, in *Jassy* (both 1947). However, it was comedy that made her name. She absent-mindedly dropped sugar cubes in to her tea during Norman Wisdom's rendition of 'Don't Laugh at Me' in *Trouble in Store* (1953) and was Margaret Rutherford's maid Spencer, in *I'm All Right Jack* (1959). In the early 1960s, she made a delightfully dotty maiden Aunt Emily in *What a Carve Up!*, played the deaf landlady in *Raising the Wind* and brought heartbreaking poignancy to the Leslie Phillips vet comedy *In the Doghouse*. On television, she played Little Lil in the BBC sitcom *The Rag Trade* from 1961 until 1962. One of her favourite television jobs involved a trip to Paris to play a sad little French spinster in *Maigret* ('A Crime for Christmas', 1961). It was definitive Esma.

Carry On credits: *Constable, Regardless, Cruising, Cabby*

find themselves being described as youngsters, although one newcomer was certainly worthy of the title: Jim Dale, who made his first appearance on location on 4 April for *Cabby* in 1963. Contracted via 'Jim Dale limited', he received £160 for five days' work on the film, during which time 'it is understood and agreed that the artiste is on first call to the BBC during the weeks commencing 8 April 1963 and 6 May 1963.' For Bill Owen, his four days work for £320 would signal his farewell to the Carry Ons. Liz Fraser too would take a sabbatical for over ten years. She had revealed at the time that she saw film as her future rather than live theatre because 'I like to have my evenings free. Besides I like the money in films.' In a conversation with Stuart Levy of Anglo

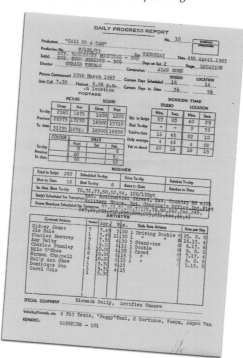

Amalgamated, however, Liz had remarked that the films could be marketed much more forcefully. Rather than admiring her business prowess, Levy telephoned Peter Rogers complaining that he didn't expect an actress to comment on issues such as distribution. 'Liz spoke out of turn,' reflects Rogers. 'I would love to have used Liz in more films, but when your distributor picks up the phone and tells you not to use someone, you have to have a very good reason for going over their heads.' Liz Fraser was unceremoniously dropped from the series.

Above: Esma Cannon as 'the mad little pixie' in a portrait from *Carry On Cruising*.

Left: An historical call sheet records Jim Dale's first official day on a Carry On film.

CARRY ON JACK (1964)

With an impending threat from the Spanish, the British admiralty is forced to accept any willing recruit to serve as an officer. And there's none more willing than the bumbling midshipman, Albert Poopdecker RN (Bernard Cribbins). Unfortunately, on his way to his ship, a couple of rascally sedan-chair-carriers (Jim Dale and Ian Wilson) advise him to get a bit of female company before the voyage. Stumbling into Dirty Dick's, Albert loses his uniform to the comely Sally (Juliet Mills), who is desperate to set sail in search of her lost love, Roger (Peter Gilmore). While still in disarray, Poopdecker and a smelly cesspit cleaner, Walter Sweetley (Charles Hawtrey), are press-ganged for the good of the nation. Poopdecker desperately tries to explain to the devilish First Officer, Jonathan Howett (Donald Houston), and the Bosun, Mr Angel (Percy Herbert), but it appears Poopdecker has already reported for duty – in the disguised shape of Sally! Still, it's the sickly Captain Fearless (Kenneth Williams) who runs the ship with lily-livered cowardice, forcing his men to drink milk instead of rum and to sail away from impending trouble. The crew mutiny and set Albert, Sally, Walter, Fearless and his cow adrift in an open boat. Howett and Angel manage to capture the entire Spanish fleet but during a makeshift surgical session on Fearless's foot, Albert manages to destroy the spoils of war.

A Spanish omelette – Bernard Cribbins, Juliet Mills, Charles Hawtrey and Kenneth Williams adopt fool-proof disguises for a bash at the enemy.

With Liz Fraser having talked her way out of the series, the new leading lady came from a very well-known theatrical pedigree, a fact that Juliet Mills was more aware of than most. With her father, John Mills, one of the most respected of British film actors and her younger sister Hayley Mills the darling of the Walt Disney Organisation, Juliet had already been cast by Peter Rogers in *Twice Round the Daffodils* and *Nurse on Wheels*, so a Carry On appearance was something of a formality.

It was the fledgling scriptwriter Talbot Rothwell who was to steer the series into uncharted waters. His provisional idea from June 1962 had taken a comment from Horatio Nelson 'in an exclusive interview with Hardy' from 1805, as its starting point: 'It is high time we saw a really funny story come out of all this silly nonsense with Spain. I am heartily sick of all melodrama and bloodshed.' The treatment also included the 'historical note' disclaimer 'Any relationship between this story and historical fact is purely accidental (fact has been purposely avoided).' Rothwell, bewitched by the Hornblower stories of C S Forrester, had originally entitled his script 'Poopdecker RN', but Peter Rogers had other ideas. He owned the film rights to James Mitchell's book *Steady Boys, Steady*, and that title was quickly adopted for Rothwell's outline. That in turn, however, was hastily usurped by Rothwell's alternative, 'Up the Armada', which remained the favourite. Importantly, not casting the outline at all, Rothwell explained in a covering note to Rogers that 'the story has been designed to feature, along with the usual bunch of screen idiots, the two excellent reproductions of men-o'-war of this period which are at this moment lying unemployed in Valencia harbour, waiting for some astute and adventurous man to make this film.'

That astute and adventurous man was Peter Rogers. After a spirited meeting with Rothwell, it was agreed on 16 August 1962 that Rogers would pay £3000 for a screenplay based on the treatment. Still, a certain 'Taxi' project would put back production on the naughty nautical romp for nearly a year, until the studio agreement was signed on 29 July 1963. When it was finally put into pre-production overdrive, it still wasn't a Carry On; Rogers liked the title 'Up the Armada' too much. This was scuppered by the British Board of Film Censors, which considered the title too lewd for general distribution – 'Despite' bemoaned Rogers, 'people shouting "Up the Arsenal" every Saturday!'

Peter Rogers decided to move the Carry On series into historical costume and the 'Armada' script was blessed with the title 'Carry On, Mate!' As usual, Rogers was at his happiest tweaking the finished screenplay. Indeed, he completely rewrote the beginning, losing entirely Rothwell's knowing prologue:

Nelson: What a tragedy it is, Hardy, that such an epic story should have such a miserable ending.
Hardy: I confess sir I would prefer to see a happy nay even a romantic one.

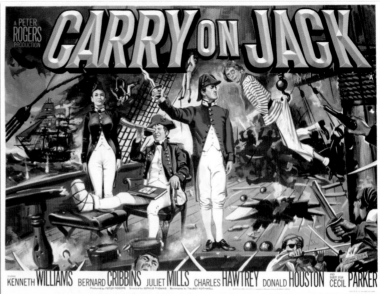

KENNETH WILLIAMS BERNARD CRIBBINS JULIET MILLS CHARLES HAWTREY DONALD HOUSTON AND CECIL PARKER

Nelson: Perhaps that can be achieved even now Hardy.
Hardy: How sir? (NELSON WHISPERS) Oh I don't think that would work sir.
Nelson: Try it man, try it.
Hardy: Very well sir. (HE KISSES HIM) Well, I told him!

Although, the finished film retains the punchline, the more serious intonation of the dramatic death of Nelson, played out against Gerald Thomas' painstaking recreation of the celebrated painting in the National Maritime Museum, was pure Peter Rogers. He also edited a proposed voiceover announcement, preferring to replace this with a montage of newspaper headlines which, in turn, was dropped.

The production was also in talks with Warner Bros at their British base at Elstree regarding using stock footage from the Gregory Peck hit *Captain Horatio Hornblower RN* (1951) and the 1952 Burt Lancaster classic *The Crimson Pirate*. Also on

Above: Talbot Rothwell's original draft script suffered something of an identity crisis.

Left: Character actor George Woodbridge relishes the ale and the pleasures of the flesh; specialities of Dirty Dick's.

TITBITS!

Rotund character star George Woodbridge, a reassuring fixture of Bray pubs for Hammer Film Productions, was paid £160 for four days work on the film. His contract dictated that he would play Ned, the jovial dweller of Dirty Dick's who gets a mouthful of Guinness, and another character, ambiguously identified as 'Clown'. This character was subsequently dropped from the film.

ON LOCATION

Kenneth Williams and Juliet Mills joined the film on the second day of production and found themselves on location at Frensham Ponds, near Farnham, Surrey, along with Bernard Cribbins, Charles Hawtrey, one cow and one horse. The exterior scenes from the beach to the scrub were filmed. Kenneth Williams remembered it as 'delightful weather with delightful people. The cameraman [Alan Hume] said, "The sun always shines for Gerald, doesn't it!" and everyone agreed that location filming went uncannily well for

him.' The open boat sequences were filmed in a water tank in the Paddock at the studios from 10 September 1963, by which time Williams was lamenting: 'all day in the bloody rowing boat, till I was aching all over. Charles Hawtrey was pissed. Breath smelled appallingly. It's a disgrace. Still, one must be charitable.' When a night shoot was scheduled in the tank on 13 September, for the Cadiz quayside scenes and the side of the *HMS Venus*, Williams's diary entry records a 2.15 am finish; 'the interim periods, we sat about singing rude songs and telling smutty jokes. The

reason for most of the smut in the world is boredom.'

Charles Hawtrey is blown away by a ribald 'life on the ocean waves'.

Pirates Ed Devereaux and Peter Gilmore rip the Pinewood scenery apart with larger than life performances.

hand to give the historical content weight was Commander Ian Cox. Although he had spent the previous six years as a poultry farmer, Cox had also served in the Navy for over twenty years and been involved with Van Heflin's Second World War adventure *Under Ten Flags* (1960) and an uncompleted film script, 'Puncher's Private Navy'.

The biggest change in style and content in the history of the series, *Carry On Jack* also pushed the budget to £169,782, a further £20,000 on top of the figure for *Cabby*. From the first day of production, on 2 September 1963, the film was referred to as 'Carry On Sailor'. On the back lot were old hands Jim Dale and Ian Wilson, with incoming star Bernard Cribbins. Gerald Thomas happily allowed him to ad lib on set, although his comment 'You must be Dick!' when encountering a filthy Charles Hawtrey in the public house, Dirty Dick's, was lost from the film.

Although the cast was awash with new faces, Kenneth Williams enthused: 'The picture was something of a reunion for me because the midshipman was played by Juliet Mills, whom I'd met doing *Twice Round the Daffodils*, and the bosun was Donald Houston, with whom I played long before that in the Festival of Wales production in 1951. Cecil Parker played the admiral, and this was a very adroit bit of casting, rather like Wilfred Hyde-White's role in *Carry On Nurse*; both of them actors who were absolutely right for the parts, but not the people you expected to see.'

But it was another star attraction that stole the producer's heart: Emma the cow played by a sea-going Jersey called Daisy Mae. Spoilt rotten on location, forbidden titbits were smuggled on-set and Peter Rogers even dutifully took her for 'walkies'. However, during post-production, it was discovered that one scene required a retake. Unfortunately for Daisy Mae's continuing screen career, she had already been 'dehorned' and so a replacement was searched out from the dairy farms around Pinewood. A near enough match

TRAILER

Bernard Cribbins as Albert Poop-Decker, as unlikely a young lad as ever went to 'see'. Juliet Mills as Sally the loveliest lass that ever loved a sailor. The order is Carry On Laughing as Peter Rogers and Gerald Thomas give you Carry On Jack, another hilarious comedy hit in the brilliant Carry On series.

was discovered and painted to achieve an exact likeness of Daisy Mae. The extra shot, of the exterior of the open boat, was filmed in a tunnel, in studio, on 19 November 1963.

In the newspapers, Kenneth Williams seemed proud and recharged about this new phase of Carry On film. 'Instead of a tyrannical Captain, and a charming sort of Mr Christian like the Bounty, we've got the very reverse situation here, we've got a Captain who is all for humanitarianism, rather a milksop himself, and a bit of a fool and a first officer who's an absolute sadist and all for flogging everybody at the slightest sign of mutiny.' The 1962 remake of the MGM classic Mutiny on the Bounty, with Marlon Brando, Trevor Howard and Richard Harris, was still fresh in the minds of the thousands of cinema-goers that saw the Carry On crew sail the ocean waves in February 1964. Despite its departure

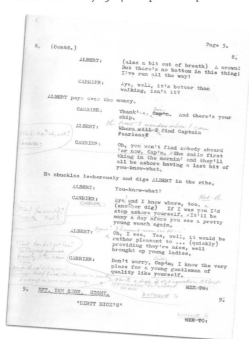

from a contemporary setting and the enlistment of new leading actors, Peter Rogers claimed that the box office takings were untroubled. Indeed, it was only Kenneth Williams who seemed disenchanted, when he wrote on Friday, 28 February 1964: 'We went to see Carry On Jack at the New Victoria. It was half empty. It was a lousy, badly made film. Really badly made. The editing was all wrong for comedy. I was astonished at the excellence of Charlie Hawtrey. He was superb. So was Cribbins – the best droll I've seen in years. But really good. The rest awful. Including me. My voice sounded so far back and so phoney. So badly recorded.'

Bernard Cribbins (1928-)

One of the most endearing comedy heroes of the last fifty years, Bernard made his screen debut in 1957 with supporting roles in The Yangtse Incident and Davy. His earliest show-stopping moment came with Tommy Steele and Sid James in the 'Watch the Birdie' number from Tommy the Toreador. He co-starred with Peter Sellers and Lionel Jeffries in the classic prison comedy Two-Way Stretch (1962) and reunited with the team for The Wrong Arm of the Law in 1963. Already a pop sensation, his 'Hole in the Ground' and 'Right Said Fred' had reached the top ten in 1962 followed by another hit, 'Gossip Calypso', that Christmas. It was a leading role in the film Crooks in Cloisters (1963), with Ronald Fraser and Barbara Windsor, that caught the eye of Peter Rogers. A hot film property, he co-starred with Peter Cushing in She (1965) and Daleks' Invasion Earth 2150 A.D. (1966). In 1967, he dutifully reprised his Carry On Spying manhole cover gag in the Bond parody Casino Royale. During the 1970s, he landed his best-loved film role as the porter in Lionel Jeffries' The Railway Children (1970) and played an unsavoury landlord for Alfred Hitchcock in Frenzy (1972). He was the unforgettable guest, Mr Hutchison, in Fawlty Towers: 'The Hotel Inspectors', and played the hard-nosed and clumsy eponymous hero of Dangerous Davies – The Last Detective for director Val Guest. A children's favourite, Cribbins holds the record of 111 appearances on the BBC's Jackanory and delighted as the voices of all The Wombles. His many commercial voiceover assignments include Busby for British Telecom. In 2007 he joined the regular cast of Doctor Who.

Carry On credits: Jack, Spying, Columbus

Left: Producer Peter Rogers may have been taken with Talbot Rothwell's work but couldn't resist a few hand-written amendments to the dialogue.

Bernard Cribbins and Jim Dale discuss where to get a bit of you know what, on Pinewood's 'F' Stage.

CARRY ON SPYING (1964)

When the cunning spy, Milchmann (Victor Maddern) of STENCH, the Society for Total Extinction of Non Conforming Humans, kills Professor Stark (Frank Forsyth) and makes off with his secret formula 'X', British Intelligence needs every man they can find. Reluctantly, the Chief (Eric Barker) and Cobley (Richard Wattis) of BOSH, the British Operational Security Headquarters, realise this includes accident-prone agent Desmond Simkins (Kenneth Williams). With new recruits Charlie Bind (Charles Hawtrey), Harold Crump (Bernard Cribbins) and the blonde babe with a photographic memory, Daphne Honeybutt (Barbara Windsor), under his wing, they trawl the Third Man territory of Vienna and the crowded streets of the Casbar in search of the Fat Man (Eric Pohlmann). Having knocked out top British agent Carstairs (Jim Dale) in a public convenience, Simkins falls under the bewitching spell of agent and cabaret artiste Lila (Dilys Laye). A tense high-speed train journey almost wipes out our heroes but the trail heats up and leads straight to the mastermind Dr Crow (Judith Furse), 'her' fiendish gadgets and sultry Amazonian guards. Crow is defeated but Simkins is elated when Lila invites him to join her organisation, SNOG!

Don't point that thing at me, it might go off!: Charles Hawtrey, Kenneth Williams, Bernard Cribbins and Eric Pohlmann are shown who's boss by Dr Crow's Amazonian guards.

Despite staking its claim as the most pun-packed, fast-paced, rollercoaster ride of a Carry On ever, *Carry On Spying*'s roots were firmly entrenched in the more sedate, community feel of the Norman Hudis scripts. Peter Rogers had registered the title as early as October 1962, immediately in the wake of the worldwide approval of the first James Bond film, *Dr. No*. In a February 1963 treatment, Hudis cast Sid James as the head of a spying fraternity, training raw recruits in the art of espionage. Kenneth Connor was to have played the potentially vibrant but ultimately cowardly secret agent, his name – Bold – being the closest thing to 007! Charles Hawtrey was cast as the equally ironic, Intrepid; Hattie Jacques would play Dauntless; and Joan Sims would provide the love interest as Valliant. Four months later, the basic concept remained the same, but Kenneth Williams was now earmarked to play the ineffectual leader, Phillip Bull. The British bulldog spirit was at the heart of the film, with the spy ring now consisting of Sid James as Lucky Dexter, Joan Sims as Janie May, Kenneth Connor as Art Accleston and Charles Hawtrey as Fingers Allen. Esma Cannon was tentatively suggested as the administrator Amelia Barley. Although a sterling cast was name-checked, Peter Rogers wasn't happy with the script. He had hoped for a fantastical James Bond parody. What Hudis had delivered had his customary heart and soul running parallel with the comedy, the plot revolving around spies infiltrating an atomic weapons plant disguised as CND activists. One scene, depicting the spies joining in with a peace rally and lying on the ground in protest, featured a disenchanted First World War veteran. He left his post as a security guard and, with a chestful of medals, proclaimed, 'They're right, this is a filthy weapon.' So saying, he lay down with the protesters.

At this point, Peter Rogers was disenchanted with the writer he would later call a 'genius'. The producer was now fully aware that there was only one man who could keep the Carry Ons going in the direction he wanted: Talbot Rothwell. Days after dismissing the Hudis scenario, Peter Rogers assigned Rothwell and Sid Colin to write a new screenplay.

By the time the studio agreement was signed, on 16 January 1964, the title had been changed to *Come Spy With Me*. Indeed, the contracts for the four principal actors all featured this new title. It proved a short-lived alteration. By the time filming began on 3 February the title had reverted to *Carry On Spying*.

It also ushered in the ultimate Carry On blonde bombshell in the curvy shape of Barbara Windsor. Still on the lookout for a replacement for Liz Fraser, Rogers and Thomas spotted Windsor teetering through the hallowed Pinewood dining room en route to a barside chat with Ronald Fraser, with whom she had just worked on the film *Crooks in Cloisters*. Aware of her television success in *The Rag Trade* and her impressive roles under Joan Littlewood, Rogers knew that Barbara's 'pedigree was impeccable'.

The first day's filming was anything but. Bernard Cribbins, another cohort from *Crooks in Clositers* and an old hand on his second Carry On, had warned the young actress about

Kenneth Williams. 'My first scene, I fluffed my lines. "Oooh, dahling, do please get it right," he said snootily from beneath the black false whiskers. Out of sheer embarrassment I went on the attack. Having heard he had fallen out with the actress Fenella Fielding [during the revue, *Pieces of Eight*], I pulled myself up to my full four feet ten and a half inches and replied, in my poshest voice, "Don't you yell at me with Fenella Fielding's minge hair stuck round your chops. I won't bloody stand for it." He just stared at me, then flared those famous nostrils, and clapped his hands. "Isn't she wonderful?"' The new girl was warmly welcomed into the Carry On family, and principals Cribbins, Williams, Hawtrey, Windsor and Dilys Laye would often fill the hours between takes playing I Spy With My Little Eye. As Bernard Cribbins explained, 'It's a great mental exercise – if you're mental!'

Above: Kenneth Williams lets the side down on the *Carry On Spying* press book. This, and the film's poster, bear more than a few similarities to the artwork used to promote *From Russia With Love* (1964).

Left: Harem honeys, Barbara Windsor and Bernard Cribbins, infiltrate Hakim's Funhouse.

ON LOCATION

The opening scene was filmed at the Timekeepers Gate entrance to Pinewood. On 29 January 1964, Dilys Laye recorded her songs for the Café Mozart scenes on the Denham music stage. Denham's long corridor was also used during the chase through Dr Crow's headquarters.

Eric Pohlmann and Dilys Laye play Film Noir for laughs.

The Carry On team's poke at James Bond caused a legal battle.

Barbara Windsor marks her Carry On debut with a whistle-worthy publicity pose.

It wasn't the title or the new leading lady that concerned another producer at Pinewood Studios – it was the subject matter. Peter Rogers recalls that *Carry On Jack* had greatly impressed Harry Saltzman, the co-producer of the James Bond films. 'He caught my eye in the bar at Pinewood and said, "Congratulations on your picture. That was marvellous. You know, Cubby [Broccoli] and I have been thinking, we might like to make a comedy." To which I replied, "I was under the impression you already had!", which didn't please him very much.'

During production in February, the matter became a legal one. The South Molton Street solicitors Harbottle and Lewis wrote: 'Dear Mr Rogers, I refer to our telephone conversation last week when I informed you of our client's concern regarding your production of this film. During our conversation you stated that you proposed to amend the script for the film by deleting reference to the name of one of the characters, namely James Bind and substituting therefore the name "Charlie Bind". I shall be grateful if you will let me know whether in fact this amendment has been made.' Rogers replied: 'I would point out that I amended this dialogue because I thought it was funnier than the original and told you about it because I imagined it might

TITBITS

Richard Wattis was recruited for three days work at a guaranteed fee of £150. His contract dictated that he be free for his West End commitment in *Six of One* at the Adelphi theatre, by 6.00 pm each evening, and exempt from work on matinee days, Wednesday and Saturday. Ubiquitous voice-over artist Olive Gregg re-dubbed the character of 'Sergeant'. The most intriguing dubbing work was taken up by Carry On debutante John Bluthal: as well as playing the Peter Lorre-styled head waiter at the Café Mozart, Bluthal provided the strangled, other-worldly voice for the evil Dr Crow. Adding to the asexual clout of the villain, 'she' was played in the flesh by the imposing Judith Furse. The 'Glamazons' included delicious dollies Audrey Wilson, Vicky Smith, Jane Lumb, Marian Collins, Sally Douglas and Christine Rodgers; dressed in sexy but imposing black kinky boots and black, body wrap outfits designed by Yvonne Caffin. It was reported that the villainous girls 'would appeal to the least interested male! It certainly got the okay from stars Kenneth Williams, Bernard Cribbins and Charles Hawtrey as well as director Gerald Thomas!' Half of that illustrious quartet were surely very uninterested indeed.

ease your anxiety. The change was not brought about because of any threat of litigation. I assure you that if I thought the original dialogue was funnier I would have retained it. I am thinking of "Carry On Lawyer".' Dutifully, the following day, the solicitors responded: 'Many thanks for your letter of yesterday's date confirming the amendments made to the script for this film. I have accordingly notified my clients of the position.' And thus a veil was drawn.

But it was with cap in hand that Rogers had to explain to Stuart Levy why the budget had escalated. Despite the fact that *Carry On Spying* was the most economically made film in the series since *Carry On Regardless* over two years earlier. At the end of April, with the film in the can and over budget, Rogers wrote: 'I feel that I owe you some explanation concerning the budget figure of *Carry On Spying*.' Various factors were blamed, not least of which, 'a chapter of accidents' (see 'Doctor, Doctor!'), 'artiste contracts went over their specified period resulting in a certain amount of daily rate overage. You will notice that it contained about fifty-four sets with not one item of location. To have concluded such a schedule in six weeks one and a half days is a little extraordinary I think. However, if you feel having seen the finished film that it is not worth £140,000 I shall stand corrected.' Stuart Levy was jovial in his next-day response: 'Thank you for telling us that on *Carry On Spying* the "event" has at last happened and that you have run over the budget on a picture. It is appreciated that a chapter of accidents aggravated the major excess

Eric Barker (1912-1990)

An actor since his youth, Barker was in films as early as 1918's *Nelson*. He made his first adult mark in 1930, playing juvenile Shakespearian roles at the Q theatre in London. He subsequently performed 'small parts' in repertory at Birmingham, Oxford and Croydon. A 1934 pantomime season at Oxford introduced him to Joan Hickson, playing the principal boy in *Dick Whittington*. Thrown together again for the first time in twenty-five years on the set of *Carry On, Constable*, the two embraced with affection. Barker reinvented himself as a cabaret artiste and radio comedian specialising in impersonations and returned to films such as *Carry On London* and *Concert Party* (both 1937). It was during a stint at the legendary Windmill Theatre that he met and married chief ballerina Pearl Hackney in 1936, with whom as wife and comic partner, he would enthral radio audiences, notably in *Merry-Go-Round* and *Steady Barker!* (his inimitable catch-phrase). But it was the Boulting brothers that kick-started his third and finest relationship with the cinema, winning a British Academy Award for his performance in *Brothers in Law* (1956). Becoming part of the Boultings' stable, memorably as the dithering vicar in *Happy is the Bride* (1957), he also became the man from the ministry in three St. Trinian's comedies (*Blue Murder at...*, *The Pure Hell of...* and *The Great St. Trinian's Train Robbery*). A leading comic actor throughout the 1960s, he was at his best in the two Dentist comedies with Bob Monkhouse and as the bemused medic in the Norman Wisdom classic *On the Beat*.

Carry On credits: *Sergeant, Constable, Cruising* (story only), *Spying, Emmannuelle*
Autobiography: *Steady, Barker!*

cost factor of set construction and you have our sympathy in this. Better luck next time. Anyhow, we trust the production will prove to be well worth the extra money!'

Eric Barker as the incompetent Police Inspector in *Carry On, Constable*.

'Our Man in Vienna', Jim Dale, disguises himself as a sheikh.

Kenneth Williams bashes funhouse doorman, Tom Clegg, on the bonce outside a notorious den of iniquity.

CARRY ON CLEO (1964)

The marching feet of the Roman army are tramping all over Britain under the leadership of Mark Antony (Sid James) and his sidekick Sergeant Major (Victor Maddern). The sickly Julius Caesar (Kenneth Williams) despairs of the filthy weather but perks up at the sight of Bristol stunna Gloria (Julie Stevens). Horsa (Jim Dale), the forlorn boyfriend of the captured Gloria, isn't prepared to let Rome take over and hatches a plan along with his reluctant new neighbour, square-wheel-maker Hengist Pod (Kenneth Connor). Captured and shipped back to Rome, the slaves escape and make their way to Egypt. Caesar and Mark Antony are also on official business, much to the chagrin of Caesar's wife Calpurnia (Joan Sims). Her father, the dirty old sage Seneca (Charles Hawtrey), goes along for the ride. But little does Caesar know that Antony is plotting his downfall so he can claim the sultry Cleo (Amanda Barrie) and the Roman Empire. Still Caesar feels easier when Hengist, having mistakenly been given the credit for Horsa's Roman slaying bravery, becomes his new champion and bodyguard. In the end, Hengist revisits his marriage bed with Senna Pod (Sheila Hancock), Horsa weds Gloria and the mighty Caesar is, quite literally, stabbed in the back.

Talbot Rothwell was officially signed up to write *Carry On Cleo* in December 1963, promising to delivery the draft screenplay by Valentine's Day 1964 and the final version by 1 May. Cameras started rolling on *Cleo* in July.

The Elizabeth Taylor and Richard Burton epic *Cleopatra* had been the most expensive, lavish motion picture of all time. Naturally, Peter Rogers wanted to poke fun at the historical excess, particularly when the production decamped from Pinewood Studios. When production had resumed in Rome in the September of 1961, it was decided it was cheaper to leave the sets standing in Buckinghamshire than to pull them down for re-use. *Carry On Cleo* was budgeted at a mere £165,802. The grand exterior sets from

Cleopatra abandoned on the Pinewood backlot were gratefully employed, as was interior scenery loaned out by actor Victor Maddern from a recent London production of *Caligula*. Having landed himself a role in *Cleo*, Maddern then discovered that the armour in which he was kitted out had Richard Burton's name in it. However, the most quoted claim – that *Carry On Cleo* moved in, shot in six weeks and beat the Elizabeth Taylor's *Cleopatra* to the cinemas – is apocryphal. The 20th Century-Fox film actually premiered in June 1963, but it was still the most talked about and reviled motion picture of the time, having rocketed from $2 million to $35 million and caused the resignation of Fox president Spyros Skouras.

The coffers weren't, however, empty enough to threaten legal action over a ribald rip-off of the *Cleopatra* poster featuring Burton, Taylor and Rex Harrison. The pose was copied exactly, with the principals replaced by the leering face of Sid James, the smouldering charms of Amanda Barrie and the pompous visage of Kenneth Williams. By this time, anybody who hadn't seen the slightest funny side to the expensive farce had left the company, so it wasn't the film poster being mocked that concerned Fox; it was the fact that the *Cleopatra* poster was, itself, based on an original portrait by Howard Terpning. Having, unwittingly, infringed copyright law, the case was taken to the High Court. 'We cast our legal team in the same way as we cast the Carry Ons,' reveals Peter Rogers. 'I selected Lord Hailsham to represent us. He had that delicious twinkle in his eye, a real sense of theatre and an eccentric, extroverted edge to his character.' He faced Sir Andrew Clark, representing 20th Century-Fox, while the Judge, Mr Justice Plowman, oversaw the case. 'Everybody seemed to enjoy the high spirits of the session, everyone was terribly polite and pleasant to each other.' The upshot was that the *Carry On Cleo* poster was changed.

Opposite: I have seen your bust! Kenneth Williams is clearly taken with Amanda Barrie as the 'Siren of the Nile'. Kenneth Connor guards his man.

Top: The poster that very nearly got away. Legal action was taken to try and prevent the Carry On gang mocking the advertising for the 20th Century Fox epic.

Right: Jim Dale and the 'disgraceful' Kenneth Williams.

ON LOCATION

The pre-production meeting for *Carry On Cleo* detailed 'two days local location at Bulstrode Park, Gerrards Cross' with hilltop shooting at Iver Heath in July. The hilltop shot consisted of a bull called Bob, two horses, Dido and Prince, marching feet, footage of Caesar's tent and the Beaconsfield Fire Department providing the rain! Lunch was skipped and the filming wrapped by 5.40 pm, when the unit returned to the studio.

Filming an ancient British settlement on the back lot at Pinewood.

Hengist Pod – Man of Action. Kenneth Connor throws himself into a macho publicity session.

Another potential lawsuit could have proved trickier. When the film was released, someone informed Marks and Spencer of their unwitting involvement. Markus and Spencius were played with streetwise panache by Gertan Klauber and Warren Mitchell, but it wasn't the parody that concerned the store, it was the unofficial use of their trademark green and white. The art director, Bert Davey, had done his job too well. 'If the Sieff family had employed an independent lawyer, like 20th Century-Fox, we would have been over a barrel,' reflects Rogers. Luckily,

Trade magazine *Kine Weekly* proudly reveals that *Carry On Cleo* is a huge box office hit.

TITBITS
Amazingly Joan Sims's supporting role was completed in just five and a half days. The title-role actress, Amanda Barrie, completed in eight days, in between stage commitments to *She Loves Me* at the Lyric. Barbara Windsor was tested for the role during the making of *Carry On Spying*. A black wig was plonked on her head and the actress exclaimed: 'Ooh, I look just like me mum!' (Peter Rogers denies this story.) Voluptuous Tanya Binning, the leader of Caesar's Vestal Virgins, was paid in cash for her three days' work and adopted more contemporary gear for a London publicity session.

says: 'Treachery! Help – I am undone!' Still, ever the armchair historian, Rothwell couldn't resist one cheeky line when Caesar, looking at Seneca's legs, ruefully comments: 'No matter what they say about me, thou art truly the knobbliest Roman of them all!' Alas, the pun was edited from the film.

Left: Talbot Rothwell's lovingly prepared draft script pays suitable homage to Hollywood's trouble Cleopatra, Elizabeth Taylor!

Below: Amanda Barrie applies the make-up for her signature comedy role as the naïve Cleo.

Marks and Spencer used an in-house lawyer and Rogers was simply obliged to write a letter of apology to the *Daily Express*, which was never passed on for publication.

The original Rothwell script lacked just one immortal touch. The unforgettable line for Julius Caesar: 'Imfamy. Infamy. They've all got it in for me!' It has become the most famous one-liner in Carry On history, much to the bemusement of Frank Muir, who along with his writing partner Denis Norden, actually wrote the line for the BBC radio comedy series *Take It From Here*. 'Most radio humour is by its nature ephemeral and it is rewarding to find that quite a few effective lines from *Take It From Here* have been preserved on film and are still quoted,' said Muir. 'This happened because a close friend and colleague of ours, Talbot "Tolly" Rothwell, was signed up to write the Carry On films, which were very much like a cinema version of our radio parodies of popular literary genres. Tolly ran out of time and asked us for help. The pleasure which Denis and I have of seeing our early quips and fancies preserved on film is tempered by the irony that it is an old *Take It From Here* line which is quoted as the archetypal Carry On line.' Indeed, as originally written, the line wasn't funny at all. In Rothwell's draft screenplay, Caesar merely

Jon Pertwee (1917-1996)

A dapper Jon Pertwee in the 1953 comedy *Will Any Gentleman?*

Something of a national treasure, Pertwee remains a television hero as the Third Doctor in *Doctor Who* and as the simpleton scarecrow *Worzel Gummidge*. A graduate of the Royal Academy of Dramatic Art, he became a professional actor in 1936. War service with the Navy interrupted a fledgling career, but he returned as a skilled character man in the radio series *The Waterlogged Spa*, with Eric Barker. In the late 1940s he became part of Highbury Studios' pool of talent and struck up a lasting relationship with writer/director Val Guest, notably starring as the detective in *Murder at the Windmill* (1948). He would later reunite with Guest as the salty lighthouse keeper in the Cannon and Ball comedy *The Boys in Blue* (1983). However, it was another long-running radio show, *The Navy Lark*, that made Pertwee a household name. Proclaiming that he was recruited into the Carry On squad because 'Peter Rogers phoned me and said, "Kenneth Williams has gone mad! Can you come down for the odd day to calm him down!"', he was determined to remain a character actor and not become part of the team. His finest film, as the wonderfully egotistical horror actor in *The House That Dripped Blood* (1970) blended into his cloak-wearing 'mother hen' of a Time Lord for five years on *Doctor Who*. He subsequently hosted the fiendish ITV panel game *Whodunnit?*, brought unexpected dignity to his private eye cameo in *Adventures of a Private Eye* (1977) and reprised his Doctor on television, stage, radio and the never-ending convention circuit. A glimpse of the great character star behind the cult hero was spotted in *Virtual Murder*: 'A Torch for Silverado' (1992).

Carry On credits: *Cleo, Cowboy, Screaming, Columbus*
Autobiographies: *Moon Boots and Dinner Suits, I Am the Doctor*

The Big Job – the final black and white film from Rogers and Thomas.

The Big Job

Writers Norman Hudis, Spike Milligan and John Antrobus had all tried to freshen up the weary old plot of a bank robber who stashes away his ill-gotten gains, serves his time and returns to find the area in which he hide the loot has been developed. In the spring of 1965, Talbot Rothwell sent Peter Rogers the shooting script for *The Big Job*, originally 'The Great Brain Robbery', named after the leader of the gang George Brain (Sid James). The location for the bank robbery that sets up the fun was the Crown Inn, Chalfont St. Giles. Now it's a restaurant specialising in Russian cuisine!

So impressed was Stuart Levy at Anglo that he wrote to Peter Rogers on New Year's Eve, 1964: 'I have pleasure in enclosing herewith the Sunday, Monday and in some cases the Tuesday, takings on *Carry On Cleo* pre-release. As you will see they are very good indeed. I tried to get hold of you once or twice on the telephone but without success, and I will let you have further news on this when I get it. It looks as though we are going to have very big weeks all over.' Indeed, within a fortnight he had provided 'some more figures on *Carry On Cleo* which, I am sure, will make you as pleased as it makes me. It is doing thundering good business all over the country and I have not the slightest doubt that we will have big figures when it goes on release next week.' On 3 February 1965, Associated British Cinemas confirmed that '*Carry On Cleo* finished London last Saturday night to the magnificent total of £103,784 beaten only once in the last twelve months by *Zulu* last Easter. This is really wonderful and fabulous and I thought I couldn't let the occasion pass without a very warm and heart-felt expression of appreciation to you and Gerald from my colleagues and myself. Carry On! – please.' Gerald Thomas was already hard at work on another film, but Peter Rogers responded to the good news: 'I thought we were just short of the £100,000. I have passed on your message to Gerald and the boys and they naturally get a kick out of having worked on a successful film. It makes them work even harder to make *The Big Job* a winner.'

Kenneth Williams (1926-1988)

The son of an East End barber, Williams discovered a love of music, history and poetry at an early age. His acting debut saw him in drag as the Princess Angelica in a school production of William Thackery's *The Rose and the Ring*. Joining the Tavistock Repertory Company as an amateur actor, he was called up in 1944 and eventually joined the Combined Services Entertainment in Singapore.

Demobbed in 1948, he joined the Newquay Repertory Theatre, before coming to national prominence as the Angel in the BBC television production of H G Wells's *The Wonderful Visit* in 1952. That same year, he played Slightly in *Peter Pan* at the Scala Theatre and appeared in the Birmingham Repertory Company's production of *Henry VI*, playing Burgundy in Part One, Hume and Smith in Part Two and Rutland in Part Three. In 1954, he played the Dauphin in George Bernard Shaw's *Saint Joan* at the Arts Theatre and the St Martin's Theatre.

Spotted by BBC comedy producer Dennis Main Wilson, Williams was cast as the resident character man on a new series, *Hancock's Half Hour*. For seven years, he played aged Colonels, frantic military officers and a spotty herbert who became known as 'Snide'. The series gave him his life-long catchphrase: 'Stop Messin' About!'

His film career started with a supporting role as an eager gardener who finds the victim in Herbert Wilcox's *Trent's Last Case* (1952) and as an airport employee in *Innocents in Paris* (1953). On stage, he played Elijah in Orson Welles' production of *Moby Dick* at the Duke of York's, was Montgomery in Sandy Wilson's staging of *The Buccaneer* at the Apollo, Maxime in *Hotel Paradiso* at the Winter Garden and Kite in *The Wit to Woo* at the Arts. A natural for

K. C. Williams [signature]

revue, he joined Maggie Smith in *Share My Lettuce* in 1957.

But it was radio that made his name. In 1958, he joined Kenneth Horne's team for *Beyond Our Ken*, creating the roles of rustic philosopher Arthur Fallowfield ('The answer lies in the soil!') and an aged man who screamed 'Thirty five years!' to almost every question he was asked.

The pantomime season saw him as Ugly Sister Portia in *Cinderella* at the Coliseum, with Tommy Steele. In the early 1960s he starred in the revues *Pieces of Eight* and *One Over the Eight*. He played the detective in the West End double bill *The Private Ear* and *The Public Eye* at the Globe Theatre and, later, played another detective, Inspector Truscott, in *Loot*, a role written for him by Joe Orton. In the 1980s, he would direct productions of Orton's *Loot* and *Entertaining Mr Sloane*, with Barbara Windsor as Kath.

As much a personality as an actor for his last twenty years, Williams was a relentless player of the Radio 4 panel game *Just A Minute*, hosted fifty-two editions of *International Cabaret* for BBC television and became a near-permanent fixture of the chat show circuit. His last stage role was as the Undertaker in Trevor Baxter's *The Undertaking*, staged at the Greenwich Theatre in 1979.

His celebrated *An Audience with Kenneth Williams* was broadcast by Channel 4 in 1983, and he became a best-selling author with two volumes of bitchy put-downs, *Acid Drops* and *Back Drops*, as well as a children's story, *I Only Have To Close My Eyes*. On television, he was a much-loved host of *Jackanory*, narrator for *Willo the Wisp* and the voice of the computers in *Galloping Galaxies* (1986).

Carry On credits: *Sergeant, Nurse, Teacher, Constable, Regardless, Cruising, Jack, Spying, Cleo, Cowboy, Screaming!, Don't Lose Your Head, Follow That Camel, Doctor, Up the Khyber, Camping, Again Doctor, Loving, Henry, At Your Convenience, Matron, Abroad, Dick, Behind, That's Carry On, Emmannuelle, Laughing's Christmas Classics*

Autobiography: *Just Williams*

CARRY ON COWBOY (1965)

The Wild West lives in fear of the black-hearted Johnny Finger, the Rumpo Kid (Sid James). It seems the only man who is pleased to see him is the local undertaker, Josh (Davy Kaye) who is kept busy with his rootin' tootin' ways. Having been warmly greeted by the saloon owner Belle (Joan Sims), the Rumpo Kid decides to settle in Stodge City for a while, much to the distress of Judge Burke (Kenneth Williams). The local law enforcer, Sheriff Albert Earp (Jon Pertwee) is hard of hearing, short-sighted and, unsurprisingly, no match for the Kid. With another body for Josh to deal with, the Judge needs someone to clean up Stodge. Enter British drainage, sanitation and garbage disposal engineer, first class, Marshall P Knutt (Jim Dale), who is mistaken for a real Marshal. The Kid is worried enough to have a hasty pow-wow with the Red Indian Chief, Big Heap (Charles Hawtrey), in the hope of planning a murderous raid on the stagecoach carrying Knutt. While the Chief's son, Little Heap (Bernard Bresslaw), is scalp-mad, Big Heap is a peace-loving sort of chap; until the taste of whiskey fires him up. Luckily for the stage, gun-slinging Miss Annie Oakley (Angela Douglas) is aboard and defeats the redskins. Planning to kill the Kid for killing her father, Sheriff Earp, it's Knutt who gets the credit and is welcomed as a hero by Burke, the Doc (Peter Butterworth) and rancher Sam Houston (Sydney Bromley). Still, with a little bit of training, Knutt should be able to handle a gun, shouldn't he?

In the light of the mounting success of *Carry On Cleo* and the expiry of Norman Hudis's six-year contract, Talbot Rothwell's position as principal Carry On scribe was considered a strong one by his agent, Kevin Kavanagh. He suggested that 'Tolly should participate in some way in a proportion of any possible profits' – a suggestion that Peter Rogers dismissed. Rothwell was happy to lay the matter to rest and get back to his Western screenplay: 'Believe me, I couldn't care less about the percentage. As you well know, where money is concerned I'm about as ambitious as a eunuch at an orgy ... There are other things that concern me more at the moment. Did you read the item in yesterday's *Mail* which said that the Beatles were going to make a "western" film? All about four cowboys from Liverpool (yes really!) riding across the wide open spaces in search of a girl or something. A further item today states that they are going to start a film on Monday at

Pinewood. Would it be this one? If so, does it affect your plans? Do let me know soon as I am quite well advanced on the script.'

The 'new' narrative Beatles film never did materialise, even though writers from Joe Orton to Dave Freeman were at one point attached to the project. Kevin Kavanagh was also wary of the Fab Four's project. 'I've got myself in a complete muddle as to the terms which Tolly can expect for the next Carry On! I see the Beatles are going to make a cowboy film – are you going to try to get in first?' The next day Rogers confirmed that 'to get you out of your muddle *Carry On Cowboy* is one of those pictures on which Tolly can expect a straight £5,000.'

The first draft was delivered in March 1965. The pre-production meeting was held at Pinewood four months later, revealing that: 'This would consist of an eight week schedule comprising location at Chobham Common, Surrey, from Monday 12th July.' Unfortunately, this time the weather wouldn't always shine down on Gerald Thomas. Preparing scenes on the open trail and the hillside with Jim Dale, Angela Douglas, Brian Rawlinson and Bernard Bresslaw, all artistes were called but not used. As the daily progress report glumly reflects: 'continuous heavy rain all day prevented any shooting. Wrapped up at 4.00 pm.' It was a wasted day that Thomas was never able to catch up with. It was all the more frustrating in that the unit had been setting up the location since the previous Thursday when they had started erecting tents close to Longcross Station Road and building loose boxes inside for the horses. The work continued on the Friday and over the weekend forty-six horses were taken from the studio lot to the tents and bedded down. The next day was no better. With Sid James, Kenneth Williams, Charles Hawtrey and Peter Gilmore

EASTMAN COLOUR

HOW THE WEST WAS LOST!!

SIDNEY JAMES KENNETH WILLIAMS JIM DALE CHARLES HAWTREY JOAN SIMS ANGELA DOUGLAS

on call at Chobham, the weather was inclement and it was decided to utilise the available actors and film interiors for the Rumpo Kid's hideout in a local barn. The scenes were completed

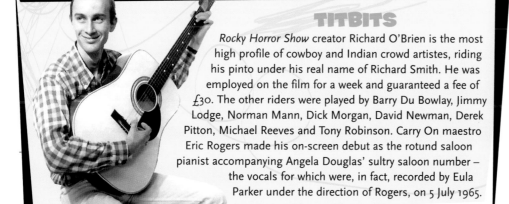

TITBITS

Rocky Horror Show creator Richard O'Brien is the most high profile of cowboy and Indian crowd artistes, riding his pinto under his real name of Richard Smith. He was employed on the film for a week and guaranteed a fee of £30. The other riders were played by Barry Du Bowlay, Jimmy Lodge, Norman Mann, Dick Morgan, David Newman, Derek Pitton, Michael Reeves and Tony Robinson. Carry On maestro Eric Rogers made his on-screen debut as the rotund saloon pianist accompanying Angela Douglas' sultry saloon number – the vocals for which were, in fact, recorded by Eula Parker under the direction of Rogers, on 5 July 1965.

Left: 'I think the check shirt is the very one I wore in the film,' says Richard O'Brien. 'In fact I'm sure it is. Thrilling stuff ain't it? You supplied your own gear as stunt riders in them there days.'

Opposite: Sid James as the Rumpo Kid, every inch the Western baddie.

High camp with Big Heap Charles Hawtrey filming on location at Black Park.

ON LOCATION

A rain-sodden Chobham Common was utilised at the start of production for the wide open prairies of the Wild West. A further location, at nearby Black Park, was used for Charles Hawtrey's Indian encampment but the shoot was similarly affected by the weather. On 10 August, the unit set up at 8.00 am but returned to Pinewood without shooting at 10.30 am; the scenes were finally filmed on 12 and 13 August. A stray totem pole, which an interested passer-by had purloined in the night, was finally located at the local police station! Esher Common was used for the Indians' stagecoach attack sequence.

between 10.00 am and 4.30 pm with no lunch break, before the unit returned to Chobham Common and waited for the weather. They soon decided 'to wrap up and return to studio'. Sydney Bromley's blood and thunder performance as rancher Sam Houston was similarly affected the next week when the unit wrapped up early owing to heavy rain.

Back at Pinewood Studios, art director Bert Davey had constructed a living, breathing recreation of a typical Kansas cattle town. With Rothwell's provocative script and a library of reference books, Davey designed the façades of houses, offices, a bank, jail, livery stables, corn chandlers, gunsmith, undertakers and saloon.

Carry On new boy Bernard Bresslaw looks ill at ease in the saddle as Gerald Thomas sets up a wide open prairie shot in wildest Buckinghamshire.

He also had to build an intricate drainage system during his six-week timeframe. 'It was amazing,' remembers Jim Dale. 'Mind you we were the only western town in history with a turning at the end of the main street! There was no rolling countryside on the Pinewood lot!'

As for his character of Marshall P Knutt, Dale says: 'I loved it because there were little moments I was allowed that I could make a little different. By now I had been lucky enough to have been considered part of the Carry On team. That meant that the writer was writing parts especially for me, which was lovely. And Gerry Thomas allowed me a little bit of time to perfect elements of my performance. Like the business with the revolver.' Asked at the time, Jim complained that 'I can't get my draws off as quick as I would like to!' Contracted for the entire eight-week shot for £1,600, Jim was also committed to the television series *Thank Your Lucky Stars* each Sunday in Birmingham, but the effort certainly paid off.

When the film was trade shown on 9 February 1966, Keith Devon, of Bernard Delfont's agency, wrote to Peter Rogers: 'Further to my brief meeting with you at the preview of *Carry On Cowboy* may I reiterate what I told you at the time that I think this is a most excellent film for the public and in my opinion will be a

TRAILER

'A smash hit by Peter Rogers and Gerald Thomas who have made Carry On the hallmark of the very best in comedy entertainment.'

Peter Butterworth was equally bowled over. Having slotted into the Carry On regime on his very first day on set, 28 July 1965, he rather endearingly wrote to Peter Rogers on 9 May 1966: 'I have now seen *Cowboy* for the third time, and with three different types of audience. How they liked it! So they bloody well should of course because it is very very good, tremendously funny, and has a wonderfully happy atmosphere. Congratulations to you both. I'm so glad I was in it.' Even the notoriously hard to please Kenneth Williams came away enthused by the product: 'It was marvellous. It's the first good

Peter Butterworth in a beaming portrait shot as Doc; his letter clearly shows how delighted he was to join the Carry On team.

Sid James, Percy Herbert and a sultry Joan Sims up the ante at the bar.

very big winner for you indeed. Might I say that I thought the entire cast was excellent and I wish to thank you for the very great opportunity that you have given Jim Dale. I do hope that after his performance in this film you will agree with me that he will be a very big comedy bet indeed.' Sid James's agent, Michael Sullivan, was impressed as well and not only with his client. He wrote on 10 February to say 'how extremely entertained I was by your film *Carry On Cowboy*. Further more, I have never seen Sidney better in any picture and I think you have done miracles for Jim Dale.'

Margaret Nolan (1943-)

The words 'buxom' and 'voluptuous' might have been invented for the blonde bombshell Nolan. She started her professional career as a model, working under the name of Vicki Kennedy. Revealing all for countless cheesecake shots, she eventually posed for *Playboy* and decorated a number of influential Swinging Sixties feature films. Notably, it was Nolan, and not Shirley Eaton, who had various images from *Goldfinger* projected on to her body in that film's opening sequence. Margaret also appeared in the film as Dink. She was also a, literally, dumb blonde, on the craggy arm of that 'dirty old man' Wilfrid Brambell in the casino sequence of the Beatles film, *A Hard Day's Night*. She proved her mettle in an impressive run in the Carry Ons, reaching her zenith as the bubbly Dawn Brakes getting frisky on a train with Bernard Bresslaw in *Girls*, and as his prissy missus in *Dick*. Maggie connoisseurs are advised to check out her strip-teasing art teacher from *The Great St. Trinian's Train Robbery* (1966) and her pouting amateur dramatic drama queen, Nemone Wagstaff, in *Steptoe and Son* ('A Star is Born', 1972). After a stint as Denise Paget in *Crossroads* in 1983, she retired from acting and moved to Spain. She is now back in Blighty looking to re-launch herself as an artist and cultural icon.

Carry On credits: Cowboy, Henry, At Your Convenience, Matron, Girls, Dick

Margaret Nolan as the newly-pregnant Mrs Tucker in *Carry On Matron* (1972).

On location, Jim Dale, Angela Douglas, George Mossman and Brian Rawlinson keep an eye out for Injuns... and the bus to Iver Heath!

British comedy in years, the first time a British Western has ever been done, and the first Carry On to be a success on every level. It's got laughs, and pathos, some lovely people and ugly people. Mind you, it's an alarming thought that they'll never top this one.'

Internationally, *Carry On Cleo* was still packing them in. Keith Moreman, managing director of the Greater Union Theatres in Australia, wrote: 'In Sydney the previous best Carry On had a run of five weeks in the city and *Carry On Cleo* ran twelve, and took more money than any Carry On before, and in fact took more than twice most of them. This is certainly a very pleasing surprise but it has just caught the imagination of the public here and pleased everyone. One exhibitor in a small country town has just played it for a third time having played it between Xmas and New Year for the first time. That is what he thinks of it. In most situations *Carry On Cleo* has beaten "hard-ticket" pictures like *Lawrence of Arabia*, *El Cid* etc. that has played in the same houses but increased admission prices.' The news was passed on to a grateful Peter Rogers by the Overseas Sales Manager, who commented, 'You will be delighted to know that once again a Carry On has broken theatre records. From my experience in that market I think that colour makes a big difference and *Cleo* looks like beating [the] *Nurse* figures. I have every hope that *Cowboy* will do equally well and I am arranging a holiday date for that later in the year.'

And Kenneth Williams need not have worried. He was already well and truly immersed in the next film...

Eric Rogers (1921-1981)

Having taken to the clarinet and piano as an infant, Rogers was composing music from the age of eleven. An airman during the Second World War, he would pound out riotous renditions of 'Roll Out the Barrel' or 'Bless 'Em All' for the price of a pint of beer. He once estimated that he had played both songs at least 10,000 times in NAAFIs, sergeants and officers messes and pubs across the country.

At the end of the war, he was serving as a Spitfire pilot. Upon demob, he used his gratuity to set up a small orchestra playing the Orchid Room in London's Trocadero. As well as playing the big band sound, Rogers was accompanist and arranger for such variety artistes as June Wilson and Fred Emney. He also helped Norman Wisdom perfect his multi-musical instrument skill for his celebrated stage routine. A friend of the untrained Lionel Bart, it was Rogers who transcribed and orchestrated the score for *Oliver!* and he would often joke that he 'wrote every note' of the hit musical. He was appointed musical director when the show transferred to Broadway, rewriting passages of the score for the bigger orchestra that the Great White Way staging required. His work on the film version, with John Green, won an Academy Award.

Having became a musical director at Decca Records, he also accompanied such singers as Max Bygraves, Julie Andrews and Anthony Newley, notably on his single 'Personality' and the 1960 album *Love is a Now and Then Thing*. His orchestra recorded such mood albums as *Percussive Twenties* and *Sizzling Twenties*, while his arrangement on 'Ill Be With You In Apple Blossom Time' for Rosemary June hit the number one spot on the US Billboard Chart in 1959. A ballet, *Nancy*, composed for a Royal Variety Show, was plundered for an unforgettable theme; 'Startime', synonymous with the ATV series *Sunday Night at the London Palladium*. Rogers would, eventually, become the musical director of the theatre.

A friend of the original Carry On composer, Bruce Montgomery, Rogers's first association with the series came as early as *Carry On Teacher*. Although not credited, Montgomery gladly paid him for additional passages, including the jaunty score during the classroom back scratching. Montgomery would often call on him for the remainder of his

Carry On scores, with Rogers contributing elements of the music accompanying Charles Hawtrey's visit to a strip club in *Carry On Regardless*. He wrote the music for Liz Fraser and Dilys Laye dressing for dinner in *Carry On Cruising* and for the ending of the film. Peter Rogers was aware that more and more of the Montgomery music was, in fact, Eric Rogers and signed him up as composer and conductor on *Nurse On Wheels*. He would be the producer's first musical choice thereafter.

Eric was confirmed as composer for *Don't Lose Your Head*, although questions were raised at the pre-production meeting over the theme song. The original Eric Rogers score of 'Here We Come Gathering Nuts in May' was rejected. Moreover, as Peter recalls, 'The Rank Organisation accused me of using relatives in my films. They thought Eric was a relation. We were so close that we might as well have been. We always worked together on film music. It was the most enjoyable part of production and even when there was no music to write, Eric and I would get together in his music room where we spent many happy hours.'

Eric would lovingly include snatches of classical music in his scores; notably in *Carry On Loving*. The Grubb household is complemented by Chopin's 'Funeral March', Charles Hawtrey tracks down Sid James to Gounod's 'Funeral March of a Marionette' and Patsy Rowlands turns sexy to a jazz arrangement of Rubenstein's 'Melody in F'. Eric also scored *The Iron Maiden*, *The Big Job*, *All Coppers Are...*, *Bless This House* and *Quest For Love* for Peter, as well as the Sid James comedy musical *Three Hats For Lisa*.

Eric Rogers in his cameo as the saloon pianist in *Carry On Cowboy* (1965).

Carry On credits: *Cabby, Jack, Spying, Cleo, Cowboy, Screaming!, Don't Lose Your Head, Follow That Camel, Doctor, Up the Khyber, Camping, Again Doctor, Up the Jungle, Loving, Henry, At Your Convenience, Matron, Abroad, Girls, Dick, Behind, That's Carry On, Emmannuelle*

CARRY ON SCREAMING! (1966)

Young romantic Albert Potter (Jim Dale) is understandably distressed when his beloved, Doris Mann (Angela Douglas), is abducted by the hulking hairy monster, Oddbodd (Tom Clegg). Reporting to the bumbling policemen Sydney Bung (Harry H Corbett) and Slobotham (Peter Butterworth), the trail leads to the eerie mansion Bide-a-Wee and a towering Butler, Sockett (Bernard Bresslaw). The mysterious brother and sister duo Dr Orlando Watt (Kenneth Williams) and Valeria (Fenella Fielding) are suspiciously unhelpful, although Bung soon falls under the spell of Valeria. With helpful notes from lavatory attendant Dan Dann (Charles Hawtrey), Albert is distressed to discover Doris as a shop window dummy. Bung and Slobotham investigate but are not impressed. But Valeria and Watt are worried. With a smoky drink, she transforms Bung into a Mr Hyde-styled creature of the night and he steals the dummy in question. His ever-complaining wife, Emily (Joan Sims), doesn't seem to notice the difference in his appearance. With Slobotham dressed as a woman to try and attract some mysterious attention and Emily petrified with Dr Watt's deadly concoction, the ghoulies seem to be getting the better of Bung. But Albert's monstrous turn and the revived Egyptian mummy, Rubbatiti (Denis Blake) put paid to the fiendish doc. Happily married, Albert and Doris find Bung even happier with Valeria as housekeeper and Emily still a dummy!

Unusually for a Carry On, the notion of a comic horror film came from the writer, Talbot Rothwell, and not from the producer, Peter Rogers. Rothwell's finished script was lovingly described as the 'final draft of a perfectly horrifying screenplay'. Still, several tweaks and alterations had taken place. Originally, Fenella Fielding's opulent and vampiric characterisation was named Verbena and was the daughter of Dr Watt rather than his sister. Even more bizarrely, Jim Dale's hapless romantic lead delighted under the name of Ken Connors! And it was written with Dale and not Connor in mind as 'a man of about twenty-five'.

Director Gerald Thomas played on the old military comrades connection when on 11 November 1965 he wrote to Lord Montague, curator of Beaulieu Abbey, home to the National Motor Museum: 'I am making a film called *Carry On Screaming!* in January of next year with my producer Peter Rogers. It is set in the early 1900s and is a comedy horror film. We shall require three cars for location and in the studios of that period and I wonder if you can help me in this matter. You probably won't remember me but we served together at OCTL at Mons Barracks and recently we met in the Mirabelle when you were lunching with Lee Patterson. If you are able to help us in this matter perhaps you would be kind enough to join Peter and I for lunch at the Mirabelle when you are next in town so we can discuss it further.' The following day, Montague's secretary sent 'a copy of our current catalogue which will give you some idea of the cars available' and explained that His Lordship would be 'delighted to lunch' and 'bring with him Mr Michael Ware who deals with all the hiring of veteran and vintage vehicles in the museum.' *The Pictorial Guide to the Montague Motor Museum* featured none other than Margaret Rutherford on the front cover, seated in a 1903 De Dion Bouton. A 1904

Brushmobile, a Renault and two mechanics were supplied from Beaulieu.

Character actor Norman Mitchell, a regular Carry On face since being picked up in *Carry On Cabby*, wrote enthusiastically to Peter Rogers in February 1966. 'I want to thank you so much for asking me to be in your current picture *Carry On Screaming!* and to say how very much I enjoyed being in it. It was rather splendid to be entrusted with the driving of a 1910 Inco taximetre carbriolette and I enjoyed that very much indeed. I am only sorry there

was no chase. Heigh Ho. I would like to take this opportunity of wishing you all the very best with the new picture I am sure it will be an enormous success. Thanking you for your courtesy and attention. Believe me to be yours truly Norman.' Alas, Norman's prolific association with the series was brought to a sudden halt. After a rainy night shoot, Jim Dale jokingly said to him: 'I'm looking round for Noah's Ark. We ought to go on strike for excess watch!' Mitchell picked up the story: 'At six in the morning Jim contacted me having been told that Peter Rogers was waiting by his phone for an explanation. I said to Jim, "Well, you can quote me that it was a joke!"' Clearly, Jim Dale was one asset the Carry Ons could not do without.

Another was Charles Hawtrey. Having heard that Hawtrey hadn't been cast in the latest Carry On, C H B Williamson wrote a small piece in

Left: Just a little prick! Kenneth Williams turns nasty with his petrifying liquid. 'I've tried it on my rhubarb with amazing results!' he revealed in a deleted line.

Opposite: Billy Cornelius and Kenneth Williams are powerless as Tom Clegg gets monstrously friendly with the ultimate comic vamp, Fenella Fielding.

DOCTOR, DOCTOR!

Junior monster Billy Cornelius doubled for Oddbodd actor Tom Clegg who was sick and unable to come to the studio. Clegg, ex-Household cavalry and professional boxer, had found his grunting creature 'great fun. The dialogue wasn't brilliant, but at least I had no trouble with learning my lines.' Cornelius, who had once rated number ten in British boxing and was the fight arranger for ABC TV, 'found the false teeth with protruding fangs rather uncomfortable. Obviously, fangs ain't what they used to be!'

ON LOCATION

The exterior of the police station was filmed in St Leonards Road, Windsor, and is now the Windsor Art Centre. Black Park was used for the interrupted romance of Jim Dale and Angela Douglas at the start of the film. Pinewood's South Lodge Drive was utilised for Dan Dann's public convenience. The imposing Bide-a-Wee Rest Home was the nearby Fulmer Grange, now a private school. Construction manager Bill Surridge had explained at the pre-production meeting on New Year's Eve 1965 that 'some construction would be needed on location at Fulmer which would consist of a door and gate only.'

Harry H Corbett and, in heavy disguise, Peter Butterworth, try to coax out a fiend on the Hocombe Woods set.

The sheet music for the opening song, recorded by Boz (session singer Al Saxone) but mysteriously credited as 'Anon' in the opening credits.

Today's Cinema, wondering whether this would have a negative effect on the film's box-office takings. 'Stuart Levy contacted me, nervous that the article could strike a chord with people in the industry,' recalls Rogers. As a result, Hawtrey was cast in the ill-fated supporting role of Dan Dann. Originally Sydney Bromley, fresh from playing Sam Houston in *Carry On Cowboy*, had been contracted for £50 a day. Hawtrey, in his best Carry On earner ever, secured £400 for his pivotal two days' work.

The guest star was also amply rewarded. Sid James was unavailable to play the bumbling detective Sydney Bung, a role unquestionably tailor-made for him. He was committed to playing one of the robbers opposite Kenneth Connor in the most prestigious pantomime in the country, the London Palladium's staging of *Babes in the Wood*. It proved so successful that it was still running in June 1966! At one stage, Sid's estranged comic partner Tony Hancock was in the frame to replace him in the Carry On. The two had recently reunited for a November 1965 Decca release, *It's Hancock*, which remade two classic *Half Hours*, 'The Missing Page' and 'The Reunion Party'. But Hancock was pickled and preparing his 'comeback'

season at the Royal Festival Hall. Moreover, he would probably have baulked at being the second choice in a Sid James cast-off. Aptly, the part went to another actor with the words of writers Ray Galton and Alan Simpson fresh on his lips, Harry H Corbett. As part of Joan Littlewood's workshop company, Corbett had become the actor's actor, excelling in the 'absolute searching truth' of Richard II and the experimental staging of Ewan MacColl's *Uranium 235*. But it was *Steptoe and Son* that had made him a star. Although he would return to the character on television, film, radio and stage, Corbett had gladly put Harold Steptoe to bed by the end of October 1965. All agreed that the series had reached the end. Just two weeks into the recording block of the 'last' series, Peter Rogers wrote to Harry: 'Will you please, please consider the part of Sid Bung in the enclosed script of *Carry On Screaming!* ... I have always wanted to make a film with you and I am keeping my fingers crossed this time. If you would like to talk about it please give me a ring and we will meet up.' Corbett accepted the highest acting fee that the Carry Ons had so far offered – £12,000 for six weeks of the shoot. It probably helped overcome his reluctance to tackle film acting after the Galton and Simpson tragi-comic effort, *The Bargee*, had failed to ignite. Ever the professional, Corbett was happy to joke about his involvement in the series, recalling 'my first bedroom scene and it had to be with a snake. Very sexy!' Jim Dale countered, 'Yes, but we had the best lines!' Ruminating on the snake, Dale revealed, 'I was very fond of it but let me tell you now we were just good friends!' The scene, utilised a real snake, complete with its handler just out of camera shot, and a prop creature for the actors to react to.

Unlike Corbett and Dale, Bernard Bresslaw didn't get the joke going round the set when everyone in the unit greeted him with ''ullo Lurch!' The American situation comedy *The Addams Family* had just crossed the Atlantic, and Ted Cassidy's lumbering, deadpan performance as the family retainer bore a striking

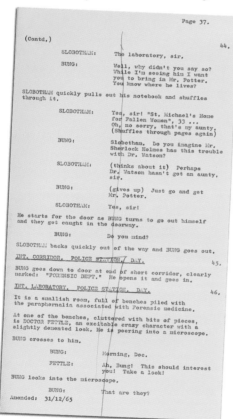

resemblance to Bresslaw. Confused, 'after my first scene I asked director Gerald Thomas if he thought the interpretation was okay and he agreed,' said Bresslaw. 'I have since seen my counterpart and it really is quite uncanny. It just goes to show that tiny minds think alike!'

Sally Douglas had already provided jaw-dropping glamour to the untaxing roles of a Dicky Dick's girl in *Jack*, a guard in *Spying*, Mark Antony's dusky slave girl in *Cleo* and Kitkata in *Cowboy*. On the first day of filming, she was at Pinewood with fellow 'dummies'

Angela Douglas and Joan Sims, being made up in her plaster mould for her role as the 'new girl', petrified in a shop window. 'They called me down the other day to do a plaster cast for the film,' commented Joan. 'I'm supposed to become a dummy, so they wanted a perfect likeness. So they sent me to the plasterer's shop and I went. A dear little man came over, looked me up and down and said, "You'll have to take that off," meaning my blouse. Well I thought, I don't mind, so off it came. He looked at me again. Eyeing my bra he was. "No you don't," I said. "You'll have to take it off," he said, "otherwise the plaster won't stick!" What do you do in a situation like that? I thought, "Oh heck, here goes," and flung it away. The man went off and came back with a great brush and pail of sloppy looking stuff. "Lift up your arms," he says. So I

A cut page from Talbot Rothwell's screenplay which includes a telling line of dialogue from Holmesian Detective Sergeant Sidney Bung, unfavourably comparing Detective Constable Slobotham to Doctor Watson.

'Fangs ain't what they used to be' for sinister siblings Kenneth Williams and Fenella Fielding.

Fenella Fielding (1934–)

Fielding is a British eccentric with Romanian ancestry. After a fledgling secretarial career, she made her stage debut in 1954 and fully came to prominence in the 1958 staging of *Valmouth* and the West End revue *Pieces of Eight* in 1959. That same year, her fruity voice was heard in her first film, the Norman Wisdom comedy *Follow A Star*. She joined Betty Box's rep company with *Doctor in Love* (1960), alsoappearing in *Doctor in Distress* (1963) and, as an injured ballerina, *Doctor in Clover* (1966). She turned down the role of Anthea in *Carry On Cabby* because the part 'was obsessed with my bust!' Her seductive, dark velvet personality was at its best in light Gothic fare, and she certainly shone in the 1962 Hammer comedy *The Old Dark House*. Her obsession with Tom Preston and a distinct talent to amuse provided useful training for *Carry On Screaming!*, although it is ironic that most of the jokes flew over her head: 'My dear, it simply didn't dawn on me that the dialogue would have meant anything other than what silly old me thought it was. I was told later that I got it mixed up and it might have offended the British censor.' Later in the decade she gave Tony Curtis a run for his money in *Drop Dead Darling* (1966) and stole the plaudits as Lady Eager in *Lock Up Your Daughters* (1969). Her voice alone enhanced such diverse fare as *The Prisoner* and *Dougal and the Blue Cat*, while her stage credentials embraced Shakespeare, Ibsen and pantomime. She made a belated return to cinema in the Rik Mayall and Adrian Edmondson comedy *Hotel Paradiso* (1999) Paradiso (1999), and played the eccentric Eve in the horror film Wishbaby (2008).

Carry On credits: *Regardless, Screaming!*

'Do you mind if I smoke?' Fenella Fielding radiates forbidden pleasures in this bewitching pose from *Carry On Screaming!*

The game's a foot! Jim Dale helps bumbling detectives Harry H Corbett and Peter Butterworth with their enquiries.

put my arms up and he dipped his whitewash brush in and slapped this stuff all over my chest. "Turn round," he said, and he did me at the back too. Then the man got some gauze and whacked that on and great fistfuls of plaster. Smack, smack, on it went, with him patting round the curves. Can you imagine what a terrible mess I looked, apart from the embarrassment. Then he did each of my legs! I had to go back the following day to get my head done!'

Kenneth Williams celebrated his fortieth birthday during production. He described his role as less frantic than earlier performances. 'Dr Watt is rather more subdued to suit the mock-eerie mood of the film. I do, however, lapse into the occasional vulgarity and a fit of the twitches.'

Amazingly, with a budget of just £179,537, the film looks rich, splendid and gloriously Gothic; a huge debt of thanks going to the director of photography, Alan Hume. Suitably enough, he had previously lit the atmospheric Hammer horror, *The Kiss of the Vampire* (produced in 1962) and the horror portmanteau *Dr Terror's House of Horrors*, produced by Amicus in 1964. 'They were very tight budgets as well, so I was used to making horror films economically before lighting *Carry On Screaming!* They were similar. Not in style, of course, although I did enjoy all the laboratory scenes with the cobwebs, bubbling vats and the like. But the actors were deadly serious about their craft. Peter Cushing and Christopher Lee never sent it up. Nor did Harry H Corbett and Kenneth Williams. They were always fun on set but focused on the work.'

Alan Hume (1924–)

Having followed in his father's footsteps, Hume worked as a storeboy at the Acton London Underground Station. He 'hated it'. Travelling in by train from his home in Uxbridge, he chatted to a gentleman who worked at a film laboratory in Acton, processing the likes of the Paramount Newsreels. Hume accepted a job offer and stayed with the labs for a year.

Hume's career in the film industry started as a clapperboy, then as loader and focus puller on such films as *They Came to a City* (1944). By the late 1940s, he was assistant to director of photography Guy Green at Cineguild. He worked with director Robert Day on the Alastair Sim comedy *The Green Man* (1956), but it was with Gerald Thomas that 'a close relationship developed.' While preparing *Carry On Sergeant* at Pinewood, Thomas invited Hume to be camera operator with director of photography Peter Hennessy. He later assisted Reginald Wyer, a veteran cinematographer since 1918 and a Sydney Box favourite, and on *Carry On, Constable* worked along-side Ted Scaife.

When Scaife landed a lengthy assignment in Turkey, Hume graduated to director of photography on *No Kidding* (1961). Hume also proved skilled at creating an atmosphere of Gothic horror for the Hammer film *The Kiss of the Vampire* (1964) and the Amicus portmanteau *Dr Terror's House of Horrors* (1965). In 1968, he turned down *Carry On...Up the Khyber* because he felt 'the title just went too far' and

instead accepted the National Service drama *The Bofors Gun* (1968).

In 1970, he lit the Stanley Baker comedy *Perfect Friday* for director Peter Hall and the Michael York and Elke Sommer adventure *Zeppelin* for Etienne Perier, before returning to Carry On and 'splitting them between Ernie Steward and myself'. Hume worked on the film version of *Bless This House*, the Leslie Phillips romp *Not Now, Darling* for Ray Cooney and David Croft, and John Hough's *The Legend of Hell House*.

In 1981, Hume lit Hough's Disney chiller *The Watcher in the Wood*. He also built up a body of work with director Kevin Connor, notably the horror anthology *From Beyond the Grave* (1973), the dinosaur drama *The Land That Time Forgot* (1974) and its sequel, *The People That Time Forgot* (1977). He joined the James Bond team with Lewis Gilbert's *The Spy Who Loved Me* (1977) and went on to enhance John Glen's *For Your Eyes Only* (1981), *Octopussy* (1983) and *A View to a Kill* (1985). He worked with Charles Crichton on *A Fish Called Wanda* (1988), Lewis Gilbert, again, on *Shirley Valentine* (1989) and the television film *Jack the Ripper*, starring Michael Caine.

Loyally, he lit the last three films for his favourite 'boss', Gerald Thomas, including the 1986 thriller *The Second Victory*. Hume reflected in 2003: 'If I could have my career over again I would do exactly the same thing. I'd sooner be working on *Carry On Henry* than *Hamlet*, thank you very much!'

Carry On credits: *Sergeant, Nurse, Teacher, Constable, Regardless, Cruising, Cabby, Jack, Spying, Cleo, Cowboy, Screaming!, Don't Lose Your Head, Follow That Camel, Doctor, Henry, Abroad, Girls, Emmannuelle, Columbus*

Autobiography: *A Life Through the Lens*

Alan Hume looks on as Gerald Thomas checks a camera angle on location for *The Big Job* (1965).

DON'T LOSE YOUR HEAD (1966)

In France, the revolution rages and Citizens Camembert (Kenneth Williams) and Bidet (Peter Butterworth) are giving the aristocrats the big chop on Madame le Guillotine! Meanwhile, in England, fancy fops Sir Rodney Ffing with two Fs (Sid James) and Lord Darcy de Pue (Jim Dale) are pursuing simple, country pleasures. But when their costumier Henri (Michael Ward) tells them of the perils in France, Ffing transforms in to the Black Fingernail and bounds to the rescue. While Darcy keeps the onlookers busy with his collection of model guillotines, the Fingernail plucks the mincing Duc de Pommfrit (Charles Hawtrey) from the jaws of death. On the run, the Fingernail baffles the authorities with a string of disguises, including an aristocratic lady and a coachman. Robespierre (Peter Gilmore) is not amused but the Fingernail reveals himself to a Gaelic stunna, Jacqueline (Dany Robin), before returning to England. Camembert, Bidet and Désirée Dubarry (Joan Sims) follow him to little avail, although true love for Jacqueline lures him back to France, and a trap in Camembert's newly acquired chateau. After the ensuing sword fight, the citizens are defeated and beheaded. And Désirée gets to marry her titled gentleman, the Duc de Pommfrit!

There is absolutely nothing that makes *Don't Lose Your Head* less of a Carry On without the Carry On prefix than, say, *The Big Job* or *Raising the Wind*. However, there is no doubt that *Don't Lose Your Head*, unlike the previous Peter Rogers comedies in the same vein, was conceived, filmed and marketed as a Carry On in all but name.

With Stuart Levy's death in 1966, the Carry Ons' reign at Anglo Amalgamated was rocked. Nat Cohen, who had pushed for more prestigious fare such as *A Kind of Loving* (1962) and *Darling* (1965) had, in Peter Rogers's eyes, 'got culture up his arse!' Besides, the home of the Carry Ons had always been Pinewood Studios, the studios that J Arthur Rank financed in September 1936. For the Carry Ons or, at the very least, saucy comedies produced by Peter Rogers and directed by Gerald

Thomas, to be protected under the wing of the Rank Organisation was the most natural progression. A contract between Rogers and Rank was signed on 22 August 1966 and with it over a decade of Carry Ons set in motion.

The minutes of the pre-production meeting record that 'Mr Rogers wondered whether the words Carry On need be used in the picture. He thought that as the film was more visual than previous Carry On productions it could stand on its own without any reference to Carry On.' By the post-production meeting on 1 February 1967, Peter Rogers, Gerald Thomas and the Rank Organisation's Frederick L Thomas were in no doubt whatsoever. It was clear that 'we were dealing with virtually the thirteenth Carry On film and as the previous films had placed the emphasis on advertising with

'Carry On' Laughing until you have hysterics....
But— **Don't Lose Your Head** A

COLOUR

THE RANK ORGANISATION Presents a **PETER ROGERS** PRODUCTION SIDNEY **JAMES** · KENNETH **WILLIAMS** · JIM **DALE** · CHARLES **HAWTREY** · JOAN **SIMS** · DANY **ROBIN**

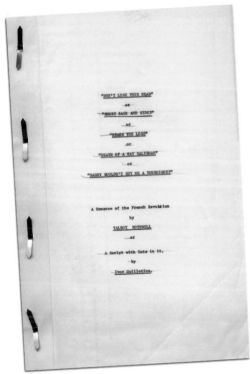

outstanding success we should continue the formula.' Rogers suggested that 'emphasis should be given to the words Carry On in the advertising copy' and several poster tag-lines featuring Carry On were considered, including 'It's the Carry On team again – sticking its neck out into the French Revolution'.

Rothwell's first draft was awash with alternative titles: 'Short Back and Sides' or

'Heads You Lost' or 'Death of a Hat Salesman' or 'Daddy Wouldn't Buy Me a Tourniquet' and the piece was subtitled 'A Romance of the French Revolution by Talbot Rothwell or a script with cuts in it by Ivor Guillotine'. All these gags were blue pencilled, although it was Peter Rogers' hand that heightened the initial guillotine dialogue 'He'll have to go' and 'and the next please' to the more pleasing, mock French 'He'll have to allez' and 'and the next one s'il vous plait'. A further comic exchange between the characters of Butterworth and Williams was completely removed:

> *Bidet*: 'Le Tent de Lafayette!'
> *Camembert*: 'Le Tent! La Marquis de Lafayette.'
> *Bidet*: 'Well, same thing.'
> *Camembert*: 'Of course it isn't the same thing. Citizen imbecile! Any child knows that a marquis is much bigger.'

Sid James's agent, Michael Sullivan, advised Peter Rogers that Sid James would be committed to a production of *Wedding Fever* at the Pier Theatre, Bournemouth, but Rogers responded that if Sid

Opposite: Glad to be bad. Peter Butterworth and Kenneth Williams sneer with gusto as revolutionaries Citizens Camembert and Bidet.

Left: The original draft script, featuring a basket-full of rejected alternative titles.

Below: Talbot Rothwell's cutting humour extended to a guillotine sketch on his draft screenplay.

ON LOCATION

Although a Paris press showing was planned, and subsequently cancelled, all the locations were found in the Home Counties. On 3 October the unit filmed at the National Trust property Waddesdon Manor near Aylesbury, the only French design chateau in the country. Eric Dunning was hired for 'supplying apparatus and services for flying artistes and stuntmen for sequences in main hall and staircase of chateau' for the Pinewood interiors between Monday 24 and Friday 28 October. On October 6 and 7 filming also took place at another National Trust house, Clandon Park, near Guildford, while the luxurious English residency of Sid James was the National Trust's Cliveden, where filming took place on 11 October. On 18 October the marriage sequence that ends the story was filmed at Denham Church, a stone's throw from Pinewood. The production manager, Jack Swinburne, gave a £15 donation to the church fund in way of thanking the aptly named, Reverend E Corr.

Sid James may have to commit to a fate worse than death in order to keep Joan Sims from screaming the house down.

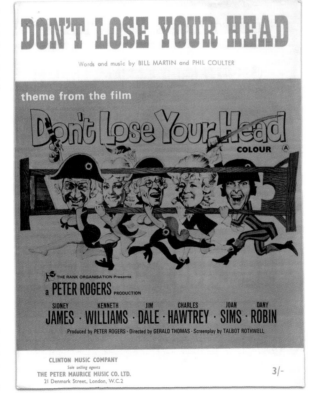

The song sheet for the title number, 'executed by the Michael Sammes Singers'.

proved unable to make the film 'I will be compelled to re-cast the part.' Sullivan turned to Gerald Thomas requesting a delayed use of Sid and an early stop date because the actor was due to start his new television series, *George and the Dragon*. In the event, Thomas utilised Joan Sims, Charles Hawtrey and Peter Butterworth for the first few days of the shoot, filming the Rose Harbour sequences on 'C' Stage, so Sid wasn't called until the filming of the guillotine sequence on the Paddock Tank stage at Pinewood. However, he wasn't released from the film until 1 November 1966, just over two weeks before the first *George and the Dragon* was broadcast. Even Sid's costumes and wigs fitting at Bermans with designer Emma Selby-Walker was a rush job, arriving for his fitting at 9.30 am then rushing back to Bournemouth before lunch – and Sid had a lot of costumes to fit for the film! All this activity took a strain. Although Sid jokingly commented 'at the end of those hectic four weeks my face was even more crumpled than any piece of corduroy ever woven' the physicality of the role and his stage and television overload may have contributed to his heart attack the following year.

Michael Sullivan's glamorous wife Dany Robin was cast as the female lead. Peter Rogers sent the script to Joan Sims with a note: 'Off to another giggle we hope, Desiree. Love, Peter.' Kenneth Williams, committed to Shepherd's Bush recording for the TV show *International Cabaret* every Tuesday evening, received: 'Wot'cher Shylock, this is for you. Love, Peter.' To Charles Hawtrey, Rogers wrote: 'Dear Duke d'Hawtrey, No one else could play the Aristocrat.' Hawtrey replied on 8 August, 'Thank you for the script of *Don't Lose Your Head* and for your letter which amused me very much. Trust all goes well and look forward to seeing you.' Hawtrey was more important to the project than he knew. It was mentioned at the pre-production meeting that 'overseas papers would be very interested in Charles Hawtrey who had made his mark already in overseas markets in Carry On pictures.'

The importance of the principal actors was never doubted and, indeed, the cast did a huge amount of publicity for this transition film. The BBC was eager to secure a Sid James interview for *Town and Around*, while Kenneth Williams was requested for *Film Review*. The producers of *Call My Bluff* promised to mention the new film during Williams' appearance on the show in

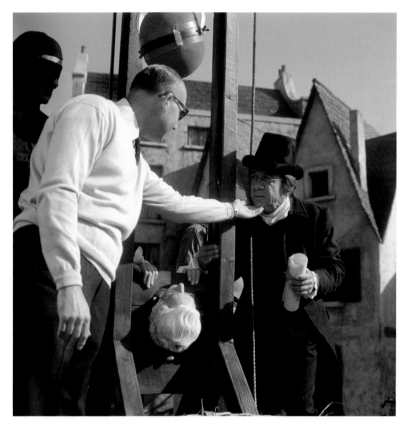

March, while the actor was asked to advertise the film in an *International Cabaret* programme broadcast at the time of the Leicester Square premiere. Independent Television had Sid James booked for an appearance on *The Eamonn Andrews Show*, and the Granada show, *Cinema*, was planning a special 'English Comedy' edition for the build-up to the general release. *Movie-Go-Round, Monday at the Movies, Roundabout*

Gerald Thomas playfully tickles Sid James under the chin, while Leon Greene waits in earnest and Charles Hawtrey gets a pain in the neck on the block.

Peter Butterworth and his young son, Tyler, on the set of *Don't Lose Your Head*. Tyler was at Pinewood filming the Morecambe and Wise comedy *The Magnificent Two*.

TITBITS

The multi-talented Diana Macnamara was extremely busy on the film, playing no less than four different parts. She was a woman at the guillotine, a double for a French soldier on horseback, the haughty Princess Stephanie during the Rodney Ffing ball and, most intriguingly of all, a double for Charles Hawtrey during the tricky horse-riding sequence that follows Sid James's duelling defeat of Kenneth Williams. Adopting Hawtrey's distinctive glasses for the full effect, she even convinced director Gerald Thomas. Fresh from undead and ghoulish turns for Hammer in *The Plague of the Zombies* and *The Reptile*, Jacqueline Pearce was allowed to remain glamorous, as a lady unimpressed with Hawtrey's tall tales. Monica Van der Zyl, dropping Hawtrey's message in the basket, dubbed countless James Bond girls (notably Ursula Andress in *Dr No* and subsequently in Hammer's *She*). And Patrick Allen did a half-day, recording the film's narration on 14 December 1966.

Michael Ward (1909-1997)

Another of Michael Sullivan's company of Carry On actors, Ward was less of a heavyweight than Sid James, but remained a familiar face. He had worked for Peter Rogers as early as 1949 in *Marry Me!* although after *Don't Lose Your Head*, amazingly, Rogers never used Ward again. Part of that indispensable backbone of British cinema character actors, Ward perfected the one-note mince machine on film and television for thirty years. His first major film, as the fussy ornithologist in *Sleeping Car to Trieste* (1948) was typical. Thereafter, his superior expression and fussy manner was put to good use as the window dresser in battle with Norman Wisdom in *Trouble in Store* (1953) and the effeminate journalist in Peter Sellers' front room in *I'm All Right Jack* (1959). Regularly employed by Rogers, Betty Box and the Boultings, film work eased in the 1970s, although he played an effete insane asylum inmate in Hammer's *Frankenstein and the Monster from Hell* (produced in 1972), an effete pub local in Hammer's film version of *Man About the House* (1974) and an effete estate agent in *Revenge of the Pink Panther* (1978). On television, he excelled as the rather effete Labour Member of Parliament in *Rising Damp* ('Stand Up and Be Counted') and as Morecambe and Wise's effete next-door neighbour.

Carry On credits: *Regardless, Cabby, Cleo, Screaming!, Don't Lose Your Head*

Michael Ward at the peak of his stooge powers in the 1950s, when he sparred with everyone from Frankie Howerd to Norman Wisdom.

and *Home This Afternoon* had all expressed interest in interviewing Sid James, Kenneth Williams and/or Joan Sims. *Photoplay* magazine planned two separate features focusing on Sid James and Kenneth Williams. *Hers, Mirabelle* and *Rave* requested photographs of all the cast members with 'emphasis on Jim Dale', while Peter Butterworth was profiled in *Weekly News*.

Filming Jim Dale, Charles Hawtrey and Sid James on the Bastille set at Pinewood.

The new boy on the block at Rank, Peter Rogers had found himself defending his moderate budget of £215,152, noting no 'increase in the budget since *Carry On Cleo* which was made exactly two years ago with the same cast and schedule.' A successful press screening temporarily put the producer at ease: 'I am very relieved because I was worried about reaction to the film.' He countered his jubilation with a very humble acceptance of the fact that, until the British public gave the film the thumbs-up, no success could be celebrated. However the relationship with Rank, particularly over money, didn't get off to the smoothest of starts. Rogers continually refused to sign production contracts until all the budget queries were ironed out. Even as late as September 1967, with *Don't Lose Your Head* released and *Follow That Camel* in post-production, there was still concern about Rank putting up seventy per cent of the budget. Rogers, although always pushing for a better deal and less financial responsibility, finally put his hands up.

Certainly many more Carry Ons were on the horizon, although the official press release which celebrated Rank's takeover with a 'Vive le Difference' unconvincingly pleaded that 'it is not – repeat *not* – a Carry On comedy.' The public knew better.

Peter Butterworth (1919-1979)

Having joined the Royal Air Force before the outbreak of war, Peter served with the Fleet Air Arm until he was shot down in 1941 during a bombing raid over Holland. Captured by the enemy and put in the prisoner of war camp Stalag Luft 3, he took part in plays and revues, deliberately staged in order to cover up the sound of digging from fellow inmates planning rescue routes.

While not performing, Butterworth took to the spade as well, although after two unsuccessful attempts at breaking out he resolved he was better at acting than shovelling. In the mid 1950s, he was tickled to be told he was 'the wrong type' for the film *The Wooden Horse*. He had helped dig the tunnel that the story was based upon.

Having joined the Navy, and still performing, he was injured out of service. A few words of encouragement from Jack Hylton after a Red Cross show at the Stoll Theatre inspired him to act in repertory and on the variety circuit. On radio he would collaborate with the Goons, in various guises, in the aborted *Sellers's Castle* (1950) and *Trial Gallop* (1952).

He starred with Michael Howard in the radio comedy *One For the Boys*, while supporting Terry-Thomas as the chauffeur and general dogsbody Lockit in the pioneering television sketch series *How Do You View?* (1949-1953). Butterworth had also been embraced by Val Guest and joined his film company with roles in *William Comes to Town*, *Murder at the Windmill* (both 1948), *Miss Pilgrim's Progress* (1949), *Mr Drake's Duck* (1950) and *The Day the Earth Caught Fire* (1961).

A pantomime regular, he created the simpleton 'Butterscoth' in many productions and became a beloved

television uncle as the skipper of *The S.S. Saturday Special*, appearing with puppets Porterhouse the Parrot and Sooty. He starred in *Peter's Troubles* (1953-1958) on the BBC's *For the Children* programme, sparred with the cartoon bird Buddy Budgerigar in ITV's

Kept In (1955) and joined forces with his wife, Janet Brown, in *For The Older Children* programmes *Butterworth Time* and *For Pete's Sake* in 1956.

He made his first film for Peter Rogers, *The Gay Dog*, in 1954, and chalked up such notable film cameos as the bandleader in *tom thumb* (1958), the train ticket collector opposite Margaret Rutherford in *Murder, She Said!* (1961) and a frantic ambulance driver in *Doctor in Distress* (1963). On television, he played the Meddling Monk, a rival to William Hartnell's *Doctor Who* ('The Time Meddler', 1965, and 'The Daleks' Master Plan', 1966). He was also a regular member of Terry Scott's *Scott On...* team.

Always in demand, he once wrote, 'when not working he goes sailing and thinks about putting up that shelf in the kitchen.' His final film roles including two for Richard Lester, *Robin and Marian* (1976) and *The Ritz* (1977), and the Sean Connery heist *The First Great Train Robbery*, as Putnam. His last appearances were in the Alan Bennett television play *Afternoon Off* and pantomime in Coventry, as Widow Twankey in *Aladdin*.

Carry On credits: *Cowboy, Screaming!, Don't Lose Your Head, Follow That Camel, Doctor, Up the Khyber, Camping, Again Doctor, Christmas, Loving, Henry, Abroad, Christmas '72, Girls, London!, Christmas '73, Dick, Laughing*: 'The Prisoner of Spenda', 'The Baron Outlook', 'The Sobbing Cavalier', *Behind, Laughing*: 'Under the Round Table', 'The Case of the Screaming Winkles', 'And In My Lady's Chamber', 'Short Knight, Long Daze', 'The Case of the Coughing Parrot', 'Lamp-Posts of the Empire', *Laughing, England, Emmannuelle*

FOLLOW THAT CAMEL (1967)

In an attempt to discredit Bertram Oliphant 'Bo' West (Jim Dale), that utter cad Captain Bagshaw (Peter Gilmore) deliberately trips during a cricket match and bags his rival's squeeze, Lady Jane Ponsonby (Angela Douglas). Humiliated, Bo and his batman Simpson (Peter Butterworth) join the foreign legion under the command of the sadistic Commandant Burger (Kenneth Williams) and the cheerful Captain Le Pice (Charles Hawtrey). The drill Sergeant, Ernie Nocker (Phil Silvers) is determined to enforce discipline but, unfortunately for him, the new recruits were witness to his dalliance with the saucy café owner, Zig-Zig (Joan Sims). The Brits threaten to expose his medal-winning bravery as a fraud so Knocker treats them with over-protective respect. Lady Jane, discovering the truth about Bo's departure, travels across the world to bring him back but, upon arrival, is drugged by Sheikh Abdul Abulbul (Bernard Bresslaw). After an evening of belly-dancing entertainment from Corktip (Anita Harris), Bo and Knocker are captured and taken to the Sheikh's desert encampment. But the passionate Burger mounts a rescue attempt. Our hapless heroes escape the Sheikh's clutches and hold the Fort Zuassantneuf.

Although the foreign legion idea had been bubbling in the writer's mind during 1966, it wasn't until February 1967 that Talbot Rothwell was contracted to write a script. Importantly, it also saw an initial return to the Carry On name. The first draft of Rothwell's Beau Geste parody is entitled 'Carry On, Bo!' or 'Across the Sahara with Spade & Bucket' or 'You've Gotta Be Tough When There's Nothing But Sandpaper – A thrilling Story of Romance & Intrigue in the glorious French Foreign Legion by Talbot Rothwell'. But Peter Rogers and the Rank Organisation got cold feet. By the end of April, the film had gone through two title changes, when solicitors Crawley and De Reye wrote to Rogers to confirm: 'whether the title had indeed now been changed from "The Foreign Legion" to Follow That Camel.'

Charles Hawtrey was dissatisfied with the role he had been offered by Rogers, writing to Gerald Thomas: 'There is little one can do about the role of "Le Pice" – but the part of Batman to Beau gives a real opportunity of being very funny. I can only hope that Peter can be persuaded to give the part to me – and am certain that both you and he would not regret so doing.' Alas, Rogers had already cast the batman; Peter Butterworth had accepted £2000, half of Hawtrey's fee, for an eight-week shoot.

The major casting cost, of course, was an American import. Talbot Rothwell, undoubtedly writing the lead role for Sid James, had been struck time and again with the fact that the character he was developing was, in effect, Sergeant Bilko in the foreign legion. He said as much in a letter to Peter Rogers: 'The only

'BILKO' JOINS THE 'CARRY ON' LEGION!

character I'm not quite sure about is the American sergeant who simply yells for Phil Silvers all the way along. I just can't get this Bilko image out of my mind; it would fit this situation so well. And it would be wonderful if you could get him.' It was the producer's job to make it happen. Sid James was in the midst of recording the second series of *George and the Dragon* for ATV and press comment that Woody Allen had been approached to replace him in the foreign legion romp appears to be just speculation. Phil Silvers' London representative agreed terms, which included a completion guarantee fee of £10,000 and a production fee of £30,000, a first-class round trip for two from Los Angeles to London and a separate limousine and chauffeur to and from the studios and all locations. Which rather put Kenneth Williams's rare fee increase to £6000 in perspective. The casting was a surprise for Williams when he went for his costume fitting at Berman's: 'met Peter Butterworth there. He told me that Sid James is out! And they're having Phil Silvers in the lead!! He is just terrible, so it's a worthy successor.'

Opposite: Harem scare 'um! Peter Butterworth, Jim Dale and Phil Silvers enjoy the scenery.

Left: Talbot Rothwell's draft screenplay reveals unused alternative titles.

Jim Dale poses as the keen but naïve action hero, 'Bo' West.

DOCTOR, DOCTOR!

Sheena the camel took an instant dislike to most of the cast and crew, spitting at both Bernard Bresslaw and Peter Butterworth, although he reportedly warmed to the soft caress of Charles Hawtrey. Having misinformed both Jim Dale and Peter Butterworth that each actor intensely disliked the other, Kenneth Williams got his come-uppance on one of the last days of filming when Dale accidentally dropped a rifle on Williams' foot.

ON LOCATION

A bulldozer was hired for the Camber Sands dunes location filming, while a foreign legion fort was erected and palm trees installed. A camel was brought in from Chessington Zoo but it had been born in captivity and couldn't walk on sand without concealed metal supports to reassure it. Rushes were screened every day at the Regent Cinema in Rye. Having scouted out hotels all over Sussex, location manager Terry Clegg secured the gang at the Yelton Hotel, Hastings. They were given £1 evening meal allowance per day, although Charles Hawtrey preferred to get fed and watered at the nearby pub, the Green Shutters. Gerald Thomas and Peter Rogers shared a double room at the Rumpels, a respected hotel in Rye. Locations local to Pinewood were utilised, with the cricket scenes being filmed over four days in the grounds of Swakeleys, a country house in Ickenham, Uxbridge, Middlesex. Osterley Park house doubled for Ponsonby's residence on 19 June 1967.

Silvers' casting helped to increase the budget to just under £290,000. In the midst of production Rogers had to defend the expense in a letter to Rank: '...this picture is cheaper than the last one. If you subtract the monies paid to Phil Silvers and take a week off the schedule – which is what I would have done without

Phil Silvers in the cast – you will see that you have more than your money's worth. Plus an artiste who should be able to help you with Paramount.' The Rank Organisation, as with every leader in British cinema, was desperate to break the American market.

Filming began in Camber Sands. The unit, in its longest period away from Pinewood, was situated in Sussex for most of May. Silvers joined Angela Douglas, Kenneth Williams, Jim Dale, Peter Butterworth and John Bluthal on location, but for Williams he quickly proved too much: 'There seems to be no respite from this kind of man,' he wrote in his diary. 'Refuses to relax and shut up. You mention the county of Kent and he says "O! you Kent do that!" and you're supposed to fall about. The awful truth is that he is not very funny. I get more laughs on the set than he does.' Professional jealousy was one thing but it is perhaps a relief that Silvers' financial package was unknown by the rest of the cast.

Silvers' failing eyesight dictated he wear contact lenses behind his glasses. Jim Dale

Charles Hawtrey and Sheena the camel snuggle up on location in Sussex.

Kenneth Williams and Phil Silvers both realise that the American star's autocue is too far away!

TRAILER

The trailer screamed 'producer Peter Rogers and director Gerald Thomas and the whole crazy Carry On company join the Foreign Legion.' And it was originally planned to start on a Phil Silvers recruitment poster 'à la Kitchener' and fade to Silvers who would introduce and voice over the trailer. On television, a quickie was filmed featuring a fare getting in to a taxi cab and yelling 'Follow that camel!' A hip teenager would confirm: 'Follow that camel! That crazy Carry On gang!'

recalls 'me and Peter Butterworth on all fours in the sand looking for the damned things that Phil kept losing!'

The problems continued when the unit arrived at Pinewood Studios. After a week, Kenneth Williams was helping Silvers 'with the lines but all to no avail. He blew on so many takes that he got humiliated and burst into tears on the set. Put my arm around him and talked and talked him out of it. He is very depressed and low. He continually says that he is "only half a person" and hints at greater powers and talents which have been taken from him when his wife and five daughters elected to leave him. I should think they were all bored out of their minds.' Never one to be too sentimental, on 7 June 'when he came out with a line today, I said "Oh! You know it? – it's fantastic, how do you do it? – go to bed with a record under your pillow or something?" Some people said it was rude of me. Angela [Douglas] said "Oh! You go too far." etc., but I'm too exhausted to care.'

In a strange twist, the original ending of the film had featured a wisecracking Phil Silvers as

A lost scene featuring Phil Silvers as Lady Jane's baby, as originally planned for the end of the film.

Anita Harris (1942-)

A graduate of the Hampshire School of Drama, it was as a singer that Anita first made her name. She represented Britain at the San Remo song festival picking up the gold medal, while her first album, *Somebody's in My Orchard*, was the Critics' Choice for Album of the Year in 1967. Peter Rogers cast her as the seductive belly dancer, Corktip, a typically pun-ridden corruption of Claudette Colbert's character, Cigarette, from the Ronald Colman film *Under Two Flags* (1936). A 'wonderfully rotund' belly dance arranger, Julie Mendez, was on set to advise Anita during her dance routine. In June 1967 Anita's hit single, 'Just Loving You', climbed to number 6 in the charts and retains the record for the longest stay in the Top Twenty; over fifteen months. On stage, she worked with such comics as Harry Secombe, Tommy Cooper, Jimmy Clitheroe and Frankie Howerd; concurrently with the production of *Carry On Doctor*, she appeared in the West End revue *Way Out in Piccadilly*. On television, she starred as Witch 'Nitty' opposite David Nixon in the children's show *Jumbleland*, picking up the *TV Times* Award for Most Popular Female Entertainer. The definitive Peter Pan under the direction of Pauline Grant at the National, she returned to the role for *The Millennium Peter Pan*. She is no stranger to more serious dramatic fare, having starred with George Sewell in a successful tour of Agatha Christie's *The Verdict*.

Carry On credits: *Follow That Camel, Doctor*

the baby of Lady Jane. Turning to the camera, the little Phil said: 'Ah well, as the old Arab saying has it – you can put many camels thru' the eye of a needle but you still know not what will come out.' The scene was certainly shot but, at the eleventh hour, replaced by a baby Kenneth Williams instead.

With the film in the bag, the Leicester Square premiere was set for 14 December with a nationwide general release in the second week of January 1968. The attachment of Phil Silvers made little difference to the film's American success, despite it being released as *Carry On in the Legion*. Gerald Thomas, meanwhile, was already up to his eyes in matters medical at Pinewood.

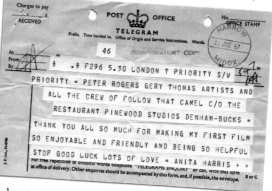

Top: Anita Harris photographed in the Pinewood gardens during a publicity session for *Carry On Doctor*.

Above: A telegram from Anita Harris following the completion of her role as 'Corktip'.

CARRY ON DOCTOR (1968)

Money-grabbing faith healer Francis Bigger (Frankie Howerd) falls off stage in mid-lecture and is rushed to hospital by cheery ambulance men Henry and Sam (Peter Gilmore and Harry Locke). The men's ward boasts such eccentrics as 'the temperature king' Charlie Roper (Sid James), Mr Smith (Peter Butterworth), Ken Biddle (Bernard Bresslaw) and Mr Barron (Charles Hawtrey), who is suffering a phantom pregnancy. All of them are under the friendly care of Dr James Kilmore (Jim Dale), who is idolised by Nurse Clarke (Anita Harris) and chastised by the rotund Matron (Hattie Jacques) – it's Dr Kenneth Tinkle (Kenneth Williams) that gets her pulse racing. But his past isn't whiter than white, and a skeleton emerges from his cupboard in the shapely guise of Nurse Sandra May (Barbara Windsor). Tinkle's medical treatment of her seems to have gone beyond the call of duty. However, internal politics sees Kilmore blamed for the ensuing chaos, while Francis, under the impression that he is dying, marries his mousy assistant Chloe Gibson (Joan Sims). The patients' loyalty to Kilmore sees a revolt against the hospital hierarchy and before long Tinkle and Matron are forced to admit their deceit.

While Kenneth Williams was still suffering on Camber Sands during the filming of *Follow That Camel*, his visiting producer, Peter Rogers, 'told me that he would like to do a *Carry On Doctor* as the last, and then "say goodbye to the Carry Ons." Rather sad really.'

This was no idle seaside chat. Rogers wrote to the Rank Organisation, sharing his concerns about registering the title of *Carry On Doctor*: 'I think we should make this in September as Nat is threatening to make a Carry On at that time and if we make *Carry On Doctor* it could be the finale of both series.' The comment concerning Anglo's Nat Cohen was crucial. At EMI, Cohen would return to lowbrow popular comedy with Frankie Howerd's *Up Pompeii* film and spin-offs and the *Steptoe and Son* films but, as early as 1967, he was indeed planning a new Carry On.

Despite the earlier claim that it was only a Carry On if produced by Peter Rogers, Rogers hadn't made an official Carry On since the last Anglo release, *Screaming!* In other words, the latest Carry On had been a Cohen product. It is more than likely that Sid James, Charles Hawtrey and the others would have accepted a Carry On from the Cohen stable – after all, it was just another job – and a Carry On with the team but without Peter Rogers would have made little difference to box-office receipts. Interestingly, Rogers seemed resigned to bringing the Carry Ons, and indeed his wife's Doctor series, to a close and a new beginning for the partnership beckoned. To that end, James Robertson Justice, who had starred as Sir Lancelot Spratt in all six Doctor films, signed an agreement to his likeness being used in *Carry On Doctor*, in September 1967. His portrait, bearing the legend 'Sir James R Justice Founder', appears in the hospital foyer in *Carry On Doctor*.

Rogers' original casting ideas for the hospital staff are interesting. On 10 August 1967 he wrote to Joan Sims: 'Will you please read the

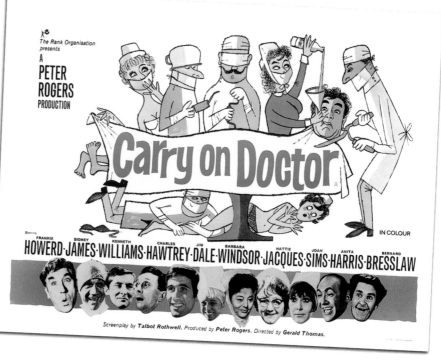

enclosed with the idea of playing the part of Matron.' In terms of Carry On folklore this seems unbelievable: Hattie Jacques *is* the Matron, a character she had created in *Carry On Nurse* in 1958. However, she hadn't made a Carry On since 1963's *Carry On Cabby*, and Joan Sims had played the Matron in the latest Doctor film, *Doctor in Clover*, on general release in 1966. But with Hattie back in the Matron's role, a later agreement insisted that Joan's name be billed even though advertising could exclude Barbara Windsor, Hattie Jacques, Anita Harris, Bernard Bresslaw and Peter Butterworth, some of whom were billed above Sims. Space was found for Butterworth's face on the poster, but not his name.

Rank still had reservations over the Carry On name. On 16 June, when contracts were signed, Talbot Rothwell's latest effort was known as 'Nurse Carries On Again', which was retained as one of the film's alternative titles; the first time the series actually included them.

Opposite: Wed in bed – Anita Harris and Bernard Bresslaw witness the marriage of Frankie Howerd and Joan Sims by a deaf vicar, played by Peter Jones.

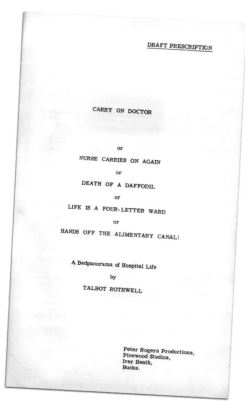

Left: Talbot Rothwell's original screenplay includes several alternative titles dropped from the opening credits.

DOCTOR, DOCTOR!

On 9 October 1967 Kenneth Williams wrote that he 'finished the operating theatre sequence and started the scene in the room with matron, Hattie. Hurt my back and moving the head forward is now painful. Always these films are painful for me. Should have stuck to my original decision not to do this one.'

ON LOCATION

Maidenhead Town Hall became a 'film star' almost as soon as it was completed in 1963; doubling for the hospital in the Betty Box comedy *Doctor in Distress*. Frankie Howerd and Harry Locke filmed the ambulance sequence for *Carry On Doctor* outside the building on the last day of shooting, 20 October 1967. Later that same day, the Masonic Hall, Windsor Road, Uxbridge was used for the exterior of the lecture hall that opens the film. The Lancaster Hotel Car Park and balcony were used for the establishing shots for the 'roof top drama' sequence.

Peter Gilmore compliments Barbara Windsor on her lovely looking 'pair' on location outside Maidenhead Town Hall.

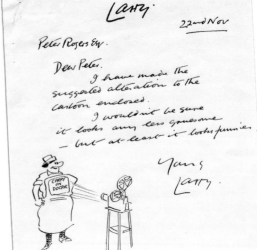

A note from cartoonist 'Larry' to producer Peter Rogers featuring an imaginative suggestion for the *Carry On Doctor* title card. Sadly, it went unused.

Jim Dale rehearses his romantic chat-up lines.

The film was also the first to benefit from title illustrations by renowned cartoonist 'Larry'. A veteran of *Punch* magazine, his real name was Terrence Parkes. 'Larry' wrote to Rogers: 'I haven't a clue how my drawings will look "blown up" to screen size – they may look bloody horrible – I await the results with some trepidation, meanwhile I'll Carry On Smoking. Yours "worried", Solihull.' He need not have worried; Rogers loved them, and a secretarial note reveals that he kept all the artwork. He did, however, request that one of the images, the trolley of spares, be toned down; 'for the sake of the customers I would prefer the spares to be arms and legs rather than "internals". If necessary you can have the fingers of one of the spare arms making the usual gesture.' 'Larry' was almost immediately

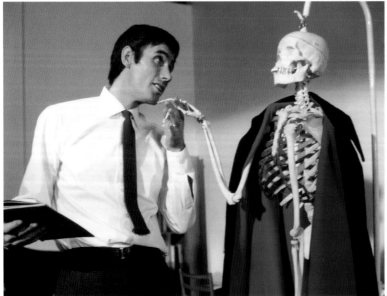

part of the Carry On furniture. As well as the next two films and *Carry On Girls*, he designed a 'Carry On Noshing' dinner menu which, as Rogers wrote, on 3 January 1968 'was a great success with visitors at Xmas'.

A warm welcome awaited Sid James, returning to duty following his heart attack, cast as the almost permanently bed-ridden patient, Charlie Roper. Co-star Jim Dale wryly notes: 'Look what they did with him, they gave him a part of a man who is constantly smoking. Bless his heart, he was choking to death most of the time!'

Rogers had big plans for the Francis Bigger character, pursuing Frankie Howerd to accept the role. He wrote to Howerd: 'Dear Frankie (if I may make so bold). Will you please read the enclosed script with a view to playing the part of Mr Bigger (with an 'I')? I'm sorry to have kept you waiting for so long but you know what typists are with holidays. I am keeping my fingers crossed and hoping. So will you please be prepared to meet and discuss the idea?' On the same day, Kenneth Williams received the script and noted that: 'It's really a very good vehicle for Frankie Howerd but all the other parts are lousy. I think that is it. This is the straw that breaks the camel's back. I wrote a nice letter to Peter Rogers saying that I didn't want to play the part.'

This was presumably a carefully considered decision as at the time Williams was under the impression that this was the last Carry On Rogers would make. The following day, Williams journeyed to Morocco where, while staying at the Rembrandt Hotel, he received a 'telegraph from Peter Rogers saying Frankie Howerd out, and offering me the part!! Of course it's impossible, so I'll have to wire or phone London or something! Stomach going over with worry about it all.' Typically, Williams resented being offered minor roles but was terrified when approached for the central turn that would hold the movie together. Baulking at the idea of carrying a Carry On, he accepted the role originally offered.

Howerd's *Way Out in Piccadilly* co-star, Anita Harris, rushed from Pinewood for a pre-arranged radio spot on *Pop In* during the afternoon of 5 October 1967. 'As Anita arrived at the programme in her nurse's uniform this aroused considerable comment, resulted in an excellent five minute radio plug for the film and drew a strong connection for her pop fans between Anita and *Carry On Doctor*,' explained her husband and agent, Mike Margolis, adding that *The Ed Sullivan Show* in the USA was interested in her chart success and had made approaches for her to appear. This 'would be a first class promotion spot for the film in view of your interest in the American market, as we would make certain that the film would be well mentioned.'

Although, the Rank Organisation was still searching for inroads into the States, Rogers was 'happy to stay in my own backyard' and even an offer of a million-pound travel insurance with Lloyds didn't impress. He denied the American opportunity, 'regardless of your generous offer of insurance, I cannot possibly free her from her contractual obligation to my company to

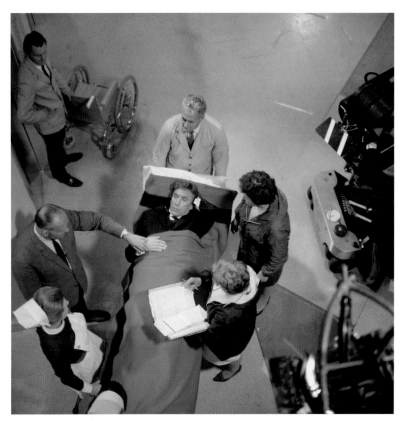

Lights, camera, action for Frankie Howerd, disproving his own lament that 'you can't be funny at 8.30 in the morning.'

appear in the show.' Rogers explained to Margolis: 'I can quite understand your attitude to what appears to be the dual career but you must try to understand that I am only concerned with the single career of Anita Harris and although you profess that the TV slots and radio spots which you arrange are calculated to enhance the value of my film I have to consider

TITBITS

Both Barbara Windsor and Jim Dale were busy with high-profile theatrical work at the time of filming: Barbara was appearing in *The Beggar's Opera*, Connaught Theatre, Worthing, while Jim was once more tackling Shakespeare in *A Midsummer Night's Dream* at the Ashcroft Theatre, Croydon. Stunt doubles Jasmin Broughton and Ken Norris were employed for their sun-bathing escapade on location while the majority of the scene was filmed on Pinewood's 'C' stage. The day before filming was completed, Joan Sims and Peter Butterworth opened in *Uproar in the House* at the Whitehall Theatre. Penelope Keith, often credited with an appearance despite continually denying any involvement in the Carry On series, did in fact film a brief cut role as 'plain nurse' alongside ambulance driver Peter Gilmore on location in Maidenhead. Distinguished voiceover artist Peter Haigh wrote to Peter Rogers 'on the off chance that there might be a bit for me in your next movie. If there was I'd be delighted.' Rogers replied that 'I think there might be a bit of narration work going on *Carry On Doctor*.' Alas for Haigh, Patrick Allen did the job. The Caffin Ward in the film was named in in-joke honour of the costume designer Yvonne Caffin.

Harry Locke (1912-1987)

A repertory actor since the late 1920s, Harry Locke's career was interrupted by war service with the Intelligence Corps. Demobbed in 1946, he returned to the stage; mainly as a cheeky chappie-styled stand-up comedian. On film, he played numerous chatty cab drivers and work-shy soldiers, making early appearances in the George Formby comedy *George in Civvy Street* (1946) and the Ealing classic *Passport to Pimlico* (1948). He made over seventy films, excelling in Disney's *Treasure Island* (1950) and Hammer's *The Devil-Ship Pirates* (1964). Still it was comedy that suited him best: Betty Box used him in *Doctor in the House, Doctor At Large* and *Upstairs and Downstairs*; he cropped up as part of Peter Sellers' union gang in *I'm All Right Jack* and 'served' with Benny Hill in the bitter-sweet RAF film *Light Up the Sky!* A couple of Terry-Thomas films (*Carlton-Browne of the F.O.* and *Kill or Cure*) and Norman Wisdom (*The Girl on the Boat* and *The Early Bird*) kept him busy, although he was also recruited for more 'worthy' fare such as *The L-Shaped Room, Alfie* and *Oh! What a Lovely War*. His last film role came as a barman in *The Creeping Flesh* (1972). On television, he starred in the civvy street comedy *Fair Game*, with Derek Farr, and played the bemused AA man in Galton and Simpson's *Comedy Playhouse*: 'Impasse' with Leslie Phillips and Bernard Cribbins. He guest starred in the first *Randall and Hopkirk (deceased)* ('My Late, Lamented Friend and Partner', 1969) and in *Just William* ('William and the Wonderful Present', 1977).

Carry On credits: *Nurse, Doctor, Again Doctor*

Corpsing in the wards, with Frankie Howerd, Anita Harris and June Jago unable to keep a straight face.

the value of personal publicity for Anita Harris in relation to her ultimate value to the film – and at this stage in her career I doubt very much if people are going to queue to see *Carry On Doctor* because Anita Harris happens to be in it.'

When Anita Harris wrote to thank Rogers for her roles in *Follow That Camel* and *Carry On Doctor*, he responded with a missive that, reading between the lines, seemed like a farewell to the actress, full of damp praise and hoped for success in other people's films: 'I would like to return your thanks for being such a good trooper and trying so hard on the two films we have made together. I am convinced that you have a big future in films, particularly in the musical field, which is obviously the sort of career you want to carve for yourself. I sincerely hope we will be able to work again some time in the future when the right part arises that we mutually feel is going to be a success for you. Lots of luck.' The role of the Khasi's daughter, Jelhi, in *Carry On...Up the Khyber* clearly called for Anita's dusky attractiveness, but Rogers obviously thought otherwise.

Lucy Griffiths seemed happy to be involved in the series for on 4 June 1968 she wrote to Gerald Thomas: 'I thought you might be interested to know that my "bit" [as a patient] in *Carry On Doctor* seems to have attracted the great British public – it's happening so often when I go into a shop not usually patronised or get on a bus – that the assistants say – "saw you in a film" – or "you do acting don't you" – or just "hello!" with a big grin – it warms one's heart and makes one want to go straight out and do a lot more for them – I expect that you are well *Up the Khyber* by now – and I know there's nothing up there for me.' Destined to return to the Carry On fold, but not yet, Griffiths was certainly right about her director's whereabouts.

Jim Dale MBE (1935–)

As part of the Carry On team, Jim is proud to say, 'We made a helluva lot of people laugh and that's what I've wanted to do ever since I was a kid.'

By the age of ten he was studying ballet, tap-dancing and tumbling. At sixteen, he was the youngest stand-up comedian on the circuit, having been discovered by talent scout Carroll Levis. And by the time he was twenty-two, he was a pop star with the number two chart hit 'Be My Girl', and regular appearances on BBC's *Six-Five Special*, the film version of which provided his 1958 film debut.

He first made an impression on the Carry On team by impersonating Kenneth Williams in his cameo as a befuddled trombonist in *Raising the Wind* (1962).

He was compère on *Thank Your Lucky Stars* from 1963, was a weekend disc jockey on *Children's Favourites* and made his West End debut at the Vaudeville Theatre in 1965 in *The Wayward Way*, a musical adaptation of *The Drunkard*, which he also produced. He was cast as Autolicus by director Frank Dunlop in the 1966 staging of Shakespeare's *The Winter's Tale*. After a run at the Edinburgh Festival, the production transferred to the Cambridge Theatre. That same year, his lyrics for

Georgy Girl won him an Oscar nomination.

In 1969 he launched a self-penned album, *Meet Jim Dale*, and a variety show for ATV, *Join Jim Dale*. He adapted the Molière farce *Scapino*, with director Frank Dunlop, and played it at Edinburgh and the Old Vic. In 1971, Laurence Olivier invited him to join the National Theatre. Credits included Barnet in *The National Health*

(which he would recreate in the 1973 film version), Launcelot Gobbo in *The Merchant of Venice*, Costard in Olivier's production of *Love's Labour's Lost* and *The Architect and the Emperor of Assyria*, a two-hander with Anthony Hopkins.

On television, he hosted *Sunday Night at the London Palladium* and, in the West End, starred as Denry Machin in *The Card*. He played Spike Milligan in the film of his wartime memoir, *Adolf Hitler – My Part in His Downfall* (1973) and released another album, *This Is Me*. The Broadway run of *Scapino* in 1973 bought him to the attention of the Walt Disney Organisation, for whom he played the villain in *Pete's Dragon* (1977) and *The Spaceman and King Arthur* (1979). In 1980, he was 'the Toast of Broadway' when he created the flamboyant title role of *Barnum*, winning both the Tony Award and the Drama Desk Award. Other on and off-Broadway successes included *Me and My Girl*, *The Comedians*, *Privates On Parade*, *The Music Man* and *Joe Egg*.

In the mid 1990s he returned to the London Palladium to play Fagin in *Oliver!* and, back in America, played to packed houses in Leslie Bricusse's *Scrooge*. He is now the 'voice' of Harry Potter, with Grammy Award winning, unabridged recordings of the J K Rowling stories, the seventh instalment of which, Harry Potter and the Deathy Hallows, saw him break his own 'Most Character Voices in an Audio Book' entry in the record books with a staggering 146 separate characters.

Carry On credits: *Cabby, Jack, Spying, Cleo, Cowboy, Screaming!, Don't Lose Your Head, Follow That Camel, Doctor, Again Doctor, Columbus*

CARRY ON...UP THE KHYBER (1968)

The British rule of Imperialistic India is under threat. Not only is the wicked Khasi of Kalabar (Kenneth Williams) plotting to over-throw the 3rd Foot and Mouth Regiment, the 'feared devils in skirts', but the governor, Sir Sidney Ruff-Diamond (Sid James) seems more concerned with polo and tiffin than keeping the British end up – in the military sense of the word at least. When devil in skirt Private Jimmy Widdle (Charles Hawtrey) faints at the sight of 'beautiful warrior' Bungdit Din (Bernard Bresslaw) whipping out his weapon, the dreaded Burpa has a crafty look underneath Widdle's kilt. The fact that he wears underpants threatens to undermine the regiment's reputation for toughness. Unfortunately, when Sir Sidney takes two of his men to disprove the rumour, both Captain Keene (Roy Castle) and Sergeant-Major MacNutt (Terry Scott) are also found to be wearing the offending garments. With a little help from Sidney's neglected wife, Lady Joan (Joan Sims), the Khasi shows the natives a photograph proving the British soldiers wear underpants. While Lady Joan hopes to play around with the Indian leader, Sir Sidney gets stuck in to the Khasi's bevy of beautiful wives. But the Khasi's daughter, the Princess Jelhi (Angela Douglas), smitten by the dashing Captain Keene, warns of her father's planned revolt. As the natives revolt, the British keep their upper lips stiff and settle down to dinner, much to the wide-eyed fear and amazement of the missionary Brother Belcher (Peter Butterworth).

Six months is a long time in filmmaking. In May 1967, Peter Rogers had been resigned to bringing the Carry Ons to an end with a medical wrap-up. By November 1967, just a month after *Carry On Doctor* had finished filming, he was trying to sell ideas to John Davis, the head of the Rank Organisation. One of his projects, *The Man in the Mirror*, fell by the wayside but he also wrote: 'I am wondering now if you are at all interested in a comedy called *Up the Khyber* (or some Carry On title) with my usual team of goons plus, probably, Frankie Howerd or someone. It would be about the British "thin red line" antics in India and so on – with all locations in and around Pinewood.'

The story's fakir was the key guest star spot. Frankie Howerd wasn't available due to a stage commitment to *The Wind in the Sassafras Trees* that had opened in Coventry in February and was preparing for pit stops at Boston and Washington before opening on Broadway. In his stead, the 'someone' that Rogers referred to was to have been comic giant Tommy Cooper. Although a stage and television legend, even by 1968, Cooper's film career had been patchy to say the least. Other work commitments prevented him going up the Khyber, allowing Cardew 'the Cad' Robinson his finest cinematic opportunity, albeit in a role much reduced from the original characterisation.

The part of Captain Keene was written for Jim Dale, who was found to be busy in the theatre during the production dates and was replaced by the song and dance man, Roy Castle.

Rothwell's draft script was, as usual, peppered with alternative titles and comic commentary. On the finished film, Rothwell's preface was drastically edited down to simply, 'The British Position in India'. This somewhat defused the joke: the entire sub-heading had been: 'A Sikh-making saga of the

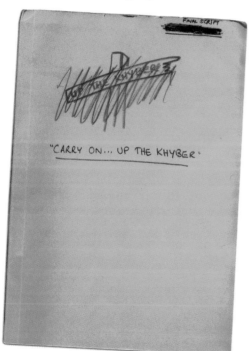

North-West Frontier Dramatised from the Best-selling book THE HANDYMAN'S KAMA SUTRA otherwise known as THE BRITISH POSITION IN INDIA.' Rothwell's script seemed to need a script doctor above and beyond the hand of his producer and in February 1968 John Antrobus was asked 'to write revisions and additions to the existing screenplay'.

Peter Butterworth and Terry Scott began filming the Town Market Place sequences on 6 May and it was noted that 'the production would utilise the "Spanish Village" set on the [Pinewood] Lot for these sequences'. By the end of May, however, Rogers was once again defending his escalating budget to Rank, having sent the unit on location for a week to complete work at the foot of Mount Snowdon, the furthest afield the Carry Ons ever travelled. With North Wales doubling for the rugged countryside of India, it tickled Rogers to receive a letter from someone who had served in the British Army during the closing days of the Raj: 'I know exactly the mountains you were filming

Opposite: Bernard Bresslaw kisses his scimitar in this stunning portrait taken on location in Wales.

Left: Talbot Rothwell's script, complete with Up the Khyber signpost doodle that clearly was surplus to requirements.

Below: Tommy Cooper, the first choice for the role of the Fakir, visits his old chum Roy Castle on the Pinewood set.

ON LOCATION

The polo match audience scenes were shot on 18 April 1968 at the cricket ground within Pinewood, with the 'polo material to be obtained from stock'. While on location at the Pass of Llanberis, Cwm-y-Llan, the team stayed at the Goat, Beddgelert and the Royal Victoria, Llaneris. Extras were picked from the locals and the vicar allowed the use of the Church Hall, Beddgelert, for the crowd artistes' changing room. On 22 May, the 'rebels' were revolting over more money. The *Daily Mail* reported: 'the extras, dressed as Scottish soldiers, "mutinied" and demanded £2 more a day to compensate for the freezing wind blowing up the kilt. Peter Weingreen, the film's assistant director, said: "We had agreed to pay the extras £3 a day. But somebody had put it into their heads that they ought to be getting £5. We told them they couldn't have any more money, and if they didn't like it there were other local people willing to do the job." One of the "mutineers", 21-year-old Geraint Pritchard, said: "The kilt doesn't keep you warm at all. Then somebody on the film crew told us that extras in London get £5 a day. We asked for more but in the end we had to climb down." Terry Scott, dressed in a warm track suit, built himself a bonfire and said "I'm not wandering about in a kilt till they want me. It's too parky."'

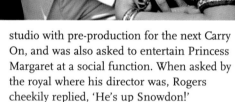

Sid James relaxes on the *Chitty, Chitty, Bang, Bang* village set at Pinewood Studios, with Vicki Woolf and Wanda Ventham.

Terry Scott promotes his latest film when receiving treatment for persistent piles at St Mark's Hospital in Islington.

in. I served there for two years. Thank you for bringing back such happy memories for me.' The producer himself did not join the location unit; he was busy at the studio with pre-production for the next Carry On, and was also asked to entertain Princess Margaret at a social function. When asked by the royal where his director was, Rogers cheekily replied, 'He's up Snowdon!'

The location filming caused some concern for the star of the film, Sid James. Sir Sidney Ruff-Diamond was nothing like the studio-bound role in *Doctor* that had eased him back into filming after his heart attack. This was strenuous stuff on a par with his energetic performance in *Don't Lose Your Head*, which had undoubtedly contributed to the strain on his health. At least Sid was saved the uncomfortable experience of sitting astride a real elephant. His scenes with Joan Sims, sitting in a howdah, were filmed with a mock elephant against a blue screen background.

A real elephant was required for certain shots. Production manager Jack Swinburne wrote to the Robert Brothers Circus, Northants, requesting 'one which is used to carrying a howdah. The action required from this elephant is just one walk past palace gates and another walk past stopping at a drinking trough. I will in due course let you know what time the elephant is required at the above studios.'

Kenneth Williams, meanwhile, was juggling his film career with an outrageous success on

A classic Carry On scene, as the British stiff upper lip is tested during an explosive dinner party.

Peter Butterworth favours the missionary position but can't seem to tempt the alluring Dominique Don to join him!

radio, in *Round the Horne*. His Carry On contract released him for the Monday afternoon recordings and for one extra afternoon show. *Round the Horne* co-writer Brian Cooke recalls the radio cast gathering at the Paris Studios, Lower Regent Street: 'We'd have the first cold read then take a break, during which showbizzy gossip was exchanged, often about the Carry On films that Williams was doing at the time. He'd clutch my knee in a fierce painful grip, staring straight into my face, frantic that I should laugh. "That Joannie Sims, she's OUTRAGEOUS! Halfway through this love scene, she lets one off. FARTS! I had to leap out of the bed... I wouldn't mind but she looks at ME as though I'VE done it! I mean, there's no PROVENANCE in a fart, is there? Once it's out, it's OWNER-LESS!"' This particular fart did, it seems, belong to Williams himself. It was a favourite chat show story, and he would remember crying indignantly 'even Rudolph Valentino broke wind!' – it was Gerald Thomas who observed that 'they were silent films Kenny!'

The most memorable sequence in the film was the climactic dinner party at the British residency. Filmed from 19 to 22 April 1968 on Pinewood's 'H' Stage it was, according to Peter Rogers, 'a great achievement of the art director [Alex Vetchinsky] and cameraman [Ernest Steward] to give the impression that the room was huge.' The actual exterior was the back of Heatherdean Hall at Pinewood Studios. The meal, as Roy Castle remembered, 'was real –

TITBITS

Patrick Allen recorded his narration on Friday 31 May 1968 for a fee of £30. On 16 May, Roy Castle, Cardew Robinson and Terry Scott were called for a retake necessary on the exterior walled garden sequence but were unable to shoot due to the bad weather. T Mitchell was released from the film on 21 May so he could start work on the big screen version of *Till Death Us Do Part* at Shepperton.

Angela Douglas (1940-)

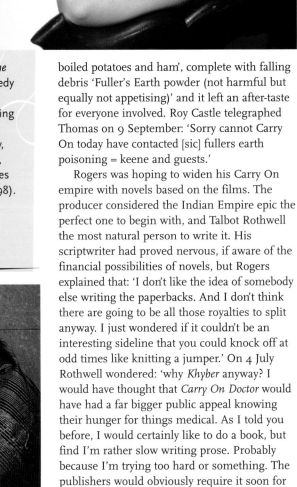

The epitome of Carry On glamour for the historical classics, Angela Douglas caught the acting bug at an early age and worked with the Worthing Repertory Company in her teens. Her West End debut came in *The Anniversary Waltz* and she made her first film, *The Shakedown*, shortly afterwards in 1959. On television she starred opposite Alfred Lynch in the celebrated play, *A Smashing Day*, while her film career reflected a light side with a romantic encounter with Tommy Steele in *It's All Happening* (1963). Her tongue-in-cheek comment about 'being a lady' was greeted with Kenneth Williams complaining, 'If you were a lady, you wouldn't be doing Carry On films!', but the actress enjoyed her 1960s brush with the comic gang. Just a month before filming began on *Carry On...Up the Khyber*, she had married the actor Kenneth More (on 16 March 1968). Having worked together in *The Comedy Man* (1963), Angela was forever known as 'Shrimp' by her loving husband. Sadly, the break-up of his first marriage and his subsequent marriage to Angela created bad feeling in the industry. She never worked for Peter Rogers again. However, she appeared in Leslie Phillips' spy production *Maroc 7* (1968), guest starred as the lovely Miranda Lockston in *The Avengers* ('Requiem', 1969) and reunited with Jim Dale in the comedy *Digby – The Biggest Dog in the World* (1974). In 1975, she appeared with Nigel Davenport in the television series *Oil Strike North*. Putting her career on the back burner to tend to her ailing husband, after Kenneth More's death in July 1982 she returned to acting. Notably, she played the Brigadier's wife, Doris, in *Doctor Who* ('Battlefield', 1989), the regular role of Isobel Trimble in *Cardiac Arrest* and James Fox's bemused wife in the Michael Caine thriller *Shadow Run* (1998).

Carry On credits: *Cowboy, Screaming!, Follow That Camel, Up the Khyber*
Autobiography: *Swings and Roundabouts*

Angela Douglas in a demure publicity pose from *Carry On Screaming!*

Angela Douglas and Peter Butterworth point out flying pigs in a break during filming the one Carry On that regularly and justifiably gets acknowledged as a classic of British cinema.

boiled potatoes and ham', complete with falling debris 'Fuller's Earth powder (not harmful but equally not appetising)' and it left an after-taste for everyone involved. Roy Castle telegraphed Thomas on 9 September: 'Sorry cannot Carry On today have contacted [sic] fullers earth poisoning = keene and guests.'

Rogers was hoping to widen his Carry On empire with novels based on the films. The producer considered the Indian Empire epic the perfect one to begin with, and Talbot Rothwell the most natural person to write it. His scriptwriter had proved nervous, if aware of the financial possibilities of novels, but Rogers explained that: 'I don't like the idea of somebody else writing the paperbacks. And I don't think there are going to be all those royalties to split anyway. I just wondered if it couldn't be an interesting sideline that you could knock off at odd times like knitting a jumper.' On 4 July Rothwell wondered: 'why *Khyber* anyway? I would have thought that *Carry On Doctor* would have had a far bigger public appeal knowing their hunger for things medical. As I told you before, I would certainly like to do a book, but find I'm rather slow writing prose. Probably because I'm trying too hard or something. The publishers would obviously require it soon for publication... or would any time do?

Carry On...Up the Khyber was the second biggest box-office hit of 1968 in the UK. And the biggest was written by Talbot Rothwell too.

Talbot Rothwell OBE (1916-1981)

Born master of the pun, when he joined the Carry On team in 1963 Rothwell explained that 'It was 12 November 1916 that I fought my way out of my first tight spot. Even at birth I was an out-of-the-ordinary child. The doctor took one look at me and said, "This child will get ahead." In fact the head arrived a couple of days later. At school I took school certificate three times and matriculation four times – failing brilliantly in all subjects. But I excelled at games of all kinds – in the first fifteen with rugger, in the first eleven with cricket and in the first twenty with the caretaker's daughter.'

After leaving school, Rothwell spent an unhappy three months as a clerk at the Town Hall, Brighton, the only compensation being it was the hometown of his comic idol, Max Miller. Despondent, Rothwell joined the Palestine Police for two years and then transferred to service with the Royal Air Force. When the Second World War broke out, he was a pilot officer with Coastal Command in Scotland. In June 1940, while flying a Lockheed Hudson on a bombing raid over Norway, he was shot down by enemy fire and captured. Imprisoned in the infamous Stalag Luft 3 camp, Rothwell began writing plays and comedy skits for the revues staged by the camp theatre. They were 'one of the tortures that the prisoners had to go through' he reflected, but the noisy reaction to the shows served their purpose; to disguise the sound of fellow prisoners tunnelling to safety. The shows also teamed Rothwell with actor Peter Butterworth for the first of many times.

Upon demob, Rothwell persevered with writing and his first play, 'a farcical comedy' called *Queen Elizabeth Slept Here*, opened at the Strand Theatre in November 1949. Starring Jimmy

Hanley, Rosalyn Boulter and Kenneth Connor, it 'evoked positive gales of laughter', according to the *Daily Herald's* P L Mannock.

Rothwell's television break came in 1950 when he and his writing partner Sid Colin were invited by Terry-Thomas to beef up his sketch series *How Do You View?* In 1954, Rothwell and Colin scripted a spin-off sitcom, *Friends and Neighbours*, starring T-T's regular gang of Peter Butterworth, Janet Brown, Benny Lee and Arvil Angers.

Later that same year, the writers wrote another show for Angers, *Dear Dotty*, set in the offices of a woman's magazine, 'Lady Fare'.

Thanks to the impact of *How Do You View?* Rothwell and Colin found themselves in demand from other top comics. From 1952, they scripted the Arthur Askey BBC sketch show *Before Your Very Eyes*, the third series of which introduced the buxom British blonde bombshell, Sabrina, who was retained when the show was snapped up by Jack Hylton at Associated Rediffusion.

Rothwell and Colin scripted the Arthur Askey and Richard Murdoch series *Living It Up* (1957-1958), *The Ted Ray Show* (1955-1958) and *The Jimmy Wheeler Show* (1956). Alone Rothwell contributed to the Crazy Gang's hugely successful revues at the Victoria Palace, and wrote television material for Richard Hearne's *Mr Pastry*, the Michael Bentine sketch show *It Pays To Be Ignorant*, the last series of *The Army Game* and *The Dick Emery Show*.

In 1960, Rothwell created the popular nautical sitcom *Mess Mates* (1960-1962), starring Sam Kydd, Victor Maddern and Fulton MacKay; writing all but one of the second series with *Carry On Laughing* scribe Lew Schwarz. But it was *Up Pompeii* that proved his biggest sitcom success. Hugely popular, it was only Frankie Howerd's reluctance to continue and Rothwell's work overload (the second series was written with Sid Colin, the film farmed out to Colin completely) that saw the show curtailed after fourteen episodes. Thereafter, it was Carry On and on and on for Rothwell. In 1966, he had hopefully written about himself that 'he is fully booked for the next twenty years to write films for Peter Rogers.' In fact, his last credit was for producer David Croft, on the 1975 special revival show *Further Up Pompeii*.

'Tolly' on set with director Gerald Thomas during the making of *Carry On Matron*.

Carry On credits: *Cabby, Jack, Spying, Cleo, Cowboy, Screaming!, Don't Lose Your Head, Follow That Camel, Doctor, Up the Khyber, Camping, Again Doctor, Up the Jungle, Christmas, Loving, Henry, At Your Convenience, Matron, Abroad, Christmas '72, Girls, London!, Christmas '73, Dick*

CARRY ON CAMPING (1969)

Plumber Sid Boggle (Sid James) and his plumber's mate Bernie Lugg (Bernard Bresslaw) are enjoying a nudist camp film at their local fleapit cinema. Their reluctant girlfriends Joan Fussey (Joan Sims) and Anthea Meeks (Dilys Laye) aren't enjoying it at all, but Sid is desperate to loosen up his frigid squeeze. In a camping store the cheeky chap seizes a leaflet about the Paradise Camp, thinking it to be the home of a nudist colony. Elsewhere, Charlie Muggins (Charles Hawtrey) has equipped himself with camping gear, while frustrated businessman Peter Potter (Terry Scott) grudgingly goes along with his wife Harriet (Betty Marsden) and their tandem for another nightmarish holiday under canvas. Dr Soaper (Kenneth Williams) is keen to get his charges, the girls of Chayste Place, out into the fresh air, although the Matron, Miss Haggerd (Hattie Jacques) is uncertain. But the young ladies, led by Babs (Barbara Windsor) and Fanny (Sandra Caron), aren't as innocent as Matron thinks. Especially when their randy driver, Jim Tanner (Julian Holloway), arrives to drive their coach. Muggins hooks up with the Potters and Soaper is tricked by the girls into getting in to bed with Matron; but the arrival of the girls certainly cheers up the depressed Sid and Bernie. Having given a wad of cash to money-pinching campsite owner Josh Fiddler (Peter Butterworth), the boys discover that Paradise is not in fact a nudist camp but a fully clothed hell! Sid chases Babs through the shower room, the monastery and an all-night rave but loses the teen only to rediscover love with Joan.

T**he quintessential contemporary Carry On, this would be the biggest cinema success in Britain in 1969. Still, the finished** article was very different from the original concept and was a very long time coming. Indeed, the title was first registered as early as May 1962, following the series' first venture into holiday mode with *Carry On Cruising*.

It was originally scheduled to go into production in October 1966, after the completion of *Don't Lose Your Head. Follow That Camel*, which had been postponed in favour of *Camping*, was put back into immediate pre-production, undoubtedly due to the extended discussions about the *Camping* script, the threat of a rival Carry On from Anglo and the continuing reluctance of the Rank Organisation to embrace the brand name. Once Rank did start carrying on officially it was all systems go for Rogers. In June 1968, Peter Rogers discussed the *Camping* idea with Rothwell and, with talk of caravans and foreign travel, the seeds for future Carry Ons *Behind* and *Abroad* were also sown.

Cartoonist 'Larry' was onboard again, while the original script was, as usual, edited and restructured by Rogers. A glut of alternative titles were dropped, leaving just 'Let Sleeping Bags Lie'. An entire roadside café scene, en route to the camping site with the Chayste

Place schoolgirls, was also cut. In it Kenneth Williams comes face to face with the café proprietor Dan, a hefty part, never cast. One of the ton-up boys chatting up Babs and the other young sexpots, cries 'Ha, listen to Marlon Brando!'; a reference to the 1953 film *The Wild Ones* and considered 'old hat' by Rogers' blue pencil.

By this time Kenneth Williams had settled back in to the regime. Having seen the threat of *Carry On Doctor*, a film he had nearly rejected, being the last in the series come to naught, he gleefully accepted a part in *Carry On Camping* 'thinking it was an appropriate title'! In particularly cheerful mood, Kenneth wrote on 12 September: 'Dear Mr Rogers and Mr Thomas. I don't think you will regret your decision to offer me this part of Dr Soaper. You have taken a step in the right direction, and I admire your perspicacity. More power to your elbows! I am not without some experience in the dramatic field,

having served with the Tavistock Players as far back as 1939 and was described by the *St Pancras Gazette* as "Bleached and boisterous Bloomsbury Blonde who reverses the late King Charles and jokes that might have been prevalent during that monarch's lifetime" and went on to serve King and country with the Royal Engineers in the South East Asia Command. I was a great favourite with the lads and was frequently called upon to render "He Tickled the Lady's Fancy with the End of His Long Cigar" which frequently brought the house down, and several pairs of trousers. But I won't bore you with the details. I have also been booked for Methodist socials (When I Was Young And Twenty I Had A Dainty Quim) and the odd séance up at Madame Rawalpindi Smiths. I was actually present when her crystal ball exploded on the fateful night she materialised Fatty Harbuckle [sic] and had to sit on a bit of the broken glass throughout. We were knee-deep in ectoplasm and the room suddenly

went cold and there was this terrible smell of haddock. I remember thinking "Hello! Someone's brought their tea!" I was also an initiate of the Septagesamites, and performed as an acolyte but was unfairly blamed when the Bishop tripped over his surplice and ruptured himself – by the size of the surplus I thought he was a canon. But I am digressing here, and I am sure you worthy gentlemen don't want to be bored with an old thespian's reminiscences. As to character references you will find glowing testimonials to my prowess written up all over the City and at the scabies cleansing station at Paddington there is a furtive fellow called Edie in Cork Street who can give you the low down on my personal proclivities should you deem it desirable. I am always good for a Barclays (no, I don't mean the card) and am a dab hand at the

Opposite: Flying tonight – Kenneth Williams get Babs' bra in the face while the full shock has yet to register for Hattie Jacques.

Left: Terry Scott and Betty Marsden consult with director Gerald Thomas on location in Pinewood Green, just outside the studio gates.

TITBITS

A canny promotional tie-in competition with Saxa salt was actually reflected in the film itself. Cheerfully naïve Charlie Muggins (Hawtrey, naturally), finally realises that he has been taking advantage of the coach party from Chayste Place Finishing School for Young Ladies. He smiles and innocently says to haughty Dr Soaper: 'I say, could I give something towards the petrol?' The disgruntled school principal finally snaps and mutters: 'Well, you could give something for all the food!' Charles is only too happy to oblige. 'Ooh, but I'll be delighted,' he says handing him a packet of Saxa salt! The first prize in the competition was the astronomical sum of £1,000. This was double what actress Sandra Caron got paid for playing the role of Babs's bosom buddy Fanny for the seven-week shooting schedule. She had trained at the Aida Foster School, Finchley, with Barbara Windsor. Anna Karen, best known as the dowdy Olive in *On the Buses*, was a lifelong friend of Barbara's, having stripped alongside her in cabaret.

ON LOCATION

From the first day of filming, 7 October, the team spent three weeks in the Pinewood orchard filming the campsite material. The tents and camping equipment had been borrowed from Sports Continental, Kilburn, London. A coach was hired for the filming from local firm Jackie Crump, and was filmed driving along the Uxbridge Road in Iver. On 1 November, 'C 'Stage was used for the interior of the cinema before, later that same day, the unit decamped to nearby Pinewood Green to film the exterior of Mrs Fussey's house. The Flowerbuds concert was filmed on the Pinewood lot over 5 and 6 November, and the following day Charles Hawtrey, Patricia Franklin and Derek Francis filmed at Dromenagh Farm. Terry Scott joined Derek Francis on local country roads for the shotgun climax to their sequence on 11 November and filmed in the field of Sauls Farm, Iver Heath, on 4 November. On 20 November, the cinema exterior was filmed on Packhorse Road, Gerrards Cross; the Courts furnishing store Sid James and Bernard Bresslaw enter is on the High Street, Maidenhead; Chayste Place is the frontage of Heatherden Hall, Pinewood; while local Iver roads, Black Park Road, Fulmer Common Road and Seven Hills Road, and Wexham Street and Rowley Lane in Fulham were also used.

Chris Finnegan, Olympic boxing gold medallist, photographs his wife, Cheryl, and daughter, Pearl, posing with Bernard Bresslaw, Sid James, Gerald Thomas and Charles Hawtrey in a break from filming.

'On location' at the main entrance of Pinewood's Heatherwood Hall, with 'Chayste Place' ladies Trisha Noble, Sandra Caron, Barbara Windsor and Elizabeth Knight.

old abdominal breathing. Very heavy down the phone. By including me in your undertaking you are setting the seal of success upon your enterprise and we shall go forward together and it will not affect the pound in your pocket so bugger the gnomes of Zurich. Remember always that I do a very good turn (see chapter 5 of Godfrey Winn's *Performers I Have Poked*) and that, thick or thin, late or tard, sickness and in health, I shall be right behind you. Your devoted serrvt. Fred Bumhole pronounced Bummel.'

In a rare correspondence, even Sid James seemed to sense the joyous times ahead, writing: 'Many thanks for the script. Very funny! I drove Val potty laughing aloud. That doesn't often happen when one reads! There are some wonderful moments. So clean too??? Many thanks again God bless Sid.'

Production started on 7 October 1968 'on location' at the Paradise Camp Site (the orchard at Pinewood) with Sid James, Bernard Bresslaw, Peter Butterworth, Joan Sims and Dilys Laye. Terry Scott also appeared, suffering with piles throughout the production: 'I had scenes in which my backside was set on fire, butted by a bull, had a thistle stuck up it, was slapped, and had shotgun pellets picked out of it. But the most painful bit of all was that I had to ride a tandem. I'm supposed to look miserable for a big part of that film. Believe me, after riding that tandem, it wasn't difficult.'

It had been a gentle nudge from Frank Kemp of the Essoldo Circuit that landed his daughter, Sally, the role of the bull-friendly farm girl who bemuses Charles Hawtrey. Rank's F L Thomas had originally suggested Sally Kemp for work in a Betty Box film, but Kemp was also a friend of both Gerald Thomas and Peter Rogers. Frank's little girl was twenty-nine years old with repertory theatre experience and her previous films had included *Behemoth the Sea Monster* and *The*

Pale-Faced Girl. Her only Carry On assignment, she wrote to Rogers on 17 November 1968: 'I would like to thank you very much indeed for finding me such a nice little part in *Carry On Camping*. I would have liked to thank you personally, but I was afraid to approach you when I saw you during the filming in case you were very busy. Thank you once again. I hope the cow enjoyed it as much as I did.'

Shooting wrapped at the end of November 1968 and the trade show in May 1969 was followed by the West End debut at the Metropole Victoria on 3 July 1969. But the film couldn't be enjoyed everywhere, as it was rejected outright by the censor in the Republic of Ireland. Despite this, the box office figures were encouraging, which was mainly down to two reasons: Barbara Windsor! The legendary exercise sequence when Babs's bits are exposed to a grateful nation, remains the ultimate, oft-repeated, Carry On snippet. And it was flogged to death: in the trailer, in the press and even on the poster. Amazingly, the facts are trivia of national importance. The freezing weather conditions with the

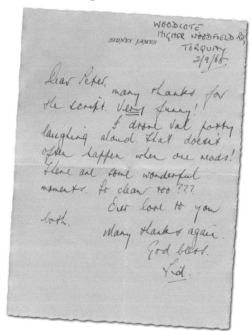

actors shivering and sinking into mud. Gerald Thomas gently telling Joan Sims: 'to think warm, think warm!' The prop guys spraying the leafless trees green to make the winter filming conditions seem like the height of summer. The shy and reserved Miss Windsor desperately trying to cover her embarrassment as Hattie Jacques whips away her hand to reveal the boob. The effects man Bert Luxford with a fishing rod attached to the bra, standing out of camera shot and ready to pluck it

Brian Oulton (1908-1992)

A Liverpudlian character actor who trained at the Royal Academy of Dramatic Art, Oulton made his stage debut in the late 1920s and spent much of his career acting, writing and directing for the theatre. Popular on BBC radio as Cyril in *Just William*, he was an instantly recognisable member of the repertory company of British cinema, playing dozens of officious clerks and belittled figures of authority. A notable comic stooge, he worked for Peter Rogers as early as 1948, in the Basil Radford and Naunton Wayne spy romp *It's Not Cricket* and *The Dog and the Diamond* (1953). He was employed by Betty Box in everything from *Doctor in the House* (1954) to *The 39 Steps* (1959) and went on to play the semi-regular character of Dr Griffin in the television series *Doctor at Large* in 1971. As well as his Carry On outings, his shocked characterisations enlivened the Boulting brothers satires, including *Private's Progress* (1955) and *I'm All Right Jack* (1959). In the 1960s, his film work included the Hammer thriller *The Damned* (1961), *Raising the Wind* (1961) and *The Iron Maiden* (1962) for Peter Rogers, and the Morecambe and Wise film *The Intelligence Men* (1965). Other cheerful escapades included Hammer's *On the Buses* (1971) and *Ooh, You Are Awful* (1972), in which he was notable as the bemused funeral director with Dick Emery in drag. Later, he played the Clerk of the Court in Richard Attenborough's *Gandhi* (1982) and Master Snelgrove in *Young Sherlock Holmes* (1985). He guest-starred in several *Hancock's Half Hour* episodes, *Steptoe and Son* ('The Piano', 1962), played the Headmaster in the ITV adaptation of *Just William* (1977) and featured in, of all things, *The Young Ones* ('Sick', 1984), knowingly sending up his 'More tea vicar?' image for the new generation of comics.

Carry On credits: *Nurse, Constable, Cleo, Camping, Christmas 1972*

off on cue. It all adds up to making Windsor a beloved British treasure chest and *Camping* the quintessential Carry On experience.

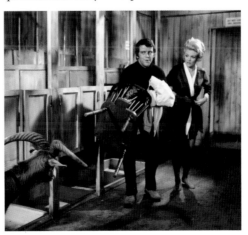

Above: A 1950s portrait of authoritative character actor Brian Oulton.

Left: A letter from Sid James to producer Peter Rogers highlights how impressed the star was with the script.

In a deleted scene Julian Holloway tries to look the hero as he protects the delectable Trisha Noble from a (supposedly) docile ram.

CARRY ON AGAIN, DOCTOR (1969)

Dr Frederick Carver (Kenneth Williams) seems to think he owns Long Hampton Hospital and happily drags his mousy assistant Miss Fosdick (Patsy Rowlands) and old medical college room mate, Dr Stoppidge (Charles Hawtrey), through his round. The Matron (Hattie Jacques), is equally cheerful in her job and even forgives the bumbling Dr James Nookey (Jim Dale) as he stumbles out of the women's washroom and, dropping his towel, terrifies nervous patient Miss Armitage (Ann Lancaster). But Jim certainly cheers up when, after chatting with his colleague Henry (Peter Gilmore), the model from his pin-up calendar, Goldie Locks (Barbara Windsor), turns up with a bruised backside! Matron is less impressed with his drooling over the scantily clad patient, while Carver is more concerned with keeping his private patient, Ellen Moore (Joan Sims), happy. She wants a doctor for the native island medical mission founded where her husband died. Nookey is approached but turns down the offer flat. But, a drink spiked by Stoppidge and Goldie's early departure, sets Nookey off on a manic crusade through the wards. He faces being struck off but Carver suggests the missionary job. On the island, Nookey encounters scheming witch doctor Gladstone Screwer (Sid James) and his miracle cure for the chronically overweight. Nookey goes into partnership with Mrs Moore and becomes a rich man back home, but Gladstone wants a piece of the action. Threatening to cut off supplies of the wonder drug, Gladstone gets his own back by providing a sex change serum!

In the late 1960s the Carry Ons were more popular than ever. On 28 October 1968, during filming for Carry On Camping, Sid James and Charles Hawtrey squeezed in a stills session for promotion of Carry On...Up the Khyber. In a letter from 'Larry' to Peter Rogers, no fewer than three Carry Ons, including the latest in pre-production, were mentioned. 'Delighted you went straight ahead with my first originals for Camping – instead of the usual farting about I get myself involved in. Of course I'm OK for staying on the "band wagon". Look forward to "Carry On Again Quak".' With the rough cut of Camping assembled, Rogers had already turned his attention to Again, Doctor. Among the problems facing Rogers was that F L Thomas of the Rank Organisation disliked the now-traditional alternative titles for the film: 'I think my main objection was to the second one [The Bowels Are Ringing]; I didn't think it was funny, merely vulgar. 'Where there's a pill there's a way' is OK and not unfunny. The thermometer gag is terribly laboured but I don't think I'd have any firm views whether they're on or off.' All three were on.

The biggest threat, however, was a question over the screenplay's originality. The problem stemmed from the ultimately unused script for *Doctor in Clover* that Talbot Rothwell wrote in 1965. It was noted by production solicitor Hugh Parton that in *Carry On Again, Doctor* 'the dialogue of Frederick Carver is so reminiscent of Sir Lancelot Spratt that I wonder whether there is any intention of parodying him and, if so, whether the character of Spratt was not originally created by Richard Gordon.' Also 'the medical mission and slimming cure provide most of the story, and I know I have read it all somewhere before. This may have been in the Rothwell scripts of *Doctor In Clover* which were not used but it is also possible that the whole plot may have originated in one of Richard Gordon's books. If it were a book in which we already own film rights, there could be no claim for copyright infringement but awkward questions would arise over credits. I feel these matters are important particularly now we know Richard Gordon is intending a

television series and wonder if you know how far the script is really original Rothwell.' To alleviate the question of 'parodying' James Robertson Justice's Sir Lancelot Spratt, Williams' character was deprived of his knighthood. Rothwell answered the question of whether the script was

Opposite: Barbara Windsor floors Jim Dale.

Jim Dale has a hasty drag as he and Kenneth Williams discuss the next shot with Gerald Thomas.

TRAILER

The trailer included a rare piece of edited Carry On comedy, for the moment as Barbara Windsor bashes the doctor on the head and Jim Dale coos 'You don't know what your kiss did to me then!' isn't in the film.

ON LOCATION

The main entrance to Heatherden Hall, Pinewood, was used as the weight-reducing clinic, while the forecourt, the ceremonial entrance and the foyer of Maidenhead Town Hall once again doubled as the hospital. The Pinewood canteen was used for the hospital dance scenes on 14 and 15 April. Jim Dale's swish consulting rooms were found in Park Street, Windsor.

May 4th 1969.

My dear Peter,

Thank you so much for a really wonderful party on Friday – it was a great send off for us all.

Bless you.

love.

Joan.

Top: Filming the end wedding sequence outside Pinewood's Heatherwood Hall.

Above: Joan Sims expresses her thanks to producer Peter Rogers for a glorious wrap celebration.

Below: Kenneth Williams is shown how to be wooed by Jim Dale.

all his own work by rather pointedly branding it the 'final screenplay of first draft of second draft of draft screenplay based on third draft of first screenplay from fifth draft of original screenplay based on first draft of an original script by Talbot Rothwell.'

Sid James sparred on camera and played poker backstage with Jim Dale during the medical mission interiors. Jim recalls that 'Sid was such a good actor he just gave all the time. He didn't need to take. I was very proud when Sid broke up with laughter due to something I was doing. I was thrilled to bits because I was

breaking up ten times more over what he was doing!'

A new face on the set was Georgina Simpson, cast as a men's ward nurse. Meanwhile, another glamour girl, Valerie Shute, enjoyed her first Carry On opportunity. She was the daughter of Warner-Pathe's Al Shute, who had got another film company to pay for a risqué photo shoot of Valerie for Gerald Thomas

TITBITS

Kenneth Williams' contract released him for his new radio series *It's Bold*, each Monday morning. Later retitled *Stop Messin' About!*, it was a reworking of *Round the Horne* following the death of Kenneth Horne. Joan Sims, originally scheduled to take over from Betty Marsden in the unrecorded new season of *Round the Horne*, was retained for the new show, although she pondered to Williams; 'Let's face it dear, our careers are in the ash-can!' Wilfrid Brambell filmed his cameo on 'F' Stage on April Fool's Day. Like his *Steptoe and Son* co-star, Harry H Corbett, his Carry On assignment was accompanied by a burst of the sitcom's familiar Ron Grainer theme music. Although the classic TV series had finished in 1965, the BBC announced its return in June 1969, so Brambell's appearance in the film was a timely one. Patricia Hayes and Valerie Van Ost also completed their roles on April Fool's Day, while Peter Butterworth filmed his role on 3 April. Miss Guyana 1967 and future Mrs Michael Caine, Shakira Baksh played Scrubba, while Pat Coombs was originally cast as the frantic Mrs Armitage; however, when Ambrosine Phillpotts proved unavailable, Coombs landed her role of the new Matron and Ann Lancaster was recast as Mrs Armitage. Hugh Futcher filmed his cab driver bit in the Pinewood car park, at which time 'Sid James said, "I knew you would be back!"' Patricia Franklyn was originally cast as the 'night nurse' before her contract was cancelled; she was replaced by Jenny Counsell.

DOCTOR, DOCTOR!

On Friday 21 March, 'statement of witness, Mr Gerry Thomas, to accident to Miss Alexandra Dane' confirmed that the actress 'was strapped in a vibration slimming machine being used during a scene in the physiotherapy department of a hospital set. The machine was placed on a circular platform which was worked with a hand-operated winch off set. The first two takes were without incident but on the third the vibrator came away from the mounting and Miss Dane fell backwards to the floor still holding the machine, hitting her left hip on a rowing machine slimming device which was also being used in the scene. I immediately stopped shooting and sent Miss Dane to First Aid for examination. She was subsequently sent to Wexham Park Hospital for an X-Ray.'

On the same day, Charles Hawtrey was dismissed at 3.30 for a wig fitting in London. However, it was Jim Dale who was in the thick of the medical action, on camera and off set. Despite a stunt double, Ray Ford, standing by, Jim was delighted that Gerald Thomas allowed him to attempt all his own stunts. Two stunts in particular, the trolley trip down a flight of stairs and through a window, and the collapsing hammock, gave the actor scars he still bears. After the trolley escapade, Jim's elbow was X-rayed at Wexham Park Hospital. For the hammock sequence, 'Gerry [Thomas] said: "Do look in to the camera as you fall so we can see it is actually you doing the stunt!" Like a fool, I did!'. On 8 April, Jim was 'called but reported sick. Due to this illness, shooting was terminated at 1.00 pm and the unit was dismissed.' Jim's 'indisposition' over 8, 9 and 10

April resulted in the loss of one day and required additional construction work, property hire and stage space.

Jim's six-week contract would be his last for Rogers for over twenty years. Because of Jim's unavailability, a Maidenhead location shoot was brought forward by three weeks. A jubilant Kenneth Williams regaled passers-by with a rendition of Ethel Merman's 'Everything's Coming Up Roses': 'I did an impromptu dance with some high kicks. One was a little too high and I landed flat on my back, ricked my neck, cut my elbow and tore my suit. Gerald appeared looking anxious and the wardrobe mistress told him, "It's all right, we've got a spare suit, there's two of them." "But only one of me," I added piteously. Gerald said, "I don't want any more injured actors on the picture."'

to inspect. The director was obviously impressed for he, rather cheekily, commented: 'I must say it is the most I have ever seen of Valerie. I am at the moment casting. You can be sure that we will find a nice little "nurse" part for Valerie.'

Of course, solid character acting was still crucial to the films. Charles Hawtrey enjoyed seven weeks on the film and, typically of the entire cast, came away from the experience with only happy memories. After a slap-up wrap party, Hawtrey wrote: 'Dear Peter, Thank you for your wonderful luncheon party at the Mirabelle yesterday – the food – the wines – the company – all of which seemed so appropriate after what was generally agreed to be the happiest production. Whilst you remained undeniably our gracious host, you complimented us not to say delighted, by being one of our motley lot. With love from your exported but never let it be said rejected Charles.' The last line of the note being both a knowing reference to his popularity overseas and a touching hint that his erratic behaviour could possibly warrant his dismissal from the team. Rogers received similar notes of thanks from Joan Sims and Hattie Jacques.

It seems everybody was happy except the censor, John Trevelyan. Gerald Thomas had an intriguing battle over certain supposed lines in the finished film. On 6 June 1969 Thomas noted that 'your examiners' words "May the God of fertility suck your coconuts" are very amusing

and probably better than the original dialogue and I can see their reason for objecting to it. However the dialogue in the picture is "May the fertility of Sumaka swell your coconuts" and I

Charles Hawtrey, as the 'hatchet-faced' Lady Puddleton, confronts a suspicious Jim Dale and a devil-may-care Sid James.

Alexandra Dane (1946-)

Busti by name and busty by nature, Dane was the perfect, over-developed, Carry On eye candy. She was born in Orange County, Bethleham, South Africa. Having made a mark as the grumpy and incompetent home help, Mathilde, in *The Saint* ('The Good Medicine', 1964), she played many, often uncredited, bits on film and television. At the time of her accident during the making of *Carry On Again, Doctor*, her agent observed that it 'appears to have resulted in publicity both for her and for the film!' This was balanced by the fact that the actress desired prominent on-screen credit for her performance. Indeed, it was noted that 'it had been included before but was omitted in *Carry On Screaming!*', Dane having played one of Dr Watt's petrified shop dummies. She also understudied Barbara Windsor during the Birmingham run of the stage show *Carry On London!* She played the taxing role of a whore in the Peter Cushing and Christopher Lee horror classic *The Creeping Flesh* (1972), delighted in the sex romp *The Ups and Downs of a Handyman* (1975) and was Bernard Bresslaw's flighty wife, Betsy, in Terry Gilliam's comedy fantasy *Jabberwocky* (1977). On television, she played Beryl in the Hylda Baker sitcom *Not On Your Nellie* in 1974 and the typically suggestively named Nefertiti Skupinski in the 1975 Spike Milligan series *The Melting Pot*. Between 1986 and 1987, she was a regular on *Alas Smith and Jones*, cropping up in the hilariously inept home movies with Mel and Griff.

Carry On credits: Screaming!, Doctor, Up the Khyber, Again Doctor, Loving, At Your Convenience (scenes cut), *London!, Behind*

The bountiful Alexandra Dane during the filming of *Carry On Loving.*

Hattie Jacques composes herself as a cheeky Barbara Windsor giggles on set.

am sure this is only referring to an abundant harvest of coconuts when they are gathered.' A reel one comment from Patricia Hayes to Jim Dale, 'You ought to have wider tops', was 'offending dialogue, which I personally think is very funny.' This 'may be considered by your examiners to be vulgar but I am sure you would not feel that it is out of place in an A certificate picture.' Thomas won the point, but he conceded to the requested cuts to reel two and 'reduced the back view shot of Goldie to a minimum'.

Sadly, Rothwell's original wedding ending was never filmed, although the following exchange was reworked and shifted to an earlier part of the film:

> *Gladstone*: All this fuss! A quick slash is so much easier.
> *Stoppidge*: I beg your pardon!
> *Gladstone*: With a knife.

Rothwell also made the sex change element of the finale much more obvious. Barbara Windsor's Goldie Locks ended up a manly 'bride' to Jim Dale's Dr Nookey, and responded to her new husband's thought that she needs a shave with: 'Don't worry old boy I'll have one before tonight!' Frederick Carver was concerned for his old flatmate's reaction to the potion: 'Good gracious, what's going to happen to poor Stoppidge.' Joan Sims' manly Mrs Moore was bitten by the marriage bug: 'I say Fred old man when's it our turn?' With this, Williams was to have looked straight into the camera and, taking a swig of the liquid, muttered: 'Oh well, if you can't beat 'em, join 'em!'

Sidney James (1913-1976)

Joining the Johannesburg Repertory Company in 1937, Sid reached the peak of his South African career as George in John Steinbeck's *Of Mice and Men*, staged at the Library Theatre in 1940. The following year he joined the Defence Force Entertainment Unit, starring in service shows with 'The Amuseliers' until his demob in 1945. Back with the Johannesburg Rep, he received a grant to study acting in England and arrived at Tilbury Docks on Christmas Day 1946.

Within days of his arrival he had secured his first film role, as Eddie Clinton in the thriller *Black Memory*. Later he joined the revue *Get In*, 'a Pleasure Cruise of Laughter and Song', starred in Jean Paul Sartre's *Men Without Shadows* at the Lyric Hammersmith and the musical *High Button Shoes* at the London Hippodrome. In 1952, he was cast as Nathan Detroit in *Guys and Dolls*, making its West End debut at the Coliseum in January 1954. On film, he played dozens of petty criminals, uneasy policemen and cheeky barrowboys and notably starred in the Hammer murder mystery *The Man in Black* (1949).

It was as Lackery, part of *The Lavender Hill Mob*, that he became a comedy star.

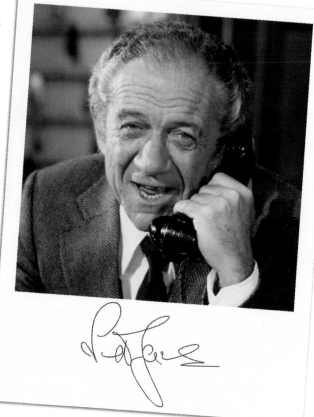

Cast as Tony Hancock's sidekick in the radio series *Hancock's Half Hour*, Sid appeared in every show – three more than Hancock himself – and remained with the television series until 1960. When the partnership folded, writers Ray Galton and Alan Simpson created *Citizen James* (1960-1962) especially for him. Still at the BBC, he also starred in the Ted Willis comedy drama, *Taxi!* (1963-1964). Happy to tackle film cameos in the likes of *We Joined the Navy* (1962) for director Wendy Toye and *The Beauty Jungle* (1964), for Val Guest, it was Carry On that dominated.

On television, Sid became the undisputed governor of Thames situation comedy; starring as crafty handyman George Russell in *George and the Dragon* (1966-1968) with Peggy Mount, and as the self-sufficient Sid Turner in *Two In Clover* (1969-1970) with Victor Spinetti. His greatest success was as Sidney Abbott, haplessly stuck in the generation gap in *Bless This House* (1971-1976). Sally Geeson, who played his screen daughter Sally remembers: 'Sid was a lovely man. He was always warm and friendly, not only to the cast and crew, but also to his fans. The atmosphere in the rehearsal room and studio was great, Sid played a large part in this, he was relaxed and fun. Sid and I had very much a father/daughter relationship, he looked out for me. His own daughter, Susan, was about the same age as the character I played in *Bless This House*, and I expect this is why we got on so well. Sid was immensely popular, whenever we were filming outside smiling crowds would gather, thrilled to see this great man who made them laugh so often. I can remember feeling terribly proud to be standing alongside him. We all wept when Sid died. He was a tonic to millions.'

Carry On credits: *Constable, Regardless, Cruising, Cabby, Cleo, Cowboy, Don't Lose Your Head, Doctor, Up the Khyber, Camping, Again Doctor, Up the Jungle, Christmas '69, Loving, Henry, Again Christmas, At Your Convenience, Matron, Abroad, Girls, London!, Christmas '73, Dick, Laughing*: 'The Prisoner of Spenda', 'The Baron Outlook', 'The Sobbing Cavalier', 'Orgy and Bess'

CARRY ON UP THE JUNGLE (1970)

Eminent ornithologist Professor Inigo Tinkle (Frankie Howerd) lectures a bored assembly and relates the story of his latest, most fascinating, expedition in darkest Africa. Joined by fellow bird-fancier Claude Chumley (Kenneth Connor) and 'Great White Tin-Opener' Bill Boosey (Sid James), the main aim of haughty Lady Evelyn Bagley (Joan Sims) is to rediscover her baby boy, who was lost in the jungle and is now fully grown into the hulking Jungle Boy (Terry Scott). Lady Evelyn's maid, June (Jacki Piper), takes a shine to the loincloth-clad youth. But, while bathing in a jungle pool, an amorous Gorilla (Reuben Martin) picks up June's discarded clothes and gets a tad frisky with the in-tents Brits. While native tracker Upsidasi (Bernard Bresslaw) is little help, he does recognise the imposing drums of the Nosha tribe, a group of feared cannibals. But an unscheduled appearance from Jungle Boy – right into the Noshas' stew pot – causes a disturbance. Unfortunately, the expedition party is immediately picked up by the ravishing Leda (Valerie Leon) and her all-female Lubi Dubbies. They are ruled over by the ever so friendly Tonka (Charles Hawtrey), who turns out to be Lady Evelyn's long-lost husband, Walter. The natives are revolting, but not as revolting as the unappealing Lubi Dubbies that 'Queen' Evelyn picks out for the captives to impregnate. Sadly, for Boosey and the others, Jungle Boy, June and a handful of soldiers, rescue them just as Leda has laid on some tasty Lubis for their attention. Back home in England, Tinkle's feathered discovery disappears and Jungle Boy sets up home with June in a suburban tree house.

As early as 26 February 1969, Richard Eastham of the William Morris Agency had detected a possible problem over a Carry On set in the jungle, particularly one with the unsubtle title 'Carry On Tarzan'. He told Peter Rogers that: 'I understand that the word "Tarzan" cannot be used by anybody other than the owners of the Edgar Rice Burroughs properties. This was explained some time ago when a television series was made in America which sounds very similar to the ideas you were telling me about for a possible Carry On.' Undeterred, Rogers began approaching his cast of actors.

First and foremost was Kenneth Williams, to play the fussy ornithologist at the heart of the tale. He was apparently happy to consider a part in the new film, but had turned down the lead role because of his television commitments, so was given 'a bit which starts on page 74 (of a 90-page script) and looks like it might have been written for Hawtrey. Right now, I want nothing to do with that set-up ever again.' That was an empty threat to his diary, of course, but Williams was right. Charles Hawtrey landed the supporting role of Tonka the Great in Williams' absence; the part that had been written for Hawtrey while Williams was still in the frame for Professor Tinkle.

Frankie Howerd wasn't approached for the role until very late in the day but he started work in mid-October with Joan Sims and Kenneth Connor on interiors for Tinkle's tent. Frankie picked up £9000 for his twenty-five day shoot. The increased cost for Frankie's services, compared to Williams', didn't ease the budget problems although, in the end, the production cost came in at just under £200,000. Even with later overheads included, this historical romp

was cheaper than *Carry On...Up the Khyber* eighteen months earlier.

Talbot Rothwell's original script credits him as 'Great White Writer' and, at various times, such unused alternative titles as 'A Safari Called Sex', 'The Game's the Thing', 'Have A Swinging Time!', 'The Lust Continent' and 'Don't Shoot Till You See the Whites of Their Thighs' were included. A lengthy explanatory commentary had also been written, used to introduce the Jungle Boy character and tap into a contemporary deodorant commercial: 'Lost when a mere baby in the jungle, found by a friendly boa constrictor, suckled by a short-sighted hippopotamus, he has never seen another human. Only the animals are his friends – and even his best friends can't tell him.' It was pointed out that the action takes place in 1873 and the Professor Tinkle character, now knowingly restructured for

Top: The original British quad for the *Jungle* epic. More politically correct times would see the native girls replaced by Caucasian glamour models.

Above: Talbot Rothwell's tongue-in-cheek suggestion for the film's set designer.

Left: You Tarzan, me Jane? Terry Scott is caught in a compromising position.

Opposite: Bird-fanciers Frankie Howerd, Sid James and Kenneth Connor detect the telltale sign of the rare Oozlum.

TITBITS

Reuben Martin would be the one-stop shop for Carry On gorillas, playing Mabel in *Carry On Laughing*: 'Lamp-Posts of the Empire' and attacking Jack Douglas in *Carry On Emmannuelle*. His wife, helpfully holding his gorilla head between takes on *Carry On Up the Jungle*, also appears as the horrible Lubi Dubbie who hoists away Frankie Howerd. Nina Baden-Semper, later a sitcom favourite in *Love Thy Neighbour*, was Lincoln Webb's girl during the Charles Hawtrey butterfly net flashback. Bernard Bresslaw learnt all his native instructions in Ndebele and couldn't wait to impress the extras on set. Unfortunately, they all came from the West Indies and couldn't understand a word, although Sid James recognised the dialect as the real thing and a Bournemouth shoe salesman commented on the actor's use of the language years later.

ON LOCATION

The actual house at which Terry Scott and Jacki Piper live is 11 Clarence Crescent, Windsor. A deal had been struck with regards damage and on 14 November Jack Swinburne issued a cheque for £15 for 'repairs to the macadam surfacing of the forecourt' on the strength of a builders estimate from E Balchin. The establishing shot of the lecture hall was filmed at the Fulmer Village Hall on 11 November. The pre-production meeting on 7 October revealed that the Pinewood Studio Paddock would be used for exterior pit scenes while 'the AFRODISIA VILLAGE will be constructed completely on 'E' Stage and during production this will be reduced in size and the surrounding jungle will then be used for tents and finally for a jungle clearing.'

A gamble in the jungle as Terry Scott, a gorilla-suited Reuben Martin, Jacki Piper and Sid James have a flutter on the Pinewood set. All but the ape were interviewed for the BBC television special *Carry On Forever*.

Bernard Bresslaw tries to make the Brits abroad feel at home during a jungle-clearing supper.

Frankie Howerd, included a lecture sequence which pre-empted the slide show introduction to the flashback sequences which make up the majority of the film. Frankie Howerd filmed this opening monologue but time restrictions saw the action cut, almost immediately, to the chase. Rogers eventually decided to retitle the film and wrote to the Film Production Association of Great Britain to register the title *Carry On Up the Jungle*. Throughout production, the film was referred to as 'Carry On Jungle Boy'. The intended Jungle Boy, however, had proved reluctant to

don the loincloth. Jim Dale, having suffered for his art during the strenuous and stunt-packed schedule for *Carry On Again, Doctor*, was offered the role but 'told Gerry Thomas that I didn't want to do it. After those great roles in *Cowboy* and the medical films I didn't want to play a part that was just grunts. It was a backward step. The part simply wasn't good enough and I told Gerry that.' Terry Scott who had seen his run in the films interrupted by Dale's return in *Again Doctor*, was less fussy and gladly accepted.

His first scenes were with newcomer Jacki Piper: 'Terry was lovely,' she recalls. 'We were doing this very romantic, touching scene and all the crew were shaking with laughter. Being the professionals we were we just carried on, but by now everybody was falling about. I hadn't noticed, but Terry had slipped out of his loincloth! The make-up lady, Nora, who was married to our chief make-up man Geoff Rodway, was a rather prim, old-fashioned person. Gerald turned to her and said, "You didn't make it up, Nora!"'

'I was watching the first day's rushes,' Piper recalled, 'and Gerald Thomas came over to me looking rather concerned. He said, "I'm afraid

DOCTOR, DOCTOR!

Terry Scott grazed his leg during a particularly energetic swing on a Pinewood vine and was tended to by the unit nurse, Sister Wells.

I've got something rather unpleasant to say," and being an actor, I thought, "They don't like what I'm doing and I'm off the film!" But Gerald continued, "We have to throw a bucket of water in your face," and I said, "Oh, that's wonderful!" This water was thrown with such force that it knocked my wig, make-up and false eye-lashes off. I'd love to see the outtakes of that!'

Frankie Howerd wrote to Peter Rogers, describing the film as 'the happiest I have ever done, and to say that if there is anything I can do nearer the release date to help with publicity I shall be happy to do so. I hope the results of the filming will be successful for all concerned and since the last time I worked for you was in October 1967, exactly two years ago, perhaps I may look forward to a similar pleasure in

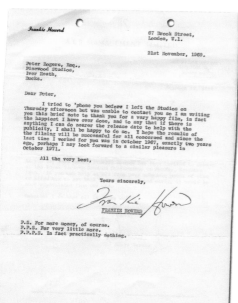

Jacki Piper (1948-)

Born in Birmingham and a veteran of the local repertory theatre, Jacki made her feature film debut in a brief, uncredited bit part as Roger Moore's secretary in *The Man Who Haunted Himself* (1970). Later that year she featured at the very end of the Betty Box comedy *Doctor in Trouble*, cadging a lift from a smitten Leslie Phillips. Finding herself in the Pinewood comedy ken, 'when I was hired for my first one Peter Rogers actually put me under contract for three years which amazed me. I was known for theatre and I thought he must have been mad. He actually told me I was the only person he contracted for so long!' Paid £600 for seven weeks on the film, it was noted that 'the first seven names are contractual and I have added Jackie [sic] Piper. However, would you like Jackie Piper with the words, for example, "and introducing Jackie Piper" or would you prefer some other similar form of introducing your new discovery?'. At the same time as her Carry On contract, Jacki continued to appear in West End productions, notably *The Secretary Bird*, during work on *Carry On Loving*, and *Big Bad Mouse*, with Eric Sykes and Jimmy Edwards. She made another Betty Box medical romp, *The Love Ban*, in 1972. In the 1970s, she played the semi-regular role of Esther Pidgeon in *The Fall and Rise of Reginald Perrin*, was Pearl, Derek Royle's assistant, in the 1975 series *Hogg's Back* and guest-starred in *The Return of the Saint* ('Tower Bridge is Falling Down'). An experienced farce actress she toured the Far East with Terry Scott in *A Bedful of Foreigners* and enjoys seasonal outings as the Good Fairy in pantomime.

Carry On credits: Up the Jungle, Loving, At Your Convenience, Matron

October 1971. Rogers replied: 'My dear Frankie it was very kind of you to write to me telling me how much you enjoyed working on *Jungle*. I must say you're bloody good in the film and I am relieved to feel that I personally may perhaps be back in your favour.' Although Howerd would be preoccupied with his own star film vehicles in October 1971, the comedian was working for Peter Rogers a lot sooner than that. A little over a week later, in fact.

Above: Jacki Piper snapped in the Pinewood gardens during the production of *Carry On At Your Convenience*.

Notorious giggler Joan Sims cracks up under the relentless pressure of comic maestro Frankie Howerd.

A cheery note from Frankie Howerd, hoping to re-join the Carry On team in 1971.

TRAILER

The mating ritual scenes, including Sid's reference to his sprinkler, the slaves downing tools and the failure of certain oysters, were in place to hopefully allow the even more risqué 'eases stiffness' line from Frankie Howerd. The trailer narration assured audiences that 'Peter Rogers and Gerald Thomas guarantee the funniest safari that has ever been disorganised'.

CARRY ON CHRISTMAS (1969)

The miserable miser Ebenezer Scrooge (Sid James) delights in his wickedness as he kicks away the stick of a street beggar (Peter Butterworth) and makes the life of his employee Bob Cratchit (Bernard Bresslaw) a misery. But the Spirit of Christmas Past (Charles Hawtrey) warns him that he will be shown the error of his ways. And thanks to visitations from the Spirits of Christmas present (Barbara Windsor) and future (Bernard Bresslaw), he is. There's Dr Frank N Stein (Terry Scott) starved of money for his experiments and poet Robert Browning (Frankie Howerd), who haplessly tries to impress his lady love, Elizabeth Barrett (Hattie Jacques), with worse and worse verse. Finally Scrooge is thrown into the world of pantomime with poor Cinderella (Barbara Windsor) at the beck and call of her ugly sisters, Haggie and Baggie (Peter Butterworth and Terry Scott). But with a little camp help from Buttons (Charles Hawtrey) and the Fairy Godmother (Frankie Howerd), Scrooge resolves to embrace the spirit of Christmas. Unfortunately he lavishes affection on a passer-by (Hattie Jacques) and is arrested by a policeman (Bernard Bresslaw).

Television had always been of crucial importance to the Carry Ons, ever since *The Army Game* had proved a useful pool of talent for *Carry On Sergeant*. BBC television cameras had been granted access to the set of *Carry On Up the Jungle* to record behind-the-scenes footage and interview Gerald Thomas and his actors for a special *Film '70* programme, 'Carry On Forever'. The rival Granada television series, *Cinema*, had also been invited when it was suggested the film would be a handy hook for a feature on Tarzan at the movies. The London Weekend Television programme, *Aquarius*, also expressed interest in tracing the humour of the Carry Ons and *This Is Your Life* contacted Pinewood with a view to 'stinging' one of the principals on set.

In fact, what eventually went ahead was a *Carry On Christmas* special for ITV's London weekday franchise Thames. Television producer Peter Eton proposed that the show woud be video-taped in colour in front of an audience and asked Talbot Rothwell to write the script. A 50/50 profit split on overseas sales between Thames Television and Peter Eton Productions was agreed. Keeping Peter Rogers in the loop, Eton wrote: 'I think *A Christmas Carol* will make a good basis for *Carry On Christmas*. The story itself is so well known that any send-up of it will be instantly recognised ... I accept Tolly's complaint that the plot is a bit thin, but I shall say that there are enough elements that can be twisted and turned and expanded and interspersed with additional sketches containing any other Dickensian characters and, in fact, any other character – especially the pantomime ones – that he wants to bring in. My suggestion is that ... we present *Carry On Christmas* as much more of a pantomime, with the cast conscious of the fact that they are playing to an audience.

'Unfortunately, the actor who plays Scrooge [Sid James] has been so busy that he has been learning his part at home – but he is utterly unflappable, knows there have been one or two alterations to the story and is perfectly happy to play it by ear and take things in his stride ... like all TV heroes, it is considered Scrooge must have somebody to talk to – how else can his thoughts be shown. He is given a secretary-cum-assistant and because there are too many old people in the cast and very few women, she

Frankie Howerd OBE (1917-1992)

Seemingly such an intrinsic part of the Carry On story, it is surprising that Frankie's sum contribution to the series was completed within a mere two years. Having become a national figure with his radio broadcasts in *Variety Bandbox* from December 1946, he was soon a familiar face on television and film, making his debut in Val Guest's comedy murder mystery, *The Runaway Bus* (1953). A memorable support as a barrow boy in Ealing's *The Ladykillers* (1955) and the lead in Val Guest's Hammer comedy, *Further Up the Creek* (1958) followed. By 1960, his career had collapsed and Michael Winner's *The Cool Mikado* (1962) proved the final straw. But, that same year, Peter Cook's Establishment Club gave him a new lease of life and Ned Sherrin invited him to comment on the budget on the BBC's satirical revue, *That Was the Week That Was*. Frankie starred in the West End as Pseudolus in *A Funny Thing Happened on the Way to the Forum* from October 1963, and was soon back with his own television series, scripted for him by Galton and Simpson. In 1966, he headed the cast of *The Great St. Trinian's Train Robbery*. Before shooting his second Carry On, Frankie had recorded the pilot for *Up Pompeii!* Always at home in a toga, a series and feature film spin-off followed, along with cinema sequels *Up the Chastity Belt* and *Up the Front*, and a television re-working, *Whoops Baghdad*. His dream film role, a sort of Bob Hope styled spooky house romp, *The House in Nightmare Park* (1973), rounded off his star film career. Still, with a new generation of 'Frankie Pankies', his television guest spots and stand-up assignments continued until his death.

Carry On credits: *Doctor, Up the Jungle, Christmas '69*
Autobiography: *On the Way I Lost It*

is young and attractive and from the opening scene in Scrooge's office, not only confuses Scrooge but also Bob Crachitt, Scrooge's nephew, who comes in to wish him Happy Christmas, and the two men collecting for charity. The rather dull spot when Scrooge goes home – when, apart from the appearance of Marley's ghost, nothing much happens – is livened up by a visit from Dick Whittington and so on.'

Rothwell developed Eton's basic premise into 'a weird sort of script' which originally included

Gerald Thomas, employed as 'comedy consultant' on *Carry On Christmas*, chats with Frankie Howerd on the set of *Carry On Up the Jungle*.

A portrait of a pensive Frankie Howerd from *Carry On Up the Jungle*.

Opposite: Charles Hawtrey in costume for his briefly spotted Dickensian goose-pincher.

Barbara Windsor's 'Ghost of Christmas Present' casts her seasonal magic over Frankie Howerd, Hattie Jacques and Peter Butterworth in this publicity still from *Carry On Christmas*.

Gerald Thomas helps *This Is Your Life* host Eamonn Andrews surprise writer Talbot Rothwell on the set of *Carry On Henry* on 28 October 1970.

a lengthy flashback sequence of Scrooge's early days. Terry Scott was to have played the rector that christens the new miser. Hattie Jacques (as Scrooge's mother) and Peter Butterworth (as the frumpy nurse) were to have had this exchange:

Mrs Scrooge: Yes?
Nurse: I'm a wet nurse.
Mrs Scrooge: Oh, I didn't realise it was raining. May I see your credentials? (*Nurse looks a bit taken aback, swells her large bosom*)
Mrs Scrooge: Yes, that seems to be satisfactory.

Barbara Windsor was earmarked for the part of Glory, Scrooge's cousin, Terry Scott would have doubled up as the Doctor and Bernard Bresslaw's Fagin would lead the young Scrooge in to a life of crime. In a spot of dream Carry On casting, alas never to be realised, Charles Hawtrey would have played the sweet innocent, Oliver Twist, whose pocket Scrooge happily picked! Later, Terry Scott would appear as a haughty school teacher, Barbara as a sexy pupil and Bresslaw as another rector. One typical, groan-worthy visual joke was to have centred around the Charge of the Light Brigade: 'officer 2/- NCOs 1/- men 60 horses 1 pail manure.' Eventually, Rothwell managed to remove a lot of the Dickensian material, the Scrooge back story being largely replaced by the Hammer horror pantomime featuring a fang-tastic Count Dracula from Peter Butterworth with Bernard Bresslaw as the Creature, a role he had originally lost to Christopher Lee during his Hammer contract days because 'I was too 'orrible!'.

Frankie Howerd, a last-minute guest star added to the Christmas mix, originally made his entrance as Robert Browning in a hot air balloon. Barbara Windsor, kitted out in a natty safari outfit, joined Sid James and Bernard Bresslaw, in *Up the Jungle* character, on the *Up the Jungle* set. This was never intended for the film and these scenes weren't cut from it; it was only a photo opportunity to promote the Christmas show.

Rehearsals for *Carry On Christmas* started in earnest at the Teddington Yacht Club on 1 December then moved to rehearsal room 3A at Thames' Teddington Studios. Vince Powell, who had co-written the Sid James sitcoms *George and the Dragon* and *Two in Clover* for Thames, was on board as script editor and was impressed with Gerald Thomas. 'He knew exactly what did and didn't work with Carry On,' recalls the writer. 'We read through the script together and he was making notes: "page five, two shit jokes, no prick jokes. Page twelve, too many tit jokes not enough prick jokes." Here was this debonair, well-dressed man with a complete breakdown of what made the Carry Ons tick.'

The cast and crew then decamped to Studio 1, Teddington, for pre-taping and a camera rehearsal on 13 December. A further rehearsal was held on Sunday 14 December and at 8pm on that same day the show was recorded in front of an invited studio audience. A final cut was edited together by 19 December, just five days before its Christmas Eve broadcast.

Bernard Bresslaw (1934-1993)

The son of a Stepney tailor's pressman, Bresslaw won a scholarship to RADA. Graduating with the Emile Littler Award as the Most Promising Actor in 1953, he made his West End debut, chosen by Laurence Olivier to appear in *The MacRoary Whirl* at the Duchess Theatre.

In 1955, Bresslaw played Leroy in Maxwell Anderson's *The Bad Seed* at the Aldwych Theatre. He was put under contract by Hammer Film Productions, appearing opposite Don Taylor's Robin Hood in *The Men of Sherwood Forest* (1954) and playing the hulking, bearded circus freak in *The Glass Cage* (1955). But it was as the slow-witted Private 'Popeye' Popplewell in the ITV sitcom *The Army Game* that Bresslaw became a national obsession.

He toured the variety circuit, recorded the hit single 'Mad Passionate Love', and starred in the Hammer film version *I Only Arsked*. From September 1958, Bresslaw supported the wisecracking dummy Archie Andrews in the radio series *Educating Archie*. Writer Marty Feldman gave him a new catchphrase: 'Ullo, it's me, Twinkletoes!' Later that year, Bresslaw made his pantomime debut, as Popeye in *The Sleeping Beauty* at the London Palladium.

On television, Sid Green and Dick Hills scripted four editions of *The Bernard Bresslaw Show* (1958-1959) for ATV. In 1959, he starred in the Hammer Jekyll and Hyde comedy *The Ugly Duckling* and joined the criminal gang of George Cole and Sid James in Mario Zampi's black comedy *Too Many Crooks*. Bresslaw was given his own BBC sitcom, *Meet the Champ*, starring as Bernie, an idiotic boxer, alongside Jimmy James as his scheming manager,

J J. Sid Colin wrote the scripts and Peter Butterworth provided support, but the series was cancelled after just six episodes. When his ITV sketch show,

Bresslaw and Friends, was curtailed after just one episode in March 1961 and *Our House* – which he joined in September 1961 – came to an end, a despondent Bresslaw decided to ditch the comic character that had made his name. He preferred to turn down lucrative variety dates in favour of Shakespearean roles for Equity rates.

After joining the Carry On team, Bresslaw happily balanced comedy roles

with serious drama. He starred in another BBC sitcom as the frustrated actor Leonard in *Mum's Boy* (1968) with Irene Handl and guest starred in *Doctor in the House* ('The Rocky Mountain Spotted Fever Casino', 1969) and *The Goodies* ('Scotland', 1971). He acted with the Royal Shakespeare Company, the English Stage Company and at the National, replacing Laurence Olivier as the cunning lawyer A B Rayam in their 1969 production of *Home and Beauty*.

In 1980, he joined the New Shakespeare Company, playing Dogberry in *Much Ado About Nothing*, Bottom in *A Midsummer's Night Dream* and Ferrovious in *Androcles and the Lion*. In 1983, Bresslaw gave one of his most subtle screen performances as Rell the Cyclops in *Krull* and, two years later, provided aggressive support for Fulton Mackay in Roy Clarke's Thames sitcom *Mann's Best Friend*.

Notable theatre credits included the murderous Jonathan Brewster in *Arsenic and Old Lace* at Chichester, Prospero in *Hamlet* at the Ludlow Festival, Detective Sergeant Porterhouse in *Run For Your Wife* at the Criterion and Abanazar in *Aladdin* at Richmond. In 1989, he played a lecherous Centurion in *The Swagger* at the Regent's Park and it was there that he gave his last performances, as Merlin in *A Connecticut Yankee in the Court of King Arthur*, and Grumio in *The Taming of the Shrew*.

Carry On credits: *Nurse* (feet only), *Cowboy, Screaming!, Follow That Camel, Doctor, Up the Khyber, Camping, Up the Jungle, Christmas '69, Loving, At Your Convenience, Matron, Abroad, Girls, London!, Christmas '73, Dick, Behind, Laughing*: 'Under the Round Table', 'And In My Lady's Chamber', 'Short Knight, Long Daze', 'Who Needs Kitchener?', 'Lamp-Posts of the Empire'

CARRY ON LOVING (1970)

Girl-shy innocent Bertram Muffet (Richard O'Callaghan) is determined to get a piece of the permissive society so he enrols with the Wedded Bliss Agency. But all at the agency is not so blissful. Sidney Bliss (Sid James) isn't even married to his supposed 'wife' Sophie (Hattie Jacques). Sophie is convinced that Sidney is enjoying himself with one of the clients, Esme Crowfoot (Joan Sims), so fixes the firm's unorthodox computer to match Bertie with Esme, much to Sid's displeasure. He cancels the date and allows Bertie to make his way to the meeting place and meet a complete stranger, model and film star Sally Martin (Jacki Piper). Bertie thinks she's Esme and Sally thinks Bertie is a photographer. When she strips, he makes a bolt for the door. Meanwhile, Sophie has employed a private detective, James Bedsop (Charles Hawtrey) to follow Sid. Hopeless, unmarried marriage guidance counsellor Percival Snooper (Kenneth Williams) has been ordered to get to know his job properly and get married himself. Sophie takes a shine to the supercilious gent but his faithful home help, Miss Dempsey (Patsy Rowlands), decides to spice up the evening meal in retaliation. Cheeky playboy Terence Philpot (Terry Scott) strikes lucky when the dowdy Jenny Grubb (Imogen Hassall) scrubs up very nicely, but a celebratory dinner turns to mayhem as Esme's boyfriend, wrestler Gripper Burke (Bernard Bresslaw), recognises Sid's jacket and the bored, mismatched couples throw themselves into a food fight!

The notion of a Carry On set in and around a marriage agency was first discussed during the lengthy debate about the Christmas special. Before filming had even begun on *Up the Jungle*, Talbot Rothwell wrote to Peter Rogers: 'Yes, I'm very happy to have a go at 'Courting'. I feel that it falls into the same sort of pattern as *Camping*, that is to say nice and elastic and not too bound down by one storyline. I have already got a good general "line" for it, I think, which leads to a finish comparable with the *Khyber* finishing routine. When I have filled in the sixty-odd minutes of "middle" a bit more I'd like to chat it over with you.' When Rothwell signed his contract on 3 November 1969, the film was still to be called 'Carry On Courting', although the following day Rogers registered the title *Carry On Loving*.

The mood of Kenneth Williams was black when he received the script for *Carry On Loving* on 7 March: 'I am offered the part of Snooper (which looks interchangeable with Charlie Hawtrey) which is certainly a small part – well no – a support, but really thankless. The end is a big party shambles where everyone throws custard pies and seems to be the bottom of the barrel, but for Talbot Rothwell bottoms are capable of infinite variety.'

Richard O'Callaghan was unquestionably being groomed as the new leading man of Carry On, and he joined seasoned veteran Sid James on Pinewood's 'C' stage for the first day of filming, 6 April 1970. Hattie Jacques joined the duo to complete the early scenes in Sid's Wedded Bliss Agency office. Kenneth Williams was enthused when he returned to the series two days later: 'seems strange to be starting a Carry On after so long an absence. We are the only film being made down there! I've never

known it so desolate: but of course it means we have the lovely dressing rooms and the best stages instead of being shoved into I-block like the old days. Oh! It was all just marvellous, I can't express the joy of it.'

Having been upset at the size of his role, Williams found that most of his colleagues were restricted to even smaller supporting turns. Charles Hawtrey, for example, completed his work in just six days while Peter Butterworth, adapting to life as a Carry On cameo player, filmed just one scene on 10 April and was identified as simply 'Client' ('mushrooms') on his contract.

O'Callaghan remembers Bernard Bresslaw with great affection: 'I was terribly nervous, of course, but

Left: Cupid Sid James and Hattie Jacques are destined to break more hearts than bring them together in Carry On Loving.

Above: Talbot Rothwell's doodles took on a romantic air before he submitted his script.

Opposite: A naïve Richard O'Callaghan and concerned Jacki Piper gatecrash the disastrous night of groping that a depressed Imogen Hassall and Terry Scott had hoped for.

TITBITS

Photoplay magazine requested large photographs of Alexandra Dane, while Imogen Hassall was featured in *Parade*, *Weekend* and, along with Jacki Piper, *Titbits*. Bill Pertwee made his Carry On debut, playing a barman. His agent advised Peter Rogers to watch him in *Norman* (Wisdom's short-lived ATV sitcom) where he was displaying his comic skill. He returned for an edited role, as the Whippit Inn manager in *Carry On At Your Convenience*, and the supporting role of the fire chief in *Carry On Girls*. The photograph of Sally Martin, film star, that Pertwee shows Sid is, of course, a *Carry On Up the Jungle* publicity shot of Jacki Piper, film star. Fred Griffiths filmed his one day's work on location outside Windsor and Eton Central railway station, on 11 May 1970. It was Sid James's last day on the film. Hattie Jacques's costumes were the most expensive in the budget, with her navy, green and brown dresses and brown bag, totting up to almost £100. Jacki Piper's grey frock, beret and bag, turquoise jumper, pink and white dress, flowered dress and brown bag were purchased by cheque by the costume department for £23.15.6.

ON LOCATION

For the Wedded Bliss Agency, the crew returned to the corner of Park Street, Windsor that had doubled for the Helping Hands agency in *Regardless*. The block of flats where Joan Sims lives is on Atherton Court, off Meadow Lane, Eton. Windsor also provided the homes of Joan Hickson, on Queens Road, and Kenneth Williams, at Adelaide Square. Richard O'Callaghan looks at the dummy in the shop window in Thames Street, Windsor. The exterior of Richard's meeting place with Jacki Piper is Ye Harte and Garter Hotel, Thames Street, Windsor, and Charles Hawtrey follows Sid James into the public conveniences at Windsor and Eton Central railway station. The bus sequence with Richard O'Callaghan and Kenny Lynch was filmed on the dog track roundabout, Slough, now the site of a Co-Op. The hospital ward scene was shot on Pinewood's 'B' Stage on 30 April 1970. Eric Rogers reused part of his *Carry On Doctor* score to heighten the medical atmosphere.

A heavily disguised Charles Hawtrey caught short in the gents.

Bernard Bresslaw lets his muscle man persona slip as he shares a laugh on set with Joan Sims.

Bernard would be sitting there doing the crossword and say, "Do you want to give me a hand?" He was very friendly. Poor Imogen [Hassall] was very distant. She came onto the set and told us her place had been broken in to. Kenneth Williams was typical. He explained that they were welcome to break into his place because he had nothing to steal!'

The legal side of the production was dealt with by the production secretary, Sylvia Pyke, and Hugh Parton. The Bank of England was happy about the use of real bank notes in the film but requested approval on stills featuring notes. The banqueting hall for the final sequence was to have taken place in the Parkway Hotel's Marie Antoniette Room, although 'Is there not one at the Savoy or somewhere similar?' was asked. All names were dropped as irrelevant and not worth legal concern. Even the music for the scene had to be changed. Eric Rogers had scored an arrangement of 'Love is the Sweetest Thing', but the US rights, which had recently lapsed, were now claimed by Warner-Seven Arts and were about to be licensed to Peter O'Toole's Keep Films for *Country Dance*. In the end, Eric Rogers substituted an arrangement of Johann Strauss's 'Laughing Song' from *Die Fledermaus*.

In an earlier scene where Charles Hawtrey peers through a newspaper advertisement for Slumberland 'where the eye-holes are positioned directly through the posteriors of the naked man and woman', the company confirmed that: 'I came to the conclusion that there was not any defamatory innuendo here.' In any event, the scene was edited from the finished film.

At a direct cost of just under £170,000, *Carry On Loving* was one of the most inexpensive – and consequently profitable – films in the series. It premiered at the Metropole, Victoria, on 5 November 1970. Business was certainly booming. At the start of May, Peter Rogers had registered the title for his next film, *Carry On Henry*, along with an unmade Bonnie Prince Charlie romp,

Patsy Rowlands makes mischief as the usually dowdy Miss Dempsey.

'Carry On Charlie'. Other titles in the producer's schedule included 'Anything For Baby' and 'The Navy Game', a belated attempt to reacquaint *The Navy Lark* with big-screen audiences.

But it was Talbot Rothwell that was still happily in the Carry On catbird seat. It was

Richard O'Callaghan (1940-)

The son of Patricia Hayes, Richard made his film debut in *The Bofors Gun* (1968) with Nicol Williamson and Ian Holm, and had embarked on a West End run in *Three Months' Gone* at the Duchess Theatre, when he landed the hapless romantic lead in *Carry On Loving*. Critically acclaimed, his performance as Bertie Muffet prompted the *Times* reviewer to remark he 'plays the obligatory innocent with absolutely the right single-minded seriousness and apparent unconsciousness of the humour of his own situation.'

Convinced that he didn't quite make the grade as the producer's 'new Jim Dale', O'Callaghan joined the American Film Theater Company, playing Joey Keyston in Harold Pinter's production of *Butley* (1973) and appearing in Joseph Losey's epic *Galileo* (1975) opposite Topol. He later provided the voice of the rabbit Dandelion in *Watership Down* (1978). Notable television guest appearances included *Public Eye* ('Divide and Conquer', 1972) and the Ronnie Barker sitcom showcase *Seven of One* ('I'll Fly You For a Quid', 1973). From 1978 to 1980 he starred in two series of the Thames comedy drama *Born and Bred* with Joan Sims. He has displayed an astonishing versatility on the stage; in Ian McKellen's production of *Richard III* at the National and on tour, a West End run in *God Only Knows* with Derek Jacobi, and the lead role of Dr Frank Bryant in the 2002 touring production of Willy Russell's *Educating Rita*. On television, he starred as the ghostly Sir Walter Raleigh in *Jackanory* ('My Friend Walter', in 1990), the Agatha Christie adaptation *The Pale Horse* in 1997 and, that same year, the BBC presentation of *The History of Tom Jones: A Foundling*. He also enjoyed the regular role of Bobby Sykes in the ITV crime drama *McCallum*, with John Hannah.

Carry On credits: *Loving, At Your Convenience*

noted, by the legal department, that Tolly's agent, John Hayes, 'tells me that the deal previously made whereby Talbot Rothwell would write six scripts over a period of three years has now been varied to the extent that his film scriptwriting services will be exclusive to you.' Rogers commented, on 11 May 1970, that: 'Talbot Rothwell's exclusivity should extend as long as his contract for scripts.' Presently, that was a continual renewal of three-year intervals.

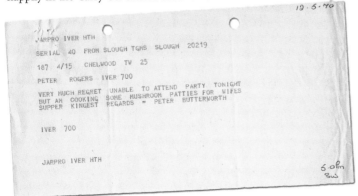

Above: Richard O'Callaghan poses in the Pinewood gardens for a publicity session promoting his first film with the gang.

Left: Life imitates art in this tongue-in-cheek telegram from Peter Butterworth.

TRAILER

'Yes, everyone's at it these days. The birds, the bees and those hilarious Carry On characters.'

CARRY ON HENRY (1971)

Having dispatched one Queen (Patsy Rowlands) on the execution block, merry monarch King Henry VIII (Sid James) rushes into another marriage with Marie of Normandy (Joan Sims). His not-so-loyal courtiers, Thomas Cromwell (Kenneth Williams) and Cardinal Wolsey (Terry Scott) despair of their King's matrimonial arrangements but each is corrupt enough to cream some money off the bungs that are keeping the Pope happy in Rome. But Henry isn't satisfied with his new, garlic-loving Queen. He can't get near her because of the pong and demands an immediate divorce. The royal taster, Sir Roger de Lodgerley (Charles Hawtrey), isn't so fussy – he chomps some garlic and keeps the King's bed warm. The King's desire to divorce Marie increases when he meets the saucy daughter of Charles, Earl of Bristol (Peter Butterworth). Charlie's girl, Bettina (Barbara Windsor), displays a talent for dancing and a lot of cleavage. As the King whisks her off, the Queen looks daggers. But there is worse in store when the King orders she be confined in the Tower. Francis, King of France (Peter Gilmore), unexpectedly turns up at the palace and threatens war if the love match between Marie and the King is faltering. Discovering Bettina in the King's bed doesn't help the situation. But the King's blonde babe ends up Queen of France instead, royal plotter Lord Hampton of Wick (Kenneth Connor) is knighted, and the King settles down to wedded bliss with Marie before catching a glimpse of the ravishing Katherine Howard (Monika Dietrich)...

There was already concern in the Pinewood camp that *Carry On Henry*, the twenty-first film in the series, would overshadow publicity for the twentieth, *Carry On Loving*. It didn't. But it is true to say that the industry gleefully recognised the milestone that *Henry* marked.

Tony Wells was appointed unit publicist by the publicity controller, Norman Martlew, because of the bigger than usual publicity push for the film and because there was already 'a considerable amount of reaction from all media of the press, television and radio. I know that you will be able to cope very well with this unique situation.' He was awarded the stills photographer Albert Clarke and secretary Doris Spriggs to help handle the influx of publicity requests. A pre-production meeting recorded 'congratulating the production company on attaining their twenty-first Carry On film and wishing them every success for the future'.

In their most ambitious location bid, Gerald Thomas and art director Lionel Couch attended a meeting with the Windsor Great Park superintendent in September 1970 to discuss filming on royal property, Queen Anne Drive and the Long Walk. On 28 September, production manager Jack Swinburne confirmed that he had heard from Major Haig MVO of the Crown Estates Office: 'I have today received formal permission for our company to shoot in Windsor Great Park and the Long Walk, in connection with *Carry On Henry*. One of the conditions is that there shall be no publicity or mention of Windsor Great Park or the Long Walk. I should be glad if you would pass this information to Tony Wells.'

A special cocktail party was arranged to launch the new film on Wednesday 7 October 1970. Although Kenneth Williams' diary entry is typically downbeat, it remains a vital record of the event: 'To the Dorchester where Peter Rogers held his champagne party for launching of his twenty-first Carry On. The only actors there were: Charlie Hawtrey and me, and Joan Sims and Barbara Windsor. The reporters all asked me "What are you doing in these sort of films?" and one man from the *Guardian* said "Why are you associated with this chamber-pot kind of

comedy?" I said that in our kind of society there was and should be room for all kinds of entertainment if it worked on its own level and that the only charge to be taken seriously by us would be the one that the comedy (burlesque in this case) didn't work: that it wasn't funny.'

Unbelievably, this landmark film was almost without its foundation-stone leading man, Sid

Opposite: Joan Sims and Sid James regally perch upon their thrones.

Sid James thinks his luck is in as Barbara Windsor saucily places her 'marrows' in his hands.

TITBITS

The medieval dance routine captured in detail in the Southern Television report was choreographed by Jack Carter. Valerie Shute was called again, this time playing a regal maid and subject to Thursday and Saturday matinees in *Oh, Clarence* at the Wimbledon Theatre. Barry De Boulay, David Dillon and Mick Dillon, cast as litter men, had a contract clause detailing work of an 'abnormal hazardous or dangerous nature'. Ray Ford was cast as a French Knight but was uncredited. James Lodge and Gerry Wain were employed as riding doubles while Mike Stevens and Les Clarke are the dog handlers during the King's 'hunting trip' through Windsor Great Park. The bald but beautiful Milton Reid was cast as the burly executioner. He went on to play Tim Brooke-Taylor's effeminate minder in the 1972 Montreux version of *The Goodies*' 'Kitten Kong'.

ON LOCATION

On 13 October, Sid James, Margaret Nolan and the unit filmed the barnyard scenes at Southlea Farm, Datchet, Buckinghamshire. The next day, the unit was joined on location by actor Derek Francis, playing his one day as Nolan's distraught farmer father. The owner, W H Berryman, was paid £25 for the use of the property. Stock footage of the Tower of London from British Movietone News was used for the opening credits, while the Palace courtyard was situated on Pinewood's Paddock Tank, where Patsy Rowlands contributed one day's work on 6 November. The Pinewood gardens, a stone's throw from the back of Heatherden Hall, were fully utilised for the Sid James and Barbara Windsor royal garden sequences and an aborted scene of 'strip croquet'. The final day of shooting, 19 November, saw the unit filming the torture chamber scenes on 'J' Stage and completed exterior palace grounds material at the Paddock Tank.

Top: Tortuous laughs for Charles Hawtrey and Kenneth Williams.

Right: Congratulations in the shape of a Peter Rogers stork – the Carry Ons come of age with film number twenty-one.

Below: William Mervyn as the cricket-loving Sir Cyril Ponsonby in *Follow That Camel*.

James, thanks to scheduling clashes with his other work commitments. A lengthy appearance in South Africa was pared down and Sid joined the film on the second day of production, 13 October 1970.

The final budget for the film stood at £225,398.49. Sadly, some of the money was wasted. David Essex was paid £40 for his one day's work on 16 October 1970. Unfortunately his Speakers' Corner scene filmed at the Paddock Tank, with equally redundant John Clive, was cut from the film probably because the whole rally scene was ruined by the prominent banner reading 'Down with SET Tax' – which of course translates as 'Sex Enjoyment Tax Tax'! The whole day was lost, for the unit later moved to the studio gardens to film the edited croquet sequence with Sid James and Barbara Windsor.

Kenneth Williams and Terry Scott were encouraged to change the final, scripted line

William Mervyn (1912-1976)

A stage actor since 1934 and in films from 1947, he found his niche as the authority figure whose pomposity was fit for bursting. Part of Betty Box's repertory company, he appeared in *The 39 Steps* and *Upstairs and Downstairs* (both 1959) for her. On television in the 1960s he starred as Chief Inspector Rose in *The Odd Man*, *It's Dark Outside* and *Mr Rose*, while he made a memorable murder suspect in the Miss Marple film *Murder Ahoy*. The film teamed him with Derek Nimmo, with whom Mervyn would became a sitcom star in *All Gas and Gaiters* (BBC, 1966-1971); he went on to play the eccentric 43rd Duke of Tottering in *Tottering Towers* (1971-1972). On film he played the kindly old gentleman in Lionel Jeffries's *The Railway Children* and mugged as Lord Twithampton in *Up the Front*, with Frankie Howerd. Notable television guest appearances include *Hancock's Half Hour*: 'Lord Byron Lived Here', *Doctor Who*: 'The War Machines' and, his last role, as the landed gentry fox-hunter, Osborne, in *Raffles*: 'The Spoils of Sacrilege'.

Carry On credits: *Follow That Camel*, *Again Doctor*, *Henry*

Congratulations to Peter Rogers and Gerald Thomas and their team on the successful delivery of their 21st Carry On
"CARRY ON HENRY"

PINEWOOD STUDIOS LIMITED

DOCTOR, DOCTOR!

Julian Holloway fell from his horse and was apparently unhurt, according to the daily progress report, but fellow thespian Alan Curtis, playing the Conte di Pisa, remembers it slightly differently: 'I had to do some exterior involving riding a horse. I was given this horse and warned, "Watch this one because he threw Julian Holloway last week!" If you watch the film you will see this quite obviously in Julian's limp.'

Curtis wasn't feeling 100 per cent himself. He appeared in the *Royal Variety Show* on 10 November, the night before his exterior filming: 'It was a tremendous night and I got to bed very late and a bit hung over' he admits.

from 'Strike, strike!' as their heads are resting on the block, to the more provocative, 'Carry On Executioner! Carry On!' Scott was now getting the meatier Carry On roles formerly the preserve of Peter Butterworth, while Butterworth himself was now the first standby for showy, walk-on parts. For one day's work as Barbara Windsor's father, Butterworth was simply credited as 'Bristol'. He subsequently wrote to Rogers, 'just to thank you for the very enjoyable and happy day I had on *Henry* last week. It was nice to be part of it again.'

Above: A devilishly dashing portrait of Kenneth Connor as Lord Hampton of Wick.

Below: Terry Scott gets to the bottom of things with a cheeky serving wench, played by Marjie Lawrence.

John Bluthal (1929-)

At his best in the surreal company of Spike Milligan, Bluthal remained a loyal stooge through his numerous *Q* series, plus *Oh in Colour* (BBC, 1970), *Milligan in...* (BBC 1972-1973), *The Last Turkey in the Shop Show* (BBC, 1974) and *The Melting Pot* (BBC, 1975). He had supported Michael Bentine in *It's A Square World* in 1960 and director Joe McGrath used him in all manner of off-the-wall ventures, most effectively in *The Great McGonagall*, with Milligan and Sellers. Bluthal was the blind beggar in *The Return of the Pink Panther* and was a natural guest star for *The Goodies*, playing the manic Major Cheeseburger in 'Clown Virus'. He was the hapless car thief in *A Hard Day's Night*. He also appeared in *Help!* and *Superman III* for director Richard Lester. A valuable part of the Carry On squad, his uncredited vocals for Dr Crow in *Carry On Spying* proved his versatility and willingness to help out during his filming of his credited role as the Peter Lorre-styled henchman. Latterly, he has appeared as Frank Pickle in the Dawn French situation comedy *The Vicar of Dibley* and gave an unforgettable turn as the bitter comedian Jack Holiday in *Jonathan Creek* ('Jack in the Box', 1997).

Carry On credits: *Spying, Follow That Camel, Henry*

John Bluthal, as Corporal Clotski, fears the vultures under the scorching desert sun in *Follow That Camel*.

Bill Maynard (1928-)

Having been advised that Bill Williams wouldn't get noticed on a playbill, the fledgling comedian took his stage name from Maynard's wine gums and made a mark as 'the sweater boy' on variety bills across the country. Maynard had started his career in 1951 supporting Terry Scott, and the two formed a double act soon afterwards. The BBC saw them as the cutting edge of comedy and gave them their own series, *Great Scott – It's Maynard!*, from 1955 to 1956. Shirley Eaton provided the glamorous support. Maynard's greatest television triumph came in 1974 with the hit ITV series *Oh No, It's Selwyn Froggitt*. His catchphrase, 'Magic!', was on everybody's lips, although he had already proved himself a stalwart character actor. In 1968 he played Bert, Alf's friend in the film version of *Till Death Us Do Part*, and Maynard was still playing the character twenty years later for the 1989 Christmas special of *In Sickness and In Health*. He also featured in the feature films *Bless This House* (1972), *Steptoe and Son Ride Again* (1973) and all four Confessions comedies as Robin Askwith's work-shy father. He played Sergeant Ellis, opposite Jim Dale, in *Adolf Hitler – My Part in His Downfall* (1972) and a more bumbling Sergeant Beetroot, with Jon Pertwee, in *Worzel Gummidge*, from 1979. He was Bernard Cribbins' sidekick, Mod Lewis, in Val Guest's *Dangerous Davies – The Last Detective*, on ITV in 1981, but remains best loved as the scruffy rogue Claude Jeremiah Greengrass in *Heartbeat*. He starred in the show from 1992 until 2000 when health problems dictated his retirement. But he was back as Greengrass in the 2003 spin-off series, *The Royal*.

Carry On credits:
Loving, Henry, At Your Convenience, Matron, Abroad (scenes cut), *Dick*
Autobiography: *Stand Up And Be Counted*

Butterworth missed the arrival of Southern Television by just one day: on 5 November 1970, television cameras invaded Pinewood studios to record a behind-the-scenes look at the making of the film, complete with interviews with Sid James, Kenneth Williams and Terry Scott. The piece was edited down to five minutes, losing filmed interviews with Joan Sims and Barbara Windsor. The 16mm footage was subsequently acquired by Rank and included on the special edition DVD release of *Carry On Henry*, released by Carlton in 2003.

Far right: Peter Butterworth was clearly delighted to be back with the gang when he wrote to producer Peter Rogers.

Right: Filming Sid James in the Pinewood gardens on 16 October 1970.

Terry Scott (1927–1994)

The son of a Watford postman, Terry was convinced his future was on the stage from the age of five. Unfortunately, after he left Watford Grammar School, his parents insisted he get a 'proper' job with an accountancy firm. A hated part of his life, he served with the Navy during the Second World War and used his £39 demob money to break in to show business. He developed a comedy routine and would entertain unsuspecting drinkers in pubs and clubs for twenty-five shillings a performance. Joining the Grange-over-Sands Repertory Company for the (unpaid) experience, he then accepted a paying position with the Denville Players in Jersey.

By 1949, his talent had been recognised by the BBC and he landed a regular broadcasting contract, notably on *Variety Bandbox* and *Workers' Playtime*. But it was a stint on Clacton Pier where he learnt his craft and created the character that would make his name, the irritating schoolboy 'Knocker'. The character, eventually to record the song, 'My Brother' and used to advertise Curly Wurly chocolate bars, proved an instant hit and BBC television offered him an experimental sketch show, *Great Scott – It's Maynard!* (1955-1956). After a flop in a now-forgotten series – the Lew Schwarz-scripted BBC sitcom, *Scott Free*

Terry Scott

(1957), which cast him as an out-of-work actor opposite Norman Vaughan – he 'found himself at the bottom of the bill again'.

He nevertheless went on to make a number of notable cameo appearances in films; notably as bemused policemen in *Blue Murder at St. Trinian's* (1957), in

Double Bunk and *What A Whopper!* (both 1961), and in *Murder Most Foul* (1964), where his glee at discovering a murder is made a mockery of by Margaret Rutherford's Miss Marple. Brian Rix invited him to join his Whitehall theatre

company, playing farce for eighteen months. He was also a regular on his 1962 television series, *Dial RIX*.

Terry ruefully wrote that 'the BBC decided I might be funny after all, and *Hugh and I* emerged.' John Chapman created this series for Scott and Hugh Lloyd and it ran from 1962 until 1968; the last series re-titled *Hugh and I Spy*,

to spoof the popular American series.

The following year, they were reunited for Jimmy Perry's *The Gnomes of Dulwich*, and starred in the BBC Christmas Day 1973 pantomime, *Robin Hood*. Terry was also enjoying success in his sketch series, *Scott On...*, which had started with a 1964 special, *Scott On... Birds*, and, over a decade, went on to encompass everything from 'Food' and 'Money' to 'Christmas Trees' and 'The Permissive Society'. A short-lived 1973 sitcom, *Son of the Bride*, cast Terry as a besotted mummy's boy, distraught that his mother, Mollie Sugden, is planning to remarry. The writer, John Kane, worked on several episodes of the 1974 sitcom *Happy Ever After*, which brought the domestic pairing of Scott and June Whitfield fully to the fore. Kane would go on to write the best of *Terry and June*, which kept millions laughing until 1987.

Terry subsequently joined Eric Sykes's team for the 1988 slapstick comedy, *Mr. H is Late*. But it was theatre that kept him active in his later years. Long recognised as Britain's best pantomime dame, he discussed the role alongside such skilled exponents as Billy Dainty and Arthur Askey in the 1982 Channel 4 documentary *The Pantomime Dame*. He had starred as Nurse Teresa in *Babes in the Wood* at the Richmond theatre the previous season. He was also an expert farceur, playing the bigamist cabbie, John Smith, and his friend, Stanley Gardner, in West End productions of Ray Cooney's *Run For Your Wife!* Beloved by children of all ages as *Dangermouse*'s sidekick, Penfold, his greatest ambition was: 'to be a grandfather and to see Watford stay in the Second Division'.

Carry On credits: *Sergeant, Up the Khyber, Camping, Up the Jungle, Christmas '69, Loving, Henry, Again Christmas, At Your Convenience* (scenes cut), *Matron*

CARRY ON AGAIN CHRISTMAS (1970)

Short-sighted Dr Pavingstone (Kenneth Connor) greets 'Jim' Hawkins (Barbara Windsor) outside the Admiral Benbow public house. She tries but fails to make him understand that 'he' is a 'she', while Squire Treyhornay (Terry Scott), potless but thirsty, hopes to cadge a drink from a kind-hearted soul inside. Pirates Long John Silver (Sid James) and Rollicky Bill (Bernard Bresslaw) certainly aren't kind hearted, but when they arrive at the disreputable dockside pub they pretend to be two innocent seamen. Inside, old Blind Pew (Charles Hawtrey) is continually banging on about the Black Spot but it's Kate (Wendy Richard) and the shapely bott of Hawkins that interest Long John. Particularly when he discovers the map to the secret treasure island is tattooed upon it! Setting sail, Nipper the Flipper (Charles Hawtrey) keeps the ship ship-shape while Hawkins sorts out the Bristol fashion. But when the party arrive, they discover the island is 'ruled' by the wild-haired madman Ben Gunn (Bob Todd). Long John is stranded on the island as the others enjoy a slap-up Christmas feast on the voyage home, but the naughty pirate isn't too upset. The island is populated by a week's worth of scantily clad girls!

Wendy Richard's serving wench isn't impressed by the familiar piracy of Sid James!

Linda Regan (far left) and Carol Hawkins (sixth glamour girl in line) make their Carry On debuts opposite Sid James and Bob Todd.

producer. Eton didn't take any chances over the casting, suggesting Sidney James, Jim Dale, Charles Hawtrey, Bernard Bresslaw, Terry Scott, Peter Butterworth, Kenneth Connor, Hattie Jacques, Joan Sims, Barbara Windsor and Kenneth Williams. He thought a *Treasure Island* parody a 'very strong idea' and one that 'incidentally we have established is in public domain'. A spirited yuletide take on the Robert Louis Stevenson classic appealed to Talbot Rothwell, although he decided against writing for the show: 'After the awful experience of the last one, the mental and physical drain of it ... I just couldn't face up to another.'

A workable script was conjured up by Rothwell's old partner, Sid Colin, although writer Dave Freeman recalls that it was: 'a rush job. Sid Colin was commissioned first but went down with flu and Peter Eton rang me up in desperation about three days before it was due to go into rehearsal. All they had was the outline. The plot concerning a treasure map tattooed on a pretty bottom has since been used extensively [notably in Colin's *Up the Front* for

TITBITS

The closing scene, with Sid James's pirate surrounded by bouncy Christmas babes includes at least two uncredited starlets on the verge of Carry On stardom: Carol Hawkins, who would kick-start her association with the series proper with 1972's *Carry On Abroad*, and Linda Regan who would be recruited for *Carry On England* in 1976.

When *Carry On Loving* went on general release on 29 November 1970, the stage was already set for a sequel to the biggest Christmas hit for Thames from 1969; the previous Carry On special.

Peter Eton was, once again, in the driving seat although now in the role of executive

Frankie Howerd] but I think this was the original version. Sid played Long Dick Silver, the brother of Long John, and was quite supreme.' Somewhere along the way, the actual dialogue establishing Sid as Long Dick rather than Long John was lost from the script and, indeed, it would have conflicted with Peter Rogers's alternative title, 'Carry On Long John'.

The film producer also had a hand in editing down the flamboyant opening as all the male cast members vie for the key role of Long John. Stepping completely out of the storyline, Sid James was to have bellowed, 'Silence the lot of you.' With that, he was to have looked directly in to the camera and muttered, 'Just run the titles will you, while we sort this lot out!'

The actual broadcast wasn't without its problems either. Although the cast were in the familiar environs of Teddington Studios under the direction of Alan Tarrant, who had recently proved his mettle with the Joe Baker collection *Baker's Half-Dozen* for ATV in 1967 and the Sid James sitcom *Two In Clover* for Thames, a threatened technician's strike at Thames Television had taken hold. Demanding more money for working with the new colour-camera technology, their mass walk-out dictated that Thames had to broadcast in black-and-white over the crucial Christmas and New Year period and into March 1971. The show was broadcast at 9.10 pm on Christmas Eve.

Wendy Richard MBE (1943-)

Making her first mark on television alongside Terry Scott and Hugh Lloyd in the BBC sitcom *Hugh and I* from 1962 to 1966, Wendy had also made the British pop charts with a few choice cockney phrases on Michael Sarne's hit record 'Come Outside' in 1962. She guest starred in such classic BBC sitcoms as *The Likely Lads* ('Last of the Big Spenders', 1965) and *Dad's Army* in four episodes, 'The Two and a Half Feathers', 'Mum's Army', 'Big Jake' and 'My British Buddy'. She appeared with Frankie Howerd in a cut scene in the Beatles film *Help!* and gave blink-and-you'll-miss-her appearances in *Doctor in Clover* and the Hammer comedy *On the Buses*. But it was the down-to-earth and no-nonsense Miss Brahms in *Are You Being Served?* that made her a television star. She was with the series from the *Comedy Playhouse* pilot in 1972 to the end in 1985, cropping up in the 1977 feature film along the way, and reprising her role for the short-lived follow-up, *Grace and Favour*, in 1992. Her return illustrated her affection for the role because, almost immediately after the original series had finished, Wendy had been cast as the downtrodden housewife Pauline Fowler in the flagship BBC soap opera *EastEnders*. She finally left Albert Square in 2006.

Carry On credits: *Again Christmas, Matron, Girls*
Autobiography: *My Life Story*

The return to black-and-white broadcasting might explain why the viewing figures for *Carry On Again Christmas* didn't match those for the previous year.

Wendy Richard as the naïve beauty queen, Ida Downe, in *Carry On Girls* (1973).

The legendary Bob Todd, at home as part of the *Benny Hill Show*'s rep company.

Bob Todd (1921-1992)

A Second World War bomber pilot and ex-cattle breeder, he broke into acting opposite Sid James in *Citizen James*. In 1962, he had an uncredited bit part as a musician in the Peter Rogers comedy *Raising the Wind*. In 1970 Hammer Film Productions cast him as the burgomaster in *Scars of Dracula* (the film's star, Christopher Lee, subsequently described Todd as the funniest man he had ever worked with) and as a funeral director in *That's Your Funeral* (1973). Todd enriched several 1970s sex comedies, notably as Mr Barnwell, seducing Carol Hawkins, in *Confessions of a Pop Performer* (1977). On television, he played Cyril, the entertainment officer in *Doctor at Sea* (1974) and became an invaluable stooge for Marty Feldman, Spike Milligan and Jim Davidson. He appeared in Eric Sykes's silent comedies *Rhubarb, Rhubarb* (1980) and *Mr. H is Late* (1988) and played Professor Crankshaft alongside Glynis Barber's *Jane*. However, it is for his work with Benny Hill that 'Toddy' became internationally famous. He walked with ease through Richard Lester's homage to slapstick at the start of *Superman III* (1983) and, in 1985, received the ultimate accolade when Half Man Half Biscuit released *Back in the DHSS*, featuring the track '99% of Gargoyles Look Like Bob Todd'.

Carry On credits: *Again Doctor, Again Christmas*

CARRY ON AT YOUR CONVENIENCE (1971)

The century-old lavatory manufacturer, W C Boggs and Sons, faces some changes when its owner (Kenneth Williams) is forced to consider manufacturing new-fangled bidets designed by the floral-shirted Charles Coote (Charles Hawtrey). Boggs's son, Lewis (Richard O'Callaghan), is all for the new idea but works foreman Sid Plummer (Sid James) isn't convinced. It's the steady old lav that fills W C Boggs with pride, ably demonstrated by his faithful secretary Miss Withering (Patsy Rowlands). Pride in the workplace is the last thing that concerns bolshie union man Vic Spanner (Kenneth Cope). Along with his bumbling mate, Bernie Hulke (Bernard Bresslaw), Spanner is continually trying to get the workforce out on strike. Worker Chloe Moore (Joan Sims) isn't interested, but the girls are outvoted and it's 'Everybody out!' Young Lew Boggs is pleased, because this gives him some free time to woo Plummer's canteen-worker daughter, Myrtle (Jacki Piper) much to the outrage of Spanner, who also fancies her. The strike threatens to ruin the company and the workers return; but only for the works outing to Brighton. W C joins in the fun for the first time and wakes up in the bedroom of Miss Withering, while Sid tries his luck with Chloe. The ladies, led by Spanner's overbearing mother (Renee Houston), get the factory up and running, Spanner buckles down to it and Sid's bird-fancying wife, Beattie (Hattie Jacques) joins the firm and brings an end to her husband's own bird-fancying!

With Christmas audiences sated with small-screen Carry On, the next cinema release was to prove the least commercially successful entry in the series so far. A sort-of 'Carry On I'm Alright Jack', it was a slap-and-tickle take on unions and petty-minded union bosses, initially developed as 'Carry On Comrade'.

Perhaps it was felt that there was a risk of alienating the Carry Ons' traditional constituency, because the project was soon re-titled 'Carry On Working'. Although that title was retained for the final line of the film (a line that doesn't appear in the original script) by the time of the pre-production meeting on 15 March 1971, Peter Rogers had registered the title *Carry On At Your Convenience*.

Carry On At Your Convenience went into production on 22 March 1971, with romantic leads Richard O'Callaghan and Jacki Piper filming the interior of the Whippit Inn restaurant scenes on 'C' Stage with Julian Holloway, Shirley Stelfox and a subsequently edited Bill

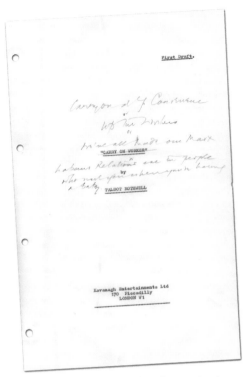

Talbot Rothwell's draft screenplay still carries the title 'Carry On Worker'. An alternative title from Peter Rogers, 'We've All Made Our Mark', was also dropped.

teller's tent and the ghost train. Joan Sims joined the cast in a blaze of glory on 29 March, filming the classic condensed Carry On sequence in the works canteen on 'D' Stage.

The eagerly awaited location trip to Brighton came at the very end of the shoot. Richard O'Callaghan remembers that: 'I wasn't a regular

Opposite: Up the Workers! The resolve of faithful union members Bernard Bresslaw and Kenneth Cope begins to crumble when faced by the girl power of Renee Houston, Marianne Stone, Hattie Jacques and Margaret Nolan.

Pertwee. 'C' Stage was also used for Miss Withering's bedroom, the interior of Sid Plummer's house and all the interiors for the pier, including the rifle range, the fortune

Quest for Love

Quest for Love was another Peter Rogers production released in 1971. Based on the John Wyndham novel Random Quest, this was a hauntingly ephemeral science fiction romance, adapted for the screen by Terence Feely. Peter Rogers was executive producer, working with Carry On Christmas producer Peter Eton and director Ralph Thomas.

Joan Collins and director Ralph Thomas on the set of Quest for Love.

DOCTOR, DOCTOR!

Peter Rogers relished contributing to the musical score of his friend, Eric Rogers. The sequence in the Whippet Inn as Richard O'Callaghan asks Shirley Stelfox for 'another couple of those, please!' is accompanied by Peter's 'Ottilie Theme'. Shirley Stelfox, the wife of Carry On Columbus bosun Don Henderson, appeared as the bunny girl waitress and her contract recorded the fact that: 'the artist understands that there will be a degree of nudity as indicated in the script.' Bill Maynard, in his third Carry On, was committed to a week on stage in The Ghost Train in Wolverhampton from 10 May, and his contract agreed to release him for the performances. Marianne Stone, another treasured Carry On support, enjoyed her most prominent role in the series. On 11 May Gerald Thomas wrote: 'I have just seen the rough cut and must say it looks very funny. You really ought to try your gorgeous giggle out on Peter, I am sure he would appreciate it.' On 14 May, Stone wrote to Rogers, explaining that: 'I enjoyed myself so much on Carry On At Your Convenience that my instinct was to send the money back! However, I have conquered that, but want to thank you for all the nice work you are putting my way. Please keep it up. All luv Marianne.' The tasty, hot-panted filly who catches Kenneth Cope's eye at the close isn't credited, despite having some dialogue. It is Anouska Hempel, who retired from the business to marry London hotelier Lord Weinberg. She had already made her mark in Bond (On Her Majesty's Secret Service), and Hammer (Scars of Dracula) before her Carry On foray. However the ultimate uncredited appearance is made by GSE Limited employee Peter Govey. It is his hand that pulls down the sheets of toilet paper during the film's opening credits!

ON LOCATION

As well as three days in Brighton, the unit filmed the works gate sequences outside the carpenter's shop at Pinewood. One day's filming, 26 April, was disrupted by continuous rain. On 28 April, an extended day at the home of Sidney Plummer in Pinewood Green was required for the night shoot with Sid James and Joan Sims. On 30 April, Vic Spanner's house and the betting shop was filmed on the Baker Street set at the Pinewood studio lot, a leftover from Billy Wilder's underrated film *The Private Life of Sherlock Holmes*. The coach pulled up at the Ghurka pub in Iver and the scene featuring Sid James and Kenneth Williams unloading beer from the back was filmed at the bus stop opposite the pub. The cinema where Richard O'Callaghan picks up Jacki Piper was the Odeon, on the High Street, Uxbridge.

Top: Joan Sims and Charles Hawtrey share a joke on location in Brighton.

Above: *Kine Weekly's Carry On Henry* special included an early good luck message for the twenty-second Carry On film.

so it wasn't a big deal for me but Kenneth Williams and Joan Sims, who had been in them for years, were saying, "Ooh. Are we actually going somewhere that isn't Pinewood!"' Considering that the material is a big chunk of the end of the film, the unit wasn't down in Sussex by the sea for very long, with all the location filming in Brighton completed in three days. The return journey from Brighton was actually filmed on local roads around Pinewood Studios. The montage of pub-sign footage was from stock and only the Red Lion, Iver, was actually utilised as a location.

Revenge

Sydney Hayers had directed the 1965 comedy musical *Three Hats For Lisa*, starring Sid James and from a script co-written by Talbot Rothwell. But his first collaboration with executive producer Peter Rogers was *Revenge* (1971), a return to the thrillers that had made his name. George H Brown was the producer and John Kruse wrote the taut screenplay.

In post-production Gerald Thomas faced the massive task of editing down the lavatorial epic he had created into a workable Carry On length. But the director still didn't go soft on the censors when a threatened line was one he wanted to retain. It was suggested that the Bernard Bresslaw line 'pencil-doings' be cut, along with Joan Sims's 'prodding at my vitals' observation and Kenneth Williams's 'meat and two veg' limerick. Thomas fought and won for these classics from his established team but conceded to John Trevelyan's request that the line 'All the time it's prick, prick, prick' and the reaction 'So the girls say' be removed.

One major cut had nothing to do with the censor. Terry Scott, in what would have been his sixth consecutive appearance in the Carry Ons, was signed up to play the satirically scripted leader of the union, Mr Allcock. With his permanent tan, union business in sunny climes and opulent manner, the depiction of the union boss was particularly right wing. Perhaps it was cold feet on the

Peter Rogers helpfully pencilled his suggested credit for Royal Doulton's support of his toilet epic.

Renee Houston (1902-1980)

Houston was a dedicated music hall performer from 1916, when she first performed with her sister, Billie. In the 1930s, she played the lead in such films as *Come into My Parlour* (1932) and the autobiographical *Happy Days Are Here Again* (1936). She later became an experienced character actress, playing Miss Brimmer in *The Belles of St. Trinian's*, Ebbey in *A Town Like Alice*, Alec Guinness' faded muse in *The Horse's Mouth* and Mrs Tucker in Hammer's *The Phantom of the Opera*. For Peter Rogers, she played the Matron in *Twice Round the Daffodils* and Mrs Beacon in *Nurse On Wheels*. Her last film role was as the flamboyant show-woman Chou-Chou in *Legend of the Werewolf* (1975).

Carry On credits: *Cabby, Spying, At Your Convenience*
Autobiography: *Don't Fence Me In*

part of the distributors that finally swung the balance. In any event Terry's entire contribution was cut from the film. Although only a showy guest-star performance, Terry's clout within the Carry On gang and his national popularity on television would have been exploited on the poster: a caricature likeness was to have been included and the billing to read: 'Sidney James, Kenneth Williams, Charles Hawtrey, Joan Sims, Bernard Bresslaw, Kenneth Cope, Patsy Rowlands, Hattie Jacques, Terry Scott, Jacki Piper, Richard O'Callaghan.' Gerald Thomas reluctantly wrote: 'My dear Terry I am writing to you personally because I do not want you to

hear second hand that we have cut your sequence from *Carry On At Your Convenience*. This is in no way any reflection on you or your performance but the film finished 50 minutes over length and we felt rather than cut your sequence down so that you were only on the screen for a flash it would be kinder to remove the entire scene as really it had no effect one way or the other on the story, such as it is.'

Top left: Sid James is confronted by chief picket Kenneth Cope.

Below left: Suzy Kendall is in for a big surprise in Assault.

Below: Factory floor frolics with Kenneth Williams and Charles Hawtrey.

Assault

Peter Rogers was also executive producer on *Assault* (1971), a psychological thriller from director Sydney Hayers, producer George H Brown and scriptwriter John Kruse. Based on the novel *The Ravine* by Kendal Young, it starred Suzy Kendall as Julie West, an art mistress who helps Detective Chief Superintendent Velyan (Frank Finlay) when one of her students, Tessa Hunt (Lesley-Anne Down), is raped.

Kenneth Cope (1934–)

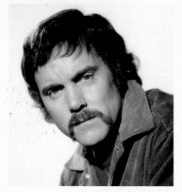

Making his film debut as a British soldier discovering something nasty in Hammer's *X the Unknown* (1957), Kenneth enjoyed a string of military roles in such films as *The Yangste Incident* and *Dunkirk*. On television, he made various appearances in costume serials like *The Adventures of Robin Hood*, *William Tell* and *Ivanhoe*, but it was the regular role as Jed Stone in *Coronation Street* from 1961 until 1966 that made his face known to millions. During his time in the soap, he was also recruited for the influential BBC satire programme *That Was the Week That Was* and, in 1965, teamed with a fellow *TW3* survivor for *The Lance Percival Show*. He wrote the first Thames sitcom, *Thingumybob*, for Stanley Holloway in 1968 and enjoyed guest spots in *The Avengers* ('The Bird Who Knew Too Much', 1967 and 'The Curious Case of the Countless Clues', 1969). But it was for the ghostly detective, Marty Hopkirk, in *Randall and Hopkirk (deceased)*, that TV enthusiasts love him best. After his brush with Carry On, he starred in the crime romp, *Rent-a-Dick* (1972) and featured in the 1980 film version of *George and Mildred*. Notable television guest appearances included *Doctor Who* ('Warrior's Gate', 1981), a seedy bus company owner Jackie Afflick in *Miss Marple* ('Sleeping Murder'), *A Touch of Frost* ('True Confessions') and *Last of the Summer Wine* ('The Love-Mobile'). He wrote for such television hits as the drama *Village Hall* and the David Jason sitcom *A Sharp Intake of Breath* in the 1970s. In 1999, he returned to the world of soap as Ray Hilton in Channel 4's *Brookside*.

Carry On credits: At Your Convenience, Matron

Terry would return with a leading part in the next film, *Carry On Matron*.

Carry On At Your Convenience remains the definitive ninety-minute encapsulation of lavatorial humour. Indeed, regular Carry On character actor Hugh Futcher considered the theme an overplayed one: 'A mention would always get a laugh but we had everything that goes into a bathroom suddenly everywhere on set!' The marketing men seized upon the lavatory however. A nationwide tie-in with Wolfe Publishing and their book *The Good Loo Guide*, was suggested. An internal memo reveals that: 'we have secured a quantity of display units to be placed in stores and foyers throughout the UK which will have a cross reference to *The Good Loo Guide*. We are still endeavouring to persuade a newspaper to run a nationwide contest to find the best talking budgerigar in the country with appropriate prizes of cages, bird seed etc, etc.' A week before the London release *Reveille* were to run a tie-in competition to win a fully-fitted bathroom, while the help of Royal Doulton and Co Limited was gratefully thanked on screen. But the 'convenience' double meaning wasn't amusing to all. In foreign territories like Australia and America the title was changed to *Carry On Round the Bend*.

Richard O'Callaghan, Jacki Piper and Kenneth Cope as Carry On's next generation.

Sid James with his spoilt horseracing expert budgie, Cleopatra.

TRAILER

A teaser toilet trailer was commissioned, while regular trailer scribe Tony Church worked on the main advertisement. He submitted his draft script on 28 June 1971 delighting in describing the film as 'the biggest basin-full of fun since the invention of WATER-LOO!'.

Joan Sims (1930-2001)

The daughter of the Laindon stationmaster, Joan remembered that 'from a very early age my great passion was performing. The station offered a readymade stage in the form of the loading bays in the goods yard.'

She graduated from the Royal Academy of Dramatic Art in April 1950 with the Mabel Temperley Prize for Grace and Charm of Movement. But life after RADA was no fun. She joined the Chorlton-cum-Hardy Players, playing small roles before landing the lead in *Sarah Simple*, opposite Harry H Corbett. By Christmas 1951, she was appearing with Stanley Baxter in a new pantomime, *The Happy Ha'penny*, at the Glasgow Citizens' Theatre, and later landed her first television job, voicing Millicent Mushroom, Barbara Beetroot and Oscar Onion for the children's show, *Vegetable Village*.

Her first 'on-screen' television credit was as Boris Karloff's secretary, Marjorie Dawson, in *Colonel March Investigates*. A film version was cobbled together from the series and, in 1953, Joan made her first film proper when she supported George Cole, Jon Pertwee, Sid James and William Hartnell in *Will Any Gentleman?*

On stage, she had become a star of West End revue, with *Intimacy at Eight* and *High Spirits*, with Dilys Laye and Ian Carmichael, at the London Hippodrome. In a revamped version of *Intimacy at 8.30*, Joan stole the show with her husky delivery of the 'Siren Song', and was personally chosen by Terry-Thomas to support him in his 1953 radio hit, *Top of the Town*.

In 1954, she played Dirk Bogarde's reluctant girlfriend, Rigor Mortis, in *Doctor in the House*, the sultry schoolteacher Miss Dawn in *The Belles of St. Trinian's*, and a telephone operator in *To Dorothy A Son*, for producer Peter Rogers. Her future as the darling of British comedy cinema was assured.

She would appear in four more Doctor comedies, as the heartbroken Wendy in *Doctor at Sea* (1955), a stripper in *Doctor in Love* (1960), Matron in *Doctor in Clover* (1966) and a Russian sea

captain in *Doctor in Trouble* (1970), while the Carry Ons and other Gerald Thomas comedies gradually came to dominate her work. On television she recaptured her stage triumphs in BBC's celebration of the revue *Before the Fringe* (1967), played Eric's on-off romantic interest in *Sykes* and twice guest starred on *The Goodies* ('Wicked Waltzing', 1971, and

'Way Outward Bound', 1973). She created the pathos-tinged role of the woebegone, booze-addled Gran in Johnny Speight's *Till Death Us Do Part*, despite being over twenty years younger than her screen daughter, Dandy Nichols! Chosen to replace Betty Marsden in *Round the Horne*, the sudden death of Kenneth Horne in 1969 dictated that the series Joan ultimately appeared in was centred around Kenneth Williams and renamed *Stop Messin' About*.

In 1980 she played Amelia Elizabeth Dyer in *Lady Killer*: 'Suffer Little Children' for producer Pieter Rogers. Her last stage appearance was as Fairy Sweetcorn with Suzanne Danielle and Kenneth Connor in *Jack and the Beanstalk* at the Richmond theatre for the 1984/85 season. Later television guest appearances included Miss Murgatroyd in *Miss Marple* ('A Murder Is Announced', 1985), Katryca in *Doctor Who* ('The Trial of a Time Lord', 1986), Auntie Reen in *Only Fools and Horses* ('The Frog's Legacy', 1989) and Betsy Prig in *Martin Chuzzlewit* (1994). She played Dennis Waterman's housekeeper, Mrs Wembley, in *On the Up* (1990-1992) and Madge in *As Time Goes By* (1994-1998), with Judi Dench and Geoffrey Palmer. Her last television role was as Betty the pianist in *The Last of the Blonde Bombshells* (2000).

A portrait of Joan Sims from *The Belles of St. Trinian's* (1954).

Carry On credits: *Nurse, Teacher, Constable, Regardless, Cleo, Cowboy, Screaming!, Don't Lose Your Head, Follow That Camel, Doctor, Up the Khyber, Camping, Again Doctor, Up the Jungle, Loving, Henry, At Your Convenience, Matron, Abroad, Christmas '72, Girls, Christmas '73, Dick, Laughing*: 'The Prisoner of Spenda', 'The Baron Outlook', 'The Sobbing Cavalier', 'One in the Eye For Harold', 'The Nine Old Cobblers', *Behind, Laughing*: 'Under the Round Table', 'The Case of the Screaming Winkles', 'And In My Lady's Chamber', 'Short Knight, Long Daze', 'The Case of the Coughing Parrot', 'Who Needs Kitchener?', *England, Emmannuelle*

Autobiography: *High Spirits*

CARRY ON MATRON (1972)

Sid Carter (Sid James) is the cunning head of a criminal gang that includes the long-haired drip Ernie Bragg (Bernard Bresslaw), the cheeky Freddy (Bill Maynard) and Sid's son, Cyril (Kenneth Cope). Cyril disguises himself as a new nurse in order to case a maternity hospital and the booty – the hospital's stock of contraceptive pills. The Head Chopper at the hospital, Sir Bernard Cutting (Kenneth Williams), is convinced he's undergoing a sex change while the nutty Dr F A Goode (Charles Hawtrey) dishes out psychiatric mumbo jumbo. The hardworking Matron (Hattie Jacques) has more than enough to contend with on the wards, with the troublesome Mrs Tidey (Joan Sims) who seems more interested in eating than producing a baby, and her loyal, British Rail worker husband (Kenneth Connor) who continually hangs around the waiting room. Waiting. Cyril is picked out by notorious 'bird-watcher' Dr Prodd (Terry Scott) and goes back to his place in order to get a map of the hospital. The poor doc gets a shock when the lovely nurse turns out to be a crook in a frock. But 'she' makes headline news when film star Jane Darling (Valerie Leon) hails 'her' a heroine for helping her through her pregnancy. The Sister (Jacki Piper) desperately tries to keep the ward in order, while Cutting's secretary Miss Banks (Patsy Rowlands) keeps her employer in check, but nothing can cool his pent-up desire to prove himself as a man. And it's Matron who is in his sights. The criminal gang don disguises – Sid dresses as the foreign Dr Zhivago and Ernie as a heavily expectant mum – but the crime is thwarted by the mothers-to-be. The medical hierarchy's threat to call the police is halted when Sid reveals the heroine of the day to be a man. Cyril weds his shapely nurse, Susan Ball (Barbara Windsor), and Matron finally gets her doctor.

During the correspondence over the first Christmas television special, Peter Rogers had reminded Talbot Rothwell that *Carry On Matron* was a film he wanted to make. Indeed, he had registered the title on 26 September 1968, along with *All Policemen Are Bastards* which, retitled *All Coppers Are...*, was put into production just before the maternal comedy.

Rothwell wasn't Rogers's first choice as writer for *Carry On Matron*. Over seven years since his last Carry On script, the man behind *Carry On Nurse*, Norman Hudis, was initially approached. Within a couple of months, however, this intriguing Carry On comeback was off, thanks to difficulties arising out of Hudis' membership of the Writers' Guild of America.

The film began shooting on schedule, with Kenneth Williams, Hattie Jacques and Patsy Rowlands gathering on Pinewood's 'B' Stage for scenes within Sir Bernard Cutting's office. Patsy completed her role on the second day, and Sid James joined the production in the second week of filming.

Thomas was doubtless delighted with the speedy progress he had made on the film. It

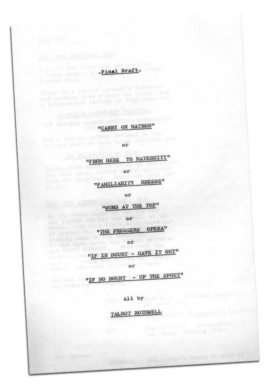

was to get better. As Kenneth Williams recorded on Thursday 18 November: 'The end of picture party was held in the Green Room at Pinewood and there was a superb buffet spread and lots of drinks. I talked to Hattie and Sid. Ken Cope, Ken Connor, Bernard Bresslaw, Charlie

Hawtrey and two policemen from Langley. Gerald told me that he was six and a half days ahead of schedule. He said it was a record for him. I should think it's a record for the industry!'

Ever since Alexandra Dane had alerted Peter Rogers to the comedic talents of Jack Douglas in 1968, the comedian had been in the sights of the producer. Jack performed a one-day cameo as the greatly blessed father staggering in to the waiting room and muttering down the phone, 'Can you get me the *Guinness Book of Records* please?', on 'B' stage on 25 October 1971. The apocryphal story goes that as this was a try-out for the actor, Jack wasn't paid for his performance in the film. 'Equity would have caused trouble if we had done that!' assures Peter Rogers and, indeed, Jack was contracted at a 'special rate' of £25 for his inaugural Carry On, subject to his commitment to *The David Nixon Show* for Thames Television. The makers

Opposite: Crooks anonymous – Sid James, Bill Maynard, Kenneth Cope and Bernard Bresslaw 'case the joint' for a spot of pill plundering.

Left: Talbot Rothwell's original draft script, complete with alternative titles both adopted and discarded.

All Coppers Are...

A hard-hitting police drama from executive producer Peter Rogers, also released in 1972. This was Rogers' final film with director Sidney Hayers and producer George H Brown. In October 1971 Rogers wrote to a Rank executive: 'the police like this film themselves and I only hope that your enthusiasm filters down through the ranks of Rank – who are inclined to "turn when father turns" – and then perhaps this film won't be pissed against the wall as the others were.'

Robin Askwith shows an unhealthy disrespect for the law in *All Coppers Are...*

DOCTOR, DOCTOR!

The health of title-role actress Hattie Jacques was causing concern. Dr Black noted that 'since my last examination on 24 March 1970 there has been an impressive drop in blood pressure 170/130 to 150/110 [and] she is receiving hypertensive drugs from her own doctor. A fall of this magnitude must, I think, imply an improved prognosis even though her weight has increased from 18 st 10 lbs to 19 st 7 lbs. She is now making a determined effort to reduce her weight.' Lloyds of London, on the other hand, were 'unhappy that since Miss Jacques was examined last March she has discontinued medical treatment', which certainly conflicts with the medical report.

ON LOCATION

For once it was a real hospital, Heatherwood Maternity Hospital, Ascot, that provided the forecourt for the film's Finisham Maternity Hospital. The maternity wing amenity fund was given £250 in thanks. The unit used the location for three days, including a night shoot for Terry Scott's ambulance mayhem. Denham Church played host to another Carry On wedding, following its use in *Don't Lose Your Head*. The Rev E Corr received £25 towards church funds, while Diana Copisarow, the owner of the White House, Denham Village, received £25 and flowers that were, 'exquisite, thoroughly undeserved but so much appreciated'.

A pregnant pause on the set, with Bernard Bresslaw dragged up to the hilt and Terry Scott once again fooled in to thinking a man is a woman.

Brian Osborne as Bob, one of the randy archaeology students in *Carry On Behind* (1975).

were so impressed that a crate of Dom Perignon champagne was delivered to his house bearing the note 'Welcome to the Carry On team'. 'So' chuckles Jack Douglas, 'I was literally launched in champagne. Everybody was so welcoming, Sid James said "Welcome to the madhouse, mate. Fancy a cup of coffee?" We were just chatting amiably when Kenneth Williams walked over. "Sid! You haven't offered Jack a biscuit. Where's yer manners, man?" Sid gave a gravelly chuckle as Kenneth flared his nostrils and flounced off to fetch some biscuits.'

For Jacki Piper, filming completed her three-year contract with Peter Rogers and a

Brian Osborne (1941-)

Having made his film debut as a miner in Ken Russell's ebullient *Women in Love* (1969), Osborne happily joined the Carry On team for a myriad of supports on film and television. He played the removal van driver in the 1972 Peter Rogers film *Bless This House* and was cast in the semi-regular role of Pearce in *Upstairs, Downstairs* between 1971 and 1972. Later he supported the star in *Frankie Howerd Reveals All* (1980) and played Farmer Goodrich in *Lord Peter Wimsey* ('Strong Poison', 1987).

Carry On credits: *Matron, Abroad, Girls, Dick, Laughing*: 'The Baron Outlook', 'The Sobbing Cavalier', 'Orgy and Bess', 'One in the Eye For Harold', *Behind, Laughing*: 'Under the Round Table', 'Short Knight, Long Daze', 'The Case of the Coughing Parrot', 'Who Needs Kitchener?', *England*

commitment to her family life saw her leave the team: 'It was at the time of the premiere of *Carry On At Your Convenience*, and after we had finished *Carry On Matron*, that I found out I was pregnant. I was appearing in the West End at the same time as filming and obviously all that time surrounded by babies in a maternity ward had rubbed off because I was too tired to get pregnant the usual way!' Jacki started on the film on 22 October and completed her farewell appearance in seven days.

Valerie Leon made a return to the series for the first time in two years having dropped Rogers and Thomas a note detailing her recent four-month tour with Brian Rix in *She's Done It Again*, and her starring role in Hammer's *Blood From the Mummy's Tomb*. Rogers replied that: 'so long as "experience" is the only thing you've broadened there is every chance of your working for me again.' She was cast as the expectant film star, Jane Darling. Valerie's husband in the film was played by Robin Hunter, son of British character actor in Hollywood Ian Hunter and husband of Carry On starlet Amanda Barrie. He had just wrapped Hammer's *Vampire Circus* at Pinewood before landing his one and only Carry On role.

The last day of filming, 18 November 1971, concentrated on the interior of Sid's car and the gang of crooks. Some of the material, as scripted, was altered in discussion between Sid and Gerald Thomas. While casing the maternity hospital for contraceptive pills, Sid was to have said he knew a country that would 'pay handsomely for 'em'; this was changed to, 'pay a bloody fortune for them'. Moreover, the country in question was originally identified as Ireland. The criminals' discussion about breaking into a nudists' camp was originally extended beyond his gang quickly making their exit. Sid was to have grumbled: 'Hey come back here,' then break into a smile – 'Oh well, perhaps it's a job I could get more out of on my own!' chuckling dirtily.

The finished film also lost an extra element of the wedding between Kenneth Williams' doctor and Hattie Jacques' matron. The happy ending would have been tarnished by showing a billboard: 'It shows an obvious actress in classical costume, looking worried and, in big letters we have "Do you suffer from 'First Night' nerves? Then take Amalsan".' At this point Williams, obviously suffering from first night nerves, collapsed in a heap outside the church. This was subsequently dropped. Yet another abandoned ending would have seen Charles Hawtrey's Dr Goode reacting to the marriage without the collapse and looking

Sid James sweet talks his way past hospital receptionist Gwendolyn Watts.

A star delivery grabs the interest of ambulance man Brian Osborne, medics Kenneth Williams and Hattie Jacques, and dogged reporter Bill Kenwright.

DOCTOR, DOCTOR!

Dependable character actress Marianne Stone was cast as the eccentric Mrs Putzova although her performance was cut from the finished film. Regular Carry On faces Michael Nightingale and Margaret Nolan both had one-day assignments on the film on 14 October 1971. Director of photography Ernest Steward is credited as the author of *The Psychology of Jealousy*, the book hypochondriac surgeon Kenneth Williams consults!

Derek Francis (1923-1984)

Although excellent as the working-class father of Janet Munro in *Bitter Harvest* (1963), the prolific Derek Francis was happily cast time and again as men of the cloth. At his best as the sub-prior Father Matthew in the Derek Nimmo sitcom *Oh Brother!* for the BBC, he joined the cast from the second series in 1969 and reprised his role for guest spots in the follow-up, *Oh Father!* in 1973. He was promoted for the ITV sitcom *Bless Me, Father* (from 1978), playing Bishop O'Reilly alongside Arthur Lowe. He cornered the market in the late 1970s, playing a Bishop in Terry Gilliam's *Jabberwocky*, Prudy's bishop stepfather in *The New Avengers* ('House of Cards') and the bishop in Hammer's *To the Devil a Daughter*. Notable television guest spots included Emperor Nero in *Doctor Who* (*The Romans*, 1965) with William Hartnell, John Scott Eccles in *Sir Arthur Conan Doyle's Sherlock Holmes* ('Wisteria Lodge', 1968) with Peter Cushing and Umberto Bellini in *Jason King* ('Wanna Buy a Television Series?', 1971) with Peter Wyngarde. He delighted in his Carry On roles, writing to Gerald Thomas on 23 October 1971 after wrapping on *Carry On Matron*: 'Thank you so much for letting me play "Arthur" – I haven't enjoyed myself so much for ages!' His talent for comic pomposity was fully explored as Abu ben Ackers the Wazir in the sitcom *Whoops Baghdad!* with Frankie Howerd. In the 1980s, he featured in *The Professionals* ('You'll Be All Right', 1982) and played Lord Kingclere in *The Wicked Lady* (1983). In March 1984, Francis played Ernest in Channel 4's *Winter Sunlight*; in the same week that the character died of a heart attack, so did the actor who played him.

Carry On credits: Doctor, Camping, Loving, Henry, Matron, Abroad

directly into camera and cooing: 'I do love happy endings, don't you?' and winking.

The film was, typically, affected by the two bugbears of Carry On: the censors and the budget. Firstly, the British Board of Film Censors requested the removal of the line 'If you can't be good keep your hand on it!' and Madeline Smith's Mrs Pullet reflecting on her newborn babe's bent little thing, 'unlike his father's!'. The censors wanted Thomas to 'remove all shots in which girl's [Gilly Grant] naked breasts are seen in bath' and Sid James's 'cock line outed'. That scene, with Kenneth Connor and Jack Douglas, was fought for by Thomas, who explained that it 'would be impossible to remove without adversely affecting the continuity of scenes on either side.' Thomas agreed to remove the nudity although, despite further concern from the censors, it ultimately remained intact.

The film came in at a direct cost of a little over £200,000, although the Rank Organisation commented on the doubling of the publicity budget – Peter Rogers blamed this on 'far too many newsmen, far too many photographers, far too many VIPs visiting us on the set and costing us money in entertainment'!

The trade show for *Carry On Matron* took place at Studio One on 18 May 1972, by which time *Carry On Abroad* was already in its last week of filming.

Far right: He may be covered in foam but that doesn't stop Charles Hawtrey promoting the latest Bush television set.

Right: Barbara Windsor radiates the Florence Nightingale spirit as Nurse Susan Ball.

Hattie Jacques (1922-1980)

Although she would be immortalised as the strict hospital Matron in the Carry Ons, even the coldest of characterisations were touched by Hattie's big-hearted personality. Having served as a Red Cross nurse for two years during the Second World War, she joined the Players Theatre in 1944 and became one of the company's mainstays.

For Christmas 1949, she played Marrygolda, one of Beauty's sisters in *Beauty and the Beast*, at the Theatre Royal, Covent Garden and, again for the Players, adapted *Riquet with the Tuft*, with Joan Sterndale Bennett, as 'a magnificent new fairy extravaganza'. In the production, Hattie played her favourite character, the immortal Fairy Queen with 'wanderful' powers. She would regularly perform with the Players until 1962.

She had crafted vignettes of Dickensian whimsy on film in Cavalcanti's *Nicholas Nickleby* (1947) and David Lean's *Oliver Twist* (1948), but it was as a latecomer to Tommy Handley's radio team in the morale-boosting *It's That Man Again* (1947-1949) that she became best known. As the greedy schoolgirl Sophie Tuckshop, she would gorge herself during midnight feasts, happily proclaiming, 'But, I'm all right now!'

From 1950, she played Miss Agatha Dinglebody supporting Max Bygraves in his efforts in *Educating Archie*. Archie's second tutor was Tony Hancock and, from 1956, Hattie joined his regular *Hancock's Half Hour* team as no-nonsense secretary, Grizelda Pugh, not only a dreadful secretary but also dreadful in the kitchen: Hancock memorably commented in 'Sunday Afternoon at Home' that 'I thought my mother was a bad cook but at least her gravy used to move about!' She was retained for just three

Hattie Jacques

television *Hancock's Half Hour* episodes ('The Russian Prince', 'The New Neighbour' and 'The Auction') in 1957.

Eric Sykes – who had co-written *Educating Archie* with Sid Colin – wrote his own BBC television series, *Sykes*, from 1960. Having rejected the husband-and-wife domestic sitcom as hackneyed, he wrote the role of his twin sister for Hattie Jacques. The series ran until 1965. Eric and Hattie reunited for such sketch shows as *Sykes Versus ITV* (1967) and *Sykes and a Big, Big Show* (1971), before embarking on another batch of *Sykes* from 1972 until 1979.

Richard Wattis returned as the nosy neighbour, Charles Brown, and Deryck Guyler was recruited as friendly police constable 'Corky' Turnball.

On film, Hattie had performed a delightful dance routine to Arthur Lucan's music-hall warbling in *Mother Riley Meets the Vampire* (1952) and proved an expert stooge for Norman Wisdom, notably as the Germanic temptress in *The Square Peg* (1958). She appeared with Peter Sellers in *The Bobo* (1967), *The Magic Christian* (1970) and a legendary episode of *Sykes*: 'Stranger' (1972) which spiralled into ad-lib hysteria.

Television guest spots included *Howerd's Hour* written by Eric Sykes, the first series of *The World of Beachcomber* with Spike Milligan (both 1968) and *Doctor At Large* ('Cynthia Darling', 1971), scripted by John Cleese. Hattie's last television role was, suitably enough in Sykes's remake of *Rhubarb, Rhubarb*. It was broadcast posthumously, in December 1980. Kenneth Williams wrote: 'Curiously, I'd always thought of Hat as living for a long long time. Oh! The blow will really hit me later on.'

Carry On credits: *Sergeant, Nurse, Teacher, Constable, Regardless, Cabby, Doctor, Camping, Again Doctor, Christmas '69, Loving, At Your Convenience, Matron, Abroad, Christmas '72, Dick, Laughing*: 'Orgy and Bess'

CARRY ON ABROAD (1972)

Publican Vic Flange (Sid James) always holidays abroad because his nagging wife, Cora (Joan Sims), doesn't like flying and has to stay and look after the pub. Unfortunately for Vic, twitching regular Harry (Jack Douglas) lets it slip that the package holiday he has booked to the Mediterranean island Els Bels also includes much-married saucepot Sadie Tompkins (Barbara Windsor) on the guest list. Suddenly Cora changes her mind and decides she wants to go on the trip. Stuart Farquhar (Kenneth Williams) is the representative of Wundatours and, with the help of employees Miss Dobbs (Patsy Rowlands) and Moira (Gail Grainger), welcomes the motley passengers. They include the hen-pecked Stanley Blunt (Kenneth Connor) and his bossy wife Evelyn (June Whitfield), a bowler-hatted mummy's boy, Eustace Tuttle (Charles Hawtrey), ebullient Scot Bert Conway (Jimmy Logan) and a monk with potential bad habits, Brother Bernard (Bernard Bresslaw). Unfortunately, the hotel they are to stay in isn't finished. Pepe (Peter Butterworth) desperately tries to run the place in a myriad of different guises and his wife, Floella (Hattie Jacques), struggles with the temperamental stove. Pepe is soon overrun with complaints, when Vic discovers Sadie naked in the shower, sand pours out of Moira's sink and the lavatory drenches Bert. Although agreeing to play leapfrog with Tuttle, bathing beauties Lily (Sally Geeson) and Marge (Carol Hawkins) have their eyes on other things. Marge takes a shine to Brother Bernard, while Lily lures the dashing Nicholas (David Kernan) away from his disgruntled companion, Robin (John Clive). While most of the party go off to the village and get arrested for causing a scene at the establishment of Madame Fifi (Olga Lowe), Evelyn is left behind and seduced by Pepe's son, Georgio (Ray Brooks). With the last-night bash swinging thanks to a local mixture that blesses the drinker with X-ray vision, the party goes with a bang as the hotel collapses. But alls well that ends well, when the holidaymakers reunite at Vic's pub.

With no new Christmas special, the 1969 Thames show was repeated on 20 December 1971. There was no holding back on a new film, however. A Carry On set within and around a British package holiday to sunnier climes had been touched upon during discussions surrounding *Carry On Camping* in the late 1960s. The subject arose again with Peter Rogers confirming in February 1972 that Talbot Rothwell was working on *Carry On Abroad* as the next film.

Peter Butterworth, who had missed the previous two films and not had a major role since Josh Fiddler in *Carry On Camping* four years earlier, took the bull by the horns and wrote to Peter Rogers, asking 'If there is anything I can play in the next Carry On I would love to do it. I was so very disappointed I couldn't make the last one because of that Italian job.' [Peter had been cast as Freddy, a member of Sid's gang in *Carry On Matron*. The role was subsequently played by Bill Maynard]. The letter certainly worked. He enjoyed three weeks work on *Carry On Abroad*.

A letter from Carol Hawkins also helped secure her a part in the film. Writing to Peter Rogers, on 6 March 1972 she explained that: 'as

I have recently completed the film *Please, Sir!* and the comedy TV series *The Fenn Street Gang* playing the part of Sharon, I thought perhaps you would like a photograph of myself to keep in your files for future casting reference.' Not only did Rogers employ her in his next two films; he also, on 11 May 1972, gave her a

financial contribution towards her special day: 'Please take your horses [for a horse-drawn carriage] out of this and use the rest for a wedding present from me.'

Also on 6 March 1972, Gerald Thomas approached assistant director David Bracknell in the 'hope there will be a spring Carry On. In fact I received a major portion of the script this morning. If all goes well we hope to start around 17 April and of course I would offer it to you before anybody else. Carry On non-smoking. I hope I am not going to have a miserable basket on the floor. If so, please buy a packet of

Opposite: Olga Lowe and her girls have had enough of Jimmy Logan, Sid James and Charles Hawtrey.

The daily progress report for 26 May 1972 – Charles Hawtrey's last day of Carrying On.

Hattie Jacques, as the frantic Floella, saw her role drastically cut because of health problems.

TITBITS

Barbara Windsor was committed to her stage role in *The Threepenny Opera* at the Piccadilly Theatre during the production, while Gail Grainger was appearing in *The Man Most Likely To* at the Duke of York's and was released from the film for Friday and Saturday matinees. At the time of the film's release, Kenneth Williams, June Whitfield, Carol Hawkins and Sally Geeson took part in a Christmas stills publicity session. Williams had been decidedly taken with the trio of glamour girls 'new' to the Carry Ons; although Carol had appeared in *Again Christmas* and Sally in *Regardless*, both were uncredited. Williams had written on 20 April that: 'I sat next to Gail Grainger on the bus coming out. I rather like her. She is a good actress and a sincere person with a willingness and a kind of humility which means you can make a suggestion and she will act on it. There is another girl called Carol who is sweet and a girl named Sally who is adorable. When you meet girls like these you understand why men fall in love with the opposite sex: they're gentler, kinder, and understanding about vulnerability.' Olga Lowe, cast as the Els Bels brothel-keeper, was an old friend of Sid James's from the Defence Force Entertainment Unit during the war. She was also with the actor during his last stage tour in *The Mating Season*. Note the film's technical advisor is credited as 'Sun Tan Lo Tion'!

ON LOCATION

The Slough location for the Wundatours office was filmed from outside the Bargain Centre, 65 High Street, on 20 April 1972. This was John Clive's first day on the film, Clive having inexplicably been absent from the closing reunion scene. The pre-production meeting on 12 April detailed that Pinewood's 'J' and 'K' stages would be used, while the studio lot would stand in for the island village and the exterior of the Palace Hotel would be built on the lot. A location trip to Gatwick airport was also arranged.

Sid James looks after the 'new girls', Sally Geeson and Carol Hawkins, on the Pinewood back lot.

Barbara Windsor is caught unawares in the shower!

Carol Hawkins as the saucy holiday-maker Madge.

Carol Hawkins (1949-)

Having provided glamorous support in *Zeta One* and Hammer's *When Dinosaurs Ruled the Earth* (both 1969), Carol replaced Penny Spencer as the sexy schoolgirl Sharon Eversleigh in the film version of the ITV sitcom *Please, Sir!* and went on to play the role on television in the spin-off series *The Fenn Street Gang*. On film, she played Terry Scott's daughter in *Bless This House*, tried to seduce Leigh Lawson in *Percy's Progress* and stripped in the street for *Not Now, Comrade*. Her television credits include *Porridge* ('No Way Out'), *Blake's 7* ('City at the Edge of the World') and *Trial and Retribution II*. An experienced farceur she has starred in West End and touring productions of Ray Cooney's *Run For Your Wife* and *Caught in the Net*.

Carry On credits: *Again Christmas, Abroad, Behind, Laughing*: 'And in My Lady's Chamber', 'Who Needs Kitchener?'

Woodbines. Love to the family.' Bracknell got the job.

Filming began on *Carry On Abroad* on 17 April 1972, with Sid James, Barbara Windsor, Joan Sims and Jack Douglas shooting the interior saloon-bar sequences on Pinewood's 'K' stage. The pub was identified as the Bull and Bush, but not referred to as such in the film. Almost the entire cast had been called and were on standby on the first day, as it was originally hoped they would shoot the reunion scene later that day. It was ultimately filmed the day after.

On 4 May 1972, Sid James was given a clean bill of health after five years of monitoring following his heart attack. The Central insurance office confirmed that 'after a series of restrictions in cover on this artist under-writers have agreed for the above production to grant full cover. It is to be hoped that this will be available for any future productions in which the artist appears. This, however, remains to be seen.'

Hattie Jacques, however, was restricted by health and weight concerns. Immediately after filming, it was noted that 'our insurers have now informed us that no cover whatsoever can be given in respect of the above for any future films while the existing provisions apply.' Originally with a major role written and a fifth billing position, Hattie's part was drastically trimmed back to just one week's work and she was demoted to eleventh billing.

Abroad saw Charles Hawtrey film his very last day of Carry On. A rather ignoble end, this

DOCTOR, DOCTOR!

During the filming of the village market-place siege, Kenneth Connor suffered an injury. The progress report for 27 April 1972 notes: '9.00 am Kenneth Connor arrived with swollen and bruised right elbow as a result of action on SL.136, shot at 4.16 pm Wednesday 26th April. He attended Wexham Hospital for X-ray. No bones broken, but elbow badly sprained. He resumed work.' While filming the collapsing hotel sequence, on 18 May, at 2.40 pm David Kernan slipped and grazed his back. He continued working after treatment.

The gang's all here – filming the hotel lobby sequence on Pinewood's 'K' Stage, May 1972.

Sally Geeson as Sally Abbott in the feature film version of *Bless This House*.

was the arrival of the coach along dirt roads filmed on location at Bagshot. Hawtrey's last line of Carry On – 'Oh, what a wonderful idea!' – was actually shot on his first day of filming.

For the first time in many years, there wouldn't be a second Carry On film in production in October. The production company wasn't idle, however; less than two months after *Carry On Abroad* had wrapped, they started another film: *Bless This House*.

The direct cost of *Carry On Abroad* was almost £205,000, of which £36,000 was spent on the actors' salaries. The final cut was ready on 24 November and premiered at the Metropole, Victoria, on 30 November. It went on general release around London on New Year's Eve 1972.

The enrolment of Jimmy Logan into the Carry On team had been a conscious effort to increase interest in Scotland. Indeed, a similar plan had seen Chic Murray briefly considered for the role of Sergeant Wilkins in *Carry On,*

Bless This House

At the behest of Philip Jones at Thames Television, Peter Rogers and Gerald Thomas delivered a feature-film version of the company's popular situation comedy in 1972. A farcical, frantic and faithful representative of the small-screen classic, it was given a Carry On makeover, with Peter Butterworth replacing Anthony Jackson as Sid James's neighbour and friend Trevor. Terry Scott and June Whitfield, before becoming a permanent domestic fixture on television, were cast as the new neighbours, and Carol Hawkins joined the cast, eventually becoming the newest member of the family during the wedding climax.

Sally Geeson (1950–)

A model and actress since childhood, Sally's early film credits include *Desert Mice*, *The Millionairess*, *The Pure Hell of St. Trinian's* and *The Young Ones*. She burst into the limelight as the female lead opposite Norman Wisdom in the 1969 comedy *What's Good For The Goose*. She played Christopher Lee's cheeky maid, Sally Baxter, in *The Oblong Box* for director Gordon Hessler, who also cast her as the ill-fated peasant girl in the Vincent Price horror *Cry of the Banshee* (1970). She guest-starred in *Man in a Suitcase* ('Day of Execution', 1967) and *Strange Report* ('Kidnap: Whose Pretty Girl Are You?', 1969). From 1971 until 1976, she would enjoy her biggest success as Sally, the daughter of Sid James in the hit ITV sitcom *Bless This House*.

Carry On credits: *Regardless, Abroad, Girls*

Jimmy Logan (1928-2001)

A legendary Scottish entertainer from a legendary family of entertainers, Jimmy started in showbusiness at the bottom. He sold programmes before working theatre lights at the age of eight, and started performing his cowboy act at the age of ten. He became an assistant manager at fifteen, played the accordion on stage, tackled juvenile leads and finally landed his own show at the Metropole Theatre, Glasgow, at the age of nineteen. By 1950 he had his own radio show, *It's All Yours*, and successfully broke into television across the border with his own sketch series for ATV. Simply entitled, *Jimmy Logan*, these were broadcast under the *Saturday Showtime* banner and scripted for him by Eric Sykes. Popular across the country, in Glasgow, he was idolised. He practically held court at the Alhambra Theatre, appearing in six-month runs of the revue *Five Past Eight* and four-month pantomime productions. He played to over 320,000 in just twenty-one weeks in 1957 and, that same year, was invited to perform before the Queen at the Royal Command Performance at the London Palladium. With a hit recording, 'Loganberry Pie', and a contemporary slant to his performance which now included his popular 'teddy boy' skit, he was still a true Scot at heart. Indeed, he revelled in recreating Harry Lauder's numbers. During filming, Gerald Thomas had released Logan to fulfil a commitment as host for a Dr Barnardo's charity cabaret at the Rose Ball, Glasgow, in front of Princess Margaret. He continued in variety, with the occasional foray into straight acting including a stint as Uncle Vanya in 1991.

Carry On credits: *Abroad, Girls*
Autobiography: *It's a Funny Life*

Constable. When *Carry On Abroad* was released, Logan was starring in pantomime at the King's Theatre, Edinburgh, and he was invited to the Scottish premiere at the Odeon, Glasgow: 'We rushed along and this huge cinema just had a couple of cleaners' lights and no sign of life anywhere. I banged on this side door and a fellow came out and I said, "Is the premiere on today?" and he said "Oh aye, come in Jimmy, the audience are all in." I said my piece to the audience, we sat down and a sign appeared on the screen explaining that since there would be no interval people should get their ice creams now! I went off to buy them and when I returned my friend was laughing his head off. He said, "I've never been to a premiere before, but you don't expect to see one of the stars queuing up for ice cream!"'

TRAILER

GCE Limited, fully aware that the series and its star was a national institution, suggested a novel idea for the trailer. 'For the opening of the *Carry On Abroad* trailer we would like to do a montage of cuts from previous Carry On films and then pick it up with a special shooting of Sid James as per the attached draft. This would then link onto the trailer proper for *Carry On Abroad*. Perhaps you would be kind enough to let me know how you feel about it (without being rude). 1. We open on a fairly rapid sequence of close-ups on Sid James. We see him in all his best known Carry On roles. 2. As his face continually changes we hear Sid's voice. (Ad libs on these lines). "That was in... Ee, you know... Gor! Remember that? Oh blimey! Oh no! Me life in moving pictures! Gordon Bennett!" (The number of roles is beginning to wear Sid down). 3. Suddenly the real Sid is on camera. Sid: 'No wonder me face is like a bit of crumpled bog-paper!' (Shot pulls out to reveal Sid as a tourist type). 'I don't know about you lot, but I think it's about time I went abroad.' 4. From out of frame, someone throws a hefty case to Sid. He pratfalls, hugging the case. Facing camera on the case *Carry On Abroad*. 5. Sid shrugs, accepts the inevitable, and camera tracks in to titles. 6. Title dissolves, bringing on first trailer scene.'

Right: Abandon hotel! Peter Butterworth panics as June Whitfield and Kenneth Connor adjust to their new surroundings.

Barbara Windsor MBE (1937-)

Born in Shoreditch in the East End of London to a dressmaker mother and a bus conductor father, Barbara trained at the Aida Foster school. She landed her first stage role in Foster's 1950 pantomime at the Golders Green Hippodrome. Later she was cast as one of the orphans in the musical *Love From Judy*, which opened in the West End's Saville Theatre in September 1952.

It was with that show's star, Johnny Brandon, that she made her first television appearances, on *Variety Parade* and *Dreamer's Highway*. She made her film debut, as a schoolgirl extra, in *The Belles of St. Trinian's* (1954). By 1957, she was performing at London's Winston's Club with Amanda Barrie and, two years later, was auditioned by Joan Littlewood for *Fings Ain't What They Used To Be* at the Theatre Royal, Stratford East, and was cast as Rosie. The show opened at the Garrick Theatre and ran for two and a half years.

As a result, Littlewood cast her opposite James Booth in the East End film comedy drama, *Sparrows Can't Sing* (1962). Pure cockney, the film caused headlines in America as the first British film that required subtitles! In 1961, Barbara had appeared in the BBC sitcom *The Rag Trade*. She returned for the third series, in 1963, as Reg Varney's girlfriend, Judy. She has been the definitive cockney 'sparrer' ever since.

After filming *Carry On Spying*, she starred on Broadway in Joan Littlewood's production of *Oh! What A Lovely War*. She returned to England to play Delphina in Lionel Bart's Sherwood Forest musical *Twang* in 1965, partnered with Bernard Bresslaw as Little John. In 1967, she appeared with Danny Le Rue in *Come Spy With Me* at the Whitehall Theatre.

Film roles included ill-fated young ladies in *Too Hot To Handle* (1960) and *A Study in Terror* (1965). During her return to the Carry Ons at Pinewood, she was offered a cameo role with

Arthur Mullard and Dick Van Dyke in *Chitty, Chitty, Bang, Bang* (1968). Later that year, she toured with Frankie Howerd in *The Wind in the Sassafras Trees* and starred as Millie in the sitcom *Wild, Wild Women* – 'like *The Rag Trade* but set at the turn of the century'. Television guest appearances included

Dad's Army ('Shooting Pains', 1968) and *Up Pompeii* ('Nymphia', 1970).

At the end of 1969, Ned Sherrin cast her as music hall legend Marie Lloyd in the musical he had co-written with Caryl Brahms, *Sing A Rude Song*. It opened at the Greenwich Theatre in February 1970. By the close of the year, she had been cast as Hortense, the saucy French maid, in Ken Russell's film version of the Sandy Wilson musical *The Boy Friend*. Starring Twiggy, it was shot on location at the Theatre Royal, Stratford East.

Notable stage credits included a two-month tour of the two-hander comedy *The Owl and the Pussycat* with Simon Oates, and Maria in *Twelfth Night* with the Chichester Festival Company. In 1982, she starred in a national tour of *Calamity Jane* and has enjoyed regular pantomime and summer season-credits, including *The Mating Season* (1989) in Blackpool, and the Fairy Godmother in *Cinderella* (1990) at the Wimbledon Theatre.

Cast as Peggy Mitchell in *EastEnders*, she has played the role on and off since 1994. Other television appearances include Myrtle in *You Rang, M'Lord?* ('Current Affairs' and 'Please Look After the Orphans', both 1991), Millicent in *One Foot in the Grave* ('The Affair of the Hollow Lady', 1995) and the first BBC *Hall of Fame* (2000).

Carry On credits: *Spying, Doctor, Camping, Again Doctor, Christmas '69, Henry, Again Christmas, Matron, Abroad, Christmas '72, Girls, London!, Christmas '73, Dick, Laughing:* 'The Prisoner of Spenda', 'The Baron Outlook', 'The Sobbing Cavalier', 'Orgy and Bess', 'The Nine Old Cobblers', 'And In My Lady's Chamber', 'Who Needs Kitchener?', 'Lamp-Posts of the Empire', *That's Carry On, Laughing's Christmas Classics*

Autobiographies: *Barbara – The Laughter and Tears of a Cockney Sparrow, All of Me – My Extraordinary Life*

CARRY ON CHRISTMAS (1972)

A rollicking Christmas feast at the Turnit Inn is enlivened by a roaring fire, a comely serving wench (Valerie Leon) and some tall tales introduced by the Club Chairman (Kenneth Connor). Lady Rhoda Cockhorse (Joan Sims) introduces the first gift-givers Adam (Jack Douglas) and Eve (Barbara Windsor) in the Garden of Eden. The aged General Ffingham Clodhopper (Kenneth Connor) is awoken from his slumbers to relate 'The Last Outpost', his experience when the natives revolted and peppered his dinner party with bullets. Thompson (Norman Rossington) determinedly continues to serve the food when cowardly Captain Alastair Dripping (Peter Butterworth) belatedly joins the company and woos the General's daughter (Barbara Windsor). A game girl, she decides that it's probably time to reverse her usual maxim of 'death before dishonour'. Back at the feast, Sir Francis Fiddler (Peter Butterworth) introduces a selection of Elizabethan madrigals before 'The Sailor's Story'. Esmeralda (Joan Sims) and Harriet (Hattie Jacques) stitch in a spooky house as the butler, Ringworm (Jack Douglas), makes the tea and wrecks the kitchen. Lt Banghem (Kenneth Connor) and Lt Trembler (Peter Butterworth) are unexpected guests but, revealing himself as Inspector Knicker, Banghem reveals Ringworm is none other than Charles Burke the body snatcher! Knicker's reward is a quick fumble with the saucy maid (Barbara Windsor). Finally, Miss Molly Coddle (Hattie Jacques) introduces the pantomime, Aladdin, with the Fairy Godmother (Hattie Jacques) overseeing the rhyming couplets as Hanky Poo (Kenneth Connor), Widow Hole in One (Peter Butterworth) and the well-endowed Aladdin (Barbara Windsor) go through the motions.

A rich mixture of mirth: members of the *Carry On* gang. Under the head-dress of holly is Jack Douglas and that's Charles Hawtrey, centre. Peter Butterworth grins down on Kenneth Connor. And the girls, from left to right: Joan Sims, Hattie Jacques and Barbara Windsor.

Charles Hawtrey was dropped from the show so late in the day that the actor was erroneously credited in the *TV Times* for the 20 December 1972 broadcast.

As filming was coming to an end on *Carry On Abroad*, agent and promoter Michael Sullivan was instigating a television Christmas special for later in the year. Confirming the deal with Peter Rogers, Sullivan noted 'that you have appointed me your agent to negotiate with Philip Jones in respect of this year's Carry On presentation for television ... I also confirm I have arranged a meeting with Prince Littler for Wednesday next to discuss the proposals of a Carry On pantomime presented by yourself at the London Palladium for the season of 1973/74.' Sadly, the very appealing idea of a Carry On pantomime for the stage never came to fruition, but Michael Sullivan did strike a deal with Philip Jones, Head of Light Entertainment at Thames television.

Clearly losing interest in the television project, Rogers pencilled a note suggesting that they cancel the Christmas show. He considered it an overkill threat to the Carry On franchise: 'I can't accept either offer suggested by Philip Jones for a Christmas Carry On. I would prefer to forget the whole thing.' This was a short-lived reaction however. By 17 July, Rogers was mapping out what he didn't want for the show, writing to Sullivan that: 'I wondered if you were going to write and confirm details of our deal with Thames Television regarding *Carry on Christmas*. I particularly do not want Frankie Howerd in the cast.'

Why Frankie Howerd was not wanted for the show is inexplicable. Ironically, the comedian could have proved very useful as, unbeknown to Peter Rogers, the much-needed element of camp was severely threatened. Kenneth Williams was as reluctant as ever to tackle a television Carry On, and was committed to his stage hit *My Fat Friend*. Charles Hawtrey was signed up for the show, but then the old question of billing was raised. Peter Rogers and Gerald Thomas were adamant that Hattie Jacques was to be awarded top billing on the show. Charles Hawtrey considered it his right and that seemed a reasonable assumption on his part, since Williams, Sid James, Frankie Howerd and Terry Scott, the only regulars to be billed above Hawtrey, were all out of the show. Barbara Windsor recalls: 'Charlie threw a moody. He went off to Bourne & Hollingsworth to have something to eat and he said "If they want to talk to me I'll be having Brown Windsor at the restaurant!"' Gerald Thomas telephoned the department store restaurant and gave Hawtrey an ultimatum: accept second billing or nothing. Hawtrey refused second billing and hung up. Barbara laments that: 'Charles let Gerald Thomas down badly just two days before filming and so he was never used again, which was a great shame because he was my favourite actor in the team.'

During the pantomime season, numerous Carry On regulars were already committed to stage activities across the country. Thomas restructured Hawtrey's roles for Brian Oulton, returning to the series for the first time since *Carry On Camping*, and Norman Rossington, who hadn't been with the gang since *Carry On Regardless* in 1961. Hawtrey's absence also allowed Jack Douglas to grab more roles than originally intended. Hattie Jacques's contribution was fairly restricted. If anything, Kenneth Connor had the greatest claim to star billing.

Ironically it wasn't Hawtrey but Williams who was missed by Stanley Reynolds in his review of the show in *The Times*. Celebrating Rothwell and Freeman's 'monstrously vulgar wit', he wrote that 'without Kenneth Williams the magic was not quite there for me, a Carry On is not a carry on without the nasal Williams mincing tall.' But 'Barbara Windsor busting out of her shirt front as Aladdin, coming striding in to the rolling goggle eyes of Norman Rossington who says: "Well, you've got to have boobs in any show", was for me a hilarious comic moment. By that time I was actually laughing out loud and Christmas seemed to be getting started on television.'

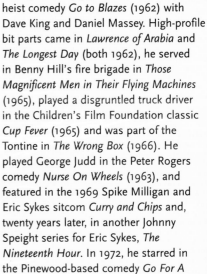

Norman Rossington reports for duty in *Those Magnificent Men in Their Flying Machines* (1965).

Norman Rossington (1928-1999)

Solid, stocky and totally reliable character actor with a skill for accents; he was at his most relaxed in his native Liverpudlian. Historically Norman was the only actor to work with both the Beatles and Elvis Presley on film. He was memorably exasperated as the Fab Four's manager in Richard Lester's influential *A Hard Day's Night* (1964) and supported the King in *Double Trouble* (1966). Trained at the Bristol Old Vic, he became an instant star as the work-shy Private 'Cupcake' Cook in *The Army Game*. Early films included *Three Men in a Boat* (1956, memorably as the young lover who tows his girl's mother behind them) and *Doctor in Love* (1960). He starred opposite Albert Finney in *Saturday Night and Sunday Morning* (1960) and revelled in the heist comedy *Go to Blazes* (1962) with Dave King and Daniel Massey. High-profile bit parts came in *Lawrence of Arabia* and *The Longest Day* (both 1962), he served in Benny Hill's fire brigade in *Those Magnificent Men in Their Flying Machines* (1965), played a disgruntled truck driver in the Children's Film Foundation classic *Cup Fever* (1965) and was part of the Tontine in *The Wrong Box* (1966). He played George Judd in the Peter Rogers comedy *Nurse On Wheels* (1963), and featured in the 1969 Spike Milligan and Eric Sykes sitcom *Curry and Chips* and, twenty years later, in another Johnny Speight series for Eric Sykes, *The Nineteenth Hour*. In 1972, he starred in the Pinewood-based comedy *Go For A Take* with Reg Varney, and was unforgettably brittle in the London underground horror, *Death Line*. He made sporadic film appearances thereafter, notably with Peter Sellers in *The Prisoner of Zenda* (1979), as the mysterious train stationmaster in *House of the Long Shadows* (1983) and a shopkeeper in *The Krays* (1991). He was prolific on the stage and was appearing in the West End run of *Beauty and the Beast* at the time of his death.

Carry On credits: *Sergeant, Nurse, Regardless, Christmas '72*

CARRY ON GIRLS (1973)

The seaside town of Fircombe is facing a crisis – it's always raining and there's nothing for the tourists to do. So Councillor Sidney Fiddler (Sid James) hits on the notion of holding a beauty contest. The Mayor, Frederick Bumble (Kenneth Connor), is taken with the idea, but feminist councillor Augusta Prodworthy (June Whitfield) is outraged. She storms out of the meeting in disgust. The motion is carried in Augusta's absence and Sid contacts publicist Peter Potter (Bernard Bresslaw) to help with the organisation. Sid's girlfriend, Connie Philpotts (Joan Sims), runs a hotel and soon her residents, including the eccentric Mrs Dukes (Joan Hickson) and the Admiral (Peter Butterworth) are outnumbered by dolly birds, including the feuding biker babe Hope Springs (Barbara Windsor) and the bountiful Dawn Brakes (Margaret Nolan). A fight orchestrated by Hope provides better newspaper copy than bringing a donkey off the beach which, despite the bucket and spade of hotel employee William (Jack Douglas), ruins the plush carpets! Press photographer Larry (Robin Askwith) happily snaps the Mayor losing his trousers at a most awkward moment and nervously gulps his way through a nude session with Dawn. Eventually, the Mayor's wife, Mildred (Patsy Rowlands), joins Prodworthy's bra-burning movement and plots the downfall of the Miss Fircombe contest on the pier. Peter Potter reluctantly becomes a man in a frock for another publicity gimmick for the television show, Women's Things, *for producer Cecil Gaybody (Jimmy Logan) and researcher Debra (Sally Geeson). Prodworthy and butch feminist Rosemary (Patricia Franklin) call in the police (David Lodge and Billy Cornelius) but Peter's girlfriend, Paula (Valerie Leon), steps into the breach as the mystery girl.*

While the rest of the country was already laughing at *Carry On Abroad*, it was noted, on 10 January 1973, that the film had finally been passed in Eire with an 'under 16 restriction' placed upon it. Times were indeed getting saucier and nowhere more so than within the Carry On series, when Talbot Rothwell was commissioned to write a film centred on a seedy beauty contest.

The draft ending was a dramatic and exciting chase sequence in which Mayor Firkin (the original name for Kenneth Connor's authority figure) embarks in a small car and, en route, hilariously loses his trousers for the umpteenth time in the film. Sid and his beauty queen would depart the scene with a 'Just Married' sign on the back of their vehicle upon which, 'between the words of which Hope [Barbara Windsor] has scrawled the words "about to be".' The notion of impending wedded bliss was dropped in favour of Sid's 'Not bloody likely!' reaction to the sign urging them to return to the seaside town. With an understanding of the budgetary limitations, Rothwell conceded that his initial draft script might be a tad ambitious.

He wrote to Rogers that: 'I would like to discuss this with you before outlining it in detail as you may consider it impractical or unnecessary.' The producer did.

Although there wasn't quite the fanfare that had greeted *Carry On Henry*'s 'coming of age' for the series, the pre-production meeting of 10 April 1973 did conclude with: 'there being no other business to discuss the meeting terminated with those present wishing the production company every success with their twenty-fifth Carry On production.'

The six-week shooting schedule began on location in Brighton, on 16 April. Thirty years before it was ravaged by fire and the elements, the historic, Grade I listed West Pier was already in a dangerous state of repair. At the pre-production meeting, 'special note was made of the fact that the pier is in a dangerous condition and no member of the unit is to pass beyond the Pavilion.' Brighton filming was completed in three days. The West Pier go-karting was filmed on 16 April with exteriors of Clarges Hotel shot the following day.

Casting hadn't proved a smooth affair however. Renee Houston, who had last graced the series as Kenneth Cope's uncouth mother in *Carry On At Your Convenience*, was originally contracted for the role of dotty Mrs Dukes. Her contract was cancelled for health reasons and Joan Hickson returned to the series. Bill Maynard, who had filmed contributions for the previous five films, was cast as the no-nonsense police inspector. Although he had begged his agent, Richard Stone, to accept any film

assignment, the actor proclaims that: 'The Carry On movies have become the strangest cult I have ever been involved with, although, quite frankly, I thought most of them were awful.' Maynard was offered a lucrative television assignment that clashed with the filming schedule, so David Lodge, out of the series since *Carry On Regardless* in 1961, was cast in his stead.

Robin Askwith joined the cast as a nervous photographer by the name of Larry. Destined to have the best-known bum in the British film industry, thanks to his starring roles in the Confessions films, Askwith had just worked for Gerald Thomas on the *Bless This House* film: '[He] told me at the end of film party that I

Opposite: Margaret Nolan feels a perfect ass on set.

Angela Grant, Laraine Humphreys and Barbara Windsor put on the style as an awkward Bernard Bresslaw finds it hard to turn away. The scene was filmed back stage at Pinewood's ballroom.

An irresistible wink from Sidney James as *Film Review* promotes the latest film with glamour girls Barbara Windsor, Valerie Leon and Margaret Nolan.

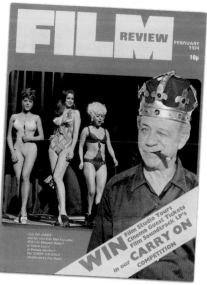

ON LOCATION

As well as Brighton, the unit filmed in the extremely local location of the boardroom at Pinewood Studios, which stood in for the Council Committee Room on 14 May. The previous day, Committee Room scenes were filmed on 'C' Stage and featured Arnold Ridley, beloved as Private Godfrey in *Dad's Army*. Fellow *Dad's Army* actor Bill Pertwee appeared on location in Slough and Windsor, at the Slough Fire Station, Tuns Lane, on 17 May. On 15 May, The unit filmed the tube train debacle with Valerie Leon and Michael Nightingale on the studio lot and decamped to Marylebone station to film the train-boarding scene with Bernard Bresslaw, Margaret Nolan and Valerie Leon. The Slough Town Hall on the Bath Road was used for the exterior of the Fircombe council offices.

Sid James has fun on location in Brighton, April 1973.

would be offered a part in the next Carry On film. *Carry On Girls* was like a continuation of *Bless This House*. Exactly the same unit, exactly the same location and virtually the same cast. Richard O'Sullivan would wend his way down to the studios in the evenings and we would laugh until closing time. Gerald Thomas was also extremely encouraging and by the end of the film my part had increased somewhat. "Cor, your bleedin' part is getting bigger and bigger darlin'," screamed Barbara Windsor.'

Jimmy Logan, signed up for the showy guest part of mincing Cecil Gaybody, was happy to

return to the series but 'I didn't quite get the character right. I know what I was trying for, a sort of cross between Charlie Hawtrey and Terry Scott's schoolboy character, but it turned out to be one of my most embarrassing performances.' Charles Hawtrey, although not approached for the role, was keen to get back to the Carry Ons and, as Peter Rogers explained, 'No one is dropped from the Carry Ons forever!' The role of Gaybody was certainly tailor made for Hawtrey, as is shown by this original exchange, altered in the final film:

> *Gaybody*: I do women's things.
> *Sid*: You could have fooled me.

Prominent amongst the decorative beauties in the film is Angela Grant, who had been decorative before in *Follow That Camel, Carry On...Up the Khyber* and *Doctor in Trouble*; they 'didn't require much acting', she remembers. Her route into film was typical: 'I became a model at the age of fifteen, I was very keen to enter the world of glamour and my mother was a fashion buyer for Marshall's at the time. I took a course with Michael Whittaker and walked my way through the show until I was about seventeen and a half and suddenly found myself in the movies. I had more to do in *Carry On Girls* with all that itching powder and the women's lib movement. Talk about the glamour of showbusiness!'

Valerie Leon reveals herself as the real 'Miss Potter' in front of Bernard Bresslaw, Sid James and Joan Sims.

DOCTOR, DOCTOR!

On 26 April, Joan Sims slipped and fell when leaving her dressing room to return to work at 2.00 pm. No injury was sustained apart from slight bruising and, with no irony at all, the progress report reveals that 'Miss Sims carried on working.'

Sid James pulls some birds at Pinewood Studios.

All the glamour girls and a more relaxed attitude to nearer the knuckle innuendo created a lot of headaches for the censors. Stephen Murphy, the new Secretary of the BBFC, wrote to Gerald Thomas with an extensive list of required cuts. Thomas responded on 13 July: 'The dialogue you object to, "You lecherous sod", is, in point of fact, as I explained "You lecherous so and so". We have checked this again on the moviola and I can assure you this is what Joan Sims actually said. Reel 4: I am resubmitting this reel to you for your reconsideration because Peter and I both feel that there is really nothing objectionable in the fight sequence between Barbara Windsor and Margaret Nolan, when Barbara attempts to get her bikini back, but does not actually do so. I am sure you will find this acceptable for an A category. With other cuts agreed, Murphy

Patsy Rowlands joins the bra-burning movement in this uplifting publicity pose.

TITBITS

Honda provided a Hunda ST70 Funbike free of charge for Barbara Windsor to ride. Unfortunately, she couldn't handle the complicated scenes so a very butch Nick Hobbs doubled for her in the hotel exterior scenes and the initial getaway from the West Pier. Dubbing editor Martin Evans got out of jury service to fulfil his contract for the film, thanks to an excuse letter from production manager Roy Goodard. Dubbing work involved June Whitfield inexplicably voicing the character of Paula Perkins, as played by Valerie Leon.

Joan Hickson (1906-1998)

A national treasure amongst character players, Joan Hickson found lasting fame and critical plaudits on television with her incisive performance as Agatha Christie's spinster detective, Miss Marple. Ironically, her tail-end fame seemed to overshadow her past achievements, a stage and film career of sixty years standing. Trained at the Royal Academy of Dramatic Art, she made her professional debut in 1927 and broke into film in the early 1930s, making an early mark as the typically 'plain Jane' Effie Brickman brought out of her shell by Roland Young, *The Man Who Could Work Miracles* (1936). An indispensable part of the backcloth of British cinema, she was often called upon for a brief turn as a charlady or nosy neighbour or disgruntled barmaid, although the Boulting brothers gave her stronger meat as Richard Attenborough's mother in *The Guinea Pig* (1948). She became part of the Betty Box and Peter Rogers pool of talent, with appearances in *Marry Me!* (1949), *Doctor in the House* (1954), *Please Turn Over* (1959), *The 39 Steps* (1959) and *Raising the Wind* (1961). In 1955 she excelled as the myopic Lady Emily Cranfield in the Frankie Howerd comedy *Jumping For Joy*. In the 1970s, her roles included Arthur Lowe's wife; who finds his decapitated head in *Theatre of Blood* (1973), and John Le Mesurier's wife, who finds Robin Askwith wooing their daughter, Linda Hayden, in *Confessions of a Window Cleaner* (1974). On stage, she played the mother in *A Day in the Death of Joe Egg*, Madame Acarti in *Blithe Spirit* in 1976 and won a Tony for *Bedroom Farce* in 1977. When Hickson played Miss Pryce in a 1946 stage production of *Appointment with Death*, Agatha Christie wrote: 'I hope you will play my dear Miss Marple.' A near brush came in 1961 when she played an aggressive and ill-fated home help in the Margaret Rutherford film *Murder, She Said!* In 1980, Hickson played Mrs Rivington in *Why Didn't They Ask Evans?* and, finally, in 1984 landed the title role in the BBC *Miss Marple* production *The Body in the Library*. She would play the role in a further eleven television adaptations, sold worldwide, ending with *The Mirror Crack'd* in 1992.

Carry On credits: *Nurse, Constable, Regardless, Loving, Girls*

put out that the advertising of *Carry On Girls* does not carry your caricature. This is not an omission but the obvious decision of the distributors bearing in mind, presumably, that you have only been in three of the films and only this last one is anything like a sizeable part ... But this I can tell you without fear of contradiction – you're bloody good in the film and I'm very happy that you "happened along" and I look forward to the next film with you.' By the time of this missive, Jack's visage was already gracing the poster for the latest Carry On wheeze; an all-singing, all-dancing stage revue in the West End.

June Whitfield radios the BBC that she should be free to start filming Happy Ever After once she has completed her role.

slightly relented about the cat-fight: 'I think we would settle for this if you could get rid of the very close shots of the bikini bottoms. Thomas, reluctantly, agreed.

The billing was never set in stone either. The poster and all paid advertising was to have bunched the glamour girls under the banner of 'Beauty Contestants' while the original roll-call of stars was to have been Sid James, Joan Sims, June Whitfield, Barbara Windsor, Bernard Bresslaw and Kenneth Connor. Windsor was elevated to second billing, while guest Whitfield was moved to sixth.

Although billed on the poster, Jack Douglas was distressed, and on 8 November Rogers reassured him. 'I am sorry that you feel rather

Patsy Rowlands (1934-2005)

Educated through several convent schools, Patsy had no particular ambition in life until her parents arranged for her to take elocution lessons. Greatly encouraged by her teacher, at the age of fifteen she won a scholarship to the Guildhall School of Speech and Drama. She graduated with the top marks across the United Kingdom.

She made her stage debut, in the chorus, of a touring production of the musical *Annie Get Your Gun*, in 1951. Patsy then joined the Players theatre company, singing traditional music-hall numbers and appearing in their experimental pantomime seasons. In 1958, actor and director Vida Hope cast her as Thetis Cooke in Sandy Wilson's musical adaptation of the Ronald Firbank novel *Valmouth*. Patsy's mischievous performance, as a simple country girl longing for the return of her sailor boy sweetheart, won critical acclaim. Her show-stopping number, 'I Loved A Man', allowed her some wickedly funny business with a fish. Indeed, at the close of the number, she would be flat on her back with the fish between her toes! The production transferred to the Saville Theatre in 1959; marking Patsy's West End debut.

She was a vibrant part of the 'new wave' theatre, relishing her favourite role as Sylvia Groomkirby in

N F Simpson's surreal comedy *One Way Pendulum* (1959), and playing Avril Hadfield opposite Laurence Olivier in Tony Richardson's production of David Turner's *Semi-Detached* (1962).

She made her film debut in *On the Fiddle* (1961) and followed it with a supporting role as June Ritchie's friend in John Schlesinger's *A Kind of Loving* (1962) and Norman Wisdom's 'fantasy' operating assistant in *A Stitch in Time* (1963). Tony Richardson cast her as Honor, a saucy young miss in his Oscar-laden film classic *Tom Jones* (1963). She would later appear in

Richardson's equally bawdy romp *Joseph Andrews* (1977).

But it was another champion of her talents, Sid James, who helped her land the role of neighbour Betty in the Thames sitcom *Bless This House*. An irregular fixture of the show throughout its run, Patsy also reprised her role for the feature-film version in 1972. She starred as Mrs Evans with Stratford Johns in *The Galton and Simpson Comedy* ('An Extra Bunch of Daffodils', 1969), while guest starring in sitcoms from *George and Mildred* ('The Twenty-Six Year Itch', 1979) to *Bottom* ('Parade', 1992). In 1980, she played Mrs Body in the classic detective show *Cribb* ('Abracadaver') and went on to star opposite Thora Hird in the Salvation Army series *Hallelujah!* (1981).

On stage, she appeared in Lindsay Anderson's 1975 production of *The Seagull*. She played Netta Kinvig in Nigel Kneale's science fiction comedy *Kinvig* (1981), Flossie Nightingale in the repertory company comedy *Rep* (1982) and landed one of her favourite television assignments, as Thelma, in *Emery Presents... Legacy of Murder* (1982), with Dick Emery and Barry Evans. She featured in the Ray Galton and John Antrobus comedy *Get Well Soon* (1997) and gave memorable character studies in BBC costume dramas *Vanity Fair* (1998) and *The Cazalets* (2001). Her later stage appearances included the housekeeper in *Oliver!* at the London Palladium, Mrs Potts in *Beauty and the Beast* at the Criterion and Mrs Pearce in the 2002 revival of *My Fair Lady* at the National Theatre.

Carry On credits: *Again Doctor, Loving, Henry, At Your Convenience, Matron, Abroad, Girls, Dick, Laughing:* 'The Nine Old Cobblers', *Behind*

CARRY ON LONDON! (1973-1974)

A rousing revue which kicked off with the instrumental 'What A Carry On!!!' before the stars, Sid James, Barbara Windsor, Kenneth Connor, Bernard Bresslaw, Jack Douglas and Peter Butterworth, took up residence with the dancing girls and boys for 'Round-About Victoria!!!' Dr McAndrew (Sid James) operated on a terrified patient (Jack Douglas) as Dr Ram (Kenneth Connor) and Matron (Bernard Bresslaw) aided and abetted, while the evening went historical with the principals singing Elizabethan madrigals and Miss Barbara Windsor shining in 'Curtain Time' at the Royal Standard Music Hall. After a spot of 'Carry On Loving!' with Trudi Van Doorn, the second-half comedy programme started with 'Be Prepared!' Sexy young things Barbara (Windsor, of course) and Ethel (would you believe, Peter Butterworth) are spotted by the randy scoutmaster (Sid James) and his boy scouts Babcock, Muggeridge and Pennimore (Bernard Bresslaw, Jack Douglas and Kenneth Connor). Caesar (Sid James) takes a fancy to Cleo (Barbara Windsor) in the 'Cleopatra's Boudoir' sketch, much to the displeasure of Mark Antony (Kenneth Connor) and Titus Atticus, Captain of the Guard (Jack Douglas). Abdul, a hefty, dusky eunuch (Bernard Bresslaw) and High Priest Grabatiti (Peter Butterworth) also joined the fun before the gang became themselves again for the closing number.

lthough the possibility of a Carry On pantomime at the London Palladium for the end of 1973 came to naught, the inspired notion of a Carry On stage show didn't go away.

During the pre-production of *Carry On Girls* in September 1972, wheels had been set in motion between Peter Rogers, theatrical impresario Louis Benjamin and theatre-owners Moss Empires Limited. The Palladium connection was retained with Albert Knight, producer of some of the theatre's most successful pantomimes, appointed to stage the show. A collection of old jokes, music hall turns and big production numbers, *Carry On London!* was set to take over the Victoria Palace, of which Benjamin was the managing director.

Sid James, Kenneth Connor and Jack Douglas all agreed to appear in the show, and Peter Rogers appointed their agent Michael Sullivan as his representative. However, fellow stars of the upcoming *Carry On Girls* proved reluctant. Bernard Bresslaw's agent held out for second billing after Sid James, but eventually accepted the billing offered.

Barbara Windsor was also reluctant to take part. En route to the Brighton location for the first day's filming of *Carry On Girls*, Sid James shared a car with Windsor: 'Sid said, "I know what I was going to say to you, Barbara. This show, *Carry On London!* I've only just heard you won't do it." "That's true. It's not right for me." "Why's that, then?" "Well, I'm doing OK as I am," I said. "I'm doing films, theatre, a bit of telly. I don't want to do the Carry On girl on stage. The theatre's too special to me to play that character there."' By the end of the journey, however, a very persuasive Sid had coaxed Barbara to talk to her agent, Richard Stone, and accept the stage assignment.

The original casting suggestions for the show utilised the six team members who did appear, along with three others. Joan Sims was approached but declined due to her dislike of theatre work. June Whitfield, committed to the new film, was also shortlisted. Her agent explained that she continually turned down theatrical engagements for June because of her 'domestic' commitments, but that June had been 'very, very tempted' by the Carry On stage show. 'It was the fact that the performance would be twice nightly that finally helped her to reach a negative decision.'

The most surprising casting suggestion of all was Charles Hawtrey. Even after the *Carry On Christmas* situation, he was included on the proposed cast list for the stage show but, although he would remain active in summer season and pantomime roles until 1979, his reaction to the Carry On stage offer is unrecorded.

The show was officially launched at a Victoria Palace press junket on 18 July 1973. Barbara Windsor, Jack Douglas, Bernard Bresslaw and singer Trudi Van Doorn were on hand to talk to the media while Sid James stood by in New Zealand to speak to reporters via telephone. When Sid returned from his tour in *The Mating Season*, he had 'something missing' according to Barbara Windsor. When he entered the upstairs room at the Palladium for rehearsals, he 'greeted everybody warmly [but] he had no enthusiasm, and didn't seem to care.' Michael Sullivan revealed that the initial Crazy Gang concept had been elbowed in favour of a revue show highlighting exotic continental acts and, in Barbara Windsor's opinion, 'We were just a warm-up act for them.' Indeed, although the production was billed as 'the costliest in England' with a costume budget of over £50,000, Barbara Windsor felt 'as if I'd been forgotten'. Jack Douglas's brother, Bill Roberton, was directing the show and seemed to have formed an alliance with Sullivan concerning the format.

The team opened in a three-week try-out season of *Carry On London!* at the Birmingham Hippodrome from 14 September: 'The audience reaction was everything we thought it would be,'

says Barbara Windsor. 'We took our bows to polite, lukewarm applause. No actor ever likes that, of course, but since I was well aware that I could have phoned in my performance, personally, I felt it was all we deserved.' During this Birmingham run, the show was fleshed out and improved upon by the cast and co-writer Dave Freeman. Although the theatre programme only credits Freeman for the Elizabethan Madrigals section which was lifted from his own *Carry On Christmas* television show from 1972, the writer recalled that: 'Talbot Rothwell was supposed to be writing all the comedy sketches but, as with the Christmas show the previous year, he became ill and couldn't finish it. Sid James liked my material and was pleased when I was asked to write for the show. The King Henry madrigal was one of his favourites. Eric Merriman and I were called in and I went to Birmingham to see the try-out. I

Top comics like Morecambe and Wise, Michael Bentine and Dick Emery were invited to the opening night in the West End.

Scoutmaster Sid James gets his woggle in a twist with Siren of the Nile, Barbara Windsor.

DOCTOR, DOCTOR!

Cast as Britannia for the Conservative 'Get Britain Back to Work' campaign, Barbara Windsor was weighed down with a breastplate, steel helmet, trident and a union flag. After an hour of waiting, in costume, the photographer was ready for action, whereupon Barbara tripped and injured her back. Rallying round for the two performances of *Carry On London!* that evening, Barbara was told to rest and was out of the show for three weeks. Anita Kay stepped in to the breach. On Barbara's return: 'Sid and Peter Rogers had bought the entire stock of a flower stall outside the theatre and had wheeled it in by the barrowload.' Later, 'bad vocal chords' saw Barbara out of the show again. Having spent £100 on flowers, Rogers was less than impressed, although he handpicked Janet Mahoney as her replacement. Another Richard Stone client, Mahoney had appeared as Gay, the 'flatmate' in *Carry On Loving*, and was considered a good substitute for Windsor in both the sketches and the musical numbers. In the end, Windsor returned to the show with Rogers complaining to Benjamin on 28 February 1974 that: 'If *Carry On London!* survives, it will be against more odds than have ever been ranged against any production – strikes, three day week, fuel cuts, Barbara Windsor and Richard Stone.'

It was suggested that Jack Douglas pose as a street cleaner and Peter Butterworth as a street musician when the first night and a television presentation of *Carry On London!* coincided in October 1973. The television show was originally entitled 'Carry On Tonight' and was to have been presented by *Carry On, Constable* actor Robin Ray before Shaw Taylor landed the job.

remember sitting up with Bill Roberton half the night trying to rewrite the opening sketch, which didn't work. The old gang was just a fill-in really and our sketches just appeared without any fanfare. I think Jack Douglas suggested some sort of old-time music hall routine and I wrote some extra lines to bridge the songs with the comedy.'

Jack's idea reflected the pre-destined residency at the Victoria Palace, for the comic knew that between 1863 and 1910 the historic Royal Standard Music Hall had stood on the same spot. This gave the show a rousing climax to the first half.

Barbara Windsor recalls 'a sketch in which I played Cleopatra to Sid's Caesar' that began as four male dancers carried me on and rolled me out on stage à la Eartha Kitt'. This routine also resurrected memories of the original *Carry On Cleo*, Amanda Barrie, unfurled by Sosages as played by Tom Clegg.

'The show was much better than it had been',

reflects Dave Freeman, 'but wasn't as good as it could have been either. The opening sketch we had slaved over in Birmingham was cut when the show opened in London. It wasn't the happiest show I ever worked on. There was an undercurrent of squabbling over the material.'

The show opened at the Victoria Palace on 4 October 1973 and, Barbara Windsor relates, the critics 'were disappointed and picked up on the faults we knew were still there, but we didn't get panned.' That same evening, the ITV network broadcast an edited highlights package from the show's Birmingham run, *What A Carry On!*

Peter Rogers, in attendance again on the second night, noted: 'We saw the whole show and the place was packed. But it seemed that only the ladies (middle-aged) were laughing. And this has been my experience in films. It is the ladies who enjoy the dirty jokes and innuendo.' Indeed, Rogers overheard one customer complaining to her friend that she thought the show would have been more 'cheeky!'

Having seen the show three times in one week, Rogers subsequently pondered, 'What on earth would we do if Barbara Windsor had to stay away?'

But the audience certainly seemed to enjoy themselves. And for one star, it was a learning curve. Jack Douglas recalls: 'Sid James was a great actor but not a great comedian, which surprised me at first. Kenny Connor and I would ad lib material and Sid would stare at me with a blank expression on his face. After the show he said, "Jackson, don't ever do that again!" "What?" "Ad lib!" "You're joking!" "No, I know my lines and can do it the same every night but if you throw me something I don't know, I'm finished." I promised, it wouldn't happen again.'

Appearing alongside the plucky spirit of Barbara Windsor, Jack Douglas found his talent to ad lib came in useful on one December night: 'I looked up to see that the safety curtain was descending on our performance. It's scary when you consider these curtains actually weigh about

ten tons. "Um, Barbara. Step forward, will you?" I said. "What are you doing, Jack?" asked a confused Barbara, realising this impromptu man-handling wasn't in the script. "You don't want to end up like a fly, do you?" "What!" "Squashed!" I said, pointing up at the curtain's menacing progress towards us. "I'm afraid that the safety curtain seems to be suffering from a bad case of stage fright," I told them. "So, Barbara and I will be keeping you amused for the next twenty minutes or so, while it tries to pull itself together." I got a round of applause, not for the groan-inducing joke, but because I'd told them the truth and they appreciated the fact that we'd have to ad lib for a while.' The safety curtain, being controlled hydraulically by water pressure, had reacted to the River Thames running at a third of its usual capacity and started to descend.

Jack was, seemingly, instrumental in bringing Sid James closer to his leading lady: 'That was my fault!' Jack admits. 'The Pete Murray show, *Open House*, wanted to interview us all. It was a live broadcast, from the Victoria Palace, and we had to be on-air at 9.30 in the morning. I protested to Peter Rogers that some of us had to travel in from out of town and very early for this and he agreed. We were all put up overnight in a London hotel. Sid and Barbara were thrown together and what happened, happened.'

Dave Freeman also recalls Barbara Windsor's husband, Ronnie Knight, 'ranting at me about

Sid and her having an affair. I tried to calm him down, "Oh come on, look at him!" sort of thing, but we all knew about it. Sid was a very attractive and gentle man.' Jack Douglas concurs, 'People used to laugh at me, but Sid James was a sex symbol. The women loved him.'

Carry On London! proved a financial albatross. Dave Freeman remembers: 'It was losing money all the time but the Victoria Palace stuck with it

Valerie Leon (1945-)

A stunning and statuesque model and leading lady who enhanced British cinemas' three most successful threads of popular culture. As well as seven Carry On credits, she appeared opposite the James Bonds of Roger Moore (*The Spy Who Loved Me*, 1977) and Sean Connery (*Never Say Never Again*, 1983), and starred in the Hammer horror *Blood From the Mummy's Tomb* (1971). Adding decoration to *The Italian Job* (1969), as the Royal Lancaster Hotel receptionist, and *Zeta One* (1969), as a bizarre leather-clad alien, she landed a singing role in the 1970 television show, *The Man Who Had Power Over Women*. Invaluable as a comic support, she posed with Charlie Drake on his greatest hits album, *Hello My Darlings*, joined forces with Margaret Nolan as a scantily-clad attraction in *No Sex, Please – We're British* (1971) and bewitched Peter Sellers in *The Revenge of the Pink Panther* (1978). Perhaps her most celebrated role was as the domineering Hi Karate aftershave girl in a string of adverts during the 1970s. She was so identified with the part that she parodied it on stage in pantomime and in a guest spot in *The Goodies* ('It Might as Well be String', 1976). Other notable television guest appearances include *Randall and Hopkirk (deceased)* ('That's How Murder Snowballs', 1969), *Up Pompeii* ('The Senator and the Asp', 1970) and *The Persuaders!* ('The Long Goodbye', 1971). She was dynamic as Miss Hampton in *Can You Keep it Up For A Week* (1974) and smouldered in *The Ups and Downs of a Handyman* (1975) and *Queen Kong* (1976) with Robin Askwith.

Carry On credits: *Up the Khyber, Camping, Again Doctor, Up the Jungle, Matron, Christmas '72, Girls*
Autobiography: *Into the Leon's Den*

because they had nothing else to put in until the autumn. If *Carry On London!* folded the theatre would have been dark. Amazingly, they kept it going for over twelve months.'

Giving Peter Rogers the customary four weeks notice in September 1974, Louis Benjamin revealed 'our intent to terminate the run of the production after the second performance on Saturday, 12 October, 1974.' With tongue firmly planted in cheek, Rogers replied on 19 September: 'Formal notice formally received. Sad but necessary. I don't think I realised until lunchtime yesterday just how much your sense of professionalism has been hurt by the behaviour of certain of my "children" at the Victoria Palace. I can assure you that they will never have the chance to do it again.'

Valerie Leon, set to stun, in this publicity pose for the current film, *Carry On Girls*.

The cover for the Pye single that featured Sid James's 'Our House'. The b side was the plaintive 'She's Gone'.

CARRY ON CHRISTMAS (1973)

Mr Belcher (Sid James), a department store Father Christmas, tries to eat his breakfast sausage sandwich. But he's caught in the act by the slimy manager Mr Sibley (Kenneth Connor) who is showing his line in beds to a customer (Laraine Humphrys). Santa happily sits teenage sexpot Virginia (Barbara Windsor) on his knee as her mother (Joan Sims) looks on. Reflecting on Christmases past, Belcher ponders on prehistoric festivities. Senna Pod (Joan Sims) moans about her lot in life, aged Anthro Pod (Kenneth Connor) sleeps most of the day, while hulky Bean Podkin (Bernard Bresslaw) tries hard to keep up. Seed Pod (Sid James) has it taped, however. He wages war on a friendly Angle tribesman (Julian Holloway) and escapes family life with saucy Crompet the Pit Girl (Barbara Windsor) in his arms. Santa recalls a scene of drawing room manners from 1759, with Sir Henry (Sid James) losing his wife, Lady Fanny (Barbara Windsor) to the dashing Captain Rhodes (Julian Holloway) during a game of 'Postman's Knock'. Life in the trenches during World War I is no fun at Christmas, although Sergeant Ball (Sid James), Private Parkin (Kenneth Connor) and Captain Ffing-Burgh (Bernard Bresslaw) make the best of it. A couple of French fillies (Joan Sims and Barbara Windsor) brighten the day before the Germans (Peter Butterworth and Jack Douglas) turn up. Robin Hood (Sid James) has his own troubles, with a limp bow, songs from Alan-a-Dale (Jack Douglas) and nagging from Maid Marian (Joan Sims). Friar Tuck (Peter Butterworth) and Will Scarlet (Kenneth Connor) attempt to keep their boss happy at Christmas time!

Saucy Santa Claus, Sid James, and Santa baby, Barbara Windsor, happily get on their sledge for a *Carry On Christmas* promotion.

After two months of performing *Carry On London!* the cast had relaxed into the sketch revue format and were enjoying the experience. While performing twice nightly at the Victoria Palace, Sid James, Barbara Windsor, Kenneth Connor, Bernard Bresslaw, Jack Douglas and Peter Butterworth were also rehearsing for that year's Christmas television special. They were joined by Joan Sims, who replaced an indisposed Hattie Jacques. Joan clearly relished some choice and outrageous characterisations, notably the mother of the sexy schoolgirl played by Barbara Windsor. The entire script was written by a back-to-full-power Talbot Rothwell.

The Thames Christmas show did allow the gang to break into musical mode with a balletic sequence featuring the petite Barbara Windsor and her dragged-up co-stars. The Thames show was originally saddled with the mouthful of a title 'Carry On Once Again Christmas', but was quickly abridged to just *Carry On Christmas*. The budget was just over £25,000 but clearly couldn't stretch to a proposed finale featuring Sid as Santa dishing out toys to kids in Great Ormond Street Hospital. To the strains of the *London!* song, 'Smile, Smile, Smile', the rest of the cast – still in Robin Hood gear – were to join the party.

In January, Mary Whitehouse (of the then influential National Viewers and Listeners' Association) wrote to Thames Television, complaining about *Carry On Christmas*: 'Its very title would be likely to attract the family, particularly on Christmas Eve when the children are likely to watch to a later hour. Viewers who spoke to me found the programme highly offensive in its sexual innuendoes and general attitudes. More than one mentioned the episode in which Barbara Windsor and Syd [sic] James made a joke of a thirteen year-old girl having sex. Unfortunately, it seems to be accepted that the viewer will "take" anything so long as it is presented as "humour". This is not at all so... Another point was made to me – the fact that the programme was called *Carry On Christmas* and yet turned out to be highly suggestive was in itself offensive.'

The matter was dealt with by Philip Jones at Thames. '*Carry On Christmas* was in fact the fourth Christmas television spectacular which Thames have produced with the Carry On team and it has become almost an annual institution. But aside from television, there have, of course, been no less than twenty-five Carry On feature films during the last fifteen years and many of these have been seen on both television channels. In addition, most of the artistes are currently appearing in *Carry On London!* at the Victoria Palace and from all this exposure there can surely be no doubt in any viewers minds regarding the content. Our shows are exactly in the style of the pictures and, in fact, are produced by the same highly respected and professional production/writing team. Naturally none of us would wish to offend any section of our viewers but I think the majority of

Julian Holloway (1944-)

The son of music hall star Stanley Holloway, Julian had entered films as a bright young thing of the Swinging Sixties scene, notably in classics for director Richard Lester, the Beatles romp *A Hard Day's Night* (1964) and the Michael Crawford comedy *The Knack* (1965). He had made three forays into the world of Peter Rogers comedy before receiving his one and only star billing for *Carry On Camping*. The part was originally earmarked for Jim Dale although a huge chunk of his romantic storyline was edited. At the time of filming, Julian was appearing in *Spitting Image* at the Duke of York's Theatre and was on tenterhooks over his wife's pregnancy. Gerald Thomas sent him a telegram on 24 October 1968: 'Wishing you every success. Hope it's twins. Love Gerald.' On BBC television in 1968, Holloway played Corky opposite Anton Rodgers's tour de force as P G Wodehouse's Ukridge and the following year cropped up in the intriguing British horror film *Scream and Scream Again*. Just before his Carry On career came to a halt he guest starred in *The Sweeney* ('Big Spender'), wowed the West End in *The Norman Conquests* and, later, appeared in *Elizabeth R* and as the corrupt Jack Favell in the 1978 television production of *Rebecca*. Payback came when, in 1979, he was killed by a giant sewer rat in *The New Avengers* ('Gnaws') and played Bainbridge in the big screen spin-off of the Ronnie Barker situation comedy *Porridge*. Later he guest starred in *Hallelujah!* ('Repentance', 1983) and played Sergeant Patterson in the final episodes of the original run of *Doctor Who* ('Survival', 1989). In 1992 he toured America playing his father's signature role, Doolittle, in *My Fair Lady*.

Carry On credits: Follow That Camel, Doctor, Up the Khyber, Camping, Loving, Henry, At Your Convenience, Christmas '73, England

the public enjoy and expect the long-established Carry On team to offer that measure of robust and bawdy comedy which is surely not far from the best traditions of British music hall. I am sorry you received several phone calls but I have had no other criticisms.'

Although 1973 saw the last completely original *Carry On Christmas* special for television, it is unlikely that Mary Whitehouse's complaint struck a chord. Television was clearly the place for the Carry Ons, be it specially produced programmes or screenings of the old films. With his cast still packing them in at the Victoria Palace, Peter Rogers was already in pre-production for the twenty-sixth feature film and an ambitious television series for ATV.

Carry On hero Julian Holloway, at his most persuasive as Sir Thomas in *Carry On Henry* (1971).

Sid James and a bountiful Barbara Windsor were the biggest attraction for the *TV Times* holiday edition.

CARRY ON DICK (1974)

Highwayman Big Dick Turpin (Sid James) is terrorising merrie olde England with his henchmen Harriet (Barbara Windsor) and Tom (Peter Butterworth). When he robs the powerful Sir Roger Daley (Bernard Bresslaw) and his prim wife (Margaret Nolan), the befuddled Bow Street Runners are determined to track him down. Captain Desmond Fancey (Kenneth Williams) and Sergeant Jock Strapp (Jack Douglas) are ineptitude personified and can't see through Dick's disguise as the local Reverend Flasher. The Reverend's faithful housekeeper Martha Hoggett (Hattie Jacques) is also blind to his mischievous double life. But with a tip-off from the greasy old hag, Maggie (Marianne Stone), Fancey and Strapp discover their man has a curious birthmark on his manhood. Strapp wastes no time in carrying out an inspection in the public convenience of the Old Cock Inn and is unceremoniously dumped in to a horse trough for his troubles. Madame Desiree (Joan Sims), a travelling show-woman with her Birds of Paradise (Laraine Humphreys, Linda Hooks, Penny Irving and Eva Reuber-Staier), having been robbed by Dick Turpin, also fails to make the connection with the kindly Reverend. But Desiree does swallow his story that the undercover Bow Street Runner, Fancey, is, in fact, the wanted highwayman! The girls pull down his breeches but fail to find an incriminating birthmark. Miss Hoggett begins to put two and two together when Mrs Giles (Patsy Rowlands), apparently sick and used for a cover-up story for Dick's raids, is seen fit and well at the church jumble sale. Not only that, but Harriett is caught wearing Lady Daley's bracelet. With the net tightening, the Reverend Flasher gives an elongated sermon before outwitting his would-be captors and making a speedy getaway across the border.

With Talbot Rothwell's contract coming to an end after *Carry On Girls*, Peter Rogers once again turned to Lee Wyman and George Evans to write another script, *Carry On Dick*. However, Rothwell's three-year contract was renewed as planned, with *Carry On Dick* the first of another six films, and Wyman and Evans were given a credit of 'based on a treatment by' in the film's opening titles.

While the rollicking feel of a restoration comedy is apparent in the Wyman and Evans treatment, Rothwell basically reworked his old *Don't Lose Your Head* plot and fitted the Turpin elements in around it. Sadly it was to be his final Carry On script: 'I was nearing the end of my work on *Carry On Dick*,' he explained. 'It seemed a normal sort of morning when I awoke. I had my breakfast, then went to my desk to begin my day's work on the script. I sat down opposite my electric typewriter, but instead of working I found myself staring at the keys. I couldn't work. I had a sort of mental blockage. I just stared at those keys and thought, 'What is all this ASDFG? What do they mean? It's ridiculous. It wasn't that I couldn't think up dialogue. I could. It wasn't that I couldn't physically type. It was simply that every time I went to type, my brain said "No". My brain said it was ridiculous. In the end I had to get my daughter Jane to type it for me. It wasn't all that much of a problem because I had done a pretty fair copy of a draft. She just typed from that.' Rothwell's doctor confirmed he was suffering from eyestrain and mental fatigue brought on by overwork and that the condition would ease with lots of rest. In effect, Rothwell retired from the business and his three-year contract produced just the one Carry On film script.

For Sid James and Barbara Windsor, the continual pressure of an affair was increased with stage, television and film commitments that kept them working together constantly. In April 1974, Barbara's six-month contract for the *Carry On London!* stage show came to an end and she informed Sid that she intended to leave the show at this point: 'He was devastated. "If you leave, I'll go as well, and then the show will

DICK TURPIN CARRIES ON WITH HIS FLINTLOCK COCKED!

fold," he said.' With that ultimatum, Barbara stayed in the show and, with her five *Carry On London!* co-stars, found herself making the film *Carry On Dick* and performing in the evenings for the duration of the shoot.

Although enduring a heavy workload, Sid James seemed in good health for the film. Indeed, when Hattie Jacques was cleared for insurance on the film on 26 March 1974, 'subject to exclusion of incapacity directly or

indirectly arising from the cardio vascular system', it was noted that, 'there was a similar exclusion for some years for Sidney James.' But not for this production. His position as the King of Carry On was such at this stage that it was: 'in order for Sidney James' name to appear on a line by itself with the names of the other star artistes in two rows beneath his name provided always that all names on the card appear in the same size lettering.'

For Jack Douglas, finally granted a caricature on a Carry On film poster, the production was a joy from start to finish: 'Gerald Thomas was the most brilliant of comedy directors. "I want a shot of you riding down here chasing Dick Turpin through the forest," he said, indicating the route he wanted me to take. I climbed on board and awaited further instructions. "Action!" shouted Gerald. I squeezed my heels into the horse's sides and we set off at a gentle canter. Suddenly, my mount swerved sideways, straight into the path of a chest-level branch. The impact swept

Opposite: Joan Sims looks decidedly unimpressed with the size of Sid James's weapon as her Birds of Paradise look on in amazement.

Left: Barbara Windsor as Harriet, the most unconvincing highwayman in film history.

Below: The alluring Penny Irving snapped in a 1974 publicity session at Pinewood.

TITBITS!

Although their scenes were heavily edited in the finished film, Patsy Rowlands, Michael Nightingale and George Moon completed their work in one day, 18 March 1974. Patsy was 'happy to play anything, just to be with the old team again'. The stunning Birds of Paradise included one ex-Miss UK, Linda Hooks, and one ex-Miss World, Eva Reuber-Staier. Laraine Humphrys was fresh from raising temperatures in *Carry On Girls* and the recent *Carry On Christmas* special. Penny Irving had appeared with Benny Hill and would set pulses racing again in 1974 with a sultry turn in the Betty Box comedy *Percy's Progress*.

ON LOCATION

The church was located in Hitcham Lane. The Reverend Bayley-Jones wrote on 6 March: 'As far as we are concerned it will be quite in order for you to do a day or two filming of the exterior and entrance of Hitcham Church. You will have to cover up the notice boards which contain many things unheard of in 1750.' Filming commenced on 20 March. A church interior and vestry was constructed on Pinewood's 'C' Stage for filming from 25 March. Both Black Park and Langley Park were utilised, with the latter used for the 'blasted oak' sequence on 21 March. The rectory was the Manor House, Stoke Park, Stoke Poges. The Jolly Woodman pub at Littleworth Common, Buckinghamshire, was well versed in filmmaking: *Genevieve* had also used it for a location. Production manager Roy Goddard thanked the pub for its hospitality on 11 April, saying that it 'was most successful (I believe the takings went up quite a bit the day we were there).'

Bernard Bresslaw and Margaret Nolan emerge from the Old Cock Inn – The Jolly Woodman in Littleworth Common, Buckinghamshire.

Bernard Bresslaw chats up the faux French minx, Joan Sims.

me clean off the horse and I landed heavily on my back. "You didn't tell me my character was in Special Branch, Gerald!" I said breathlessly.'

Having shot arguably the most robust and bawdy of the Carry On romps, Gerald Thomas had a particularly strong battle with the censors on his hands. Such lines as 'always on the job', 'the size of his weapon', 'my organ in use again', 'diddler', 'Jock Strapp doesn't hang about', 'twice nightly', 'most treasured possession' and 'I'm a silly old cunt-stable!' were considered 'dubious dialogue' by the examiner. In the event only one line, Bill Maynard's pillory-encased observation 'I shall piss in your ale!' to Peter Butterworth, was toned down with a musical flurry covering the offending word. A 'quick flash of Barbara Windsor's tits as her blouse

Marianne Stone (1923-)

The omnipresent Marianne Stone is undoubtedly the most prolific character actress of post-war films, enhancing literally hundreds since her debut in the early 1940s. She first worked for Peter Rogers in *Marry Me!* in 1949 and enjoyed a lengthy association with him, Betty Box and the Rank Organisation. She was a favourite too of Val Guest, appearing in *Mr. Drake's Duck* and *The Runaway Bus* and his Quatermass films for Hammer. She had also appeared in Hammer's *Spaceways* (1953) for director Terence Fisher. The Boulting brothers found her invaluable in their classic satires *Private's Progress*, *Brothers in Law* and *I'm All Right Jack*. In fact, she was everywhere in the 1950s, appearing with Norman Wisdom in *Man of the Moment*, *Just My Luck* and *Follow A Star*, with Cardew Robinson in *Fun at St. Fanny's* and with Max Bygraves in *Charley Moon*. She wasn't just an outstanding comic support, she excelled in the Diana Dors drama *Yield to the Night*, and was memorable as the mysterious Vivian Darkbloom in *Lolita*. In 1963, she appeared in sixteen films and in 1964 eleven, unforgettably asking Ringo whether he was a mod or a rocker in *A Hard Day's Night* and getting involved with Lon Chaney Jnr in *Witchcraft*. Her many other credits for Peter Rogers include *You Know What Sailors Are!*, *Watch Your Stern*, *All Coppers Are...* and *Bless This House*, as nosy neighbour Muriel, having guest-starred in the April 1972 television episode 'Wives and Lovers'. She was directed by Charlie Chaplin in *A Countess in Hong Kong*, played the semi-regular role of Lena Van Broecker in *Secret Army* and eventually embraced the world of saucy sex comedies such as Val Guest's *Confessions of a Window Cleaner*, *I'm Not Feeling Myself Tonight* and, as a humourless waitress, *Confessions From A Holiday Camp*.

Carry On credits: *Nurse*, *Constable* (voice only), *Jack*, *Screaming!*, *Don't Lose Your Head*, *Doctor*, *At Your Convenience*, *Matron* (scenes cut), *Girls*, *Dick*, *Behind*, *Laughing*: 'The Case of the Screaming Winkles'

buttons burst' was also questioned but retained. Thomas agreed to remove the line 'whores de combat'. Dick Turpin quoting the psalm with the phrase 'goes a whoring' was also removed, as was, for some bizarre reason, the Kenneth Williams line 'cold water – I'd shrink even further in that'. After all the cuts, the director wryly commented, 'I hope this meets with your approval as we now have a rather short film.'

Gerald Thomas told Kenneth Williams that 'South Africa banned *Dick* 'cos of our use of the

church, playing Sid as a crooked Vicar.' Williams commented, 'Ironic that it takes a government like that to do something about such appalling sacrilegiousness while our government pass it without a qualm.'

Marianne Stone as the frantic Mrs Putzova – her character was completely edited from *Carry On Matron* (1972).

The last stand – Sid James winks a fond farewell to the Carry On films.

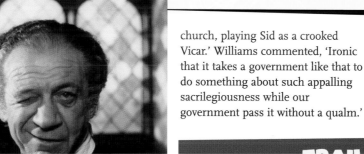

TRAILER

'Only Sid James could play Big Dick with such a flourish and he's a bit of a flasher too, on the quiet. Barbara Windsor fills two roles very nicely. Kenneth Williams is a rather thick dick and Hattie Jacques is marvellous on an organ. Bernard Bresslaw: there are no flies on him! This is Joan Sims doing the turn of the century. Kenneth Connor doing his bit. This wench is Peter Butterworth though he's really a Tom. Who else but Jack Douglas slashing his way to fame.'

CARRY ON LAUGHING (1975)

The Prisoner of Spenda
(first broadcast 4 January 1975)
The Baron Outlook
(first broadcast 11 January 1975)
The Sobbing Cavalier
(first broadcast 18 January 1975)
Orgy and Bess
(first broadcast 25 January 1975)
One in the Eye For Harold
(first broadcast 1 February 1975)
The Nine Old Cobblers
(first broadcast 8 February 1975)

Barbara Windsor and Sid James as the newly-married Vera and Arnold Basket in 'The Prisoner of Spenda'.

Opposite: David Lodge as Captain Bull in *Carry On England* (1976).

The premiere of *Carry On Laughing* was greeted with this splendid *TV Times* front cover.

With plans for a Carry On television series having been discussed between Peter Rogers and Talbot Rothwell as far back as 1969, it was Lew Grade that finally made the project a reality. Rothwell was unavailable to pen any of the episodes but his original suggestion of a series called *Carry On Laughing*, with self-contained episodes that could utilise the same sets for more than one show, was an exact blueprint for the ATV series.

The programmes were all geared towards headlining Sid James, and the star was determined to include Barbara Windsor in the series. To that end, Sid managed to up Barbara Windsor's salary to £900 an episode. As it happened, Sid himself was only available for the first four programmes, as he was committed to another Australian tour of *The Mating Season*.

All the shows were recorded at ATV's Elstree Studios, which were equipped with seven separate sets for the series, leading to confusion as Sid James jokingly asked an interviewer: 'How do I get out of this place?' The majority of the first batch of shows was penned by Dave Freeman.

Some of the regular team were anxious that such a major venture in to television would spell the end of the film series. However, Sid James revealed in a *TV Times* interview: 'We hear we're doing yet another film some time in 1975 so we're carrying on just as before. Sometimes I think we'll carry on till we drop, but it will have

TITBITS

John Levene plays the British soldier who apprehends Barbara Windsor in 'The Baron Outlook'. He had been popular as Sergeant Benton, alongside Patrick Troughton, Jon Pertwee and Tom Baker in *Doctor Who*. Patsy Smart, the sex-mad old hag in 'One in the Eye For Harold', also had a connection with *Doctor Who*, gleefully watching a rat-gnawed corpse being dredged from the Thames in 'The Talons of Weng-Chiang' (1977), although she is best remembered as the dotty neighbour in *Terry and June*. Bernard Holley, suspicious of a dragged-up Sid James in 'The Sobbing Cavalier', is also fondly remembered for his appearances in *Doctor Who* ('The Tomb of the Cybermen', 1967 and 'The Claws of Axos', 1971), as well as the Power Master in *The Tripods*. Veteran BBC broadcaster McDonald Hobley crops up as a Quaker reporter in 'Orgy and Bess'. Simon Callow remembers the same episode as 'one of the most tragi-comic episodes of my career – my first television, there I wasn't until the credits!', although he can be spotted bearing a 'pressie for Bessie!'

ON LOCATION

For 'The Nine Old Cobblers', the Carry On unit returned to a couple of familiar locations. The country roads, with Jack Douglas and Kenneth Connor, were shot in Black Park, while the public house the two detectives stay at was the Jolly Woodman, Littleworth Common in Buckinghamshire, previously used in *Carry On Dick*.

been a giggle – for everybody.' Barbara Windsor played up to her image while talking to the *TV Times*: 'Usually I don't read the script very carefully when they send it to me. I only get stuck into it when I start rehearsals. Then one day, they turn round and say, "Well, Barb, this is the bit where you lose your bra and your knickers fall down," and I say "No. Is it?" and of course I have to get on with it.'

Jack Douglas recalls that Barbara Windsor tried for a change of image. 'In the ['Nine Old Cobblers'] script there was a part of an old pub landlady. I thought Gerry would cast Joan Sims or Hattie Jacques but no. In came this little old lady with granny glasses, grey hair and a shawl. We played the scene and she was excellent. I ran over to Gerry shouting, "Who is she? She's fantastic!" at which point Barbara pulled off the grey wig and spectacles!' However, before filming, it was decided that the public wouldn't stand for 'Carry On Barbara' in any role which wasn't typically bubbly and bawdy, and the actress reverted to her usual comedy performance.

The series was a justified success. Indeed, never again would such a high quantity of Carry On team members appear together. 'Orgy and Bess', the fourth episode, signalled the Carry On farewell of Sid James and Hattie Jacques, while Barbara Windsor gives some of her most polished contributions in her final Carry On character assignments. As for Peter Butterworth, Kenneth Connor and Jack Douglas, their places as the indispensable backbone of the comedy were successfully utilised by producer Gerald Thomas under the assured comic direction of Alan Tarrant.

The shows were used not as a replacement for the film series, but as a profitable and publicity-geared exercise to fully embrace the small screen and try out new actors earmarked for the film series.

The necessary element of camp was brought to the shows by John Carlin, whose effeminate

serf, Ethelbert in 'The Baron Outlook', even resurrects Hawtrey's old entrance line, 'Oh Hello!' Diane Langton cropped up in the first two episodes and fully turned on the blonde, busty charms in 'One in the Eye For Harold', the only episode in the series that Windsor missed.

The first episode, 'The Prisoner of Spenda', was broadcast on 4 January 1975 and heralded the series as a flagship venture for ITV, blessed with a *TV Times* cover that promised 'Happiness is ITV and a New Year Carry On.'

David Lodge (1921-2003)

A singer of comic songs at school and a circus clown and ringmaster before breaking into acting, it was Lodge's stint in the Royal Air Force during the war that really shaped his destiny, when he met his life-long friend, Peter Sellers. Having made his film debut in the Sellers movie *Orders Are Orders* (although his dialogue scene was cut), he made his mark in *Cockleshell Heroes* (1955). He would notch up over a hundred appearances over the next thirty years, as often as not as comic support for Sellers. He played a suspicious policeman in *The Naked Truth* (1957) and the knuckle-headed cellmate 'Jelly' Knight in *Two-Way Stretch*. He partook in the Goon anarchy of Richard Lester's *The Running, Jumping and Standing Still Film*, turned nasty for *Never Let Go* (all 1960), and fought against corpsing opposite Inspector Clouseau in *A Shot in the Dark* (1964) and *The Return of the Pink Panther* (1974). Forever loyal, Lodge was also there on the troubled set of *Ghost in the Noonday Sun* (1974), and for Sellers' last hurrah, *The Fiendish Plot of Dr Fu Manchu* (1980). A favourite of Norman Wisdom, Lodge was the perfect authority figure in *The Bulldog Breed* (1960) and *On the Beat* (1962). He barked out orders to Bernard Bresslaw and the *Army Game* gang in *I Only Arsked* (1958) and worked for Peter Rogers in comic bits in *Watch Your Stern* (1960) and *Raising the Wind* (1961). His finest film performance was as the punch-drunk Mr Wickens in Lionel Jeffries's *The Amazing Mr Blunden* (1972), and he remained dignified in the Kenny Everett horror comedy *Bloodbath at the House of Death* (1983). On television, he proved a reliable and understanding stooge for Spike Milligan and relished guest spots in *The Saint* ('The Man Who Liked Toys', 1964), *Father Brown* ('The Man With Two Beards', 1974), *It Ain't Half Hot, Mum* ('The Grand Illusion', 1976), *Bless This House* ('A Matter of Principle', 1976) as the grizzled convict Slasher McQuirk, and *Worzel Gummidge* ('Dolly Clothes-Peg', 1980), as the strongman.

Carry On credits: *Regardless*, *Girls*, *Dick*, *Laughing*: 'The Prisoner of Spenda', 'The Baron Outlook', 'The Sobbing Cavalier', 'One in the Eye For Harold', 'The Nine Old Cobblers', *Behind*, *Laughing*: 'The Case of the Screaming Winkles', 'The Case of the Coughing Parrot', *England*
Autobiography: *Up the Ladder to Obscurity*

CARRY ON BEHIND (1975)

Frustrated butcher Fred Ramsden (Windsor Davies) and his electrician mate
Ernie Bragg (Jack Douglas) happily head off for a fishing trip while their
respective wives Sylvia (Liz Fraser) and Vera (Patricia Franklin) look forward to
their health farm holiday. Once at the caravan site of Major Leep (Kenneth
Connor), Fred starts making eyes at a couple of gorgeous campers, Carol and
Sandra (Sherrie Hewson and Carol Hawkins). But Ernie incriminates himself
by talking in his sleep! With their infidelities certain to be repeated in the marital
bed after the hols, Fred is despondent. Meanwhile, Professor Roland Crump
(Kenneth Williams) has teamed up with Roman expert Anna Vooshka (Elke
Sommer) in an archaeological dig on the caravan site. Arthur Upmore
(Bernard Bresslaw) and his wife, Linda (Patsy Rowlands), are saddled with her
mother, Daphne (Joan Sims) and her chatty mynah bird. Arthur is caught in a
comprising position with blonde babe Norma Baxter (Adrienne Posta), whose
husband Joe (Ian Lavender) is lumbered with their hefty wolfhound. After a few
pints with the amused pub landlord (David Lodge), Fred and Ernie discover
that the caravan site is riddled with holes. But Daphne is only concerned with
the discovery of her husband, Henry Barnes (Peter Butterworth) living a
downtrodden life as camp odd-job man. Major Leep is determined to give the
place a boost and arranges an evening cabaret for the caravaners, but a
mix-up over the telephone secures a stripper, Veronica (Jenny Cox), rather
than the singer he wanted. With Carol and Sandra having hooked up with
Bob and Clive (Brian Osborne and Larry Dann), a couple of likely lads from
Crump's dig, Fred and Ernie pick up Maureen and Sally (Diana Darvey and
Georgina Moon), a couple of beauties from the village. The rain and their
wives soon bring their planned night of passion to a halt!

Having resurrected the idea of a foreign
holiday for *Carry On Abroad*, Peter Rogers
commissioned a screenplay about a
holiday under canvas from Dave Freeman.
Entitled 'Love On Wheels', this new film wasn't
originally intended as part of the Carry On
series. Freeman wrote with Sid James in mind,
but Sid was still committed to *The Mating
Season* in Australia, and Barbara Windsor was
also down under in *Carry On Barbara*.

Gerald Thomas cast Kenneth Williams, Jack
Douglas, Windsor Davies, Liz Fraser, Kenneth
Connor, Peter Butterworth and Elke Sommer.
A model in her native Germany, Sommer had
broken into films in the late 1950s and won
plaudits for her performance as Helga in the
Albert Finney war film *The Victors* (1963). She
proved her comic mettle opposite Peter Sellers
in *A Shot in the Dark* (1964) and Bob Hope in
Boy, Did I Get the Wrong Number (1966), before
working with Betty Box on the slick Bulldog
Drummond thriller *Deadlier Than the Male* with
Richard Johnson. She also appeared in Box's
Percy and *Percy's Progress*, the latter the year
before landing the lead role in 'Love On
Wheels' – now retitled *Carry On Behind*.

Peter Rogers stood firm on his policy that no actor was bigger than the Carry On name. On 12 March 1975 it was contractually agreed that 'The producer would only wish to be bound to accord ALL co-stars credit in equal size type.' It was clarified that 'Miss Sommer will not be required to speak any offensive language or commit any pornographic act or appear nude' and that 'the reference to appearing semi-nude should be deleted on the basis of what does

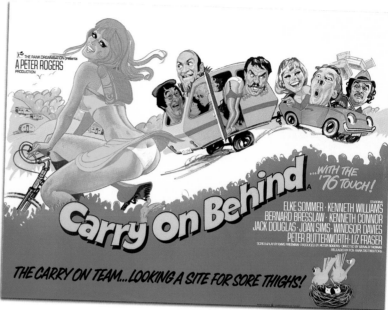

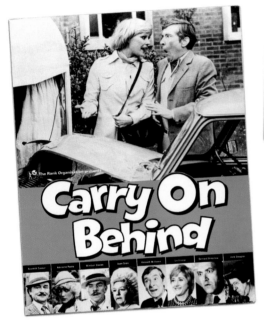

semi-nude equal?' For Peter Rogers, the actress was a joy on set: 'Elke is a very good actress, brilliant at the Carry On style of comedy and happy to behave as part of the team and not a star – which she undoubtedly is.' Elke Sommer, having worked in Britain before and being fully aware of the Carry On tradition, told the press: 'Before I started I was quite nervous. I thought they had all worked so often together it would be difficult for an outsider to break in. However, I felt like one of the family after only

Opposite: A foreign affair with Elke Sommer and Kenneth Williams getting to grips in a caravan. Sommer warmed to the most prolific of Carry On film stars and considered him as intellectual as his character.

The press agree – it's just what the public wants!

WHAT'S ON

"The art of the 'Carry On' is the simple art of suggestion. They can give the most unlikely word a sexual connotation; but they do it with robust cheerfulness. Everything, of course, is in the mind yes, and sometimes in the eye..... Elke Sommer is surprisingly successful ......" *Maurice Speed*

THE TIMES

"The perennial series is revitalised .... reinforced by Elke Sommer as a sexy archaeologist .... the sexual innuendo is about as dainty as a sledgehammer. *David Robinson*

FILMS ILLUSTRATED

"Twenty seventh in the series and liveliest in many years ...... new blood provided by Elke Sommer"

Sue d'Arcy

SUNDAY TELEGRAPH

"Kenneth Williams sneers marvellously .... the jokes have passed through the boundaries of taste and come up in the land of institution"

Tom Hutchinson

CARAVAN

"Sex larks and embarassing marital situations ...... add up to the usual sidesplitting 'Carry On' mixture.

Christine Fagg

NEWS OF THE WORLD

"Camping it up for the 27th time .... at a caravan site. Kenneth Williams and lovely Elke Sommer lead a team of loony archaeologists .... let the dirt fly in all directions"

THE GUARDIAN

"I find the Carry Ons funnier as I, and they, get older. It's something to do with the unique way they illuminate the barely-masked lechery, coarseness, greed and sentimentality behind the respectability they parody"

Derek Malcolm

EVENING NEWS (London)

"The excavation is near a caravan site where the amorous activities are far from academic. It is good to have Elke Sommer and Windsor Davies to assist the old gang in keeping seaside postcard humour alive"

Felix Barker

As this publicity brochure reveals, even the critics seemed to be delighted with the first Carry On film effort from writer Dave Freeman.

ON LOCATION

Maidenhead Town Hall was used once again and the Royal Borough of Windsor received £50 as a donation to the Mayor's Benevolent Fund for the half a day of filming there on 24 March. Later that same day, an exterior country road scene was filmed in Iver Heath. The first two days of April saw the unit in Pinewood's grounds and orchard, while the butcher's shop was found at 3 Robin Parade, Farnham Common and used on 26 April. Later that day, Bernard Bresslaw filmed some of his home exterior scenes in Pinewood Close.

On location in Pinewood's orchard with director Gerald Thomas delighting in the company of Kenneths Williams and Connor, both veterans from *Carry On Sergeant*.

Dave Freeman's much-renamed screenplay. At one stage, the film even went under the title *Carry On Carrying On*.

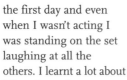

Hugh Futcher enjoys location filming in Brighton for *Carry On At Your Convenience* (1971).

the first day and even when I wasn't acting I was standing on the set laughing at all the others. I learnt a lot about life and people on *Carry On Behind* and never had so much fun in my life while I was doing it.' Sommer was also well-versed in Carry On: 'Oh, I'd seen so many, I knew what to expect. They're so funny, so ridiculous, I love them. The British sense of humour, anyhow, is much down my alley. The British are the funniest people in the world.'

Although there were some noticeable absences from the cast, Peter Rogers was delighted to welcome back Joan Sims in her eighteenth consecutive Carry On film. 'Apart

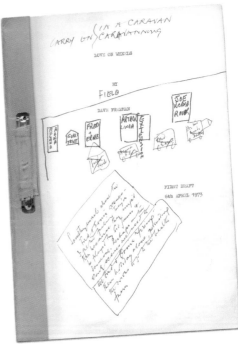

Hugh Futcher (1937-)

Having appeared with the Leatherhead repertory company, Futcher created the role of Dodger in *Chips With Everything* at the Royal Court theatre in 1963. The production transferred to the Vaudeville and ran for over a year. It was in 1964 that he joined the Carry On team, playing the man on a bed of nails in *Carry On Spying*. A regular fixture of the series, his last assignment would constitute three days filming as a disgruntled chair painter in *Carry On Behind*. Other film highlights include Reggie in Roman Polanski's *Repulsion* (1965) and as the terrified Sapper West in Hammer's *Quatermass and the Pit* (1967). Television guest appearances included Hickman, killed by 'The Sea Devils' in the first episode of that *Doctor Who* adventure (1972), and as advertising man Sidney Mayer, in *Selling Hitler* in 1991. In 1984 he created the role of Barry in the West End musical *42nd Street*.

Carry On credits: *Spying, Don't Lose Your Head, Again Doctor, At Your Convenience, Abroad, Girls, Behind*

from being wonderfully talented – one of the best comediennes in this country in fact – she is also a lovely person, amusing and marvellous company to be with.' The first day, 10 March, saw Sims and another Carry On veteran, Peter Butterworth, film their emotional reunion scenes within Barnes's caravan. On the second day, Kenneth Williams and Sam Kelly, in one day's work, filmed the opening lecture sequence on the same stage.

Typically, the location filming weather was inclement and reminiscent of the conditions for *Carry On Camping*. On 3 April Kenneth

Williams wrote that they 'started filming in sunny weather, then at 10.40 there was a blizzard with snow whirling everywhere and we all sat in the caravan.' Elke Sommer was happy to grin and bear it: 'I was "scantily clad" – isn't that how they say it, that's a Carry On expression isn't it? – and absolutely freezing, standing in the middle of this field in the shortest dress I'd ever worn. "Oh dear," I said, worrying more about my goose pimples showing than the falling snow, "how is this going to look on

Having broken off a stage run in Chicago to make the film, Elke Sommer returned to star in the Greta Garbo vehicle, *Ninotchka*, for the 1975 season. Bernard Bresslaw was also committed to a theatrical production, rehearsing *Son of Oblamov* at the Young Vic at the time of the filming. Joan Sims had starred in the celebrated restoration comedy, *The Way of the World*, which was broadcast during the production schedule. And both would experience British filmmaking, Hollywood style, when they appeared in the Walt Disney comedy *One of Our Dinosaurs is Missing*. Adrienne Posta jetted off to America after filming to take over from Goldie Hawn on the television series *Rowan and Martin's Laugh-In*. Liz Fraser returned to the Carry Ons for the first time in over a decade having excelled in *Move Over Mrs. Markham* in the 1974 summer season at the Pier Theatre, Bournemouth. Jenny Cox, who had been with the Welsh National Theatre before landing leading roles in naughty stage comedies such as *The Dirtiest Show in Town* and *Pyjama Tops*, was a novice striptease artiste. Displaying a lot more than mere bravery on the set, her completed routine was greeted with a round of applause from seasoned Carry Oners, Kenneth Williams, Joan Sims, Bernard Bresslaw and Jack Douglas. Diana Darvey, aptly born in Bristol, had been discovered by Benny Hill in a Spanish cabaret and recruited for his Thames shows to great effect. Kenneth Waller, later best known as Old Mr Grace in *Are You Being Served?* (1981) and Grandad in *Bread* (1986–1991), returned from a three-and-a-half-month tour as Polonius in *Hamlet* for the New Shakespeare Company, to find that he was an eleventh-hour replacement for Chris Gannon as the *Carry On Behind* barman. Admirers of the naked form of Helli Louise Jacobson, disturbed in the shower by Peter Butterworth, should check out her work in *The Goodies* episodes 'Winter Olympics' and 'The Goodies and the Beanstalk'; she also gets into all sorts of contortions with Robin Askwith in *Confessions of a Pop Performer* (1976). The mynah bird handler on set was Mike Cullings. The bird's dirty talking was provided by the film's director Gerald Thomas!

screen?" "Don't worry," they said, "we'll pretend it's apple blossom." Mad, but delightful.'

The censors were also reassuringly unhappy about certain parts of the film but by now, even Stephen Murphy had grasped that the Carry Ons were fairly innocuous fare in comparison to other films of the time. 'But,' asserts Peter Rogers, 'we still had trouble with them. I would say, "What about that scene in such and such a film?" and they would say, "Ah, but that was an American film. And it cost much more money than yours!" I could never understand this

Jack Douglas exposes his 'behind', much to the hilarity of Diana Darvey on this publicity leaflet.

Elke Sommer blocks the passage to the 'dirty caravan', much to the chagrin of Kenneth Williams.

TRAILER

A thirty-second trailer for television fully embraced Windsor Davies's sitcom popularity in *It Ain't Half Hot Mum*. Complete with his trusty swagger stick, Windsor looked into the camera and muttered: 'You will laugh. Because I am in it!'

Windsor Davies (1930-)

Sitcom's best-loved Welshman was actually born in London's Canning Town and started a career in teaching before succumbing to the acting bug at the age of thirty-one. Having joined the Cheltenham Repertory Company, he was spotted by Royal Court director John Dexter and offered roles in *The Kitchen* and *The Keep*. Davies followed this London success as Sir Toby Belch in *Twelfth Night* at the Shaw Theatre and the leading role in *Tartuffe* in Edinburgh. He appeared in the television series *Probation Officer* in 1962 and enjoyed guest spots in such classic shows as *Adam Adamant Lives!* ('Death Begins At Seventy', 1967), *Doctor Who* ('The Evil of the Daleks', 1967) and *Bless This House* ('The Bells Are Ringing', 1974). He made his film debut in the Margaret Rutherford Miss Marple mystery *Murder Most Foul* (1964) and featured to good effect in Hammer's *Frankenstein Must Be Destroyed* (1969), *Confessions of a Driving Instructor* (1976) and *Not Now, Comrade* (1977). In the latter, he was cast alongside the diminutive Don Estelle. A match made in comedy heaven, the two both starred in the Jimmy Perry and David Croft situation comedy *It Ain't Half Hot Mum* from 1974 until 1981. Davies became a national figure as the abrasive but ultimately misunderstood Regimental Sergeant-Major Williams and, with Don Estelle's dulcet tones, scored an unlikely number one hit with 'Whispering Grass' in 1975. Estelle and Davies formed a popular cabaret act which toured until the situation comedy *Never the Twain* came to dominate his calendar. Cast as antiques dealer Oliver Smallbridge opposite Donald Sinden, the show lasted from 1981 until 1991. He played General Tufte in the 1998 BBC presentation of *Vanity Fair* and Rottcodd in *Gormenghast* (2000). Davies was suitably cast as Uncle Lon in the 1999 *2Point4 Children* episode 'Carry On Screaming' and Sir Toby Belch in the Carry On drama *Cor Blimey!* in 2000.

Carry On credits: *Behind, England*

Windsor Davies in a typically ballsqueezing portrait from *Carry On England* (1976).

Georgina Moon, Jack Douglas, Diana Darvey and Windsor Davies enjoy the cabaret night, filmed on Pinewood's 'B' Stage.

reasoning!' The censors' report of 20 May 1975 required cuts to 'remove all sight of bare breasts of dancer in film within film... remove sight of Linda's [Patsy Rowlands] dangling breasts seen through caravan window... remove dialogue "I feel a complete arse" as man [Kenneth Connor] holds girl's bottom.' Gerald Thomas made some slight edits and got the required A certificate.

With the film safely in the can, Thomas was buoyant with prospects for the future explaining that 'now that Peter Rogers has set his own limit on the series by saying that the last Carry On will be the first to lose money we continue to carry on merrily.' When the film opened in the London suburbs on 11 January 1976 it proved a huge hit. Across the nation, it scored bigger initial box office returns than either *Carry On Dick* or *Carry On Girls* immediately before it. The film, a product of 1975, was the culmination of the most high-density year of new Carry On ever; but the knowing poster tag that it was a film 'with the '76 touch!' was little to boast about. It may have started well but 1976 was to be the year that Carry On died, in more ways than one.

Dave Freeman (1922-2005)

Gerald Thomas and Dave Freeman on location in Pinewood's orchard for the filming of *Carry On Behind* in April 1975.

An ex-policeman, Freeman discovered a love for comedy during war service. In 1953, however, he was still undiscovered. Writing bits and pieces for BBC radio, he was more gainfully employed as security officer at Winfield House, the American officers' club in Regents Park, and was also in charge of booking the cabaret for the Saturday night dances.

One of the acts he booked was Benny Hill. A writing partnership developed and he scripted early television appearances for Benny in *The Centre Show*, *The Services Show* and, eventually, *The Benny Hill Show* on the BBC. Dave also co-wrote Benny's West End revue *Fine Fettle* (1959) and an award-winning series of adverts for Schweppes, on which he also stooged for the star comedian.

Dave's other television appearances included a pilot in *Hancock's Half Hour* ('Air Steward Hancock', 1957). As part of Associated London Scripts, he contributed to the small-screen Goonery of *The Idiot Weekly, Price 2d* (1956). Freeman wrote the BBC sitcom *Benny Hill* (1962-1963) and would continue writing material for his friend

throughout his Thames success, despite not receiving a credit. When the shows were becoming more and more risqué, Freeman suggested toning down the content of *The Benny Hill Show*: 'I told him I thought his material was getting too dirty and he said, "And this is from the man who writes the Carry Ons!"'

Freeman's sitcom credits include *A World of His Own* (1964) for Roy Kinnear and *The Fossett Saga* (1969) for Jimmy Edwards. He also wrote for Arthur Askey (*The Arthur Askey Show*, December 1959), Harry H Corbett (*Mr. Aitch*, 1967), Richard O'Sullivan (*Robin's Nest*: 'The Happy Hen', 1978, and 'Should Auld Acquaintance', 1979) and *The Avengers* ('The Rotters', 1968), for director Robert Fuest. He wrote some new material for Sid James's Australian trip in 1972 and also wrote eleven episodes of *Bless This House*, including Sid James's favourite show, the last-series classic 'The Frozen Limit' (1976).

Dave wrote his first film, *Jules Verne's Rocket to the Moon* (1967), for producer Harry Alan Towers and a sterling cast that included Terry-Thomas, Lionel Jeffries, Jimmy Clitheroe and Graham Stark. In 1970, he wrote additional material for Graham Stark's directorial debut, the comedy short *Simon, Simon*. The following year, Freeman contributed the 'Envy' section to Stark's feature film for Tigon, *The Magnificent Seven Deadly Sins*.

His first stage farce, *A Bedful of Foreigners*, was written in 1973 as a vehicle for Terry Scott as the bemused Brit Stanley Parker. Dave had previously written material for Scott's television shows, *Great Scott – It's Maynard!* and *Scott On...* June Whitfield provided support in *A Bedful of Foreigners* as the seductive Helga Philby, and the play has been revived the world over ever since, notably in a Far East tour, again with Terry Scott, and Jacki Piper.

Carry On credits: *Again Christmas, Christmas '72, London!, Laughing*: 'The Prisoner of Spenda', 'The Baron Outlook', 'The Sobbing Cavalier', 'The Nine Old Cobblers', *Behind, Laughing*: 'The Case of the Screaming Winkles', 'The Case of the Coughing Parrot', *Columbus*

CARRY ON LAUGHING (1975)

Under the Round Table (first broadcast 26 October 1975)
The Case of the Screaming Winkles (first broadcast 2 November 1975)
And in My Lady's Chamber (first broadcast 9 November 1975)
Short Knight, Long Daze (first broadcast 16 November 1975)
The Case of the Coughing Parrot (first broadcast 23 November 1975)
Who Needs Kitchener? (first broadcast 30 November 1975)
Lamp-Posts of the Empire (first broadcast 7 December 1975)

A portrait of Barbara Windsor from 'And In My Lady's Chamber'.

Kenneth Connor, David Lodge and Jack Douglas during the recording of 'The Case of the Coughing Parrot'.

With thirteen half-hour slots always part of the deal with Lew Grade and ATV, a second batch of seven *Carry On Laughing* episodes was put into production at Elstree Studios in May, just after the completion of *Carry On Behind*.

Of the tried and tested formats from the first series, it was decided that Dave Freeman should pen two more adventures for Lord Peter Flimsy. David Lodge returned as the ineffectual Inspector Bungler; Kenneth Connor also returned as Flimsy's faithful manservant, Punter.

A King Arthur scenario conjured up by writer Lew Schwarz, 'Under the Round Table', kick-started the second series on 26 October 1975, and cropped up again for 'Short Knight, Long Daze'. The third historical setting, also

TITBITS

The hapless trumpeter to King Arthur is played by the man soap addicts later loved to hate: Brian Capron, who played the evil Richard Hillman in *Coronation Street* from 2001 until 2003. Oscar James was another actor who subsequently found soap fame. Cast as the Black Knight in 'Under the Round Table' and the witch doctor Youranutta in 'Lamp-Posts of the Empire', he played Tony Carpenter in *EastEnders* from the start in 1985 until 1987. He had previously played Joe Phillips in the Vince Powell scripted ITV sitcom *The Bottle Boys* with Robin Askwith. Susan Skipper, the saucy Mabel in 'Short Knight, Long Daze' contrasted Carry On with high-octane action by playing Colin Welland's secretary in the film, *Sweeney!* (1976). Later she starred in *The Cedar Tree* and was the delectable Lady Maud in *Raffles* ('The First Step', 1977) with her husband, Anthony Valentine. Melvyn Hayes, meanwhile, was set for Carry On film glory in 1976's *England* and milked the flame-haired, chopper-wielding Charwallah Charlie in 'The Case of the Screaming Winkles' for all he was worth.

Jack Douglas and Kenneth Connor in 'Lamp-Posts of the Empire'.

used twice for the second series, was an *Upstairs, Downstairs* spoof starring Kenneth Connor as the head of the Bulger-Plunger family, with Jack Douglas and Joan Sims as the downstairs staff, mercilessly sending up the performances of Gordon Jackson and Angela Baddeley.

Finally, the last *Carry On Laughing*, 'Lamp-Posts of the Empire', resurrected the style and even the gorilla (Reuben Martin) of *Carry On Up the Jungle*.

Peter Rogers didn't feel the series achieved what he set out to do, but in terms of capturing the fun and games of the Carry On team in a twenty-five minute format, the series kept the Carry On gang fresh in the minds of the television audience and proved that the Carry On series could carry on without its leading star, Sid James, and its most prolific writer, Talbot Rothwell.

Indeed, the series proved so successful that, a week after the first broadcast of 'Lamp-Posts of theEmpire', a first-series repeat started with 'The Prisoner of Spenda'. While plans for an ATV television special, *The Carry On Easter Parade*, were discussed, there was also a repeat showing for the 1973 *Carry On Christmas*. Peter Rogers commented, 'Not another one! When will these Carry Ons end? I suppose with a title like that they can't.' But, alas, the clock was all ready ticking.

ON LOCATION

The castle used for the two episodes set in the court of King Arthur was found at Knebworth; renowned for its rock festival. During the production, Jack Douglas set up home in a C I Caravan left over from *Carry On Behind* parked in the grounds of a local country club.

Norman Chappell (1929-1983)

With eyes wide in nervous apprehension, jowls quivering with uncertainty and mouth in a continual 'o' of exclaim, Chappell supported almost every post-war comic worth his salt. Indeed, he considered himself 'the comedians' friend', supporting Jimmy Tarbuck in *The Jimmy Tarbuck Show* (1974-1975), Les Dawson in *Sez Les* (1976) and *Dawson and Friends* (1977) and Frankie Howerd in *Whoops Baghdad* (1973) and *Frankie Howerd Strikes Again* (1981). He also played Albie, in support of Harry H Corbett, in *Mr. Aitch* (1967). Sitcom guest appearances included an effeminate choral singer alongside Frank Williams in *All Gas and Gaiters* ('The Bishop Gets Warm', 1971) and the Little Puddleton station porter in *Bless This House* ('Strangers in the Night', 1972). He appeared in Hammer film spin-offs of *Love Thy Neighbour* and *Nearest and Dearest*, played the humble Corporal Mould in *Danger UXB* and featured in the Bernard Cribbins television drama *Dangerous Davies – The Last Detective* (1981). He had just finished the Channel 4 series *For Four Tonight* at the time of his death, during a visit to his 92-year old mother.

Carry On credits: *Cabby*, *Loving* (scenes cut), *Henry*, *Laughing*: 'Orgy and Bess', 'One in the Eye For Harold', 'Under the Round Table', 'The Case of the Screaming Winkles', 'Short Knight, LongDaze', 'The Case of the Coughing Parrot', 'Lamp-Posts of the Empire'

Victor Maddern (1926-1993)

Trained at RADA, Victor became one of the most welcome of supporting actors in post-war British film and television. Making his film debut as the cockney soldier who kills Barry Jones at the end of *Seven Days to Noon* (1950), he played variations on the theme for the best part of a decade, be they serious (*The Planter's Wife*, *The Malta Story*) or comic (*Top Secret*, *Private's Progress*). In 1958, he gave a mesmerising performance as a hunchback in the Donald Wolfitt horror *Blood of the Vampire*. But it was a return to the Boulting brothers stable that ended the 1950s on a high note; as the work-shy union man in *I'm All Right Jack* who sighs 'Blimey, it's all go today in'it!' as his card game is interrupted by the dinner hooter. Peter Rogers used him to grand effect in comic bits in *Please Turn Over*, *Watch Your Stern* and, most memorably, as a furniture removal man bewitched momentarily by music, in *Raising the Wind*. Military cameos in low comedy like *Petticoat Pirates* and *On the Fiddle* stood shoulder to shoulder with prestigious assignments like *The Longest Day*, but Maddern was professional and devoted to his craft whatever the role. In 1968, he was the miserable junk man in *Chitty, Chitty, Bang, Bang* and faced the terror of Hammer's *The Lost Continent*. However, it was television that took up much of his time in the 1970s; he joined Dick Emery's repertory company, excelling as Lampwick's beleaguered son-in-law. Later roles included an aged police constable in *Miss Marple* ('The Moving Finger', 1985) and, his last assignment, Fruity Pears in *The Darling Buds of May* ('Oh! To Be in England', 1992).

Carry On credits: *Constable*, *Regardless*, *Spying*, *Cleo*, *Laughing*: 'Orgy and Bess', 'The Nine Old Cobblers', 'Under the Round Table', *Emmannuelle*

CARRY ON ENGLAND (1976)

Captain S Melly (Kenneth Connor) is put in charge of an experimental mixed-battery during the darkest days of World War II. It's a relief for Captain Bull (David Lodge) to greet his relief, but Melly isn't prepared for the ball-squeezing Sergeant Major 'Tiger' Bloomer (Windsor Davies) and the randy antics of Bombadier Ready (Jack Douglas), Sergeant Tilly Willing (Judy Geeson) and Sergeant Len Able (Patrick Mower). Forever feigning illness or hiding in their underground 'snoggery', the troops are happily getting to grips with each other rather than the enemy. Most prominent of the females is Private Alice Easy (Diane Langton) who tries to charm her new command-ing officer but only succeeds in propelling her top button into his system! Private Jennifer Ffoukes-Sharpe (Joan Sims) pines for 'Tiger' while every-body, including little Gunner Shorthouse (Melvyn Hayes) gets a piece of the action. Even after a tip-off to the medical officer, Major Butcher (Julian Holloway), segregation and rigorous training, the unit is still a shower. But an inspection by the cowardly Brigadier (Peter Jones) and Major Carstairs (Peter Butterworth) is interrupted by an airborne attack and Melly's troop prove they are real British bulldogs.

A script, 'The Busting of Balsy', had been commissioned from writers David Pursall and Jack Seddon for the second series of *Carry On Laughing*. For cost reasons, this script was abandoned as an idea for the ATV show, but Peter Rogers asked the writers 'to convert their television play into a Carry On film, tentatively entitled *Carry On England*.' The central character was changed from Balsy to Melly. Alternative titles for the film, 'How We Nearly Won the War' and 'A Cock-Up of a Cock-and-Bull Story', were dropped.

With Rank paying for only half of the film's production costs, Peter Rogers and Gerald Thomas embarked on a fruitless search for a source of funding other than their own pockets. This search even included an approach to the rock band Pink Floyd – which declined for 'tax reasons' – before Thomas and Rogers personally fronted fifty per cent of the budget of *Carry On England*, a disliked title which never got replaced.

Kenneth Williams was unavailable for the role of the Brigadier; he was committed to a theatre run in Feydeau and Desvallieres's *Signed and Sealed*, for which he had approached a host of friends to take part and all had refused. Among them were both Kenneth Connor and Joan Sims, which, had they accepted, could have seriously depleted *England*'s trawl of Carry On gang members. Peter Jones, who had last worked with the team marrying Frankie Howerd to Joan Sims in *Doctor*, was recruited in Williams' stead. Melvyn Hayes also signed up, alongside his *It Ain't Half Hot Mum* co-star Windsor Davies who, after starring in

Carry On Behind, felt 'like an old 'un.'

From Rank, there was 'no longer a contractual obligation that the film will be suitable for exhibition to family audiences, merely the best endeavours provision that you will attempt to gain a U certificate.' In light of the script material, this was always going to be a tall order, although Thomas and Rogers had always been more than aware that the family audience was their biggest target. Still, the two made a rare, fact-filling journey to the cinema together: to watch the latest Robin Askwith film, *Confessions of a Driving Instructor*. Seemingly, with Carry On reaching the family audience at home on television, it was time to give the adult fans of the series something a bit hotter at the cinema. Sex sold and, in British cinemas in 1976, nothing attracted packed houses more than nudity.

Patrick Mower, who was best known as hard men like James Cross in *Callan* and Tim Haggerty in *Special Branch* on television, was a friend of Gerald Thomas. Mower cheerfully acknowledges that he was cast in the Carry Ons because 'Gerry's daughters rather fancied me and wouldn't go to see the film if I wasn't in it!' although the actor had

enjoyed success in stage comedy and, importantly, appeared in Betty Box's *Percy* in 1971, grinning as he cuckolds Hywel Bennett.

Gerald Thomas's friendship with Mower resulted in him 'asking me to have a word with Judy Geeson. She refused to take her top off.' All the girls' contracts included the special clause that 'the artiste will be requested to appear nude

to the waist during the filming' – except that of Judy Geeson. Although she had stripped in *Three into Two Won't Go* (1969), she blankly refused within the confines of a Carry On comedy. Patrick Mower couldn't persuade her and Gerald Thomas didn't force the issue. It is never explained in the film, but Judy's character is mysteriously absent from the scene where the girls come on parade wearing nothing but regulation trousers. The defiant lines, originally written for Geeson's character, are delivered by a happy to disrobe Tricia Newby as the low-ranked Private Murray.

Mower and Geeson joined the recognised stars of the film, Kenneth Connor and Windsor Davies, on the second day, 4 May, on 'G' Stage. For Judy Geeson, the film was 'a most enjoyable

Patrick Mower watches the filming with producer Peter Rogers.

Jack Douglas keeps abreast of the situation in this outrageous out-take.

DOCTOR, DOCTOR!

Jack Douglas, who had joined the filming for the interior air-raid shelter scenes on 'C' Stage at Pinewood, was called upon for some fairly strenuous sequences. He filmed interiors in the men's hut which included several hours with Melvyn Hayes on his shoulders. During the filming, Jack strained his back and had treatment from the medical department.

ON LOCATION

Filming utilised local locations throughout, with the Green Room at Pinewood being used for the military officers' boardroom scenes with Peter Jones, John Carlin and Michael Nightingale. Two weeks were spent in studio while the unit filmed on the lot and in the Pinewood orchard for the rest of the five-week shoot. During the 'location' work, an Equity member complained about lunch breaks falling short of the agreed hour by fifteen minutes and, therefore, artistes being called too early. 'I don't have any time for that sort of thing,' says Patrick Mower. 'If the sun is shining, carry on filming and eat later. That's my attitude anyway.' The issue was dropped.

Khaki chaos as the Carry On squad grapple with a gun on loan from the Imperial War Museum.

Both Richard O'Sullivan and James Bolam were in the frame to play Len Able before Patrick Mower got the nod. Here he struggles to keep a straight face opposite Kenneth Connor. Mower was invited to re-join the team for a cameo role in *Carry On Emmannuelle* opposite his girlfriend Suzanne Danielle. Other commitments prevented his appearance.

Peter Rogers and Louise Burton adjust each other's dress while Melvyn Hayes and Barbara Hampshire keep their eye on manoeuvres.

and relaxing experience, with none of the strain and tension you get on some films. As Jack Douglas says, the director Gerald Thomas 'has a way of painting a scene visually instead of filling your head with words. The producer, Peter Rogers, is on the set every day. He even has a little office in a shed on location, and he seems to know instinctively when anyone is worried about anything and wants to discuss it with him.'

Diane Langton, as Private Alice Easy, was 'the new Barbara Windsor'. After completing the film, she was recruited for the resurrection of the ITV situation comedy *The Rag Trade*, playing Kathy, a buxom beauty in the mould of Barbara Windsor from the 1960s original. As Kenneth Connor's cheeky driver, Johnny Briggs chalked up his last Carry On appearance after getting shot in the sporran in *Up the Khyber*, painting chairs in *Behind* and shifting a mummy case in 'The Case of the Coughing Parrot'. Almost immediately afterwards, he was cast as Mike Baldwin in *Coronation Street*. As Corporal Cook, Patricia Franklin also bid farewell to the Carry Ons, after notable roles as the farmer's daughter in *Camping* and Bill Maynard's sour wife in *Loving*. She played a zombie in the 2003 comic hit *Shaun of the Dead*, and even took part in one of the film's DVD audio commentaries.

The biggest 'prop' in Carry On history was recruited for the film. Art director Lionel Couch, who had himself served in an anti-aircraft battery during the war, approached the Imperial War Museum about borrowing a 3.7 inch anti-aircraft gun retained in the museum's reserve collection. In the midst of production, Peter Rogers told the Museum 'how grateful I am to you for letting us use your beautiful gun which,

when it came through the studio gates drew gasps of approval. No one in the studios has a bigger gun at the moment, not even Bond.'

Nothing, however, could be done to prevent the BBFC awarding the completed film an AA certificate, excluding audience members under the age of fourteen. Gerald Thomas was unwilling to barter and the film was released in December 1976. Worryingly for the production company, the initial box office takings weren't good. In a last-ditch attempt to appeal to the family audiences that were denied admittance, Thomas agreed to radically reduce the topless nudity in the parade sequence that had so concerned Judy Geeson in the first place. It had also concerned Jack Douglas. 'Don't misunderstand me,' Douglas explains, 'I love seeing girls in that state of undress, but not in a Carry On. Myself and Kenny Connor, Peter Butterworth and Joan Sims, were all unhappy about that scene. I had understood it that Gerry would suggest the nudity and just show Kenny's outraged reaction. That would have been funny. The nudity was shown and the comedy was lost.' Although in the censor's version, the topless scene remains, several scenes are cropped to lose the naked breasts.

A further scene, with Windsor Davies and Patrick Mower, was completely replaced. In the original, Davies lectures his soldiers on their poor aircraft recognition and Mower knowingly comments 'but I know a Fokker when I see one!' Considered too much for an A certificate, this was changed to a reference to Bristols,

TITBITS

Eric Rogers, who had orchestrated the sound of Carry On for fifteen years, declined the film: 'The reason was because, on the budget that Peter was able to give me for that film, I could only have hired twenty musicians instead of the forty that I prefer. But I'm back next time.' Indeed he was, but in his place here was Max Harris, who had contributed to the score of *Carry On Laughing*: 'Under the Round Table', 'And In My Lady's Chamber' and 'Short Knight, Long Daze'. Perhaps best known at the time for composing the closing theme for the BBC sitcom *Porridge*, he went on to supervise the nostalgic sound of Dennis Potter's *The Singing Detective*. *England*'s score was recorded in three sessions at the Anvil recording studio, Denham, under the orchestral conductor C Katz. The score included a rendition of the non-copyright song 'Hearts and Flowers' and a Harris arrangement of 'Deutschland Uber Alles'. A special piano was brought in for Harris to record further music for the film in Theatre 2, Pinewood. Like Eric Rogers, Harris couldn't resist lifting music for comic effect, hence a burst of the Flanagan and Allen number 'Run, Rabbit Run' during the scenes of bayonet practice.

which, Mower observes, 'usually come in pairs!' Both versions survive, with the less explicit screened on television before Carlton

Gun action with Kenneth Connor and Windsor Davies.

Gerald Thomas and Peter Rogers are tickled by the comic contortions of veteran star Kenneth Connor.

TRAILER

'Leading the love parade, Judy Geeson and Patrick Mower. Twitching for some action, Jack Douglas.'

Peter Jones (1920-2000)

A treasured character actor, writer and wit, Jones entered the film industry in 1944. "*Fanny By Gaslight* was set in a brothel but they couldn't show that so when the girls are at it like knives, I was employed to look through these curtains and exclaim, 'Oh my goodness!'" Supporting roles in popular Group 3 comedies *Time Gentlemen, Please* and *Miss Robin Hood* followed in the early 1950s, but it was as a pioneering radio surrealist that he came to national prominence. Peters Jones and Ustinov created the BBC show *In All Directions*, which led to bigger roles in British film, including Ian Carmichael's sausage-eating pal, Arthur Egan, in *Private's Progress*, and an unforgettable car-dealing partnership with Dennis Price (Ustinov was originally cast but pulled out) in *School For Scoundrels*. He found his niche in television sitcoms, starring as Mr Fenner in *The Rag Trade*, appearing with June Whitfield in *Beggar My Neighbour* and Sheila Hancock in *Mr Digby, Darling*, and teaming up with Peter Butterworth as a couple of street entertainers for *Kindly Leave the Kerb* in 1971. Part of Spike Milligan's *Q* troupe, Jones became a cult hero as the voice of the book in Douglas Adams's *The Hitchhiker's Guide to the Galaxy* and was one of the most faithful players of Radio 4's *Just A Minute*, last partaking in 1999. His twilight-year television guest appearances included *Tender Loving Care* (1993), *Minder* ('The Great Depression of 1994', 1994), *Paul Merton in Galton and Simpson's 'The Lift'* (1996) as the vicar and *Midsomer Murders* ('Faithful Until Death', 1998).

Carry On credits: *Doctor, England*

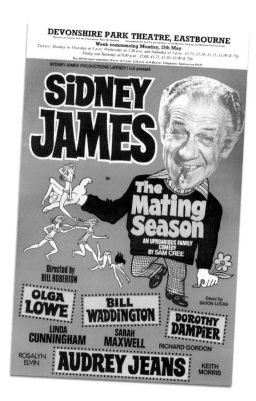

International resurrected and cleaned up the AA print for distribution.

Kenneth Connor, the only on-screen association with the film that had started it all, *Carry On Sergeant*, relished his lead role and happily promoted the film. Talking about Captain Melly – 'he is a well-meaning chap who is never taken seriously' – Connor was arithmetically incorrect but jubilant to explain that: 'It has taken me eighteen years and twenty subsequent Carry On roles to rise to the rank of Captain, however comical.'

By this stage, the association of the ongoing production of the Carry Ons and the Rank Organisation was over. 'We Have Ways of Making You Laff', a prisoner-of-war film based on Talbot Rothwell's 'Carry On Escaping' script, was shelved by Rank. And, also much to Rogers's disbelief, *Carry On England* failed to find an audience.

As the film entered pre-production, Sid James brought his tour of the Sam Cree farce *The Mating Season* to the Sunderland Empire. On the evening of 26 April 1976 he suffered a heart attack on stage and died. It was the end for Carry On.

Sid James should have been performing in Eastbourne during the shooting. It was a theatrical date he failed to keep.

Penelope Keith was earmarked for the role of Ffoukes-Sharpe, eventually played by Joan Sims. Here Linda Regan and Louise Burton stand on the shoulders of a Carry On giant, along with Diane Langton.

Jack Douglas (1927-)

Born into a showbusiness family, Jack was fascinated with the theatre from an early age. On his fifteenth birthday, his father presented him with a script for *Cinderella* with the words 'You're directing this.' The show, starring music hall veteran G H Elliott, played the Sunderland Empire.

By 1946, he was appearing in *Hi There* for the Combined Services Entertainment's Unit. His long-term partnership with Joe Baker came about by accident, when Jack had to take over the role of the Captain from an actor who had been taken ill. With Joe as the Mate in *Dick Whittington*, at the Kingston Empire, the duo were a comic hit. After a 1949 stint as children's entertainer, 'Uncle Jack of Jaywick', Douglas teamed up with Baker for pantomime (including *Aladdin* with Alma Cogan at the Empress, Brixton, in 1956), the television series *Crackerjack!* (1955-1959) and a summer season in Blackpool with Roy Castle in 1959. The following year, they toured Australia until May, appeared at the Pavilion Theatre, Weymouth, for the summer, and starred in *Robin Hood* at the Alhambra, Bradford. They also made a film appearance, opposite Kenneth Connor, in *Nearly A Nasty Accident*, before Baker broke up the act.

As a freelance stooge, Jack appeared with Bruce Forsyth, Arthur Haynes and Benny Hill in 1961 before getting the call from Des O'Connor. As his jittering character Alf Ippittimus, Jack supported O'Connor in panto, notably in *Humpty Dumpty* at the Grand Theatre, Leeds in 1963, and on *The Ed Sullivan Show* in 1966. Later that year, the act stole the plaudits at *The Royal Variety Show* at the Palladium. In 1968, Jack starred in the farce *Don't Tell the Wife* at the Grand Theatre, Blackpool. A huge success was repeated the following year at the Windmill Theatre, Great Yarmouth and,

in 1970, at the Pavilion Theatre, Torquay.

In 1971, he teamed up with John Inman for a new farce, *When the Wife's Away*, at the Windmill Theatre, Great

Yarmouth. He played 'The Reluctant Juggler' in an episode of the 1972 television drama *The Edwardians* and, in 1974, began a long association with the wisecracking television game show *Jokers Wild*. In 1975, he joined Hylda Baker for the ITV sitcom *Not On Your Nellie*. The final episode cast Jack as both

Stanley Pickersgill and his twitching cousin Alf. He ended the year playing Wishee Washee in *Aladdin*, opposite Barbara Windsor in the title role and Jon Pertwee as Abanazar, at the Richmond Theatre.

On television, he appeared in the feature-length comedy drama *The Shillingbury Blowers*. A series, *Shillingbury Tales*, and a spin-off, *Cuffy*, would see Jack recreate his role of Jake the farmer. Stage assignments ranged from a 1981 tour in *Make and Break*, the 1982 premiere of *A Sting in the Tale* at the Yvonne Arnaud Theatre, Guildford, with Bill Pertwee and Dilys Laye, and Long John Silver in *Treasure Island* at the Repertory Theatre, Birmingham. Jack also provided a stolid policeman support in Val Guest's final film *The Boys in Blue* (1983), with Cannon and Ball.

He directed and starred in a revival of *A Sting in the Tale*, at the Shanklin Theatre, Isle of Wight, and continued to appear in farce (including a revival of *Don't Tell the Wife*, at the Shanklin Theatre, 1997) and pantomime (as the King in *Cinderella* at Weston-Super-Mare in 2000, Crewe in 2001 and Eastbourne in 2003).

Jack Douglas out of character during the production of *Carry On Dick*.

Carry On credits: *Matron, Abroad, Christmas '72, Girls, London!, Christmas '73, Dick, Laughing*: 'The Prisoner of Spenda', 'The Sobbing Cavalier', 'Orgy and Bess', 'One in the Eye For Harold', 'The Nine Old Cobblers', *Behind, Laughing*: 'Under the Round Table', 'The Case of the Screaming Winkles', 'And In My Lady's Chamber', 'Short Knight, Long Daze', 'The Case of the Coughing Parrot', 'Who Needs Kitchener?', 'Lamp-Posts of the Empire', *England, Laughing, Emmannuelle, Columbus*

Autobiography: *A Twitch In Time*

CARRY ON LAUGHING (1976)

Milly (Liz Fraser) is a do-anything housemaid at the Get-U-Fit health farm owned by Mrs Babbington (Beau Daniells). Patient Alf Hardy (Jack Douglas), sent to the farm by his wife, is accompanied by a cheeky mynah bird who is there to make sure he behaves himself. The bird will tell Alf's mother-in-law if he does anything improper. Randy old soldier Major Chambers (Kenneth Connor) is at the farm to improve his physique for one final attack on the fairer sex. The stripper Candy Maple (Anne Aston) and Swedish factotum Helga (Linda Hooks) are his targets. Lazy wheeler-dealer Willie Strokes is supposed to be redecorating the premises but spends most of his time trying to get rich quick. The action took place over two acts, from Monday morning through to Thursday night.

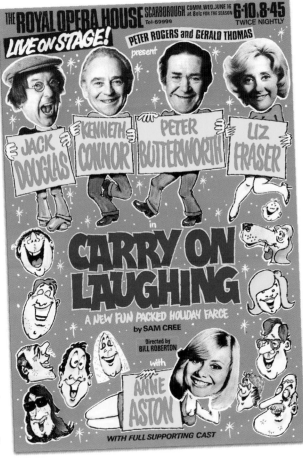

W ith *Carry On England* in the can, there was the possibility of another series or alternatively a Christmas show for Thames in the pipeline. For Jack Douglas, about to headline the Carry On summer season in Scarborough, it seemed that a film, followed by a stage show, followed by a television project, could well carry on indefinitely.

Scarborough impresario Don Robinson wrote to Bill Roberton, the director of the show, to confirm that 'Peter Rogers will present a Carry On farce with stars of his Carry On films and TV. He intends to engage Barbara Windsor, Jack Douglas, Kenneth Connor, Peter Butterworth in a farce specially written by Sam Cree [the writer of *The Mating Season*].'

Meanwhile, Roberton was assigned the task of digging out a workable comedy play, already in existence, which could be quickly reworked for a Carry On presentation. This could be a replacement for the new script or retained for the following year. Rogers wrote: 'I certainly think we should consider another Carry On stage show, particularly one with a hospital venue, perhaps with a "second eleven" as far as cast is concerned.'

Sam Cree's new Carry On play, entitled 'The Slimming Factory' and centred on a farmhouse that has been converted into a health farm, did have medical elements which suited the Peter Rogers request, and was clearly written for the cast that Don Robinson had assumed were signed up. Unfortunately, Barbara Windsor had not committed to the project although Cree's script was written with her in mind. The maid was called Babs, voluptuous, very friendly and short sighted, complete with black stockings and short skirt.

Willie Strokes, the role written for and played by Peter Butterworth, was a painter who does everything but paint; 'he has a ten minute break every fifteen minutes, is short sighted and is permanently pickled. He is also "Mr Fixit", whatever you want he can get. At a price.' Butterworth's characterisation owed a lot to *Carry On Behind* and, for good measure, a later draft introduced a talking mynah bird that spoke out at the most embarrassing of times. The bird belonged to Jack Hardy, 'a northerner sent to the farm at his wife's command, as she felt he was putting on too much weight. The experience

The Carry On gang re-opened the Royal Opera House, which had been dark since October 1971.

Linda Hooks, here publicising *Carry On Dick* (1974), offered 'Swedish manoeuvres' on stage.

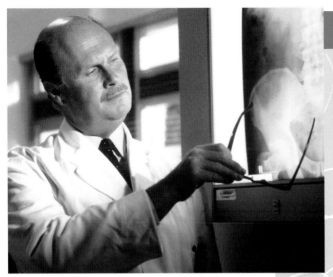

Michael Nightingale (1922-1999)

An unsung member of the Carry On team, Nightingale delivered supporting turns of pompous authority and nervous bemusement in one-day assignments throughout almost the entire history of the series. Beloved by Gerald Thomas, he fumed majestically in *Watch Your Stern*, *Raising the Wind* and *The Iron Maiden*, and returned to play the vicar in *Bless This House*. Perhaps his most high-profile film performance was as Colonel Clutterbuck in *Decline and Fall of a Birdwatcher* (1969). He later cropped up as a museum tourist in *The Return of the Pink Panther* and as the clerk of the court in the television remake of *Witness for the Prosecution*, with Ralph Richardson. Memorable guest appearances include Number 45 in *The Prisoner* ('Dance of the Dead', 1967), Leggitt the butler in *Raffles* ('The Gold Cup', 1977) and *Victoria Wood* ('Val De Ree (Ha Ha Ha Ha Ha)', 1989) as a hardy back-packer partnered with Avril Angers.

Carry On credits: *Regardless*, *Cabby*, *Jack*, *Cleo*, *Cowboy*, *Don't Lose Your Head*, *Follow That Camel*, *Camping*, *Matron*, *Girls*, *Dick*, *Laughing*: 'The Case of the Screaming Winkles', 'Lamp-Posts of the Empire', *England*, *Emmannuelle*

Michael Nightingale, looking for belly laughs in *Carry On Matron* (1972).

turns out to be a nightmare for Jack, a man fond of his food, a smoke and a drink.' The character was the leading role and especially written for director Bill Roberton's brother, Jack Douglas; albeit changed to Alf Hardy for the stage run. MILLY: 'I've a good mind to cut off your hazelnuts.'
ALF: 'Oh no – not my HAZELNUTS!?'
Was a typically ripe exchange!

Major 'P O' Chambers was designed for Kenneth Connor: 'He has come to the farm to get into shape for what could well be his last onslaught on the female race.' Candy Maple was a creation set to get the male patients excited: 'A stripper who feels her belly is getting too big for the "Belly" dance. No full-blooded male can see the reason for her concern.' Candy would be played by Anne Aston. Mentioned in the earlier casting suggestions for *Carry On England*, she had come to national prominence as a hostess on *The Golden Shot* and appeared with Frankie Howerd in the film *Up the Chastity Belt* (1971).

Bill Roberton signed both Anne Aston and Liz Fraser to the project, assets which made the cast 'a very strong one'. Roberton also hired Saxon Lucas, who 'does most of our farces', as set designer.

The show opened at the Scarborough Opera House on 13 July 1976 for a fourteen-week season. The show quickly proved disappointing at the box office – it was the hottest summer on record and 'the rest of the country' was also suffering from the sheer apathy of holidaymakers preferring to sit on the beach with a cold beer rather than bake in a theatre presenting half-baked innuendo.

The Mercury review of 19 June commented that 'it is unfortunate that the farce which puts the Carry On team on stage has not more substance... but the show is worth the money because of the quality of performance of the stars. Big Jack Douglas is the tour de force, with his nervous spasms, flying cap, wire-frame spectacles, juddering leg, and vocal mannerisms. He has so much more to offer than we have seen on television, and his enthusiasm for the show is infectious. On the distaff side Liz Fraser comes out tops. Some first night blunders by her colleagues proved to be real feed lines. Most of the laughs come from the clowning, grimacing, falling about, and double entendres so thinly veiled that even those who couldn't tell a double entendre from a bare bottom would have no communications block.'

The loss was huge. Even with artistes' fees halved towards the end of the run, final figures in January 1977 revealed that the production suffered an overall loss of £3,766.92. It was the last official Carry On stage show.

TITBITS

Danny O'Dea, a fine Irish stage comedian and close friend of Bill Roberton, was cast as Albert Waterman, Milly's lover in the play. From 1985 until the year before his death in 2003, he found a new audience on television, as the short-sighted, accident-prone Eli in *Last of the Summer Wine*.

THAT'S CARRY ON (1977)

Kenneth Williams and Barbara Windsor are imprisoned in a Pinewood projection room and trawl through film can after film can of the classic Carry On series. Kenneth is delighted with the slap-up food hamper and champagne, while Barbara loads the vintage clips. As the films remorselessly play out, Kenneth feels the need to relieve himself but Barbara is determined to plough through every film. Finally, scenes of speedy roadside urinating from Carry On At Your Convenience *prove too much for Kenneth to bear, but he holds back the flow to enjoy his finest role as the Khasi in* Carry On...Up the Khyber. *While Kenneth pontificates about the glories of the Empire, Barbara leaves the projection room and locks her co-star in. Unable to hold out any longer, Kenneth goes against the projection room door!*

That's Carry On was presented by Barbara Windsor and Kenneth Williams, seen here on location for Carry On Abroad (1972).

Talbot Rothwell in retirement, the structure of Carry On had inevitably taken a powerful blow. But, the failure of the latest film, *Carry On England*, which had failed to deliver on the financial investment of Rogers and Thomas, coupled with the unpleasant experience and financial loss of the Scarborough summer season, left the Carry Ons pretty much dead in the water. An inexpensive film was clearly the most appealing route and, at a budget of £75,000, less than *Carry On Sergeant* had cost twenty years earlier, a rummaging through the best bits for a compilation film was considered by far the best option.

That's Entertainment, the 1974 presentation of highlights from the archive of MGM, had been a surprise box office hit; so much so that a sequel, hosted by Fred Astaire and Gene Kelly, had appeared in 1976. In conversation with Nat Cohen of EMI, Gerald Thomas realised that, with twenty-eight films, a successful trawl of ninety minutes of Carry On could be easily forthcoming.

Kenneth Williams and director Gerald Thomas take a break from *Carry On Camping* at Pinewood Studios.

Peter Rogers contacted Cohen, saying that he was 'happy about the possibility of a compilation of past Carry Ons in the style of *That's Entertainment*. The idea of the compilation (which sounds like a nasty complaint) is that it should be distributed by a third party so that you and Rank benefit without prejudice. Despite concern over Herbert Wilcox's British film comedy clip fest, *To*

Gerald Thomas's 1975 comment that the last Carry On film would be the first to lose money was sounding frighteningly prophetic in 1977. With Sid James dead and

See Such Fun.' Gerald Thomas, Frank Poole of Rank and Nat Cohen continued the discussions over the official Carry On compilation film, agreeing a fiftyfifty deal for profit participation and that the Rank Organisation would, in fact, handle the film, the last of its Carry On presentations. It was settled that the film would be released as 'The Best of Carry On', a title that never sat happily with Peter Rogers.

Rogers successfully argued that 'as we progress with our compilation, it becomes more and more apparent that "The Best of Carry On" is not the best title for it. I would really like you to think about this again and reconsider the original suggestion of *That's Carry On*. Part of the reason for wanting this change is that the "best" is not everyone's idea of

Terence Longdon (1922-)

Following war service, Longdon nursed acting ambitions and trained at the Royal Academy of Dramatic Art. His height and good looks landed him humourless supporting turns in such 1950s British flicks as *Never Look Back* and *Angels One Five*. He was a revelation in comedy, supporting Peter Finch and Kay Kendall in *Simon and Laura* and Frankie Howerd in *Jumping For Joy* (both 1955) and featuring in Ralph Thomas's *Doctor at Large* (1957). In 1958, he was cast as Sean Connery's sidekick in *Another Time, Another Place* and inducted into the fledgling Carry On team. The following year, he was cast as Drusus in *Ben-Hur* and landed the starring role of ace pilot, *Gerry Halliday*, on television. He supported Adam Faith in *What A Whopper!* (1961) and when *Gerry Halliday* ended in 1963 was ripe for leading roles in such B-classics as *Clash By Night* (1963) with Jennifer Jayne. In later years, he proved himself a stolid character actor; in *The New Avengers* ('Obsession', 1977), *The Sea Wolves* (1980) and *The Return of Sherlock Holmes* ('The Man with the Twisted Lip', 1986). He enjoyed a year as the lovable rogue Wilf Stockwell in *Coronation Street* from 1981 until 1982.

Carry On credits: *Sergeant, Nurse, Constable, Regardless*

the best and if perhaps a second edition is envisaged then you are left with "second best". Also, the original MGM film created a catchphrase with *That's Entertainment* and *That's Carry On* does suggest a style. As people used to say something was "good enough for Punch", now when a certain comedy situation comes along they say *That's Carry On*.' With a brief list of props, 'film cans, hamper of food, bottle champagne', the depleted unit was installed in Pinewood's Projection Room 7. The two Carry On actors best known as personalities as well as

That's Carry On was briefly available on home video in 1990, a belated companion to Warners' release of the first twelve films.

TRAILER

'For nearly twenty years they've been the most wanted gang on earth. But now the whole lot of them have been captured at last!' Jim Dale bounced over beds from *Again Doctor* as the narration explained: 'Yes, from forty-two hours of frantic fun those ace laughter-makers Peter Rogers and Gerald Thomas have extracted the most momentous moments of mirth that have ever gone into one film. Everyone who is anyone is in it – right in it.' 'Everyone' meant Jimmy Logan, Phil Silvers, Frankie Howerd, Jim Dale, Kenneth Cope and Terry Scott. 'That's Carry On is a scream from start to finish' was illustrated by Harry H Corbett and 'it's historically hysterical' had Sid James and Barbara Windsor from *Henry*. 'You'll laugh your head off. It's just what the doctor ordered. It's highly educational. And it refreshes parts other films cannot reach.' A tagline that parodied the current campaign for Heineken lager.

TITBITS!

Having served as assistant editor on every Gerald Thomas comedy since *The Big Job* in 1965, Jack Gardener was elevated to editor for the first and only time, 'because I knew the films so well.' He really was his director's right hand man on the film, 'sitting at Pinewood for six weeks looking at every single Carry On. We picked out the best bits and made the mistake of joining them all together before editing and watching them back. They lasted six hours!' Eric Rogers returned to the films after his absence from *Carry On England*, 'to cover music editing and supervision on the film. There will be no music sessions, no recording sessions, simply a re-use and juxtapositioning of existing music from the films.' Peter Rogers was annoyed that production lawyers were reacting 'as if it were a full feature film with stills, publicity, exploitation, the lot.' In fact, *That's Carry On* was mainly distributed as a second feature with the Richard Harris thriller *Golden Rendezvous*.

A letter to Peter Rogers from Kenneth Williams following the two-day shoot on 12 and 13 July 1977.

Sid James and Barbara Windsor in *Carry On Dick* (1974).

Peter Rogers gets to grips with Kenneth Williams on the set of *Carry On...Up the Khyber* (1968).

thespians, Barbara Windsor and Kenneth Williams, proved supremely professional and at ease with the assignment, and picked up the most lucrative pay cheques of their Carry On careers. For Barbara Windsor, the experience was a sobering one: 'We were really moved by the sight of Sid James at his best. Dear old Sid had just died and we sat through two days of clips,

watching him on screen. It was so upsetting.' The selection of film clips had, inexplicably, failed to include any material from the latest film, *Carry On England*; it is only included as a mere statistic during the roll call of talent at the end of the compilation. By the time of *That's*

THE CARRY-ON BOOK

The daddy of them all, Kenneth Eastaugh's invaluable tome was the very first of many books on the subject of the Carry Ons. Published by David & Charles at the time of the release of *That's Carry On*, it was featured in a crossover promotion. Having been a Fleet Street journalist since the early 1960s, TV Critic for the *Daily Mirror* and a correspondent for *The Sun*, Eastaugh had established firm friendships with many of the cast over the years. The book featured interviews with almost everyone associated with the series, including those long since disassociated from the franchise such as Leslie Phillips, Charles Hawtrey and Jim Dale, and extracts from two interviews with Sid James from 1969 and 1974. Basically a brief history of the series packed with hilarious anecdotes from behind the scenes, the book also featured a filmography, cast lists and script extracts.

A framed cinema presentation featured on the back of the book.

Carry On's release in November 1977, *Carry On England* had well and truly been and gone from British cinemas, so it wasn't a case of ignoring the 'current' picture. Perhaps the financial wounds were still felt by the makers who had invested heavily in it. Only the first twenty-seven films were fully celebrated.

Peter Rogers wrote to Kenneth Williams: 'I want to make the credit titles of the Carry On compilation more amusing. I know that contractually your credit should read "introduced by" but I would like to put "introduced by" and then cross it out and put "interrupted by". I cannot do this without your permission. I have written to Barbara asking for permission to do the same thing to her title. I have already changed Gerald's title from "compiled by" to "confused by" so may I look forward to hearing that you agree?'

Windsor happily agreed. So did Williams, writing to Rogers: 'NEED YOU ASK? Of course, alter the titles as you wish, only do be careful not to tread on Gerald's toes. You know how sensitive he can be if he feels you're being cavalier.'

Windsor also tentatively ventured the subject of a possible Carry On for the following year. Peter Rogers was clear: 'Naturally we are planning another Carry On, but what form it will take is anybody's guess.'

Bruce Montgomery (1921-1978)

A student at St John's college, Oxford and a literary friend of Kingsley Amis and Philip Larkin, Montgomery's place as the originator of the Carry On sound is a surprising one. As Edmund Crispin, he created the detective Gervase Fen, an English professor at Oxford and, between 1944 and 1952, wrote eight novels and several collections of short stories for the character. Books like *The Case of the Gilded Fly* (his first), *Holy Disorder* and *The Moving Toyroom* are still revered as classics of the 'locked-door whodunit'. From 1955, he edited seven volumes of science fiction and these 'Best SF' anthologies are credited for introducing many renowned writers to a wider audience. From 1945, Montgomery had added a second string to his bow when his music, 'My Joy, My Life, My Crown!', was published. His first film score was *Doctor in the House* and he found himself in demand for the next three films in the series as well as the majority of Peter Rogers' output, including *Please Turn Over*, *No Kidding*, *Watch Your Stern* and, most incongruously of all, *The Duke Wore Jeans*. His most personal work was for a film he also scripted, *Raising the Wind*. It had taken him four years to complete, mainly due to trying to keep 'the Doctor films out of my hair' and 'the fact that, music teaching being such a grim business, there are no standard jokes on the subject, combined with the further distressing circumstances that the jokes I've thought up myself don't seem to me to be very good.' As for the title, it 'couldn't be more fatuous, but one has no control over these things'. His last film credit was on *Brides of Fu Manchu* (1966), though he produced one final Gervase Fen novel, *The Glimpses of the Moon*, in 1977.

Carry On credits: *Sergeant, Nurse, Teacher, Constable, Regardless, Cruising*

CARRY ON EMMANNUELLE (1978)

Emmannuelle Prevert (Suzanne Danielle) relieves the boredom of a flight on Concorde by seducing timid Theodore Valentine (Larry Dann). She returns home to London to surprise her husband, the French ambassador Emile Prevert (Kenneth Williams), but first surprises the butler, Lyons (Jack Douglas). She has left her dress on the plane! The chauffeur Leyland (Kenneth Connor), housekeeper Mrs Dangle (Joan Sims) and aged boot boy Richmond (Peter Butterworth) sense saucy times ahead, and they are right. Emile is dedicated to his bodybuilding, leaving a sexually frustrated Emmannuelle to find pleasure with everyone from the Lord Chief Justice (Llewellyn Rees) to chat show host Harold Hump (Henry McGee). Theodore is spurned by Emmannuelle, who has genuinely forgotten their airborne encounter, and despite reassurances from his mother (Beryl Reid), Theodore exacts revenge by revealing Emmannuelle's antics to the press. But, after a visit to her doctor (Albert Moses), she discovers she is pregnant and decides to settle down to a faithful marriage with Emile... and dozens of children.

Suzanne Danielle raises the hopes of prim and proper butler, Jack Douglas.

With the Rank Organisation having pulled out of distributing the series, Cleves Investments expressed an interest in backing a Carry On film and went on to plough a whopping £349,000 into a new production, over £100,000 more than *Carry On England* had cost. Peter Rogers employed a new scriptwriter for the project: Lance Peters, who delivered 'a brand new motion picture to warm the cockles'. A scribe from Australia, he had written a novel entitled *Carry On Emmannuelle*, which publishers Arrow Books had hoped would prove a useful tie-in when the film was released at the end of 1978.

The book and the screenplay, however, were totally different things, as Vince Powell remembers: 'Gerry had just produced my sitcom, *Odd Man Out*. He phoned me to say that they were about to start filming *Carry On Emmannuelle*. He basically wanted help, because the script as it was written was unfilmable in his opinion. I read it and it was filthy. Not like a Carry On at all. I was just about to fly off to Spain but I did what I could with the script and handed it over to Gerry in a lay-by on the M25 just near the particular airport terminal. It was like working for MI5!' In addition, Willie Rushton made several suggestions that found their way into the script, and Peter Rogers also claimed a credit for moulding the Lance Peters script into a workable basis for a film: 'I totally wrote his dialogue out of existence.'

Arrow Books was clearly under the mis-understanding that the film and novel would be promoted in tandem. The publishers intended to give the book a small, first edition run while the film was in production with 'provisional plans to follow it up with a reprint with a cover that would tie in directly with the film.' This was against the wishes of Peter Rogers: 'You must remember that ours is to be an A certificate film whereas, I am sure, the content of the book is X. Again, if you use photographs of any of the artistes it would give the impression that you are publishing the book of the film, which you are not. It has been necessary to revise the original screenplay considerably to make it suitable for a Carry On and any misrepresentation of content, suggested by the book, could, in my opinion, damage the film.'

Hemdale International Films had come on board as distributor, and the company was keen to return to the traditional style of Carry On after what had been seen as a departure from the series' gang unity with *Carry On England*. To that end, it was hoped that as many of the old cast members could be rounded up as possible. 'Hemdale wanted Kenneth Williams in the new Carry On almost as badly as I did,' remembered Peter Rogers. 'To secure his services I did the only thing that would change his mind about doing the film – I paid him more money!' But the bottom line was loyalty. Kenneth Williams had, for the most part, enjoyed his twenty years of carrying on. He swallowed his pride and took the film, despite continuing to nurse reservations about the script.

Hemdale were also keen to bring Barbara Windsor back to the series. She was cast as the ultimate fantasy figure for the three downstairs staff, played by Peter Butterworth, Kenneth Connor and Jack Douglas. Barbara would crop

up in 'odd appearances' during their flashback scenes and make her fourth and final appearance as the nurse who closes the film, holding Emmannuelle's babies. However, the story soon broke that Barbara Windsor had walked off the set. Barbara explained: 'I don't think I've ever

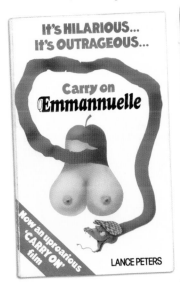

The tie-in novel by Australian writer Lance Peters.

ON LOCATION

The dining room scene was filmed in Pinewood's Green Room on 3 May, and later that same day the unit travelled to the local location of a laundrette in Bourne End. One day's filming took place at St Mary's Parish Church, Harefield, Middlesex, on 3 May, during which it stood in for the French church in Peter Butterworth's wartime memoir. On Friday 5 May, Jack Douglas, Louise Burton and Reuben Martin, as the gorilla, filmed at London Zoo. The home of Emile Prevert was 78 Addison Road, W14. The home of Theodore Valentine and his mother was found at Pinewood Green, while the Buckingham Palace sentry box was shot on Pinewood's Car Park no. 2. Second unit filming took place at Heathrow Airport and on Friday 12 May, the unit filmed Kenneth Connor, Suzanne Danielle and Larry Dann driving around Central London, while the following day the unit returned to London to film pick-up shots of landmarks like Nelson's Column, Scotland Yard, the Old Bailey and the US Embassy.

Steward, James Fagan, is tempted by the smooth caress of the seductive Emmannuelle, Suzanne Danielle, on Pinewood's 'M' Stage, 21 April 1978.

done anything on screen which would offend anyone. I couldn't believe what they wanted me to do. If I'd wanted to go into blue films, I would have done it years ago.' *The Times* reported that 'Miss Windsor said yesterday that she had refused a part because she believed it contained "soft porn". A representative of the film's producer said "Miss Windsor was understood to have had

a guest part but to have been unable to film because of other commitments. The film was not pornographic and would have an A certificate."' Upon being alerted to the news that Windsor considered the film pornography, Kenneth Williams told his diary: 'I thought, "Yes! So do I"'. But he supported the film and replied to letters with: 'I've been working on it for three weeks and I've not seen anything erotic yet!'

The first day on set was on 'L' Stage, with Kenneth Williams, Jack Douglas and a sparkling discovery in the shape of Suzanne Danielle as Emmannuelle. Known, with good reason, as 'the body', Danielle was Patrick Mower's girlfriend and had become a lifelong friend of Gerald Thomas. Employed for twenty-one days of the five-week schedule, Danielle happily concurred with the contract clause that 'the artist agrees to appear nude in certain scenes as discussed and agreed with the director.'

Amazingly, the production team was trying to gain the film not an A certificate, as revealed in the press, but a U. Clearly an impossible task given the subject matter, the BBFC still recommended various cuts, including 'Kenneth Williams standing bare bottomed. Emmannuelle seen from rear & nude in shower. Emmannuelle bends over and lifts dress in front of sentry. Dialogue referring to "making it hard for me".' 'Making it hard for me' had caused raised eyebrows in 1961, when Kenneth Connor uttered the line in *Carry On Regardless*, and it had been altered then to appease the censor. In 1978, Gerald Thomas and Peter Rogers bit the bullet and adopted the majority of the censor's recommendations for a U certificate.

Larry Dann (1941–)

An actor from the age of five, Larry Dann's credits include the 1949 Stewart Granger film *Adam and Evelyne*, as an orphanage boy, *Trouble in Store* (1953) with Norman Wisdom, *An Alligator Named Daisy* (1955) with Diana Dors and early television work with Dick Emery. Later he landed bigger roles, memorably as the boy who needs to be excused from Kenneth Williams' class in *Carry On Teacher* and Norman Wisdom's delivery boy replacement in *The Bulldog Breed*. Television appearances included Arthur Charpentier in *Sherlock Holmes* ('A Study in Scarlet', 1968). In 1974, he starred in the ambitious, low-budget horror film *Ghost Story* for director Stephen Weeks. On his first day filming *Emmannuelle*, he appeared in his re-introduction scene with Suzanne Danielle, lying face down on a sunbed: 'The first thing I did was put my hand on her bare bottom. I hadn't even shaken her hand!' On television, Larry is best remembered as the long serving Sergeant Peters in *The Bill*.

Carry On credits: *Teacher, Behind, England, Emmannuelle*

The British sex comedy, an innocent, often hilarious, occasionally jaw-droppingly embarrassing phenomenon, had reached the bottom of the barrel. Although justifiably claiming their part in kick-starting the whole movement, the Carry Ons had fully joined the sex comedy game too late. Dave Freeman believes that 'Sex comedies were the only British films making money in those days, it's true. I saw *Carry On Emmannuelle* and was shocked. Not only by the film, but by the audience. The cinema was half empty. I told Peter Rogers that he should make naughty films like we used to. Lots of innuendo and pretty girls, but not this. But, by that time, cinemas were closing, the industry was going through a very bad time. Cheaply made comedies of the Carry On sort were simply not making money. People were more interested in *Jaws* and *Star Wars*.'

Cleves Investments, though, were willing to become long-term backers of the Carry Ons, with a right of first refusal on the next five films, taking the series up to at least 1983. A buoyant

Norman Mitchell (1918-2001)

The personification of the 'old pro', Norman notched up thousands of radio and television credits and a glut of choice cameos on the big screen. As *The Encyclopedia of British Film* succinctly puts it: 'He did whatever he was asked and he was asked to do a great deal.' An evergreen policeman, he played the law in fantasy – *Doctor Who* ('The Daleks' Master Plan: The Feast of Steven', 1965), *Frankenstein and the Monster From Hell* (1974), *~~And Now the Screaming Starts!* (1973); in comedy – *Doctor At Large* ('It's the Rick Wot Gets the Pleasure', 1971); in drama – *Crossroads* (1964), *Why Didn't They Ask Evans?* (1980); and even in musicals – arresting Mark Lester in *Oliver!* (1968). A sitcom mainstay, he chalked up appearances in *Dad's Army* ('Something Nasty in the Vaults', 1969), *Ripping Yarns* ('The Testing of Eric Olthwaite', 1977), *It Ain't Half Hot Mum* ('The Pay Off', 1977), *You Rang M'Lord* ('Come to the Ball', 1993), *Last of the Summer Wine* ('Beware of the Oglethorpe', 1998) and *Up Pompeii* ('The Senator and the Asp', 1970), when he delighted in 'Frankie Howerd saying about my character, "Stovus Primus has gone out!".'

Carry On credits: *Cabby, Spying, Cleo, Screaming!, Emmannuelle*
Autobiography: *An Actor's Life For Me*

Peter Rogers wrote to Cleves: I hope that your faith in the film is fully justified and I shall cheer every time you draw blood. As Henry Hall used to say, "Here's to the next time".'

Norman Mitchell prepares to play Santa Claus at the 1999 Carry On Christmas party at Pinewood Studios.

No longer feeling himself! Kenneth Williams is welcomed back to the bed of youthful wife, Suzanne Danielle.

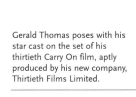

Gerald Thomas poses with his star cast on the set of his thirtieth Carry On film, aptly produced by his new company, Thirtieth Films Limited.

COMPILATIONS (AND NEAR MISSES)

The Music For Pleasure compilation album featured musical turns from numerous Carry On stars.

Gerald Thomas chats to stars Anthony Andrews and Helmut Grien on location for the West German co-production *TheSecond Victory* (1986).

The Second Victory

In a return to *The Third Man* territory, Gerald Thomas produced and directed this Morris L West-scripted whodunnit set in immediate post-war Austria. Amsterdam Olympian Renee Southendijk provided romantic interest, with support from Max Von Sydow and 'silly ass' Jonathan Cecil.

Investments and Hemdale decided to pull out of the project: 'Nobody seemed to understand that the stuff I was making could still make a fortune. No one wanted to know,' reflects Rogers.

Although it was mooted that the next would go even further than the previous film and happily accept an X certificate, Rogers denies this, confirming that: 'It would have been like the other Carry Ons. We always made family entertainment.' Hattie Jacques was approached to reprise her celebrated role as Matron. According to Peter Rogers, she accepted a part in the film, as had a traditional crop of Carry On actors, including Kenneth Williams, Barbara Windsor and even Charles Hawtrey. And it wasn't the only film in the planning stages. With *Star Wars* proving a phenomenal success across the world, an old script was briefly considered. Penned by Bob Monkhouse and his late partner Denis Goodwin, 'Carry On Spaceman' was very much in the style of the early Carry On films, with a group of ineffectual recruits learning the ropes. It was dusted off in the hope that it could be suitably rewritten for a modern audience.

But it was 'Carry On Down Under' that Gerald Thomas came closest to making. The Carry Ons had always been hugely successful in Australia. With interest from an Australian production company in backing a new Carry On film, Thomas travelled to Melbourne to scout for possible locations and finalise the budget. Peter Rogers remained at Pinewood, working out the finer points of the budget and finalising the script and the cast. The film was to be shot

Although Peter Rogers had often expressed a desire to bring the total of Carry On films to thirty, this was never intended to signal the end of the series. At the start of 1979, Rogers was looking forward to his thirty-first Carry On.

Twenty years after the original, Rogers was planning 'Carry On Again Nurse': 'I had paid for the script and I wanted someone to put up the money and provide distribution.' Taking stock after *Carry On Emmannuelle*, both Cleves

in six weeks in Australia. But Gerald Thomas was to return home despondent. When he arrived in Australia, he discovered that the secured budget of $500,000 had simply vanished. In Peter Rogers's words: 'Someone had run off with it.'

With the Australian film out of the running, Gerald Thomas turned to another script and his cast of old faithfuls. Writing in December 1980, Barbara Windsor revealed that: 'Carry On Dallas' – a send-up of TV's Ewing family saga – is also in the pipeline.' Vince Powell had scripted a spoof of the popular American show, with *Dallas* fever about to erupt around 'Who shot JR?' Gerald Thomas fully intended to pay tribute to the late Sid James in the film. The script would start with the funeral of old Jock Screwing, the Head of the Family. A portrait of Sid, in Stetson hat, would be prominent throughout. Barbara Windsor was down to play Lucy, the diminutive sexual predator played by Charlene Tilton in Dallas. With Larry Hagman

Gertan Klauber (1931-)

A swarthy and earthy character actor, Klauber, like Michael Nightingale, continually popped up in Gerald Thomas films. As well as his Carry On supporting turns, he was the milkman in *The Big Job* (1965). He also played the sweaty Pablo in Ralph Thomas's *Percy's Progress* (1974). Other film roles include the tavern keeper in the Vincent Price horror *Cry of the Banshee* (1970), Donner in the Frankie Howerd romp *Up the Front* (1972), a grinning Gestapo officer in *Soft Beds, Hard Battles* (1973), with Peter Sellers, and Bubi in the James Bond film, *Octopussy* (1983). Notable cult television appearances include the fat man in Sir Arthur Conan Doyle's *Sherlock Holmes* ('The Boscombe Valley Mystery', 1968), a cafe waiter in *The Prisoner* ('Do Not Forsake Me, Oh My Darling', 1967) and a galley master in *Doctor Who* ('The Romans', 1965), allegedly cast because of his slave marketer Markus in *Carry On Cleo*. His comedy guest appearances include the Black Rod in *The Goodies* ('The Tower of London', 1970), Major Demo in *Whoops Baghdad* ('Genie of the Bottle', 1973) and Mad King George III in *Blackadder the Third* ('Duel and Duality', 1987).

Carry On credits: *Spying, Cleo, Follow That Camel* (scenes cut), *Doctor, Henry, Abroad, Emmannuelle*

an international star all over again as JR Ewing, the oil millionaire was to be played by Kenneth Williams, as RU Screwing. Unfortunately, Lorimar Productions, who produced *Dallas* in America, failed to see the funny side and threatened legal action if the film went into

production, and so the project was cancelled.

For Rogers, the Carry Ons weren't out of his hands yet and, with almost all the old films having hit television, the small-screen premiere of *That's Carry On* in May 1981 heralded a new project. Over eleven million had tuned in for the ITV screening and Philip Jones, still at Thames, approached Rogers and Thomas with an idea for a new Carry On for television. Not specials like their old Christmas collaborations but, in light of the popularity of *That's Carry On*, a series of half hour compilation pro-grammes. With no desire to record new linking material, the shows were compiled within particular themes, be it holidays, history or hospitals. Gerald Thomas assigned Jack Gardner, who had cut *That's Carry On*, as his editor and the first batch of episodes took six months to complete. When the first episode of *Carry On Laughing* was broadcast on New Year's

Follow That Camel cast Gertan Klauber as a cheeky Arabian Spiv opposite Jim Dale and Peter Butterworth; sadly his role was cut.

In 1987, the Video Collection released thirteen Carry On films on VHS. Gerald Thomas hoped the range would revitalise interest in a new film. The *Carry On Doctor* tape credits Charlie Roper as one of the stars. Roper was in fact the character played by Sid James!

CARRY ON LAUGHING'S CHRISTMAS CLASSICS

Following the success of the compilation programmes, Philip Jones contacted Gerald Thomas about making another Christmas special for Thames, this time a compilation show. Thomas produced the programme and signed up Kenneth Williams and Barbara Windsor as the hosts. Williams met up with Thomas on 20 September and 'he talked about a Christmas Carry On Compilation with Barbara and me doing the

linking and it sounds like it could be great fun.'

And fun it was. From the off-key rendition of Irving Berlin's 'White Christmas' to Williams, dressed as a fairy, atop the tree, the half-hour romp through such Rank classics as *Doctor*, *Up the Khyber*, *Camping*, *Henry* and *Dick* proved a successful one. No scriptwriter is credited and it would appear that the actors wrote their own material. Indeed, Williams wrote on 17 November that 'Gerald Thomas

rang and asked me to think up another link for the Carry On Xmas programme.' On 24 November, the links were recorded at Teddington Studios. 'They took till lunchtime!' moaned Williams, 'and then, after that, we did the fairy bit with me dressing up in a tutu skirt and waving a wand to make snow! Gerald was there (lovely influence) and Peter Rogers turned up!' The show was broadcast on 22 December 1983.

The portrait of Kenneth Williams that appeared on the front of his autobiography, *Just Williams*. His notorious diaries can be seen in the background.

A Carry On reunion in Amersham with Barbara Windsor, Terry Scott, Anita Harris, Jack Douglas and Bernard Bresslaw promoting the video releases and gearing up for another Carry On. Later Babs and Jack would join Kenneth Connor for 'Carry On Banging'; part of Harry Enfield's *Norbert Smith* parody.

Eve 1981, an astonishing sixteen and a half million viewers tuned in; making it the second most watched show of the holiday period. It was no surprise when the BBC jumped on the bandwagon and themselves commissioned a compilation series, *What A Carry On*. Again, Gerald Thomas and Jack Gardner worked on the shows. 'They were quite difficult to do,' conceded the editor. 'The scenes were recut to try and bring them up to a more modern-day pace. We didn't record music, just rearranged the original. I'm sure if my old mate Eric Rogers had been alive he'd strangle me after what I've done to his music!'

Coinciding with the first commercial release of thirteen Rank Carry Ons on videotape in May 1987, Barbara Windsor hosted a reunion party at her pub, the Crown, in Amersham. Terry Scott, Anita Harris, Bernard Bresslaw and Jack Douglas were in attendance and Gerald Thomas announced that another film would be going into production. The new film would be 'naughty. It is in the true Carry On tradition. The only thing holding it up is finance. But I am confident it will be another winner. I hope to make the picture in the autumn.' Terry Scott, who hadn't made one since 1971, was keen to return, and 'the marvellous Russ Abbot' was also in Gerald Thomas's sights. The announced

film was 'Carry On Texas', the same Vince Powell script for 'Carry On Dallas' that had been curtailed earlier in the decade. The central family was now changed from Screwing to Ramming, although the glitz of American soaps was still to be the focal point of the comedy. Anita Harris revealed: 'I'm getting my Joan Collins impressions ready.'

Again these plans came to naught but, with it being thirty years since *Carry On Nurse* had

gone into production, Rogers and Thomas turned to the writer who had started it all, Norman Hudis, to write 'Carry On Again Nurse'. Hudis was instructed to write for the familiar gang. Williams was to have played the haughty consultant surgeon, Sir Roderick Haddon. Kenneth Connor was in mind for the Hospital Porter, Harry, and Charles Hawtrey was considered for the delusional children's author, Cecil Cholmondeley. Matron would be played by Joan Sims, as Stella Dawson, her *Carry On Nurse* character. The reason that it wasn't made was purely financial. The estimated budget of one and a half million pounds was by then considered too expensive for a film as 'parochial' as a Carry On.

'Carry On Again Nurse', or 'Carry On Nursing' as it was temporarily changed to, never got off the ground, although when its proposed star, Kenneth Williams, died on 15 April 1988, it was suggested that filming had been set to start at Pinewood in the June. Charles Hawtrey's death in October that year was another major loss to the original Carry On team.

It seemed the only sort of Carrying On that was being done was affectionate parody. In 1989, Harry Enfield and Melvyn Bragg collaborated on a *South Bank Show*-styled 'mockumentary' entitled *Norbert Smith – A Life*. Christmas 1990 saw Frankie Howerd resurrect Carry On connections when Ned Sherrin

Irene Handl (1901-1987)

Although she was thirty-six when she started acting, Irene Handl would notch up over a hundred films in a fifty-year career. She enjoyed regular support work throughout the 1930s, 1940s and 1950s, memorably playing the omnipresent musician in *Brief Encounter*. Guest television appearances in *Hancock's Half Hour* ('The First TV Show', 'The Artist' and 'The Bequest', 1956) and as Mrs Twissle in *Educating Archie* (1958-1959) led to a run of unforgettable film performances: Peter Sellers' wife Mrs Kite in *I'm All Right Jack* (1959), the psychological Miss Harker-Parker in *The Pure Hell of St. Trinian's* (1960) and Tony Hancock's landlady Mrs Crevatte in *The Rebel* (1961). She played David Warner's mum in *Morgan – A Suitable Case For Treatment* and Benny Hill's sister in *The Italian Job*. She was cast as Mrs Hudson in Billy Wilder's *The Private Life of Sherlock Holmes* (1969) and Mrs Barrymore in Paul Morrissey's *The Hound of the Baskervilles* (1977). A glut of sex comedies, including accident-prone Miss Slenderparts in *Confessions of a Driving Instructor* (1976), appeared in between television series *For the Love of Ada*, *Maggie and Her* and *Metal Mickey*. The author of two best-selling novels, *The Sioux* (1965) and *The Gold Tipped Phitzer* (1966) and an avid Elvis Presley fan, she was working until the end, playing Mrs Larkin in *Absolute Beginners*, Poppy, the Duchess of Sheffield in *Mapp and Lucia* ('Au Reservoir'), both in 1986, and appearing on Wogan's *Radio Fun* in 1987.

Carry On credits: *Nurse, Constable*

presided over a *Loose Ends* pantomime on Radio 4. 'Carry On Up Yer Cinders' cast Howerd and life-long Carry On fan Jonathan Ross as the Ugly Sisters. Barbara Windsor returned, playing Buttons in the style of Jim Dale. In association with Naff Old Jokes Limited, the show was written by Arthur Smith, who also starred as Sid James. Claire Rayner played Hattie Jacques playing the Fairy Godmother and Rory Bremner chipped in as Leslie Phillips, Barry Norman and, for some reason, Terry-Thomas.

Most intriguing of all was Julian Clary, cast as an ultra-camp Kenneth Williams, playing Cinderella. Clary was a self-confessed admirer: 'I do like vulgar humour. I never seem to tire of it. It is so English, so middle-class. Certain lines have now passed into tradition.' It was a tradition that he was destined to join officially.

A right Carry On as Santa Ned Sherrin leads his *Loose Ends* cast of Arthur Smith, Claire Rayner, Rory Bremner (in full Kenneth Williams mode), Julian Clary and Barbara Windsor. The picture was taken to promote *Carry On Up Yer Cinders!*

CARRY ON COLUMBUS (1992)

The year: 1492. The place: Turkey. The Sultan (Rik Mayall) controls the overland trade route from the Far East and with his cunning Grand Wazir (Nigel Planer) taxes merchants (Andrew Bailey and Burt Kwouk) out of all they have. When the Sultan hears that Christopher Columbus (Jim Dale) is planning an ocean route, he sends his sexy spy Fatima (Sara Crowe) to seduce him into submission. But struggling artists and mapmakers Columbus and his brother Bart (Peter Richardson) are contacted by Mort (Bernard Cribbins), who claims to hold the map for the sea route to the Far East. With backing from Ferdinard and Isabella, the King and Queen of Spain (Leslie Phillips and June Whitfield), a voyage is planned. The prison governor, Don Juan Diego (Julian Clary), jumps aboard, as do some of his inmates, including Marco the 'Cereal' Killer (Jack Douglas), Pepi the Poisoner (Keith Allen) and Tonto the Torch (Danny Peacock). Fatima, disguised as a cabin boy, and fellow spy Achmed (Alexei Sayle) join the crew. Countess Esmeralda (Maureen Lipman) and royal bookkeeper Don Juan Felipe (Richard Wilson) are unwelcome passengers on the trip which, having encountered a ghost ship and the threat of sea serpents, finally arrives in America. The natives Pontiac and Hubba (Charles Fleischer and Chris Langham) greet Columbus and fleece him of his finery, while the cigar-chewing Big Chief (Larry Miller) trades fool's gold for guns. In order to save face, Bart masquerades as a Spanish Inquisitor and confiscates the 'treasure' before the King can find out it's worthless. Back on board the Santa Maria, Christopher Columbus enjoys a right carry on with the 'unfrocked' Fatima.

F ew welcome a lifetime achievement award wholeheartedly. Although it is considered an honour to be recognised by one's peers, a lifetime achievement award suggests that you have achieved all you can. Your career is a national treasure rather than a current success. When the Carry Ons won the inaugural Jester for Lifetime Achievement in Film at the British Comedy Awards in December 1990, it was gratefully accepted by Peter Rogers and Gerald Thomas, accompanied by Kenneth Connor, Liz Fraser, Barbara Windsor and Bernard Bresslaw. Thomas dedicated the award to his departed team members.

But the award was not the end. In 1991, Gerald Thomas announced his plans for a new Carry On film. And, this time, it was going to happen. The film was the brainchild of John Goldstone. Having produced such comedy classics as Terry Gilliam's *Jabberwocky* (1977), *The Hound of the Baskervilles* (1977) and *Monty Python's Life of Brian* (1979), Goldstone had founded The Comedy House in 1990. With financial backing from Twentieth Century Fox, the company's aim was to showcase British comedy in the American arena. Following a meeting with Gerald Thomas in 1991, it was suggested that the time was right for a Carry On comeback.

With the 500th anniversary looming of Christopher Columbus having discovered America, it was a natural subject for a Carry On comedy fit for an American invasion. But the timing was of paramount importance. George Corraface was starring in John Glen's *Christopher Columbus: The Discovery*, with a budget of $17.9 million, while Gerard Depadieu was leading the exploration in *1492: Conquest of Paradise*, a film directed by Ridley Scott with a budget of $25.6 million. The Carry On film, at £1.4 million, wouldn't have covered half of Marlon Brando's salary for the Depadieu movie. Gerald Thomas observed: 'Now there will be two big Columbus epics and we'll be a comedy sitting in the middle. Perfect!'

In a natural move that should have come in 1975, Dave Freeman was commissioned to write the script 'in record time in order for us to get it into production in Columbus year. It took me less than a week.' Understandably, under such pressure, Freeman plundered his own, rarely seen television special from 1970, *Carry On Again Christmas*. Several elements, including

Jim Dale's pleas for mercy from the hangman's noose with tales of hidden treasure appeasing his captors, had been played out by Sid James twenty years earlier. The major problem facing Freeman was: 'I couldn't think of a single fact about Columbus that was in the least bit funny. You've got to start somewhere, even with a Carry On. Then I found out that Columbus took along an interpreter. He was a Jew who thought Arabic and Chinese were the same language. Now that's funny.'

With a breathtaking collection of comedy actors in his sights, John Goldstone promised that 'what we are trying to do is recreate the spirit of Carry On with a combination of the greats of Carry On and a whole new generation of talented performers.' Gerald Thomas's only concern was that the new recruits wouldn't gel with the original stars. 'The new generation tend to be stand-up comics and individual performers but they have worked in with us very well. The whole thing is a team from top to

The launch of the first Carry On film in fourteen years happily coincided with the first commercial release of the unsung ATV series, *Carry On Laughing*, from 1975.

Sara Crowe, who would woo Jim Dale on screen and his son and stand-in, Toby Dale, behind the scenes!

Opposite: Jim Dale leads the new world of comedy in to the new world... or at least off of Frensham Pond. Alexei Sayle, Keith Allen and Peter Richardson bow down to the comic master.

Jim Dale reunites with Carry On director Gerald Thomas for the first time in twenty three years. Fellow veterans Leslie Phillips and June Whitfield stand by.

ON LOCATION

With uncontrolled glee, Gerald Thomas made the film completely at Pinewood with the exception of one day's location at nearby Frensham Pond. 'It's exactly the same spot of sand I used in *Carry On Jack* nearly thirty years ago. In fact I've got the same character, Bernard Cribbins, coming out of the same rowing boat. The only difference is now he's coming out with Jim Dale and the troops. Last time he came out with Kenneth Williams and a cow.'

producer John Goldstone: 'People have asked us whether it's possible to do without Kenneth Williams, Hattie Jacques, Sid James. If indeed they were alive today, they would be very old

bottom and they have joined the team. I have great admiration for them. They are very talented and I hoped they would come down to my level. No-one twisted anyone's arms and we didn't offer them fortunes of money; they all just wanted to be in a Carry On.' The new generation included Keith Allen, Tony Slattery, Rik Mayall, Maureen Lipman and Julian Clary.

Frankie Howerd's death on 19 April 1992, just two days before filming started, highlighted the declining number of old favourites in the cast. Although Jim Dale had accepted the leading role, Joan Sims, Barbara Windsor and Bernard Bresslaw were all unenthusiastic and had other commitments. It was, of course, a major concern hanging over the head of

Right: *The Modern Review* asks, 'Can double entendres save the British film industry?' They couldn't.

Opposite: *The Observer Magazine* gaily presented young blood Julian Clary usurping the old gang. Only Jim Dale would return for the 'reunion' film.

and we wouldn't be asking them to be in it anyway.' Notwithstanding the fact that contemporaries like Peter Gilmore and Jack Douglas were cast, it was a statement that smacked of nerves. There is no question that if Kenneth Williams were alive, Gerald Thomas would have asked him to appear. Terry Scott was approached but regretted he was too ill to sign up for the five-week shooting schedule. Kenneth Connor adamantly turned down the supporting role of the Duke of Costa Brava because 'I want to be remembered as a Carry On principal not a bit-player!'

Although the film naturally introduced newcomers, just before filming began, Leslie Phillips accepted the role of the King 'as a favour to Gerry Thomas.' June Whitfield was his Queen, and Jon Pertwee accepted 'a very nostalgic and happy day' as the Duke, 'warmly embraced by Gerry Thomas and welcomed home with the somewhat ominous codicil, "You are one of the few left!"'

From the stirring, jaunty opening theme from Monty Python film composer John Du Prez to the post-punk brain attack of Malcolm McLaren and Lee Gorman's closing song, it was a Carry On for the new age. With a cast boasting some of the top comic names in the country, the right director, the right screenwriter and the right director of photography (Alan Hume), it should have worked.

What happened when Julian Clary and the Comic Strip got their hands on the Great Tradition

Model and actress Sara Stockbridge, cast as Nina the model, had been interviewed by Jonathan Ross in December 1991. Jim Dale was a guest on the same show. Carry On fan Ross was due to film a one-day cameo as the barber shop customer who has his ear cut off by Alexei Sayle. Due to his work commitments the role went to David Boyce. Peter Grant, ex-manager of Led Zeppelin, saw his scene with Jim Dale edited from the film, although he can be briefly spotted before spy Sara Crowe locates the cobbler played by Alexei Sayle. The classical Irish actor, T P McKenna was cast as the Archbishop who marries Jon Pertwee to Holly Aird. This scene was cut and McKenna's entire

performance lost. Holly Aird was fresh from starring in Soldier, Soldier, a series cast by Columbus casting director Jane Arnell. Rebecca Lacey, beloved as the dippy secretary Hilary in the situation comedy From May to December, gives a cheeky, Barbara Windsor-styled supporting turn as Chiquita, while fellow sitcom star Martin Clunes had just filmed his first series of Men Behaving Badly for ITV. The American native, Charles Fleischer, provided the voice of Roger Rabbit. Well-versed in Carry On history, in an interview with Clive Anderson, Fleischer was proud to be the first American since Phil Silvers to appear in the series. Philip Herbert, Burt Kwouk's ginger-carrier, was a camp fixture of Sticky Moments with Julian Clary. Nejdet Salih as Fayid is probably best-remembered as Ali from early episodes of EastEnders. Veteran

Harold Berens, remaining cheerful on the rack, was, at the age of 90, the oldest actor working in film and television. Arthur Smith, 'the new Sid James', dressed as Mark Antony to record an hilarious set report piece for Wogan. He was disappointed to be: 'the only comic in the country not in it!' Dancer and seventies heartthrob Peter Gordeno, as the Shaman, and Don Maclean, as the inquisitor with the ham sandwich, were both close friends of Gerald Thomas, and had long nursed an ambition to appear in a Carry On. Marc Sinden, who plays Captain Perez, was the son of Sir Donald and the godson of Peter Rogers. And, as if to bring the whole series full circle, John Antrobus is once again credited with additional material and was cast as a manservant.

June Whitfield OBE, CBE (1925-)

RADA-trained, June appeared with Wilfred Pickles in his 1947 radio *Christmas Party* and in pantomime at the Bradford Alhambra. According to Frank Muir, she is 'God's gift to scriptwriters,' and it was in his and Denis Norden's radio series *Take It From Here* that the actress first found fame in 1953. Co-starring with Jimmy Edwards, June's best loved character was 'Eff' in partnership with Dick Bentley's 'Ron', in the Glum Family sketches. The two would recreate their roles in voice only for the 1961 film *Double Bunk*. Roy Hudd, a long-running co-star in *The News Huddlines*, *The Newly Discovered Casebook of Sherlock Holmes* and *Like They've Never Been Gone*, would call her 'the comic's tart' and indeed she has worked with them all. She supported Arthur Askey in his television series *Before Your Very Eyes*, was a nurse in *Hancock* ('The Blood Donor', 1961), played a vampire in *The Benny Hill Show* (1964) and was a blind date on *Frankie Howerd* (1966). In 1970 she became part of the *Scott On...* team and was cemented as a couple with Terry Scott in the *Bless This House* film and the sitcoms *Happy Ever After* (1974–1978) and *Terry and June* (1979–1987). She guest starred in *The Goodies* ('Wicked Waltzing', 1971) and played Mother in *Absolutely Fabulous* from 1992. More serious fare included Alan Plater's *The Last of the Blonde Bombshells* and an unflappable *Miss Marple* on Radio 4. In 2002, she starred with Richard Briers in a West End revival of Alan Ayckbourn's *Bedside Manners*.

Carry On credits: *Nurse, Abroad, Girls, Columbus*
Autobiography: *... and June Whitfield*

Her four credits spanned almost the entire history of Carry On – here June Whitfield promotes *Carry On Abroad* (1972).

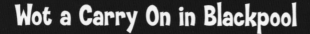

Wot a Carry On in Blackpool

It was an unofficial Carry On show on Blackpool's North Pier that gave Barbara Windsor and Bernard Bresslaw the escape clause they wanted. Neither relished the idea of returning to the Carry On films in what amounted to little more than cameo appearances, and both seized the opportunity to be rehearsing away from London during the filming. The show was written by Barry Cryer and Dick Vosburgh, who had penned one of the best *Carry On Laughing* episodes, 'Orgy and Bess'. Cryer considered the Blackpool experience as 'more a revue than a typical Carry On show, but it was fun.' A jolly collection of, literally, end-of-the-pier sketches and musical numbers, it allowed Barbara Windsor to shine as Charlie Chaplin and Betty Grable, while Bernard Bresslaw enjoyed himself as a hulking landlady and a Frankenstein Monster with a touch of George Formby about him! Frivolous and funny, the season was so successful that a nationwide tour of the material was mooted for July through to August, although health concerns with Bresslaw curtailed that.

Predictably, despite huge press coverage and media interest in a new Carry On, when the film opened at the Leicester Square Odeon on 2 October it got a beating from the critics. 'It must have seemed like a good idea at the time to gather together the remnants then stir in the new crop of formerly "alternative" comedy stars,' wrote one. 'But a lot of water passes under the poop deck between the seed of an idea and the flowering of something so stonkingly terrible that it almost defies belief. The alternative lads are patently uncomfortable with the Carry On formula, the script is inept, everyone's timing is out and it just isn't funny. Kenneth, Sid, Hattie, Charles, RIP.'

And yet one review, from *The Times* in 1966, had described *Carry On Screaming!* as 'one of the dullest and least spirited of them all' – so what did change after all? Perhaps only that the Carry Ons became an institution. Quite simply the Carry Ons were now the old team. Indeed, if Columbus had only got his skates on and discovered America twenty years earlier, the script, filmed word for word, with the old gang available, would sit more easily alongside Talbot Rothwell's *Carry On Henry* or *Carry On Dick*.

Born in Leipzig, Germany, Peter came to England in 1937 and was raised in Nunthorpe, Yorkshire. With a burning desire to perform, he left school at fourteen. However, his showbusiness dream was dampened when he was expelled from RADA. During his national service in the army, he discovered a talent for singing and broke into the business by joining the George Mitchell Singers at the Blackpool Opera House.

As a variety artiste, he stooged for top entertainers including Frank Sinatra, Danny Kaye and his favourite, 'dear Harry Secombe'. He also came to the attention of Peter Rogers when he appeared in the swashbuckling television series *Ivanhoe* (1958) with Roger Moore. Subsequently, he starred in seven West End productions: *Valmouth* at the Saville Theatre, *Follow That Girl, Lock Up Your Daughters, Love Doctor, The Fantasticks, The Beggars' Opera* and *Cinderella* at the London Palladium. Gilmore made a dashing Prince Charming in the latter, a hit production of 1966-1967, which starred Cliff Richard as Buttons, The Shadows as the

Broker's Men, Jack Douglas as Baron Hardup and Terry Scott and Hugh Lloyd as the Ugly Sisters.

In 1960, Peter featured with Sid James and Michael Sammes on the Pye recording of the hit musical *Bye Bye Birdie*. Gilmore's rendition of 'Put On A Happy Face' was one of the standout tracks. Peter's close friend Jim Dale recalls: 'I have known Peter since the early sixties. God knows how we met, but I remember visiting him and Una [Stubbs] when they were married. We got to know each other better when we appeared in Frank Dunlop's production of *A Midsummer Night's Dream* at the Edinburgh Festival in 1966. I think we all shared the same digs together with

Bernard Bresslaw. At one point he asked us to look after an old piano for him. Months later he visited the antique-crammed house in Pembridge Villas, spent the evening with us in the lounge and never even noticed his piano due to the glass domes, antique clowns, stuffed birds and bric a brac all over it.' During his years as part of the Carry On team, Peter also cropped up in other notable films. He played the ineffectual Education Ministry worker, Butters, in *The Great St. Trinian's Train Robbery* (1966), Private Burgess in Richard Attenborough's *Oh! What A Lovely War* (1969) and as Vincent Price's plane-crash victim, Dr Kitaj, in *The Abominable Dr. Phibes* (1971). That same year he was cast as James Onedin in the epic BBC drama serial *The Onedin Line*. As the hero who marries in order to fulfil his dream of a Liverpool Shipping Line in the 1860s, Gilmore starred in the show until the end of the line in 1980.

An international hit, he returned to films as the adventurous Charles Aitken in the 1978 nautical monster romp *Warlords of Atlantis*. Cult television appearances include *The Persuaders!* ('That's Me Over There', 1971) and *Doctor Who* ('Frontios', 1984). He also played Ben Bishop in the BBC zoo vet drama *One By One* (1985-1987). Later screen credits include Frank Malm in *Master of the Moor* (1994) with Colin Firth and Robert Urquhart, and *On Dangerous Ground* (1996), with Rob Lowe and Kenneth Cranham.

Carry On credits: *Cabby, Jack, Cleo, Cowboy, Don't Lose Your Head, Follow That Camel, Doctor, Up the Khyber, Again Doctor, Henry, Columbus*

CARRYING ON...

Gerald Thomas and Peter Rogers
at Pinewood Studios in 1987.

The programme for the
Barbican's 1995 season of
Carry On films.

A Carry On film may have been fourteen long years in coming, but once the cameras started rolling again at Pinewood Studios everybody was quite prepared for another.

Writer Dave Freeman was cautious when he said: 'I don't know if they will ever make any more Carry Ons, as this one was rather special, being done for Columbus year. If it does well at the box office, as we hope it will, then they may be inspired to make another one, but in the film business nothing is certain.'

Although an unofficial report circulated that a 'Carry On Buddha' was set for production, the favoured follow-up to Columbus was a medical comedy. The Norman Hudis script for 'Carry On Again Nurse' was taken out of Peter Rogers' pending drawer and dusted off.

In the end, *Carry On Columbus* was universally panned and, subsequently, few involved with the project could spare the film a good word. But rather than sinking the entire Carry On brand name, the new film was forgiven as a

misguided attempt at reheating the old innuendoes. The original films were as popular as ever and the marketing men went into overdrive.

Sadly, the man behind every Carry On, Gerald Thomas, wouldn't be around to fully enjoy the renaissance. He died at his Beaconsfield home on 9 November 1993. He was 72. Peter Rogers, his film partner for forty years, said simply: 'His epitaph will be that he directed all the Carry On films.'

Thomas' legacy was threefold. Just before his death, he had donated his production files to the British Film Institute. On television, he had walked around Pinewood Studios with Peter Rogers, happy that his work was included in the seminal BBC documentary series, *Hollywood UK*. And a final Thames compilation for Philip Jones reunited him with editor Jack Gardner for *Laugh with the Carry Ons*.

The Carry Ons refused to lie down. Another accolade came in August 1995, when the Barbican announced that they would be screening all thirty Carry Ons – the compilation *That's Carry On* not being included in the tally. Peter Rogers' reaction was typically pithy. 'What a punishment. Even the Marquis de Sade couldn't have devised a worse torture,' although he was clearly moved when he joined Jack Douglas, Patsy Rowlands and Dilys Laye at the gala screening of *Carry On...Up the Khyber*. Jack Douglas said a few words and thought that, had Sid James, Kenneth Williams and Terry Scott been alive, they would have been saying, 'We're at the bloody Barbican!'

The season was also tied in with a new 'Carry On Nibbling!' promotional campaign for KP Nuts, while Music Collection International launched their audio range of Carry Ons. Veteran Carry On narrator Patrick Allen was the natural choice to record the linking dialogue for the first two releases, *Up the Khyber* and *Up the Jungle*. Although it was planned to release the entire series, over the next two years only four more titles were issued. Allen, narrating *Don't Lose Your Head* and *Follow That Camel* was largely usurped by Peter Gilmore, in ambulance man character, for the *Doctor* release, while Joan Sims reprised her role of Joan Fussey to narrate the links for *Carry On Camping*.

In the meantime, Peter Rogers happily agreed to a series of Carry On novels written by

Norman Giller. Unlike the film novelisations that had been discussed with Talbot Rothwell in the late 1960s, these were 'wickedly funny tales taking off from where the original movie ended'. *Carry On Doctor*, *Up the Khyber*, *Loving*, *Henry*, *Abroad* and *England* were published in one batch and, wandering into bizarre territory, were generally considered unrepresentative of the series.

Continually screened on television and available on budget video cassette, the Carry Ons entered a merchandising frenzy in 1997, with the first Carry On calendar, greetings cards and pinball machine ('Carry On Winning') becoming available. The brand had now become bigger than any possibility of new Carry Ons, as the images of the greats of the series adorned phone cards, T-shirts, socks, mugs, teapots and even boxer shorts.

On 26 April 1998, the fortieth anniversary of the series was marked by a special party at Pinewood Studios and an unveiling of British Comedy Society blue plaques to Sid James, Kenneth Williams, Charles Hawtrey and Hattie Jacques in the Pinewood Hall of Fame. The event was also filmed for inclusion in the official Carlton documentary, *What's A Carry On?* produced by Chris Skinner for John Hough. For interview footage, Joan Sims, Barbara Windsor, Leslie Phillips and June Whitfield returned to Pinewood; Norman Rossington, Shirley Eaton and Terence Longdon revisited the Queens Barracks, Guildford, and Jack Douglas, Patsy Rowlands and Richard O'Callaghan reminisced on Brighton's Palace Pier. Jim Dale, in residence as Fagin in *Oliver!* at the London Palladium, reflected on his Carry On days, Peter Rogers and Norman Hudis recalled how the series had started and even Alan Hume came out of retirement to light some of the interviewees.

The anniversary was also marked by an affectionate exhibition and mini Carry On season at the Museum of the Moving Image and the National Film Theatre. It proved so successful that the exhibition dates were extended well into the new year.

Also packing them in, a little further along the South Bank, was Terry Johnson's dramatic interpretation of the Carry On saga: *Cleo, Camping, Emmanuelle and Dick*. Originally conceived as a stylised look at the relationship between an older man and his blonde obsession, Anthony Sher pulled out of the star part as the rehearsals steered more towards a Carry On romp through the relationship of Sid James and Barbara Windsor. Geoffrey Hutchings was cast as Sid in Sher's stead, while Samantha Spiro

stole all the plaudits as a note-perfect Barbara Windsor. Adam Godley flared his nostrils as Kenneth Williams, quoting verbatim rants from the Williams diaries. Gina Belman gave a hauntingly effective performance as the tragic starlet, Imogen Hassall.

In 2000, Johnson directed his own TV script – *Cor, Blimey!* – based on the National Theatre hit. Hutchings, Spiro, Godley and Belman reprised their roles. Chrissie Cotterill played Joan Sims, Steven Spiers was Bernard Bresslaw, Derek Howard was Kenneth Connor and Hugh Walters acquitted himself well as a Charles Hawtrey who looked as if he had eaten all the pies! Barbara Windsor gave the project the seal of approval, playing herself in the final scene, although Joan Sims and Jack Douglas dismissed the production as 'pure fantasy'.

Jack was, however, to join forces with Samantha Spiro for another project. Under the production eye of Ken Burns, who had edited the *What's A Carry On?* documentary and, in association with Peter Rogers, *The Carryoons* were set to launch the old Carry On favourites in a new format – as cartoon characters.

Vince Powell, a writer well versed in the Carry Ons although he had never actually received a credit for his work, was approached to write the scripts. 'It was wonderful to write dialogue for Sid James again,' he recalls. 'The scripts were written like any Carry On. Only I had the great benefit of knowing that I could write for "Kenneth Williams", "Charles Hawtrey", "Hattie Jacques" and the others.'

Jack Douglas 'was reading through the script and laughing, which is highly unusual these days.' But that was as nothing compared to the experience of returning to Pinewood Studios. A brief pilot of *Carryoon* dialogue, based around the premise of *Carry On Camping*, had been written as a promotional piece for the planned series of twenty-six episodes. 'To walk into that sound studio at Pinewood and hear Hattie Jacques's disembodied voice was the most surreal experience; especially when I realised that it was actually a young guy who was mimicking her so perfectly,' remembers Douglas. 'When we heard the voices of Kenneth Williams, Charles Hawtrey and Sid James on the loudspeakers, I just stood there open-mouthed.

Terry Johnson's controversial Carry On play opened at the National Theatre in 1998.

Next, it was my turn at the microphone and I had to swallow a huge lump in my throat before I could begin. In my mind, it was like being back with all my old pals in the Carry Ons.'

David Benson, who had wowed West End audiences and toured with his sublime self-written, one-man show, *Think No Evil Of Us – My Life With Kenneth Williams*, was the natural choice

for the Williams vocals. In an affectionate salute to his father, Carry On veteran Jeremy Connor agreed to record dialogue for Kenneth Connor, from his home in New Zealand. Even Joan Sims was keen to provide her own voice. Over the years, Angela Douglas, Valerie Leon, Fenella Fielding, Jacki Piper and Leslie Phillips have been asked to take part, and new *Carryoon* characters of Frankie Howerd and Terry Scott have been unveiled. Veteran Carry On

The cover of The Carry On Album, released in 1999.

narrator Patrick Allen recorded the trailer commentary. As usual, the only thing holding up production is the high financial demands for animation. Following the success of the fortieth anniversary party, Peter Rogers endorsed a whole host of celebrations at Pinewood Studios, welcoming both veteran Carry Oners and devoted Carry On fans. The first, in 1999, helped launch six Carry On-inspired model cars from Lledo. A *Sergeant* army truck, a *Teacher* school coach, a *Constable* police van, a *Cabby* taxi, a *Camping* camper van and a *Matron* ambulance completed the set.

Also launched at the 1999 Pinewood event was *The Carry On Album*, a specially recorded salute to the music of Bruce Montgomery and Eric Rogers. Conductor and arranger Gavin Sutherland recorded the CD in February 1999 at the Smecky Studios, Prague, with the City of Prague Philharmonic Orchestra. The result was a huge success and two follow-ups, *British Film Composers in Concert* and *What A Carry On!*, paid further tribute to the Carry On composers.

Norman Hudis had, over the years, kept his Carry On hand in with outlines for 'Carry On Under the Pier if Wet' and 'Carry On Shylock Holmes' and had even penned an opening dialogue scene for *Columbus* for his own amusement. He was subsequently moved to write another Carry On script.

But it was the old films that remained the bedrock of public interest. The launch of a new

Prototypes for the Royal Doulton Carry On...Up the Khyber Toby Jugs issued in 2001.

Carry On logo in 2002 was accompanied by trading cards and bobble-head dolls from Cards Inc, *Carry On Doctor* and *Carry On...Up the Khyber* Toby Jugs from Royal Doulton and an initiative to target the new breed of fan.

After fifteen years of exposure on the Video Club label, the Rank Organisation titles – which now include *Carry On Emmannuelle*, purchased from Hemdale – passed to Carlton, which had bought the Rank Library. The most eagerly awaited development was a special edition release of the films on DVD. *Carry On Camping* had spear-headed the series into the digital format, but now that classic was being remastered, along with seventeen others. Trailers, the ATV *Carry On Laughing* television series, rare interview footage, stills galleries and documentaries were added.

Each film was laudably treated with the same respect and a clutch of Carry On talent was happy to record audio commentaries for these releases. These were recorded over a year, starting with Jim Dale for *Don't Lose Your Head*, *Follow That Camel*, *Doctor* and *Again Doctor*. A fifth film, *Abroad*, reunited love interests John Clive, Sally Geeson, Carol Hawkins and David Kernan. Peter Rogers provided the commentary for the classic *Up the Khyber* and *That's Carry On*; running observations for the tail-ender *England* came from Patrick Mower; Jacki Piper and Richard O'Callaghan joined forces for *Loving* and *At Your Convenience*. Patsy Rowlands, Valerie Leon, Sandra Caron, Dilys Laye and June Whitfield also signed up for the project. Jack Douglas took part in four, Larry Dann joined him on two and Dave Freeman accompanied both to reflect on his script for *Carry On Behind*. Equally valued creative force Alan Hume rejoiced in the series in his *Henry* commentary. Released throughout 2003, the discs were bestsellers.

The Carry On cult was at a peak and, in February 2003, it was announced that Peter Rogers was planning another Carry On film at Pinewood Studios. 'Carry On London – the thirty-second Carry On in the series, and the first of the twenty-first century!' was officially launched at the House of Commons in June 2003. 'Promoting London and the Best of British', Peter Rogers was executive producer once again, with producer James Black in the driving seat. Inspired by the international success of the Austin Powers films, Black said: '"Carry On London" will be a blend of classic Carry On with twenty-first-century humour. Great music, stunning locations, glamorous girls, crazy characters and romantic storylines mixed with outrageous comedy and character names.'

The script was in the hands of Paul Minett and Brian Leveson, who had 'inherited' the mantle of Talbot Rothwell for the 1991 Frankie Howerd television show *Further Up Pompeii*. The press release explained: 'This is a new exciting Carry On, based around the week leading up to the British equivalent of the Oscars, "The Herberts", and the shambolic car hire firm of "Lenny Love's London Limos". "Carry On London" will bring back to the big screen, the biggest and the most famous comedy brand in the world.'

Although the launch had welcomed past Carry Oners Jack Douglas, Jacki Piper, Anita Harris, Valerie Leon and Angela Grant, 'the exciting new Carry On will establish a new Carry On team.' Confirmed casting was announced, including Daniella Westbrook as Delia Goodhand. James Black saw her as 'the new Barbara Windsor' and, as such, she was a perfect choice, having played Windsor's daughter, Sam Mitchell, in *EastEnders*. She considered Barbara 'an icon' and was looking forward to emulating her in a film which would be 'quite saucy' but the usual 'family fun' of Carry On.

Fellow Albert Square refugee Shaun Williamson was cast as limo driver Dicky Ticker. Black said, 'We see him as the new Kenneth Connor. He's got a great comedic face and there's a sort of pathos about him.' *Coronation Street*'s Andrew Whyment was cast as Dudley and *The Bill*'s Chris Ellison and Tony Scannel were to be the heavy mob element in the film. James Black's protégés Lady Isabella Hervey (as Pippa Pink), Princess Tamara Bourbon, the first cousin of King Carlos of Spain (as Always Ready) and Chloe Bailey (as K Y Yelland) were the glamorous focal point. Spandau Ballet balladeer Tony Hadley had said 'yes' to the role of pop star Tony Delmonti.

Peter Rogers was adamant that 'if the script is funny people will laugh. The cinema-going public does not even know who is alive or dead any more. Audiences do not give a damn who is in the films because the Carry On itself is the star. I will fill up the blanks with up-and-coming comedy actors, just like we always did in the old days. If the scripts are right that is all that matters. People will still go to watch the films.'

But it was soon all change. 'To be confirmed' stars were David Jason, who James Black saw as 'the new Sid James', Leslie Phillips and Christopher Lee. They all turned down the film. Shaun Williamson later revealed that 'the only original Carry On person they want now is Barbara Windsor.' In what must be seen as the curse of *Carry On Columbus*, current comedy

stars were wary of signing up for a new film. In 1992, everybody had grabbed the chance to appear. Then the bombshell of failure hit. James Black dropped out of the project and co-producer George Pavlou fully took over the reigns.

The new film was at the heart of Peter Rogers's ninetieth birthday party at Pinewood in February 2004. But no casting would be confirmed until the production was ready to shoot. However, the replacement for Gerald Thomas was announced. The new director would be Terry Winsor, who had written and directed the 1983 comedy *Party, Party*, starring *Carry On Columbus* actor Danny Peacock. By the start of 2005, all past rumoured casting had been dismissed as just that, rumour. Even an alleged quote from Peter Rogers, confirming Paul O'Grady, James Dreyfus and Johnny Vegas as the limo drivers, was unofficial.

Prospective directors, including *Columbus* star Peter Richardson and *Red Dwarf*'s Ed Bye, have since come and gone, and a new Carry On film has yet to appear. In the meantime, numerous special edition DVDs and even Royal Mail stamps have helped to keep the classic films alive. In March 2008 a fiftieth anniversary Carry On party was held at Pinewood. Special guest Leslie Phillips was there to pay tribute to the absent stars: 'All my friends have gone,' he said. 'Those wonderful actors. I've come in memory of them today.' Peter Rogers, however, is unfailing in his attitude that Carry On is unquenchable. 'I am expendable,' he says. 'When I die, someone will replace me.'

Writing in 1970, Rogers mapped out the simple appeal of his films. 'The children of seven who saw *Carry On Sergeant* back in 1958 and who came of age at the same time as the twenty-first of the series [*Carry On Henry*] grew up to appreciate the innuendoes of the script which went over the heads of the very young members of the audience. As I've always said, the Carry Ons have the same quality of innocent vulgarity as the McGill seaside postcards. Just like "What the Butler Saw". It's only the title that titillates. The Carry Ons set out with one purpose in mind – to entertain.'

And now, with those same seven-year-olds fast approaching retirement age, the Carry Ons are still entertaining audiences across the world. They look set to carry on for many more years to come.

In tandem with the 1995 Barbican season, KP Nuts used the clout of Carry On to promote their savoury snacks.

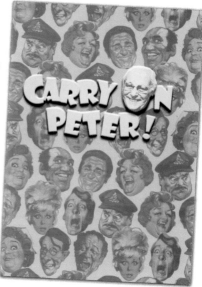

An invitation to Peter Rogers' ninetieth birthday celebration at Pinewood.

AFTERWORD

Hello Carry On fans. I was very pleased and honoured when Robert asked me to write the afterword for the new Carry On book. The eight Carry On pictures I appeared in over a period of twenty years were some of the happiest times of my career.

On my first day at Pinewood, I was very nervous about joining the already famous team. However I was welcomed with open arms by all, producer, director, cast and crew. Peter Rogers who produced thirty-one Carry Ons is a master of his craft. He is respected throughout the film world and is now, in his nineties, known as 'Mr Carry On'. Gerald Thomas was one of the best comedy directors in the film industry. From the start he gave me the rare opportunity to ad lib some of my best comedy moments. It was a joy to work with Gerald, not only was he a top director, but also a close friend. So with Peter on production, Gerald directing and top comedy writers and actors who were all household names in their own right, the recipe was perfect to make a series of pictures which are even bigger now than when they were first made.

One of my favourite stories is from *Carry On Dick*. I had to climb a certain church belfry, look out and watch Sid as 'Big Dick' riding off into the distance. Arriving on location, I found Gerald very downcast. 'What's wrong?' I asked him. 'The belfry's only five foot high,' he said. 'We can't get you and the camera in it.' Being one of the last takes of the picture, this was most annoying. So Gerald decided to build a replica belfry on the set at Pinewood. Some weeks later, I arrived at Pinewood to film the shot and found a very unhappy Gerald. He said, 'Jack, we are still in trouble. The crew have done a wonderful job with the belfry but no one told the carpenter you are six foot four. And it only measures five foot six.' 'I've got an idea,' I said. 'Can we rehearse it?' 'Yes,' said Gerald, 'get yourself up the ladder and we'll have a look at it.' Up the ladder I went into the belfry. I hit my head on a beam, on the rebound I hit my head on another beam, turned right, another bang, turned left and yet another. Then I crossed my eyes and sank to the floor. 'Did you like that Gerald?' I said. 'Great Jack.' 'Shall we film it then?' I said. 'No need,' replied Gerald, 'I've already done it!' That was typical of Gerald. He captured moments of magic and that magic is in every Carry On for all to see.

I miss the team very much and think that Robert has done a wonderful job in keeping them all alive in *The Carry On Story*.

Jack Douglas makes a memorable debut in *Carry On Matron* (1972).

Jack Douglas
Isle of Wight,
February 2005

INDEX

Page references followed by an asterisk, as 125*,
relate to mini-biographies of the players concerned.